THE TOURIST EXPERIENCE

**Also available from Continuum:**
B. Faulkner, E. Laws, G. Moscardo (eds), *Tourism in the 21st Century*
M. Foley, J. Lennon (eds), *Dark Tourism*
C. Law, *Urban Tourism* (2nd Edition)
L. Lumsdon, J. Swift (eds), *Tourism in Latin America*

# The Tourist Experience

## 2nd Edition

Edited by Chris Ryan

continuum
LONDON • NEW YORK

**Continuum**

| | |
|---|---|
| The Tower Building | 370 Lexington Avenue |
| 11 York Road | New York |
| London SE1 7NX | NY 10017-65503 |

www.continuumbooks.com

© 2002 Chris Ryan and the contributors

First published 2002

**British Library Cataloguing-in-Publication Data**
A catalogue record for this book is available from the British Library.

ISBN: 0-8264-5763-0 (hardback) 0-8264-5764-9 (paperback)

Typeset by YHT Ltd, London
Printed and bound in Great Britain by Bookcraft (Bath) Ltd, Midsomer Norton

This book is dedicated to the memory of Andrew Cliff

# Contents

# The contributors

**Tom Baum** is Professor of International Hospitality Management and Head of Department in the Scottish Hotel School, University of Strathclyde. He has professional and academic experience of the tourism and hospitality industry on five continents and has published widely in a number of related areas, notably HRM and tourism, and peripheral areas.

**Andrew Cliff** was Senior Lecturer at Manawatu Polytechnic, now UCol, Palmerston North, New Zealand. His research interests lie within issues pertaining to quality and quality management in service industries. He studied for his Master's degree at Massey University and conducted research under the supervision of Chris Ryan. Very sadly – and most unfortunately, for Andrew was a well-regarded teacher and an enquiring scholar of high potential – he was killed in an accident.

**Joanne Cheyne** has lectured since 1991 on the tourism programme at the Palmerston North campus of Massey University where she completed her Master's degree that included research on rural tourism in New Zealand. She teaches tourism management, small business management and a paper in Pacific Rim tourism and has recently been offering papers to students at the Singapore Aviation Academy. Her primary research interests are in rural tourism, resident attitudes to tourism and entrepreneurship, and small business management. She has published conference papers, book reviews and articles in journals which include *Annals of Tourism Research* and the *Journal of Corporate Citizenship*, has contributed to books and has acted as a reviewer for the journals *Tourism Management* and the *International Journal of Tourism Research*. She has, most recently, published in the area of environmental programmes in hotels and luxury lodges and is currently involved in research into environmental plans and the introduction of the Green Globe 21 certification programme to the New Zealand tourist industry.

**Donald Getz** is Professor of Tourism and Hospitality Management, Faculty of Management, at the University of Calgary. Previously he was at the University of Waterloo in Ontario, in the Department of Recreation and Leisure Studies, and early in his career he worked as a city and regional planner in Ontario. He undertook graduate and postgraduate studies at the University of Waterloo (Bachelor of Environmental Studies in Urban and Regional Planning), Carleton University (Master of Arts, Geography) and the University of Edinburgh, in Scotland (PhD in Social Sciences – Geography). His doctoral research examined the development and impacts of tourism in the rural Scottish Highlands and involved a considerable amount of fieldwork which he periodically updates.

Professor Getz teaches, conducts research, writes and consults in the field of tourism and hospitality management. He has developed an international reputation as a leading scholar and proponent of event management and event tourism. Related areas of expertise include destination management and marketing, family business and entrepreneurship, rural tourism, impact assessment, and special-interest travel. He has authored three books: *Festivals, Special Events, and Tourism* (1991), *Event Management and Event Tourism* (1997) and *Explore Wine Tourism: Management, Development and Destinations* (2000). He has also co-edited and contributed to a fourth book, *The Business of Rural Tourism* (Thomson International Business Press, 1997), and has worked with several colleagues to produce a detailed workbook entitled *Planning for Sustainable Tourism Development at the Local Level* (The Centre for Environmental Design and Outreach, University of Calgary, 1997). He co-founded *Festival Management and Event Tourism: An International Journal*, and currently serves as editor-in-chief of the journal renamed *Event Management*. This is the only research-based journal covering the entire events field. He is also on the editorial board of several international tourism journals including *Tourism Management*.

**Keith Hollinshead** lectures at the Tourism Programme of the Luton Business School. He has previously taught at Leeds Metropolitan University, UK and at the Department of Parks, Recreation and Tourism Sciences at Texas A&M University in the USA. A prolific writer and commentator on tourism research epistemologies, he has contributed to journals such as *Annals of Tourism Research, Tourism Management, Leisure Studies*, and *Society and Natural Resources*. He has strong interests in issues relating to the interpretation of places, heritage and history and the effects of such interpretations upon contemporary concepts of culture.

**Stephen J. Page** is Scottish Enterprise Forth Valley Chair in Tourism in the Department of Marketing, University of Stirling, Scotland. He has published widely in the area of urban tourism. He is also Associate Editor of the journal *Tourism Management* and recently completed a two-year study of urban tourism and crime in relation to the America's Cup hosted in Auckland, New Zealand. He has published a wide range of books in the field of Tourism Studies and maintains an ongoing interest in tourist health and safety. He is also series editor for a number of tourism publishers.

**Chris Ryan** is Professor of Tourism at the University of Waikato, Hamilton, New Zealand, and editor of *Tourism Management*. He has authored over 60 refereed journal articles, written several books and has advised on issues relating to tourism at local, regional, national and international level. Currently he is Chair of the Tourism Waikato Advisory Committee. In 2001 he was undertaking research for the World Tourism Organisation, Tourism New Zealand, Tourism Coromandel, Tourism Waikato and small operators such as River Valley Lodge.

# *Plates*

---

# Figures

# Tables

# *Preface to the first edition*

This book has been an enjoyable work to complete for many reasons. The publishers very kindly agreed to a proposal for a book in which it was stated that the purpose was to review the literature, draw some conclusions *and speculate*. I think it fair to say that all the writers enjoyed the freedom to speculate. Hence, a very significant debt must be paid to the editors of the series for having the faith that we could not only produce such a work, but do so within the constraints of 80,000 words. However, such freedom brings with it certain responsibilities. Our speculations must not be without foundation, and hence must evolve from the work reviewed. Equally that review must not be unrepresentative of at least a significant proportion of the literature. Thus we also owe a significant debt to our colleague co-researchers, teachers and practitioners of tourism – for it is their ideas, thoughts and research findings that we have plundered to refine, possibly even to define, some of our thoughts. Some of them may have been unaware of the purpose of the letters or e-mail requests that they may have received, and I can only hope that they will find the results of interest.

Another responsibility is that our speculation in this case must serve a function, and I think it possible to identify a number of such purposes. There are many texts which set out organized structures of theory as they relate to tourism – indeed a number of the contributors to this book have written such books. However, in writing such works any author is aware of the nature of theory; that, in attempts to simplify the complexities of the world in order to better understand the relationships that exist between variables, something is lost. For experienced researchers, that which is lost is fairly evident. But is it so evident for those starting their studies? I would expect that many students are only too aware that the phenomenon of holidaying is a complex one, with many variants upon a theme. However, possibly being in the early stages of their studies, an awareness of something being missing is not quite the same as knowing what is missing. The purpose of this book is to complement other textbooks about tourism by, in a somewhat eclectic manner, discussing a number of themes and raising questions and issues that will 'flesh out' students' other studies and resources.

Of course, it is not possible to address all the issues and complexities that pertain to tourism, so the theme of 'the tourist experience' was selected. The reasons for doing so included the fact that the structure of the industry is arguably devoted to the creation of satisfactory holiday experiences. Similarly holiday-makers are motivated by the desire for such encounters. Additionally, it was felt that holidays represent very special types of experiences. They are, as so many writers have commented, periods of escape and locations of attraction. Another reason for addressing this theme lay in an appreciation that the study of tourism has, until very recently, been fairly conventional in its adherence to a generally positivist tradition. It is of interest that John Urry's book, *The Tourist Gaze*, is much cited, yet has not, until possibly very recently, initiated a debate about postmodernistic interpretations of tourism by tourism scholars. This is not to state that John's book is alone – that would be to overstate the case, and to fail to recognize the contribution made by authors such as Chris Rojek or Keith Hollinshead. Certainly also, there have been others, like Graham Dann, whose writings illustrate the use of concepts of relative truths not utilized by a number of the earlier texts on tourism. Always aware of how it is possible to be overtaken by events, it is, at least at this time, possible to write with reasonable accuracy that, compared with other associated disciplines like leisure studies or geography, the tourism journals have been generally untroubled by the debate about postmodernism and the validity of its, at times, confused approaches. So another motivation for writing the book was to contribute to the analysis of tourism by utilizing some of the concepts that have emerged since John Urry's book.

This is not to say that this book is a primer in postmodernism applied to tourism, or to say that all the contributors would accept a label of being postmodernists. Indeed, with possibly the exception of Keith Hollinshead, who is more than capable of speaking for himself, I don't think any of us would label ourselves as 'postmodernists'. More cautiously, it is accepted that experience is, by definition, a subjective process, and thus the concepts like those of phenomenology, or of defining fields and contexts of experience, are as valid and pertinent to tourism as they are to much of human behaviour. But, equally, it would be argued that experiences can be manipulated by both planned and unplanned environments, and hence the contributions by Keith Hollinshead, Don Getz, Jo Cheyne and Stephen Page as described below.

This brings me to another reason as to why the book was so enjoyable to write and edit. It was a pleasure to be able to embark upon such a project with the support of friends; their professionalism and support made it easy to complete the task. I also owe them an apology in that initially I had not meant to write so much of the text myself. I will not embarrass friends by naming those who were unable to contribute, for quite valid reasons, and it was my own inefficiency that led to the realization that if the target date was to be met for publication it was no longer possible to ask others to 'stand in' at short notice. Hopefully, however, some advantage has accrued. By simultaneously writing and receiving the contributions of my co-authors it has been possible to avoid much of the unnecessary repetition that can sometimes occur in books that are collections of papers, and I would hope that this has resulted in more than a simple collection of essays – that there are indeed linkages even while each piece can be read separately. If this is not the case, then there is only one person to blame, namely myself, while of course any success is a success to be attributed to all. Another reason for enjoyment was that to write of the experience of tourists without reference to what tourists actually think, say or do seems an obvious nonsense. So it provided an opportunity to use materials derived from conversations with tourists not previously used, and an excuse for going out to talk even more to tourists – a process that Jo Cheyne also enjoyed.

So what is the plan of the book? In essence it is a simple one. First, it must be noted that its prime concern is holiday-making and recreational tourism – it does not consider other aspects of tourism such as conference-going except possibly in passing. The book begins by arguing that the experience of tourism is a special one, but that, in the form in which it is understood today, it is comparatively recent. Hence, adopting the terminology of John Urry's work, there is today a new 'gaze' about tourism. In order to understand this perception of tourism it is of interest to note how changes have occurred over time, and thus a brief review of past attitudes towards holidaying and leisure is undertaken. However, it deliberately avoids the usual pattern of describing the Grand Tour and coming of the railway age in detail, for, conceding that these were indeed important, there are other stories which reveal a more complex past.

Having established that tourist experiences are shaped by society, it is argued that each holiday-maker negotiates for himself his own reactions to opportunities and needs; and in order to understand this process it is necessary to comprehend motivations for holidays. However, any review of motivational studies reveals a paradox – the motives identified seem bewildering in their number, or at least in their labels, yet there seem to be underlying commonalities. Hence the chapter argues that there is a diversity of means of expression of needs, but an underlying uniformity of those needs; and to illustrate this the four needs identified by Ragheb and Beard are used as a basis for discussion – relaxation, intellectual, social, and mastery/competency needs. Chapter 3 develops this further by arguing that holiday-makers judge the satisfaction derived from their holidays through evaluating their experiences. However, if this is thought to postulate a simple gap model between expectation and perception, then it is pointed out that the space for the tourist to negotiate with their environment is significant.

After these three introductory chapters a number of chapters follow to illustrate these themes, and to introduce new ones. Cliff and Ryan adapt the gap model to analyse the importance of the travel agent. They chose this because the agent fulfils the functions of 'signposter' and 'gatekeeper' by indicating what is possible, and developing access. It is pointed out that experiences differ due to varying performances of these functions by the agent, while the holiday-maker also assesses, as part of the holiday experience, the performance of the agency.

Baum argues that the performance of such intermediaries in the holiday industry is vital to the quality of tourist experience, and as such a number of organizational implications follow. However, Baum picks up several themes from the earlier chapters to avoid his contribution being simply a restatement of the need for proper training. Thus he argues that there has been a change of 'gaze' not only by the tourist, but also by the provider of tourist services – that past traditions of servant–master are no longer pertinent, even while recognizing that echoes continue down the corridors of history.

From the importance of the human interactions with service providers, attention turns to the nature of the holiday location and the events that occur there. The themes of planned and unplanned physical and social resources are examined by Stephen Page in his chapter on urban tourism, and the role of events and festivals by Don Getz and Jo Cheyne in their section. Page confirms the complexity of the tourism experience by stating that urban tourism is far from homogeneous, and is, in any case, prone to subjective processes on the part of the tourist. Like Cliff and Ryan, he adopts a gap analysis based upon the ServQual model to analyse the nature of urban tourism, but also raises the question of the learning of the spatial characteristics of the place. Don Getz and Jo Cheyne also question their own terms – what is an event, and what makes it special in terms of producing a tourist experience? Like the earlier chapters they introduce a historical and sociological perspective to their topic, and draw upon leisure theory without repeating earlier text within the book, thus adding a new perspective of their own. Additionally, they note verbatim reports from festival-goers as to what constituted their tourist experience. The next chapter considers a well-known holiday haunt, namely the beach. What was surprising to the author was that, given the task of reviewing the literature, how little literature there was on the beach as a holiday site with the exception of past histories of the development of bathing and the impact of the railways. None the less, the beach represented an opportunity to return to a theme stated earlier in the book, which was the one of how marginal activities illustrate much within mainstream behaviours.

In the last two chapters the theme of time comes to the fore in two ways, and so completes a circle by reference to many of the themes of the first chapters. Keith Hollinshead writes about the concepts of heritage, and how heritage suppliers present a selection of images from the past based upon many assumptions about what is pertinent to the needs of the present. He then presents a detailed analysis of how Disney presents a form of heritage tourism that is significant in the way in which new interpretations are created and which are learnt through holiday activities. Thus he too draws distinct linkages between holidaying and wider social processes. The final chapter asks what does it mean 'to have the time of one's life'? Like Hollinshead, I focus on an aspect of time, but this time seek to analyse 'holiday time', arguing that it is a social construct, and that holidays offer not only 'the time of our lives', but also 'time for our lives'. This creates a link back to the first chapter by restating the linkage between holidays and a changing society. Finally, I attempt to draw the themes of the different sections together.

The approach identified above obviously ignores many issues and themes, but it is hoped that students, under the guidance of their tutors, will be able to adapt themes and approaches to those aspects of the topic not covered by the book. We have attempted to write a book that through our own speculations about the nature of the tourist experience will encourage others to speculate and to formulate research questions and modes of analysis.

Chris Ryan
Palmerston North, New Zealand
and Nottingham, England

# *Preface to the second edition*

The preface to the first edition stated that the purpose of the book was to review the literature as it related to varying aspects of the tourist experience, to draw some conclusions and *speculate*. The book was well received, and reviewers' comments could be described as being very positive towards the book. Therefore, this second edition was commissioned, by David Barker of Continuum.

In writing this second edition, significant changes have been made. First, the length of the text has been substantially expanded from 80,000 to 110,000 words. However, quantity of words might simply indicate greater verbosity! An important difference has been a greater contextualization of the material. Reviewers spoke of the richness of ideas, but perhaps in some instances, because of the tight constraints that existed on the length of the first edition, some of the referencing was unnecessarily brief. This new edition has permitted the authors to extend their literature reviews. For example, Don Getz and Joanne Cheyne have significantly extended and updated the literature review component of their chapter on event tourism and visitor experiences. Keith Hollinshead has been able to restore cuts made in his original text by what he may have regarded as an over-zealous editor, and to significantly update, question and contextualize what might be regarded as the contribution of commentators on tourism who have adopted what could be termed 'postmodern' stances towards the phenomenon of tourism. This has allowed him to include tables outlining the main themes of this debate, and the nature of contributions made by various writers as he has sought to synthesize their ideas with reference to tourism, and the implications for those involved in the chain of distribution associated with tourism.

Tom Baum has introduced to his chapter the important concept of 'theatre and skills of emotion', and makes the point that from the perspective of tourism in developing countries, the skills shown by quite junior staff responsible for daily interactions with tourists from the developed world are really of quite a high order. Further, in any tourist context, the person delivering the service – whether a waiter, booking clerk or guide – is continually having to create an experience that is fresh for the visitor, no matter how many times this is a repetitive experience for the provider of the service. As teachers of tourism in universities, this is an element of the service situation that intuitively would seem important to us.

Chris Ryan has responded to the reviews of the first edition in many different ways. First, the context of the debate has been made more explicit by describing much more fully some of the theories upon which his observations were being built. Readers of this edition will therefore find much fuller explanations of the work of the humanistic psychologists upon which many writers of the psychology of the tourist experience draw. Reasons for the attractiveness of these theories are also assessed. In another section of this book, following comments made by John Urry in his review of the original text, with reference to the analysis of 'time' in holidaying, a much extended discussion of this topic has been introduced to take into account the work of the group based at Lancaster University and their analysis of time and processes of globalization.

The early chapters have also been significantly amended. Since the first edition the editor has spent some time in Australia based at the Northern Territory University in Darwin. The Northern Territory contains many comparatively isolated communities within which Aboriginal people form a large part of the population. These encounters have added to his experience of Maori enterprise, thereby reinforcing an awareness of the ritual that is often involved in tourism, and the significance of ritual in social processes. Allied to this was his thinking involved in the writing of *Sex Tourism, Liminalities and Marginal Peoples*, co-authored with Mike Hall. Subsequently, it should come of no surprise that the first two chapters now contain much more reference to concepts of ritual and liminality as they operate within tourism. In his view, the tourist occupies a privileged position of non-work, engaged in a space between the places of home and host, a member of neither community, but a member of a tourist society. Hence, the position of marginality is a position of hybridization.

Another chapter that was changed significantly was that on urban tourism. Stephen Page has amended his chapter not only by locating his contribution within an updated literature review, but also by extending his theorization of the importance of the urban place to tourism, and tourism's contribution to the development of urban space. Urban spaces are not simply places that are visited, but ones which become almost organic in the way in which they respond to growing numbers of visitors, thereby creating changes of land use and different patterns of economic activity that represent a new form that meets both resident and visitor needs. Equally, as places change, so too do perceptions of place, partly as a result of the usage made of them. Therefore, host and guest may occupy two different places within the same physical space.

Finally, there is the chapter on service quality with its analysis of the debate that was initiated by a growing popularity of the ServQual model in a decade from about 1988 to 1998. In the first edition, this chapter emerged from research undertaken by Andrew Cliff. Andy was a student of Chris Ryan while studying for his Master's degree, and, to follow the nomenclature of university regulations, a 'mature student'. He was, in fact, a lecturer at what was then Manawatu Polytechnic, sited in Palmerston North, New Zealand. Like many such lecturers, Andy had a wealth of experience and, like many adult students, was excited by the opportunity to complete a higher degree, and produced work and research of a very high standard. From a professional perspective Andy recognized that in Manawatu Polytechnic's wish to establish degree courses, a research ethic and skill was a prerequisite for good teaching. Yet, I suspect of more importance to him in some ways was the intellectual excitement he enjoyed from having an opportunity to learn new skills and analyse ideas that had practical implementation and a conceptual contribution to the wider literature on service quality. Unfortunately, about two years ago, Andy was killed in a tragic accident, leaving behind a gap and pain for his immediate family and colleagues. His was a talent that was not allowed to develop fully. I hope that Andy would approve of the attempt made to update this specific chapter by reference to the reiterative nature of service quality, expectation and performance. This book is dedicated to his memory.

Chris Ryan
University of Waikato
Hamilton, June 2001

# Acknowledgements

The editor would wish to acknowledge the work of David Barker and Ms E. Cook at Continuum Books. David had faith that a second edition was required and indeed had pressed for such for at least two years. Ms Cook took over from David when he was transferred to the New York offices, and helped the book come to fruition, while Alan Worth sustained the effort by his careful editing of the manuscript.

# Chapter 1

# Stages, gazes and constructions of tourism

*Chris Ryan*

## INTRODUCTION

The way in which people perceive leisure and holidays is determined by the social fabric that surrounds them, and it is no new thing to observe that society has changed significantly over the decades and centuries. Thus a tension exists between, on the one hand, a viewpoint which subscribes to a common experience for all humanity, regardless of age or period, when needs for relaxation, escape and exploration are consistent, and, on the other, an explanation that the importance allocated to those needs and the ways in which they are expressed are socially determined to such an extent that behaviours are significantly different across time. These issues of subjectivity in the holiday and leisure experience, and the consistency of need and behaviour formed the subject of what Urry (1990) has called the *Tourist Gaze*, namely the ways in which tourists seek and then manipulate a context in which they find themselves to identify and meet wants. In doing so, linkages between different activities are, at varying times, weak or strong. Additionally, tourist destinations are multi-product locations, possessing a potential to either entertain or educate (Page, 2001).

The purpose of this chapter is to examine experiences in tourism by reference to popular literature, and to consider tourism from the perspective of tourists having temporary, marginal social roles that, nonetheless, possess the potential for life-change. Recreation can indeed be *re-creation*, and tourists may re-create themselves within the roles that tourists play (Yiannakis and Gibson, 1992), or effect more long-lasting changes in their personal lives. Hence an emphasis upon the individual is considered, but as social creatures, people construct themselves with reference to various norms, and thus the development of holidaying is considered from a historical perspective. Urry (1990) has also utilized Foucault's (1978) argument that society creates a framework of references – a gaze – when reviewing social changes of holiday-making from a Fordist to post-Fordist period, and this too is considered. Such a perspective requires some discussion of the terms associated with postmodernism as they apply to tourism, and thus this too is undertaken with reference to such issues as authenticity, or rather, in this instance, social and personal constructions of authorizations.

## THE FICTION OF HOLIDAYS – OR CATALYTIC DREAMS

Holidays are important periods in people's lives. They possess the potential for cathartic experiences. Willy Russell's heroine, Shirley Valentine, is not simply a figment of imagination, but a carefully observed phenomenon. For those unfamiliar with the play, the story concerns Mrs Joe Bradshaw, a 42-year-old Liverpool mother of two grown-up children, bound to preparing her abusive husband's meals as he returns from work each day. Under prompting from a friend, she takes a holiday to Greece, leaves the package holiday hotel and stays at a Greek taverna, where she falls under the spell of a Mediterranean romance and a Greek lover who says he likes her stretch marks. The issue that the play explores is whether the husband has the ability to change, while Mrs Bradshaw finds her old self as Shirley Valentine. While it is fiction, this author, when a windsurfing instructor for a holiday company in Greece, came across many such examples of tourists experiencing a life-change as the result of a holiday. In one case a former personnel manager of a major British retail chain, Marks & Spencer, had left her post to become a sailing instructor in the Mediterranean, and in another, a self-employed financial consultant sold his business to sail catamarans and offer sailing lessons in Greece. Indeed, a number of holiday companies have been founded by people who, on holiday, became enamoured with a place or imagined lifestyle, and left their jobs. Examples include companies such as Greek Sailing and Saronic Sailing, both subsequently absorbed by the major British tour operator, Owners Abroad. In one research study, when the author interviewed people seated in an open-air restaurant in Puerto D'Andraitx in Majorca, one woman even remarked she was a 'Shirley Valentine'. She had holidayed in Majorca a decade previously, returned home to the UK, left her husband and returned to the island to take up a new life (Ryan, 1995a). Other researchers have also identified the Shirley Valentine syndrome as a short-term motive for escape. For example, Wickens (1994) writes of 'women on a mono-gender holiday who hope for romance and sexual adventure with a "Greek God"'. Subsequently, Wickens (1999, 2000) amplified her typology and the behaviours associated with such classifications as 'the Lord Byron', 'Cultural Heritage Seeker', 'the Heliolatatrous', 'the Raver' and 'Shirley Valentine' by reference to Goffman's concepts of 'role commitment', 'role attachment' and 'role embracement'. For Wickens, the important thing is not the classification *per se*, but the way tourists change tourist roles, pursuing, escaping from and escaping to states of familiarity or fantasy. And, of course, such role change takes place within the contextual change from being non-holiday-maker to tourist. From such a perspective it is but a short step to represent tourism as being more than simply *the* destination, or *the* activity, but rather tourism achieves meaning for both the individual as a tourist, and tourists *en masse*, through relationships between roles, stages and places. In short, to understand the tourist experience requires appreciation of relationships, the network of communications that exist between competing and complementary roles, the context of place, time and action within which such communication exists and the relationship between the tourist as actor and acted upon. As Barthes (1973, p. 109) wrote, 'the universe is infinitely fertile in suggestions. Every object in the world can pass from closed, silent existence to an oral state, open to appropriation by society.' Although Wickens follows Giddens (1991) in identifying states of 'familiarity', 'ontological security' and 'flight from everyday life', the experience of tourism lies in more than simply the motivation of the tourist. As will be argued later in this book, motive alone explains action poorly, as many different actions can fulfil motive. To which it can also be observed that if de-differentiation is the characteristic of the postmodern era, then the boundaries between non-tourist and tourist are also fuzzy, through many different mechanisms that include short breaks, role of leisure within work, and the intrusion of work upon holidays through cell-phones, laptops and internet cafés, as well as socio-psychological changes.

While the life-changing experiences of a Shirley Valentine are not the norm, one cannot help asking the question, what is it about holidays that can potentially cause such change? In what ways do these periods of escape allow people to examine themselves and come to such drastic decisions? And, as noted, surely such a circumstance only has meaning in the wider context of the non-holiday daily life of people? It is not new to call holidays the vital margin of existence. Cohen (1982) described one sample of holiday-makers and their location by the sea, as a 'marginal paradise'. The beach was a margin between land and sea; the period of their stay was a temporal marginality, and they occupied a marginal social status being not of the community in which they lived. Yet this littoral strip was important in that its very marginality became illustrative of major themes of economics and lifestyles. Ryan and Kinder (1996) in their study of tourists and prostitutes make the same observation that tourism lends itself to

> an ethnomethodological perspective which concentrates on the marginal nature of the activity; a marginality which assumes an importance because the relationship between tourist and prostitute provides insights into what might be described as 'main-stream' activity.

What is true of this activity is arguably true of the whole of tourism. The two weeks break in the sun or the country contains much potential to sustain or change people's lifestyles. Ryan and Hall (2000), albeit in the specific sub-sector of sex tourism, draw attention to Turner's (1982) concept of the liminoid phenomenon. Turner wrote:

> In the so-called 'high culture' of complex societies, liminoid is not only removed from a rite de passage context, it is also 'individualised'. The solitary artist creates the liminoid phenomena, the collectivity experiences collective liminal symbols. This does not mean that the maker of liminoid symbols, ideas, images, etc., does so *ex nihilo*; it only means that he is privileged to make free with his social heritage in a way impossible to members of cultures in which the liminal is to a large extent the sacrosanct. (p. 52)

Following Ryan and Hall (2000), but generalizing their argument to encompass the whole, tourism might be called a liminoid phenomenon because:

1. it is individualized and contractual;
2. it occurs at 'natural disjunctions with the flow of natural and social processes' (Turner, 1982, p. 54);
3. it is co-existent with, and dependent upon, a total social process and represents its subjectivity and negativity;
4. it possesses the nature of being profane, being a reversal of roles, an antithesis of the collective, but possessing its own collective representation;
5. it is idiosyncratic, quirky and ludic. 'Their symbols are closer to the personal-psychological than to the objective-social typological pole' (*ibid.*, p. 54); and
6. ultimately they cease to be eufunctional, but become a social critique exposing injustices, inefficiencies and immoralities of mainstream economic and political structures.

At the heart of the interactions and relationships that arise from communication lies the interpreter of the metanyms and metaphors that is the tourist. In short, touristic experiences might be shared, but they are individualistic. It can be objected that this is true of every facet of human existence, and that tourism is thus no different from any other human experience in this regard. Much of human experience is concerned with a dialectic of the individual and the collective, the experience of each person and the consensus of sharing with others, but the claim that tourism is specifically marginal rests on this determinant in combination with the other factors listed above. Tourism is an experience born of travel, it occurs at other than the normal milieu. It happens away from home. By reason of adopting the tourist role, events occur at 'natural disjunctions with the flow of natural and social processes'. By definition though, as argued above, the meanings associated with these disjunctions possess truths through comparison as well as through the events themselves. To understand the holiday experience by solely describing, for example, interactions between tourist and tourist, tourist and courier, and tourist and hosts can ever only be a partial analysis, for the interaction takes on a new meaning by reason of its displacement away from 'normality'. Indeed, the interaction at the disjuncture is uneven from many perspectives, not least of which is, in the case of tourist–courier interaction, the fact that the courier possesses a location in time and place which, while often isolated from their own home (e.g. the English seasonal courier dealing with clients in Spain), has a temporary stability by reason of being the milieu of work. That which is absent (in this example, English customs, law and climate) helps explain the actions that take place within that which is present (Spanish customs, law and climate); yet to complicate the matter further, although out of the United Kingdom, both client and courier incorporate a mental framework of common understanding into the foreign place.

Inherent in this lies a 'quirkiness' that exists apart from any tourist behaviour that is ludic and idiosyncratic. For Huizinga, play was an act of differentiation, a stepping outside of the normal. He wrote that play is:

> considered as a free activity standing quite consciously outside 'ordinary' life as being 'not serious', but at the same time absorbing the player intensely and utterly. It is an activity connected with no material interest, and no profit can be gained by it. It proceeds within its own proper boundaries of time and space. It promotes the formation of social groupings which tend, among other things, to stress their difference from the common world by disguise or other means. (Huizinga, 1950, p. 13)

Holidays are periods of play, social irresponsibility, and the escape from home is often an escape from obligation. As socially sanctioned periods of play and relaxation, tourism fully meets the condition of being 'limonoid'. While each tourist may be hedonistic, or self-actualizing by preference or in turn, collectively the actions of individuals create what may be termed 'tourism'. In Huizinga's terminology, social groupings are formed, distinguished from the rest of the world. For Leiper (2000) a distinctive feature of the definition 'tourist' is distinctive behaviour that revolves around leisure derived from places visited. But as 'players' distinct from 'workers', holiday-makers possess the paradox of being beyond the norm. Rewarded for work by the power of money earned from work, they take upon themselves the role of non-workers, and as non-workers may be subject to the derogation of their role. Thus Feifer (1985, p. 219) caricatures the tourist as, in his straw hat, loud Hawaiian shirt, being:

'armed for action'. He has a camera slung round his neck and a wad of bills in his pocket. But like a newborn chick to its mother hen, he stays close to the big bus. Nobody knows his name ... staggering off the bus in another quaintly imposing grand place, he has no way to identify where he is except by dazedly scrutinizing his itinerary – blinking, he utters the familiar caption: 'If it's Tuesday, this must be Belgium' ... universally 'distasteful', but every marketer's favorite dish, he's simply and starkly the tourist.

But, whether caricatured or not, the act of travelling often breaks down conventions by reason of existing outside conventional structures. For example, in 1910, Mary Hall in her tramping of the Milford Track, wrote of taking cover from the rain in Quintin Huts, a refuge for walkers in that part of New Zealand. She wrote that

> False modesty had no show that night, as we sat brazen-faced watching our clothes drying on a line drawn across the open fire-place. The unmentionables of a strange gentleman might have been seen in close proximity to the corsets of a lady unknown to him, and an interesting contrast was created by the hobnobbing of something white and lace-trimmed with a pair of weather-beaten gaiters. (Hall, 2000, p. 221)

Whether it be the 'hobnobbing' of ladies and gentlemen's 'undies' or, as described below, the more blatant view of the female form by Edwardian gentlemen at the beach, tourism has often been associated with the profane, but by legitimizing the profane through processes of habituation, it is no idle claim to say that tourism has had significant impacts upon the daily lives of many over the years, whether it be in the stocking of Mediterranean foods in London supermarkets, the relaxation of norms in dress or in other intrusions that question daily construction of self. In the final resort, therefore, tourism ceases to be a carefully demarcated activity. It is both eufunctional and isolated. Tourism possesses the potential to challenge the status quo – not directly, but through its sheer existence as a world of non-work, of a world wherein tourists might find themselves as re-created persons, as an alternative means of ordering structures for individuals, both individually and societally, then tourism has a potential to challenge accepted ways of doing things. That it does not represents the ways that tourism has become part of a global, commercial structure. Yet examples of tourism as offering alternatives can be found. For example, the processes of cultural tourism based upon the culture of indigenous peoples has created a legitimization of aspiration on the part of such peoples, and, furthermore, developed a means by which they are able to access levers of economic and political power. Additionally, it can be argued that to some extent such leverage has been achieved partly upon their own terms. In the case of Australian Aboriginal peoples, while tourists may complain about a lack of achieving desired contact levels with Aboriginal people (Pearce and Moscardo, 1999), none the less Aboriginal and Torres Straits Islander peoples have been successful at generating incomes from the sale of arts and crafts without exposing their communities to an influx of tourists, and in the case of the York Peninsula, Torres Straits Islanders have successfully generated businesses selling to the tourists through retail and garage outlets without a need to commodify their own culture. The relationship between tourism and attitudes towards power structures in the case of Australian Aboriginal peoples is further evidenced by Palmer's (1998) work at Warradjan Aboriginal Cultural Centre at Cooinda in Kakadu National Park where, as a result of the visit, evidence was found of shifts in attitude towards Aboriginal land claims. Also of interest in Palmer's work is that the research also provided evidence that the research process itself, that is the actual asking of questions, enhanced the visitor experience by requiring the tourist to articulate thoughts applying to the cultural centre, thereby creating a more active than passive relationship between the subject of the tourist gaze and the onlooker.

For individuals, the continued growth of tourism has meant a challenge to the supremacy of work. Even in the decades since Feifer's caricature, cited above, was penned, a new millennium serves only to confirm Vukonić's contention that 'A new kind of consciousness seems to have arisen: free time is increasingly the content of life, and work, on the contrary, as a necessity' (1996, p. 7). However, the contention has not taken the form that Vukonić propounds. While he writes of a reduction in working time, he cites figures that even by the time of his writing, were eleven years old. The latter years of the twentieth century saw the development of a harassed leisure class, and the role of leisure as 'the content of life' has been played out not in the mere counting of hours but in an increasing de-differentiation of work and leisure, whereby work resumes a different hegemony based on contribution to self-actualization. It is probably no coincidence that the growth of non-marriage among better educated, young, single high earners has emerged as a factor for both genders in the period from 1995 in many countries, for it is not simply a choice to place career above family but a recognition that, psychologically as well as financially, new patterns of work and new occupations meet many psychological needs of stimulation, achievement and a sense of belonging to groups with shared norms, combined with freedoms to travel, change jobs and retain independence. The role-switching of tourism pervades the workplace. Recreation and leisure become part of the node of work as gymnasia, spas and showers invade the physical space of the office – and in new, imaginative software-based industries young workers create working space within which to skateboard.

Approximately 100 years earlier Georg Simmel had explored the need for individuality in the face of a growing metropolis. In *The Metropolis and Mental Life* Simmel had written:

> The deepest problems of modern life derive from the claim of the individual to preserve the autonomy and individuality of his existence in the face of overwhelming social forces, of historical heritage, of external culture, and of the technique of life. The fight with nature which primitive man has to wage for his bodily existence attains in this modern form its latest transformation. (Simmel, 1909, translated to English by Wolff, 1950, p. 409)

Simmel had seen an explicit and symbiotic relationship between 'the money economy and the dominance of the intellect' (*ibid.*, p. 411), and he analysed the tension between calculating economic egoism and the need for social warmth, and the means by which the city extends freedoms through its economic and psychosocial systems. For Simmel, born in a society creating capitalism from scientific rationalism, freedoms were the result of the triumph of the 'objective spirit' over the subjective. The paradox of the postmodern is that freedom comes from the recognition of the importance of the subjective by the rational, and the de-differentiation of the two in work patterns that recognize leisure and touristic needs even while work is conducted. Not only has there been a growth of non-marriage, but also a longer history of business travel provides testimony to the role of travel in work. Additionally, increasing amounts of evidence indicate the contemporaneous nature of work and leisure that is involved in such patterns of work. For example, in a survey of 1824 passengers at Hamilton International Airport the author found 47 per cent of business travellers stated that they would be seeing friends and relatives, attending sports events, taking a holiday and/or attending a conference even while travelling for business purposes was designated as the main purpose of the trip (Ryan and Birks, 2000).

From the perspective of the individual tourist, it is true that the cathartic experience is not the norm, but even so it must be worth examining what people actually experience on holiday. From a purely pragmatic viewpoint, consider the fact that people repeatedly spend large sums of money each year on an activity that results in no ownership of physical assets, that takes them from the comfort of familiar environments to possibly strange places where they do not speak the language, know the customs and where they run a real risk of catching 'the runs' (Cartwright, 1996, provides a literature review of travellers' diarrhoea, quoting various rates of the incidence of diarrhoea, which ranged from 5.8 to 72 per cent depending upon country visited). When described in these terms it seems hardly a rational mode of behaviour! Rationality might only be discerned if the motivations are known and if the experience actually meets the needs. However, such a statement raises questions like Why assume rationality exists, and whose rationality is being discerned – that of the participant or the observer?

The literature is rich in studies that seek to examine the motivations of holiday-makers. Such studies encompass a wide number of techniques and sources; from the empirical to the fictional. *Shirley Valentine* has already been mentioned, but the holiday has other places of literary fame. Among contemporary works, David Lodge's novel *Paradise News* has often been quoted approvingly by academic researchers (for example in the *Times Higher Educational Supplement* of 10 March 1995, p. 24), and this author will do likewise. The opening pages of Lodge's novel describe the airport concourse:

> choked with delayed passengers sleeping under the fluorescent lights in their soiled, crumpled clothes, sprawled promiscuously all over the furniture and the floor, mouths agape and limbs askew, like the victims of a massacre or a neutron bomb, while the airport cleaners picked their way through the prone bodies like scavengers on a battlefield ...
>   'What do they see in it?' he asks again. 'What are they *after?*'
>   'The free esses, innit,' says Trevor Connolly ... 'Sun, sand and sex,' Trevor elaborates with a smirk. (Lodge, 1991, p. 4)

Lodge, in his guise of the worldly-wise recent recruit to the travel agency, is simply repeating the well-worn cliché of the holiday trade, but the very experience of his hero indicates a much more complex pattern of motivations and experiences (even if it does include sex as well as sun and sand). Lodge (1996) returns to the theme of contemporary holidays as a means of self-discovery in a later novel, *Therapy*, where the relationship between self-discovery, love and pilgrimage is made all the more explicit as 'tubby' Lawrence Passmore rediscovers a love from 40 years in his past, and traces a pilgrimage of search both for life's meaning and his love through the medieval pilgrim's route to Santiago de Compostela.

Journalists have often found tourism to be valuable copy that sells newspapers and books. Moynahan's book *Fools Paradise* (1983) was sold as an exposé 'to the great tourist rip off'. Moynahan writes that:

> The sad fact is that cheats have always preyed on tourists. A pair of loaded dice were found under the lava of the Roman resort of Pompeii. A typical medieval diceman, Elmer de Multon, was sentenced in twelfth-century London for 'enticing strangers to a tavern in chepeside and there deceiving them by using false dice.' (p. 182)

Authors have found inspiration from their holidays which are subsequently transferred to their fictional heroes. Sue Townsend so enjoyed her holiday that Adrian Mole had to go to Greece, while of course Peter Mayle encouraged many British to seek their dream existence in Provence (Swarbrook, 1992). The relationship between fiction, dreams and tourism impacts has long been established. Jarvis notes how, in 1887, a visitor to north Devon wrote: 'Each town, each hamlet, hill or heath is associated either with *Lorna Doone* or with *Westward Ho!* ... Kingsley and Blackmore ... have stamped out the individuality of their genius on districts so rich in all the materials for romance' (Jarvis, 1993, p. 171).

Today, the novel is combined with the power of television and cinema to inspire the need to visit a place of dreams. Riley (1994, p. 455) has noted how the film *Deliverance* became a catalyst for a thriving river rafting operation, while Historic Fort Hays, used in *Dances with Wolves*, recorded a 25 per cent increase in visitor figures in 1991 after the release of the film. The Baseball Diamond used for *Field of Dreams*, located in a hitherto ignored farmland location, attracted 140,000 visitors between 1989 and 1993. The effects of films and television series can be long enduring. *The Prisoner*, a British television series of the 1960s which has reached cult status (as evidenced by its appearance in an episode of another cult series, *The Simpsons*) and which is still shown on television today, attracts visitors to Portmeirion in North Wales, where it was filmed, long after it reached its puzzling conclusion.

The experience of holidays is important in many ways. They may be periods of escape for people, and catalysts for change for both individuals and communities. Yet the process is partly based upon dreams and hopes about places and what they mean, and the manufacturing of images by industry sources. The tourist is both spectator and actor upon a world stage in a process that is itself part of the entertainment business. Tourists flock to MGM and Paramount Studios to further live out a fantasy seen on the screen. Disney represents a mixture of well-known world sites in Florida and portrays and reinforces a pattern of easily recognized icons of American history (Fjellman, 1992; Hollinshead, 1994a, b). Locations like Disney World, Universal Studios, Las Vegas, Fox Studios, medieval banquets, western dude ranches and similar theme-oriented attractions around the world make fuzzy the boundaries of reality. Hence Disney, on its website in 2001, described its Animal Kingdom Lodge thus:

> It's a Resort adventure in the making. Here, most balconies overlook a picturesque savanna where giraffe, zebra and other exotic animals roam about a spacious wildlife reserve. Hand-crafted furnishings and African decor welcome you to a world of comfort complete with all the beauty of nature ... and all the magic of Disney.
> (http://asp.disney.go.com/disneyworld/db/seetheworld/resorts/facilities/
> resorts.asp?id = 1015 – 15 March 2001)

Perhaps the use of the word 'exotic' is justified by the fact that the location is in Orlando, Florida. Yet the accompanying photograph portrays an image associated with African game parks as giraffes wander past a lodge. Wang (2000) identifies three forms of authenticity within tourism, namely:

(a)  Objective authenticity – corresponding to the uniqueness of the original;
(b)  Constructive authenticity – a projection of authenticity onto toured objects; and
(c)  Existential authenticity – the potential existential state of Being that is activated by tourist activities.

Of this last, Wang notes that 'authentic experiences in tourism are to achieve this activated existential state of Being within the liminal process of tourism. Existential authenticity has little to do with the authenticity of toured objects' (p. 49). Given that existential authenticity relates to states of Being, and the seeking of senses of freedom, of being one's self, the philosophies of Maslow (1970) possess paradox in the sense that according to Wang's categorization, there exists the potential for the act of self-actualization to occur at places that are constructed authenticities, lacking objective reality, and thus states of Being one's self can be located in places of artificiality. While appearing a paradox, this is not entirely inconsistent with Maslow's original work. The whole point of Maslow's theorizing was that the self-actualized person was qualitatively different from others, since he characterized the self-actualized personality as being:

> relatively spontaneous in behavior and far more spontaneous than that in their inner life, thoughts, impulses etc. Their behavior is marked by simplicity and naturalness, and by lack of artificiality or straining for effect . . . His unconventionality is not superficial but essential or internal. (1970, p. 157).

Hence, the self-actualized person can sustain a lack of artificiality in artificial places just as effectively as in the prison cell or the place of work. It is to be noted that it is clear from his diaries (Maslow, 1979) that Maslow was concerned about moral issues and questions of how people become evil when writing *Motivation and Personality*. Indeed, in his preface he notes that the motive for the book was 'the solution of various personal moral, ethical and scientific problems' (Maslow, 1970, p. 149). Hence, theoretically, the catharsis that tourism offers a Shirley Valentine can just as likely occur in Disney as on a Greek caique in the Mediterranean. It might be said that St Paul found his conversion on a road to Damascus, so the idea of self-actualization in Disney is not, perhaps, so far-fetched. If, therefore, existential authenticity can occur within manipulated places, then the crisis noted by Williams, that there has been a spiritual breakdown in the modern period,

> that humanity's decision to *unbind* itself from the soil – not return to a nomadic existence, but to bid itself to a predominantly technological environment – has provoked a similar profound spiritual crisis. We are now embarked upon another period of cultural mourning and upheaval, as we look back to a way of life that is ebbing away. (1990, p. 2)

This represents not a crisis *per se*, but a transition whereby as a species people can continue to find a spirituality not dependent upon romantic notions of naturalness. From a tourism perspective, the wider implications include the questions To what degree is eco-tourism required for a sense of better self being? Does adventure have to take place in natural settings? and Can tourists separate senses of freedom away from natural places? The answers to these questions pose serious implications for the development of tourism, and the nature of longings that arise within contemporary late- or postmodern societies.

What this analysis also renders of importance is the issue of who authorizes the constructive authenticity? Indeed, the term *authorizations* might be better in that it more clearly makes the break between issues of uniqueness as authenticity lying in the original, implying, therefore, that authenticity is permanent and possesses an inability to change, and authenticity as arising from concepts of ownership by reason of given traditions or past claims, as is the case, for example, with the art of Maori and other traditional peoples (Aotearoa Maori Tourism Federation, 1994, 1995; Ryan, 1997). The issue thus becomes clearer in posing a number of questions: Who has authorized a given representation? For what purpose has it been authorized? and Under what limits, and for whom has it been authorized? It thus becomes possible to discuss an authentic tourism representation of a given culture where that presentation differs from that used by a given group, for the authenticity lies in the choice made by a people to represent their culture in ways specific to the purpose of educating and/or entertaining tourists, just as under other circumstances, the same people selected from their culture those things thought pertinent to other uses. The silent issue implicit in such discussions is that of power: Wherein does power lie that sanctions the representation seen by the tourist? It also implies that this latter form of authorized authenticity is the subject of negotiation, is impermanent and thus changes over time.

## FROM PAST TO CURRENT GAZE

To specify that each individual imposes their own meaning within frameworks of the exercise of power is a stance akin to that adopted by Urry in his book *The Tourist Gaze* (1990). The viewpoint of contemporary commentators upon the meaning and significance of current trends in tourism that are labelled 'postmodernism' or 'deconstructionism' are examined in much greater detail elsewhere in this book (Hollinshead in this volume, pp. 172ff), but the significance of the changing perspective cannot be underestimated. Today, arguably, tourism is perceived primarily as an individual good, and is of comparatively recent origin in its form of jet travel to far-off places undertaken in periods of short duration. It is an individual good in the sense that tourists pursue the holiday for selfish reasons dominated by needs for relaxation, and many tourists do not question the impact that tourism as a phenomenon creates.

How did this occur, and was it ever otherwise? To answer this question we can utilize one hypothesis suggested by Rojek that contemporary holiday-taking is an evolution of a process that for long periods of time was organized and, to a lesser or greater degree, controlled as a means of sustaining preferred social arrangements. Thus Rojek (1993, pp. 11–50) presents a detailed description of the changing nature of leisure in western societies from the twelfth century.

At that time, Rojek observes,

> The state machines were agencies of moral regulation and they operated, directly, to manage association, organisation and practice geared to pleasure ... The state regulated ... in three ways. First, by *licensing*, the state labelled some activities as acceptable and others as not. Second, by *policing* and *punishing*, the state enforced its values upon popular culture. Third, by *stereotyping* certain forms of association, organisation and practice in pejorative terms as 'vulgar', 'unseemly' or 'riotous', the state established and reinforced a moral and aesthetic hierarchy which devalued and marginalised certain forms of being human. (p. 25)

In a world of embattled monarchy, monastic privilege and the personal dynastic ambitions of princes, the ascribed status and reciprocal obligations of feudal society led to sports like archery being approved by royal decree. Periods of misrule were also permitted, but short-lived, thereby creating certainty out of the potential for chaos.

Rojek characterizes this period as one when sport and recreation were 'accepted as fulfilling rational ends, notably recuperation for physical efficiency' (1993, p. 27). It was to cast a long shadow when, in the seventeenth century, the Puritan ethic maintained suspicion of pleasure as being both ethically immoral and wasteful of time.

Yet concepts of pleasure as something to be managed for the ethical good of the individual have long been retained within western society. Indeed, the very word 'recreation' has been generally understood as an opportunity for the *re-creation* of the positive aspects of the human psyche, i.e. it is time spent in a search for psychological health to correct the stresses caused by current stressful work patterns. The Judeo-Christian tradition implies an ethos of striving for perfection, and although today many might reject harmony with God's Word as a goal, the concept of harmony with self or with nature is still perceived as a form of searching approved by the *mores* of modern society. In some instances the search is explicit, as Ryan (1991, p. 22) notes of the *Skyros Experience*, the objectives of the holiday are spelt out by its promoters as a period of escape when, in the company of like-minded people, holiday-makers are able to explore their deeper selves.

In the nineteenth century many middle-class organizations sought to provide recreational opportunities for the working class as a means of combatting the evils of drink and gambling; to promote an awareness of higher goals. Of these, the Lord's Day Observance Society, founded in 1831, was, and remains, one of the more famous. Rojek (1993, p. 34) describes in some detail Canon Barnett's scheme of bringing art to the poor in the East End of London through an annual art exhibition which lasted from 1881 to 1898. The leisure time of youth in the late nineteenth century was provided for through organizations such as the Boy Scouts, the Girl Guides, the Boys' Brigade and other organizations which imparted an ethos of self-sufficiency combined with a respect for authority, Empire and God.

Such a view of leisure as a process of self-improvement was not restricted to the middle class. The mining communities of South Wales, Yorkshire and elsewhere created their own recreational activities aided by the growth of the night school and apprentice training. The strong acceptance of education as a means of achieving several ends: self-improvement, morally and economically; the maintenance of strong and effective trade unionism; and as a means of access to the middle-class citadels of power, led to significant leisure activities within a sense of community. From brass bands to rambling, from debating clubs to Christmas Clubs, the new industrialized working classes developed a culture of working and playing hard.

Consequently, it might be argued that the holidaying patterns that emerged in the latter part of the nineteenth century for both the 'respectable' working class and those of the 'middle class' who discovered Europe with Mr Cook, were characterized by group activities and thoughts of self-improvement. Many from that period would have agreed with Slavson (1948, p. 20) in saying that

> because recreation is a response to pleasure cravings, it must needs be regulated by society or becomes a menace ... when pleasure becomes indulgence, one grows unable to organise his life; he loses hold on self and situation. (cited in Rojek, 1993, p. 47)

Two questions can be raised about Rojek's thesis of a societal approach towards an ordered recreation. First: Is the process more apparent than real? Second: If real, did inconsistencies exist? Thus both questions might be viewed as observations or alternative means of interpreting the data. Rojek notes that the process of nineteenth-century reform possessed its own dialectic of leisure which led to its breakdown. Inconsistencies and tensions could not help but exist within the ordered approach to the role of leisure. The process of 'ordered recreation' from the twelfth to the nineteenth century had undergone significant transformations of purpose. While Edward III had sought to encourage archery as a means of improving military prowess, the nineteenth-century reformers sought material and psychological, if not spiritual, improvement of the individual. Such attempts were motivated by a mixture of Christian concern and altruism on the one hand and, on the other, a concern that a regulated society should not be threatened by either poverty or the lawlessness to which a lack of money might give rise. However, whatever the motivation, it gave birth to an increased critical awareness by growing numbers of people (Rojek, 1993, p. 48). An appreciation of nature was no longer the prerogative of turn-of-the-century romantic poets – a century after Wordsworth had wandered through dales, the embryo of a working-class movement that would, in the 1930s, challenge the rights of landowners to restrict public access to the moors and hills had been laid. The energy and concerns of Victorian reformers meant that in leisure, as in education, shopfloor relationships and politics, the old certainties based upon received biblical notions would be increasingly questioned, so that which was 'normal' became fragmented and diffuse. The late nineteenth century thus becomes a period of rupture, when old systems of knowledge begin to be replaced by alternative processes of thought.

In the *Birth of the Clinic: An Archaeology of Medical Perception*, a work which Foucault states is 'about space, about language, and about death; it is the act of seeing, the gaze' (1963, p. ix); it is noted that 'What counts in the things said by men, is not so much what they may have thought beneath or beyond them, but what systematizes them from the outset' (Foucault, 1963, p. xv).

In Foucault's terms, however, not only are there underlying systems of knowledge (*epistemes*) of which the participants may not always be aware, but there are also ruptures between these structures. Hence, within tourism literature there are references to the Grand Tour as a predecessor of modern travel, but in Foucault's terminology it was a period of a different *epistem* – of different knowledge structures – and it can be argued that our histories of it impute meanings to the Grand Tour that might not have been recognized by those who participated in it. Meanings, argues Foucault, were, in the nineteenth century, imputed through a process of classification, wherein, too, mechanisms of power came to be exercised. In *The History of Sexuality* Foucault wrote:

> But so many pressing questions singularised the pleasures felt by the one who had to reply. They were fixed by a gaze, isolated and animated by the attention they received. Power operated as a mechanism of attraction; it drew out those peculiarities over which it kept watch. Pleasure spread to the power that harried it; power anchored the pleasure it uncovered. (Foucault, 1978, p. 45)

Foucault conceptualizes a passing from an ordered world of feudal times into a more uncertain period. The process of 'ordered recreation', predominant until the latter part of the nineteenth century, was one based upon an interpretation of an individual's role within a wider society. By the late nineteenth century an increasing emphasis upon the individual became more important. Like many social movements and currents it was not a sudden appearance. It might be argued that the eighteenth century, with its tradition of rationalization that gave rise to declarations of the rights of man in France and America, was a precursor of a movement that still echoes today. However, the industrialization of the second half of the nineteenth century created a wealth and technology that permitted individual travel for larger numbers of people, and which slowly reduced the modes of social control. Did this lead to a recent period of rupture so strong that, in fact, the process of ordered recreation (that Rojek discerns until the 1950s) became displaced by a new, individualistic consumption of symbols and icons in an iconoclastic age? Or have ordered recreation, commodification and individualism become but separate, parallel strands within an increasingly complex thread of leisure and holiday-taking behaviour?

From 1843 the working classes of the South Wales mining communities were able to take steamer trips across the Bristol Channel to the sedate north Cornish resort of Ilfracombe. The first such trip was of 400 teetotallers (Jarvis, 1993, p. 132), but by June 1849 the local newspaper, the *North Devon Journal*, reported that 'over 400 of the human swarm of Swansea' had invaded Ilfracombe. Donkeys were raced down the street, whereafter

> Many of them went on board drunk; and what shocked our townspeople more … there were women – that ever we should have to write – women who were tumbled aboard in a state of – we cannot write that name of shame – a state not to be mentioned. (cited by Jarvis, 1993, p. 149)

Not that such 'shameful' behaviour was the monopoly of the working classes. In an earlier period the gentlemen of the Grand Tour eagerly awaited their visit to Venice, known as the brothel of Europe (Hibbert, 1987), while in the nineteenth century the gentlemen of the bourgeoisie would be drawn to views that overlooked the bathing huts allocated to females in a continuous hope that the waves would wash the bathing garments over the heads of the bathers, or that the effect of the sea water would permit sharp delineation of the female form. It is of interest to trace a history of hedonism, exemplified by Club 18–30 holidays in Mediterranean islands, to earlier Victorian norms. In his work *Don Juan*, Byron wrote:

> What men call gallantry, and gods adultery,
> Is much more common where the climate's sultry.

> Happy the nations of the moral North!
> Where all is virtue, and the wintering season
> Sends sin, without a rag on, shivering forth …
>
> (Byron, *Don Juan*, 1819, canto 1, st 63)

Hence an association with free-thinking, and freedom of action, was associated in the Victorian mind with warmer climates from the commencement of the nineteenth century, and as Ryan and Hall (2001) discuss, from this to a subsequent exoticism (if not eroticism) of the Far East and Polynesia was but a continuation of a theme. Equally, the seaside, as indicated above, was associated with new freedoms that set aside a prurience that existed side-by-side with Victorian sexual interest, and brought the unspoken into the open. The bathing-hut was invented to assure the modesty of females but was, at best, of limited success in achieving its objective. Sprawson (1992, p. 29) remarks that the women were encased in waisted, bloomered, skirted swimsuits, made of 'woven cotton, which when wet tended to become transparent and cling to the body, revealing more than they concealed'. He continues:

> But whatever the restrictions, they (bathing-huts) failed to prevent women from becoming objects of the greatest curiosity. In the Victorian coastal resorts, when the sea, commented

one onlooker, was normally 'black with bathers' ... The females did not venture beyond the surf but lay on their backs, waiting for the approaching waves, with their bathing dresses in 'a most dégagé style. When the waves came, they not only covered the bathers, but literally carried their dresses up to their necks, so that, as far as decency was concerned, they might as well have been without any dresses at all.' (*Ibid.*)

However, were these simply activities tolerated by a system, exceptions that prove a rule, symptoms of deeper-lying processes that co-existed with, but were secondary to, the attempts of regulation as defined by Rojek, or exhibits of a much wider social context which meant that regulation was but one theme of many co-existing themes of equal importance? Rojek argues that one sign of the regulation of leisure was the loss of 'Saint Monday'. Cunningham (1980) observes that in the eighteenth century, workers had a high preference for leisure, and long periods of it. Past working habits continued into the period of industrialization, and the long weekend was the result. Rybcznski (1991) comments on a regular custom of taking Monday off as a holiday thus:

> Among some trades the Monday holiday achieved what amounted to an official status. Weavers and miners, for example, regularly took a holiday on the Monday after payday ... This practice became so common that it was called 'keeping Saint Monday'.
>   Saint Monday may have started as an individual preference for staying away from work – whether to relax, to recover from drunkenness, or both – but its popularity during the 1850s and 1860s was ensured by the enterprise of the leisure industry. During that period sporting events, such as horse races and cricket matches, often took place on Mondays, since their organisers knew that many working-class customers would be prepared to take the day off. And, since many public events were prohibited on the Sabbath, Monday became the chief occasion for secular recreations. (pp. 43–4).

Thus the religious reformers of the mid-nineteenth century found that attempts to 'organize' recognition of the Sabbath led to the very things that they held abhorrent. A curious combination of Evangelicals and factory owners consequently led to the acceptance of half-day working on Saturdays as an alternative to Saint Monday. While, on the one hand, this supports Rojek's thesis of a social process which was in itself a form of industrialization and professionalism of leisure, recreation and holiday-taking, from another perspective closer inspection shows considerable regional variations in holiday-taking patterns. Cunningham (1990) emphasizes two theses. First, working-class leisure was no pale imitation of that of the upper classes. From dog-baiting, prize-fighting, rambling, cycling and staying at Blackpool B&Bs, the working classes developed patterns of leisure that created their own norms and emphasized strong feelings of communality. Secondly, there was significant regional variation. Past historic studies of the railways in nineteenth-century Britain have called attention to the emergence of the seaside resorts of Blackpool, Morecambe and others, but, in doing so, they have overshadowed other developments. McInnes (1988) has shown how Shrewsbury emerged as a leisure centre for the rural areas of the Marches between England and Wales prior to industrialization, while Towner (1994, p. 723) notes that while 'Railways created certain *patterns* of tourism ... growth may have occurred in different ways without them'.

It is also interesting to observe the process of democratization that occurred in the nineteenth century; a process not unique to the UK but also applying to other countries, including the USA. The trip to the beach was indeed an escape. The beach at places like Blackpool or Coney Island became precursors of a new age. Shields (1991) summarized the carnival of the beach as being vulgar:

It is this foolish, impudent, undisciplined body which is the most poignant symbol of the carnivalesque – the unclosed body of convexities and orifices, intruding onto and into others' body-space [which] threatens to escape, transgress, and transcend the circumscriptions of the body. (p. 95)

These then new leisure complexes like Coney Island, Blackpool Leisure Beach or Porthcawl represented not just a relaxation of Victorian corsetry by the 1880s and 1890s, but also an invasion by, and an excitement about, a new pattern of life. Such fairgrounds welcomed the new technology of electricity to create a wonderful new world of light which extended holidaying and leisure into the hours of darkness. Their vulgarity included the blasts of air up ladies' skirts, and a chance for young men, in public, to cling to their girlfriends as they raced down the racetrack on simulcra horses, or held their loved ones on the carousel. At the same time as Canon Barnett was enticing the East End into exhibitions of art based on wholesome themes of the virtues of family life, Blackpool was establishing a reputation that was to be later encapsulated in 'kiss-me-quick' hats. The very people that saw the East End displays of pictures would also embark, *en masse*, to the hop fields of Kent in annual excursions of work and fun. In the USA the pleasure park of Coney Island was not simply a playground but a melting pot, where the later immigrant groups from Eastern Europe that flooded into New York in the latter part of the century could escape from their ghettos and mix with earlier established groups. New Americans from Ireland, Italy, the Ukraine and Poland could mix in an environment of swimsuits, waves and wonderment at the grotesques and lights of the fun parks that represented a brave new future. Tourism and holidaying, as it is known today, was a result of, and a contributor to, the democratization of western societies.

Rojek's analysis of the development of leisure from the twelfth to the earlier half of the twentieth century is based upon a systematic interpretation of trends identified in this period. However, it is a complicated pattern, as described in his book. Further, there is significant evidence to suggest that even within the period often regarded as the modernistic, that is a period of rationalization that led to the systematization of production in the late part of the nineteenth century, an emphasis upon the particular as required by writers such as Foucault, shows many contrary patterns of the development of leisure and holiday-taking. For example, Scott Haine (1994) in an analysis of working class adolescence and leisure in Paris between the period of 1830 to 1940 argues that behaviour associated with adolescence was apparent in the old system of apprenticeship. While, in English terms, there was the growth of a 'respectable' working class, both in France and England there is evidence of an alternative youth culture – the precursors of 'mods and rockers' of the 1960s, and the soccer hooligans of the 1980s and 1990s. Scott Haine (1994, p. 459) provides evidence of 'apache' brawls and comments:

By the Belle-Epoque, working-class youth had articulated their own subculture through the abundant and varied diversions of the 'city of light': dance halls, cafés, cinemas, sports, and newspapers. Leisure activities were central to their adolescent development because, in these informal leisure institutions and activities, a sense of moratorium developed that allowed identities to be tested and created, sexuality discovered, and revolt and rebellion enacted. The result was a working-class adolescent youth subculture largely autonomous from both adult working-class culture and politics and the dominant middle-class society. These youths defined themselves less in terms of their class and labor and more in terms of their age and leisure pursuits. (p. 452)

The complexity of developing leisure which included day trip and holiday patterns is further described by Fischer (1994) in his study of three American towns in the period 1890 to 1940. He argues that theories of leisure development imply a displacement theory, whereby commercialization and commodification, as exemplified by the growth of organized sport, displace more spontaneous, informal and private entertainments and activities. Based upon interviews with older citizens, and an analysis of 9700 items in the local press over the period, Fischer concludes that

> assumptions in the displacement argument may be wrong. What probably happened between 1890 and 1940 was an increase in the total volume of recreation Americans engaged in. Americans' leisure time included organised and informal activities, commercial and self-generated ones, private and collective ones. Although the mix may well have changed, and many specific recreations – vaudeville shows, hayrides, etc. – declined, the different types of leisure persisted. (pp. 469–70)

Nowhere, perhaps, was the distinction between public and private space more dominant as a factor determining leisure behaviour in the nineteenth century than the convict ships taking men and women to Australia from Britain. If ever there was a denial of private space, it might be said to be the cramped nature of these sailing vessels. Bateson (1959, p. 70) quotes a surgeon of the 1820s describing the ships as having berths, 'being 6 feet square, and calculated to hold four convicts, everyone thus possessing 18 inches space to sleep in'. Damousi (1995), in her research of sexuality on female convict ships, finds evidence of unsettling sexual liaisons, punishment, church services, dances and concerts. Thus, she argues, the 'private' spaces became hidden, but present, and sexualized.

Thus, although writers have identified broad themes in leisure and holiday-taking, closer examination shows a much more complex and bewildering pattern of activity. Towner (1994) adopts a view very close to that of Carr's (1961) examination of what constitutes history. Carr notes the selectivity of history when commenting, 'Knowledge is knowledge for some purpose. The validity of the knowledge depends upon the validity of the purpose' (p. 27). Towner has pointed out that the histories of tourism are likewise selective, arguing that 'Past research into tourism history has thus developed a number of particular themes. Despite evident strengths in ancient tourism, Grand Touring, spas, seaside resorts and aesthetics, a distorted picture of the past was, nevertheless produced' (1994, p. 722). And again, 'The self-help creation of holiday homes by the relatively poor or the development of a weekend cottage zone around Paris becomes obscured by a focus on Thomas Cook's tours abroad' (p. 724).

Hence, if the social context of tourism and the nature of the holiday experience are to be understood, of necessity it becomes a study of the particular – it is, in Urry's terms, a study of the gaze and the pattern of surveillance.

## THE GAZE OF SURVEILLANCE

As noted, both Urry (1990) and Rojek (1993) have been much influenced in their analysis of contemporary tourism by the concepts associated with French thinkers such as Foucault and Derrida. It is of interest to note that Rojek's three processes of the control of leisure, namely *licensing*, *policing* and *punishing*, and *stereotyping* (1993, p. 25) are consistent with Foucault's approval of Marx when, in *Discipline and Punish*

(1975), the French thinker notes that 'The work of directing, superintending and adjusting becomes one of the functions of capital, from the moment that the labour under the control of capital, becomes cooperative. Once a function of capital, it requires special characteristics' (p. 175).

The modernist period brought into being by the Industrial Revolution created a demand for surveillance which permitted judgement, evaluation and ranking that created distinctions and individualized those being observed. Today, in what some have described as the postmodernistic period, tensions can be seen from the way that technology both sustains and undermines surveillance in many senses. To adopt a literal interpretation, surveillance cameras sustain the processes of licensing, policing and stereotyping, while the free flow of opinion through technology such as the internet undermines the relationship between credibility of data and information while also creating difficulties for those who would survey the world. Opinion and contention become a substitute for what previously was conceived as being empirical fact. Yet the existence of the opinion is itself both a fact and an interpretation, which gives meaning for individuals about places, events and things.

The same processes, as will be described by Hollinshead later in this book, occur in tourism. Surveillance is part of the experience of modern tourism in many senses of the term. Security is part of modern international travel. Tracing of movements through Eftpos and credit card transactions is a possibility. Hotels give guests personalized security cards that cease to function once guests check out, and ensure payment through credit card 'imprints'. Surveillance cameras overlook the shoppers and tourists in centres such as the Metro Centre in Northumbria, or those who walk through red-light areas like those of Auckland's Fort Street. Cameras at traffic lights in cities like Nottingham possess the capability of zooming in to identify drivers and their passengers. These techniques of surveillance, however, possess potential but limited power to interfere with the movement of tourists. The millions who travel leave a confusing track of records, and their very volume makes it difficult for law enforcement agencies to track people unless specific individuals have been previously identified. Thus, while such potential surveillance is a common experience of travel, for many tourists the effect of the technology is benign in that, for example, it permits guaranteed occupancy of a hotel room in a strange location regardless of whether a plane is late in landing.

The process of surveillance can hence be interpreted in many ways. The above discussion relates to surveillance as it is understood by law enforcement agencies and put into practice by the computerized systems that survey the movement of people. From this perspective the relationship with categorization and codification becomes evident. Those who stay at hotels become targets for frequent stayer programmes; those who travel frequently with airlines might earn 'airpoints' and those who constantly use credit cards may become targets for other marketing purposes. The completion of attitudinal questionnaires permits categorization based upon socio-demographic data, behaviour patterns and psychological profiling. These processes of classification generated through policing in the sense of tracking, license individuals as eligible for various services, whilst 'punishment' is exercised through exclusion from discounts, special offers and other inducements to the loyal traveller. Given the advent of the internet, marketers are able to establish direct relationship marketing not with groups, but individuals.

Such a view of surveillance seems consistent with the concept of modernism expressed by Marx, and thus at odds with the concept of the Gaze as expounded by Urry. But is it? The Marxian (and scientific management) concept of classification is the expression of the Gaze of the modern period. Rojek (1993, p. 201) presents a different aspect of surveillance when he asks, 'Why be a Tourist?' He notes (p. 201) the concern of a journalist, David Beresford, seeking to cover the release of Nelson Mandela from prison. The reality of the release, a scrum of competing television personnel, meant that participants had less of a view than those at home in their armchairs. Whose was the reality? Which is the authentic experience? Again, on attending the Mandela Concert at Wembley stadium, how did most people get a view of the stage? Not through their own vision but through the intermediary of two gigantic television screens on either side of the stage. The living-room view is replicated to provide the veracity of the view lost by actually being there!

The simulation of events becomes omnipresent argues Baudrillard. He notes: 'the unreal is no longer that of dream or fantasy, of a beyond or within, it is that of a hallucinatory resemblance of the real with itself. To exist from the crisis of representation, you have to lock the real up in pure repetition' (1983, p. 142).

Rojek (1993) notes the repetition of the 'fatal attraction' – the continued tourist tour of the death sites of Kennedy, the pilgrimage to Gracelands – are almost fantastic in their weaving of modern myth, past events and current observation.

The Gaze of Surveillance is to look upon a confusing and complex world of symbols, chaos and uncertainty. But such a state is not just negative; it, too, offers opportunities for affirmation of that which is positive. In this postmodernist world, as Urry (1990, p. 100) notes, the tourist can play at many roles in the guise of the 'post-tourist'. Feifer (1985) has noted that three factors characterize modern tourists. First, there is no need to leave home to see many places of the tourist gaze. Television programmes about travel are notably popular. In the UK the *Holiday Programme*, or *Wish You Were Here?*, have, for many years, attracted audiences in excess of 10 million viewers. In New Zealand, the television programme *Holiday* attracted 750,000 viewers, which was 54 per cent of the viewing audience in the week ending 13 May 1995. In that week it became the programme with the highest viewing figures in spite of competing television coverage of the first rounds of the final of the America's Cup; an event which appealed to New Zealanders as 'their' boat won the event. Thus, as Urry comments, 'The typical tourist experience is anyway to see *named* scenes through a *frame*, such as the hotel window, the car windscreen or the window of a coach. But this can now be experienced in one's own living room, at the flick of a switch' (1990, p. 100).

The ludic nature of tourism with reference to framing is explicitly exemplified by the framing of views by the Auckland Regional Council's Parks Authority when, at some sight-seeing locations in its parks, it erected large picture frames through which visitors could take photographs. This is echoed in the website http://www.arc.govt.nz/about/parks/p24-15.htm, where a picture frame is partially used to define the limits of a view (as at 20 March 2001). This postmodernistic commentary was, however, lost upon several members of the Auckland public, who wrote letters to their local paper decrying the wasted expenditure.

The second dimension of being a post-tourist is that there is an awareness of choice. Much earlier, Iso-Ahola (1982) noted the 'dialectical tensions' between the factors that pull and push the tourist, and how the tourist could move between the cells of the

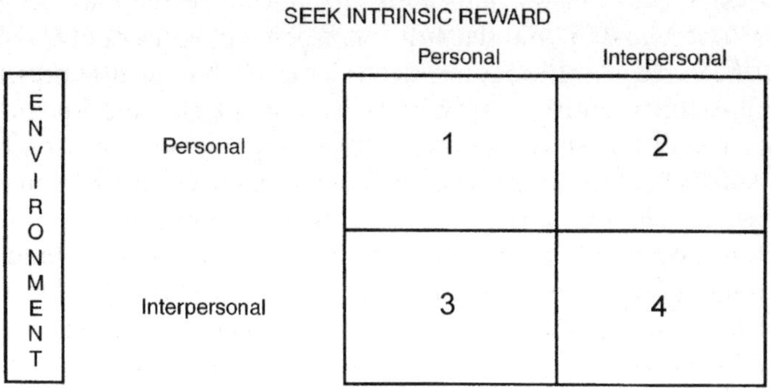

SEEK INTRINSIC REWARD

| | | Personal | Interpersonal |
|---|---|---|---|
| E N V I R O N M E N T | Personal | 1 | 2 |
| | Interpersonal | 3 | 4 |

*Figure 1.1* The matrix of motivations

matrix of motivations that is shown in Figure 1.1. Thus, an individual may seek personal intrinsic rewards and wish to escape a specific environment, in which case the type of motivation that may be dominant is shown in cell one as being ego-enhancement, an escape from responsibility, or an interest in aesthetics. The diagram in one sense represents a form of factor analysis in that different motivations might be traced to two subsets of two prime motivations, namely an escape from and an attraction to a place. However, Iso-Ahola emphasizes the nature of the experience when writing, 'Tourism is a dialectical-developmental process – individuals change through inner experience of contradiction and conflict ... Tourism behaviour is a dialectical optimizing process – it seeks to avoid and to acquire a new experience' (1982, p. 261).

Feifer (1985, p. 270) notes how the post-tourist can manipulate the symbols and places of tourism; so that the purchase of a replica of the Eiffel Tower becomes a parody of the very kitsch that would not normally be purchased. The tourist is a games-playing creature; indulging in that which is not to be taken seriously, parodying those who take it seriously and themselves for actually purchasing the souvenir known to be little more than 'airport art'. Souvenirs are not simply trophies of having 'been there'; but statements of either taste or anti-taste. Thus even the most high-brow will purchase *Mannikin Piss*. Thus the third characteristic of the post-tourist is their ludic involvement.

The comments about play that writers like Mercer (1983) and Urry (1990) make about the contemporary tourist are very different in nature to those made by Crompton (1979) and Ryan (1991). Ryan reiterates notions of tourism as periods of play, but as periods of childhood regression in the sense that childhood games like cricket on the beach are played. For Ryan (1991, p. 26) play is fun, a spontaneity divorced of meaning other than the sheer delight of senseless physical exertion. On the other hand, Urry's (1990) ludic involvement contains overtones of a studied perversity of the sophisticate. They are the refinements of the cosmopolitan citizen (Urry, 2000).

## RATIONALITY, SUBJECTIVITY AND POSTMODERNISM

Postmodernism challenges rationalism, but in doing so it perhaps emphasizes the unusual to denote the diversity of life; it seeks novelty, it describes the richness of difference. But rich diets create illness, and richness can become a meaningless concept if diversity is the norm – richness exists only as a comparison to that perceived as 'sameness' – diversity has an appeal only as an escape from that 'sameness'. But the 'sameness' instils order at an individual level from which to seek the differences.

From this perspective the interest of postmodernist writers with the meaning of leisure and tourism becomes understandable. It does so from a number of viewpoints. First, this interest arises from the nature of postmodernist thought, and secondly, it arises from the character of tourism. Postmodernism might, in part, be understood by reference to what it is not. In the literature of tourism a number of writers have described tourism as a 'system'. For example, Mill and Morrison (1985) and Leiper (1990) have both written books using the words 'Tourism System' in the title. Figure 1.2 illustrates the components of Leiper's system. Leiper, quoting Bertalanffy, notes that 'A system may be defined as a set of elements standing in interrelation among themselves and with the environments' (p. 11). Thus, for Leiper, tourism is to be analysed under the headings of the tourist, the traveller-generating region, tourist destination regions, transit routes and units in the travel and tourism industry (p. 10). Each has specific functions and roles to perform. Yet, as Ryan (1996) points out, there was, originally, an inconsistency or tension in Leiper's writing, for in the same work Leiper wrote: 'Tourism is, in essence, not a market, not an industry, not a system, but the ideas or ideologies of tourists and the behaviour of people in touristic roles' (p. 14).

It is this concept of tourism being the ideologies of tourists with which this book is concerned. However, it is in the nature of tourism that, in order to function, systems are required. Airlines fly to schedules, based upon internationally recognized systems of air traffic control, and maintained in accordance with internationally recognized schedules

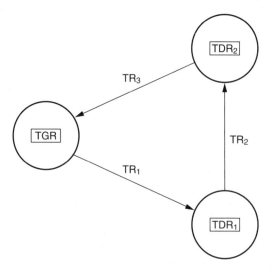

*Figure 1.2* Geographical elements in a tourist system with two destinations

as recommended by the aircraft manufacturers. Ryan (1996) has described tourism as a postmodernistic systematic industry, noting that domains of both the rational and the irrational are required to understand its working. The distinction between the two domains is placed within the dimension of motivation. Systems, it is argued, are motivated by the need for certainty of performance. Thus this aspect of tourism is located in the modern period of the late nineteenth century with Weberian concepts of bureaucracy. Further, as Ryan (1996) argues using concepts of organization borrowed from the work of Parsons, such modernism cannot but help to create processes of goal determination and to seek legitimization of power structures. However, as Leiper (1990, 2000) notes, and as Ryan (1991, 1994) has previously argued, tourism is essentially about the experience that the tourist has within a place and with the attributes of that place and the people found there. Therefore, to understand the tourist experience it is necessary to understand the con*text* within which the tourist operates. *Textuality* is important in the postmodernist approach to understanding human behaviour. Sontag (1978), with reference to medical practice and interpretation, has asked Why cannot illness just be illness? Why surround it with metaphors such as describing cancer as an 'enemy'? Is it not a case of DNA, microbes and bacteria? But Foucault, in the *Birth of the Clinic*, directly addresses this question, indicating through detailed notes of clinical practice over the period of the late eighteenth and early nineteenth centuries that this is simply not the case. Culture is constituted in language, and thus nothing is knowable outside of language. Language is the expression and determinant of the Gaze, and thus the expression of the text assumes overwhelming importance. The debate about ecotourism expresses this well. A debate in 1993, through the e-mail pages of Trinet, the international internet service used by tourism researchers, considered ecotourism as including *eco*nomically sustainable tourism, with some arguing that Disneyland is a good example of ecotourism from both environmental and economically sustainable perspectives. Wheeller (e.g. 1990, 1993) has, on more than one occasion, argued that ecotourism is about the good *guise* (*guys?*) of tourism that panders to *ego*-tourism, that it is a misplaced search for answers to the perceived problems of mass tourism.

## POSTMODERNISM: MODES OF ANALYSIS

Constructionism, as a form of academic critique, is like the individual tourist; both are concerned with the minutiae of experience. Postmodernism is concerned with actions, events and interpretations within the text – it *deconstructs* the grand design of the system. It is thus both consistent and inconsistent with another important stream of tourism literature that relates to the quality of service. As a service, tourism is concerned with performance associated with the provision of intangibles. Each interaction is different and lacks homogeneity. The customer is a party to the determinants of service performance. Thus the *text* of the interaction is all important. Yet, as Parasuraman *et al.* (1985, 1988) have pointed out, the customer, in seeking reassurance and empathy, also requires reliability of performance, and thus service providers introduce systems of staff training in attempts to develop reliability. Service is 'reduced' to blueprints in accordance with ISO 9001-style mandates.

Postmodernism thus poses a significantly important alternative to viewing the tourist experience and the systems within which that experience occurs. The nature of this alternative perspective has been described by many writers, and here two summaries of its challenge to orthodoxy will be summarised. From Fraser (1989) and her discussion of the need for discourse in health and its consequences for power, control and knowledge, the following themes can be identified and adapted:

### De-construction

There is a concern to explore discourse and discursive formations in terms, not of the grand designs which they are supposed to constitute in social theory, but with 'small designs' that possess meaning to their participants. Exploration of these 'small designs' involves the action of deconstruction.

### Fragmentation of power

With a focus upon the nature of subjectivity, revealed through discourse, the unitary, prior, essential subject is replaced by difference. Power is evaluated not as a negative, constrained action but as a positive, constitutive activity, contested and resisted.

### Scepticism

The received notions of social structuring, organization and continuity of the world are questioned.

### The acceptance of emotion

Understanding based upon empiricism is insufficient; paradoxically, it is irrational to exclude the irrational from discourse – emotion, subjectivity and a concern with the repressed are part of the discourse.

### Intertextuality

There is a concern with intertextuality (the 'play of texts' upon each other), and a reflexiveness over the production of the player's own text.

Flax (1990) has noted that the concerns of postmodernist thought can be categorized as being:

(a)   contemporary Western culture – its nature and how to understand it;
(b)   knowledge – What is it?, Who constructs it?, Who uses it? – its relation to power;
(c)   philosophy – its crisis;
(d)   power – if, where and when domination exists, and is it maintained, overcome?;
(e)   subjectivity and self; and
(f)   difference, how to conceptualize, preserve or rescue it.

From this brief review of the issues discussed by postmodernist writers it can be noted that they observe a society that is increasingly one of fragmentation, and that part of this fragmentation involves a rejection of megatheories and an emphasis upon the language and symbols of discourse. As Urry (1990) has noted, post-tourists involve themselves in ludic cynicism manipulating the symbols and meanings of the theme park or shopping mall as suits their own immediate need. The fragmentation of society is reflected in the paradox of integration, where shopping malls take on the features of theme parks (e.g. Edmonton Mall or the Metro Centre), while theme parks make more money from merchandising than rides.

What is the intellectual basis for such observations, and how might they apply to the tourist experience? It may be observed that there are sociological reasons for arguing that society is more heterogeneous than in the past. Patterns of marriage today are such that the conventional life-cycle of independence, young married, 'nesters' and 'empty nesters' is the norm for increasingly smaller proportions of the population. Increasing divorce rates mean individuals may have extended families of step-siblings and two groups of parents with whom to relate. On the other hand, 'career women' may choose to delay marriage and/or children, thereby delaying until older age the 'empty nester' stage (Ryan, 1995b). Consumers are increasingly faced with wider choices, and modern technology permits the retention of the advantages of mass production but with an added ability to 'customerize' items to meet individual preferences. The systems heralded by the mass package holidays of the 1950s now permit boutique holidays where individual activities can be catered and booked for prior to departure. On a political front one of the trends of the late twentieth century was the re-emergence of national identities based upon smaller groupings, whether it be the emergence of a new sense of political power by indigenous peoples, the claims of Serbs, Croats, East Timorese, Catalans or others, while, of course, the uniformity of the former USSR has apparently all but disappeared.

For some writers, including Baudrillard (1981) and Lyotard (1984) it might be said that such changes are part of a process which values fragmentation, openness and multivocality. Thus comments Fox (1993, p. 7): 'there is clearly an attraction in a fairly eclectic approach, and indeed "post-modernism" is, by its very nature, impossible to delimit and define'. As will be noted, its very open-endedness is an object of criticism, but it does postulate a specific worldview. Figure 1.3 is adapted from Fox's proposal that postmodernism can be illustrated by expressing alternatives to central tenets of modernism.

Futurists, like Toffler, have argued that one important distinction of the future will be between those who do or do not have access to information. This implies that information possesses an objective reality, and thus those who possess this possess authority. Postmodernism would reject this by arguing that information possesses value only within the context of the text. As noted, it has been argued that the internet undermines the 'objectivity' of information through the prioritization of opinion, while those not accessing such systems still retain knowledge of their own situation. Hence, the communication of information is not the communication of 'objectivity' but a transmission of values and persuasions, and the subjectivities of those exercising various forms of power.

The basis of postmodernism lies in its emphasis upon language – upon the text. Thus, for Derrida (1976, p. 158) 'there is nothing outside the text'. For Derrida, there is

| Tenet | Modern reading | Postmodern response |
|---|---|---|
| Logocentrism | Authority is based upon access to knowledge of reality. | Knowledge is an effect of power, and constituted in language, not in an access to 'reality'. |
| Phonocentrism | Privileging of authorial voice 'speaking from the heart'. | Speech is not privileged over writing; both show the traces of production as means of persuasion. |
| Ethnocentrism | Knowledge is transcultural and transhistorical. | Knowledge is applicable in context. Values and commitments should be exposed. |
| Phallocentrism | Privileging of the masculine voice, possession and dominance. | Masculine values have been privileged in claiming knowledgeability. |
| Egocentrism | Privileging the human subject as prior, an essence, foundation point of reference. | Subjectivity is fabricated through the accretion of acts of power. The human subject is a modernist concept. |

*Figure 1.3*  Comparison of modernism and postmodernism
From Fox, N. J., (1993) *Postmodernism, Sociology and Health*. Buckingham, Open University Press, p. 11.

nothing that is not conditioned by the structure and practice of language, and he has analysed the *différance* as containing a fundamental *undecidability* which resides in language. Thus, any attempt to define a meaning inevitably leads to a deferral of meaning; the concept slips into continuously refined shades of meaning that possess significance for the signifier. Hence, take the very concept of tourism. What is it? At one level it simply means the numbers of people who spend more than one day away from home and thus need accommodation, so long as that stay does not involve study or work or being away for more than six months. But does this technical definition say anything about the nature of the transport patterns, industry structures or experiences of tourist, employee, attraction owner or host community? Apparently not, but attempts to include these other legitimate interests produces not one but several definitions from the perspective of economics, sociology and psychology (see Ryan, 1991, 1994). Meanings are not the prerogative of individuals alone, according to Barthes, but words have unstable meanings within language.

While this may appear abstract and divorced from the daily realities of the business of tourism as perceived by its practitioners and their clients, it possesses a reality clearly seen in issues of interpretation of heritage sites. Hollinshead (1999) has highlighted four components of surveillance, namely, identifying the silent others in tourism; understanding the contextuality of competing logics of power in tourism; analysing the quiet power of the text in tourism; and comprehending the critical infinity of interpretation in tourism. For Hollinshead, Urry's history of tourism is not authoritative but a context by which tourism thrives in a wider social context. Thus, as argued above, tourism is understood by reference to the context whereby the boundaries between tourism and non-tourist activities become blurred, and the subject of tourism loses its focus and its distinctiveness. The difference between the non-tourist and tourist roles is what creates an experience that may be termed a 'tourist experience', and the difference is dependent upon a spatial dislocation of the tourist away from home; but the meaning of the disjunction and the nature of the interpretation of the experience is bound up with the wider context. A dialectic exists between space, the interpretations of that space and the de-differentiation of tourist and non-tourist roles, which is expressed in oral terms through the structures of language. In short, the harder we look at the nature of tourism the more it slides uneasily into ambiguity. Yet the issues are of immediate importance, because even as the blurring occurs, the labels being used carry implications for power structures. For example, an interpretation of Pearl Harbor, visited by many Japanese tourists, that omits a Japanese perspective effectively de-powers by silence. The issue of whether the Allies were aware of a potential Japanese strike against Pearl Harbor likewise enforces a conventional history. To what extent might speculation be voiced within differing interpretations of past events?

Does this mean that postmodernism is little more than a question of semiotics, a confusing babble of relativity? There are some who hold to this view, but a moderate perspective is provided by Curry (1991), who has criticized postmodernistic literature in geography. Curry argues that in many respects it is little more than a continuation of the debate that postmodernists themselves characterize as 'modernist', and that they have failed to transcend the limitations that they perceive and criticize. Curry implicitly criticizes postmodernists such as Lyotard and Rorty as being selective in their use of the works of predecessors to the point that 'Those earlier works have been flattened as they have come to be merely representatives of familiar and comfortable positions. As a result, both the intellectual vitality and the deep ambivalence of those earlier authors have been lost' (p. 224). Curry concludes that a concern about change has actually blinded postmodernists to a range of works that tackle the issues with which they concern themselves, and which possesses more detail and technique than that advanced by postmodernist commentators. Is there such a fundamental change in society as to constitute a crisis? Does over-emphasis upon the individual imply little more than a relativism that, in turn, implies an impossibility of structuring knowledge? And is it so very new to argue that views are dependent upon the context in which the viewer finds themself? It can be noted that the concepts of phenomenology predate the popularization of some French writers. The American psychologist, Rogers, explored the concept of knowledge and an individual's field of reference, and writing of that field, Rogers commented: 'It can never be known to another except through empathic inference and then can never be perfectly known' (1959, p. 210). Thus behaviour depends upon the phenomenal field (subjective reality) and not upon the stimulating conditions (external reality).

## RATIONALITY AND HOLIDAY-TAKING

How is this debate pertinent to the understanding of holiday-makers' experiences? Hegel had written of a *Volksgeist*, a genius or spirit of a nation working through individuals, but independent of conscious will. We are prisoners of our own time, and of the spirit of that time which shapes our perceptions and fields of reference. It is not necessary to agree with postmodernistic thought in order to appreciate that contemporary society is one of significant changes in values, and that a high level of individualism is being emphasized. But equally, that individualism is perceived not simply through the rationalism or empiricism of past decades. Tourism sells the 'experience', and if that is what the tourist buys, then it is the intensity of the experience that is the criteria used for evaluation, not the purpose of the experience.

It was noted initially that tourism has little rationality except in relation to sets of motives. The challenge of postmodernism is that it changes the analysis of motivation. As the following chapters will indicate, motivations have been conventionally explained in systematic models of purpose which assume a rationality. But possibly this is not enough. For example, Ryan (1995c) has sought to explain the distinctive nature of the island as a holiday destination by a comparison of the *is*-land with the *in*-land, arguing that the distinctiveness of islands lies not in a geographical uniqueness but rather the culture that results from, and the meanings imposed upon, a set of geographical attributes. This analysis implies deeper needs than those assessed by the rational, and, in turn, implies that it is contemporary society that concerns itself with such issues in a way not necessarily previously discussed.

Tourism as an educative process, or even as a means of relaxation, implies that it is a process of self-regeneration. But it can also be a process of extreme indulgence, and not necessarily socially, or possibly individually, responsible. The sex tourist in the massage parlours of Bangkok is driven by a need for experience; the 'playfulness' of young men with too much beer in their belly is 'an experience'. One perpetual problem with any concept of humans as the measure of reality is how to tackle issues of ethics. So, too, with tourism. If tourism is indeed about experience, what is the distinction between the search for experience and the search for indulgence? Bordessa (1993) is optimistic on this point, arguing that

> a revision in the definition of what it means to be a human being reinforces the general collapse of the world into a unitary whole: we are now more prone to see ourselves as a constituent part of this whole, within which everything is ultimately connected to everything else ... Without denying our individuality, we can foreground our melding into the wholeness of the world, whose fate thereby becomes part of own destiny. (p. 150)

In short, the tourist perceiving self as a seeker of experience, and thus dependent upon external stimuli for that experience, appreciates the importance of that externality. Bordessa concludes that not only will a much greater awareness of environmental issues emerge, but also a rejection of the 'turning a blind eye to the moral dimensions of environmental realities' (p. 155) that is inherent in modernistic thinking.

But there are significant paradoxes inherent in tourism. To return to the opening themes of the chapter, tourism represents, for some, an escape from the realities of a current environment – a chase of dreams – but what Shirley Valentines do is to substitute one experience for another. That which was once exciting and different becomes the new daily sameness. The success of a Shirley Valentine lies in the catharsis of personal change. For others, perhaps the approaching end of the fortnight in the sun brings with it a relief that the familiar begins to beckon, for the dream has faded. It is time to end the play.

Tourism has many dialectical tensions – not only the oft-remarked one of the search for the new and a lingering want for the familiar, but also the realization that the relationship between purpose and intensity of experience is a complex one. If 'experience' is the objective of holidaying, then, as commented, intensity of experience is sought, thereby re-emphasizing the significance of the holiday as a period of contrast with 'normal' life. But will *any* experience do? Are all experiences of equal validity? In the next chapter a review of the role and types of motivators will be essayed to further examine 'the tourist experience'.

# Chapter 2

# Motives, behaviours, body and mind

*Chris Ryan*

## INTRODUCTION

The previous chapter looked at general trends in both society and thinking as they affect our understanding of the nature of tourism. However, 'the gaze' of a tourist requires a physical body. While western societies create contexts for competing viewpoints, nearly all such views attribute importance to the individual. Social *mores* are individually interpreted: intellectually, sensually and emotionally. The experience of being a tourist is one that engages all the senses, not simply the visual. For example, the tourist tastes new foods and feels the warmth of the sea in which he or she swims. 'The gaze' implies an involvement of the intellect as it interprets the visual, but tourism can be an epicurean experience, an indulgence, an enhancement not only of ego and mind but also of body. Like many human activities, it has both a positive and negative side. To try to understand the tourist experience requires consideration of perceived needs and actualities of not only the beach and the 'great outdoors', but also the noise and din of the disco and the sweat of the massage parlour.

Therefore, this chapter will attempt to weave together notions of body and mind through theories primarily derived from humanistic psychology. Consequently, the role of intrinsic motivation will be discussed with specific reference to the work of commentators and researchers such as Allport, Frankl, Ragheb, Beard, Csikszentimi-halyi, Diener and Pearce, among others. Initially, the work and influence of Maslow will be described with reference to his concept of a hierarchy of needs. In describing these theories the role of humanistic psychology and its popularity in the tourism literature will be assessed. Within the chapter an emphasis will be placed upon four motives, identified as being important by Ragheb and Beard, on the premise that their categorization derives from humanistic psychology. Additionally, the psychometric literature within tourism and leisure research shows that not only do respondents identify easily with these motives, but the motives themselves have shown stability over time.

The primary thesis of this chapter is that tourist behaviour is multi-motivational, but, additionally, a reductionist position is initially postulated where it is argued that the motives are essentially few in number. None the less, the consequent behaviours are diverse, because while the *needs* are few, the *expression* of, and the *means* by which needs are satisfied, are many. Social contexts are pluralistic in nature and provide many opportunities for the expression of different behaviours, and it is this plurality that confuses. For example, an observer may note the young person who has drunk too much at a disco or, on the other hand, a group of elderly tourists enjoying a tea dance. Both can occur, albeit at different times, in a Spanish hotel, and there seems little in common between the two behaviours. One contains the potential for aggression, the other is a re-enactment of a more genteel past. The common motivation is, in both cases, a need for social interaction. Both sets of behaviours arise from a need to be with others. Equally, both situations may be characterized by individuals seeking to establish a sense of ego-enhancement, leadership or 'points scoring'. For an example of this with elderly tourists see Dann's (2000) description of the behaviours of elderly British holiday-makers at a Spanish resort during a long winter vacation. In short, behaviour conforms to norms consistent with the social interaction being shared. On the other hand, an observed similar action by different tourists can be motivated by different needs.

## SELF-ACTUALIZATION AND MEANING

In trying to understand these issues a number of theoretical approaches will be discussed. It is perhaps significant that three of the concepts to be described are derived from, or relate to, the work of Abraham Maslow and his notion of self-actualization. Maslow was born in 1908, the first of seven children born to uneducated Russian Jews who migrated to Brooklyn, New York. He first studied law at City College, New York, married his cousin Bertha against his parents' wishes, moved to Wisconsin to study at the University there, and subsequently became interested in psychology. In 1951 he took the position of Chair of the Psychology Department at Brandeis, and it was there that he became influenced by Kurt Goldstein, and commenced his writings in humanistic psychology. His major works are *Toward a Psychology of Being* (1968), *Motivation and Personality* (1954, 1970) and *The Further Reaches of Human Nature* (1971), plus a series of articles. The basis of Maslow's theory is well known, and usually encapsulated in Figure 2.1 that shows his hierarchy of needs.

Essentially, the needs can be briefly described as:

*Physiological needs* – needs for survival – food, water, shelter and maintenance of homeostasis;
*Safety and Security needs* – a need for stability, order, protection, structure and order;
*Love and Belonging needs* – social needs and wish for and to show affection, and a sense of community; and
*Esteem needs* – here there is another hierarchy – the lower is concerned with the respect of others, a need for status and recognition. The higher form involves self-respect, competence, independence, achievement and mastery.

All of these needs he called *deficit needs*, that is all are instinctive and needed for survival. They are also developmental, that is people move from the lower to the higher, although in times of stress regression can occur. This latter situation is illustrated by

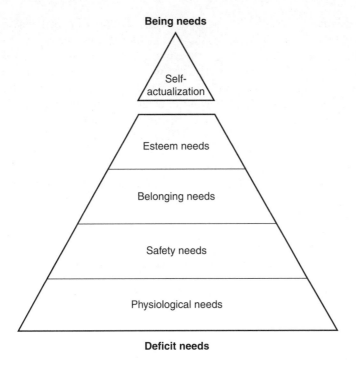

**Being needs**

Self-actualization

Esteem needs

Belonging needs

Safety needs

Physiological needs

**Deficit needs**

*Figure 2.1* Maslow's hierarchy of needs

Maslow's analysis of neurosis, shown in Figure 2.2. Essentially our salient needs may be met, but past deprivation inhibits the maturation of the personality by the individual becoming fixated on those past deficits.

The last level of self-actualization is qualitatively different, and Maslow termed it *growth motivation*. The characteristics of self-actualized people are described as being reality-centred, problem-centred, a strong ethical sense, possessing a need for privacy, showing empathy, an acceptance of self and others, spontaneous, a preference for simplicity, a freshness of appreciation; they are creative, inventive and tend to have more peak experiences than other people. Maslow also estimated that such people accounted for about 2 per cent of the human population.

Maslow's theories have been influential in informing thought, even though his critics have argued that the conventional scientific evidence is lacking. At an anecdotal level, evidence exists of peak experiences within, for example, the confines of mathematical and physical sciences. Charlton (1998) recounts the solution of Fermat's Last Theorem by Andrew Wiles who stated 'Suddenly, totally unexpectedly, I had this incredible revelation ... It was so indescribably beautiful; it was so simple and so elegant. I just stared in disbelief for twenty minutes' (p. 11). However, Maslow argued that peak experiences were available to all. There is a link between the work of Maslow and that of researchers in the area of emotional wellbeing. There exists significant evidence that the majority of people report positive levels of wellbeing (Diener and M. Diener, 1995; Diener and C. Diener, 1996; Veenhoven, 1993). A number of factors seem to operate, and they include frequency and intensity of emotions, the degrees of independence

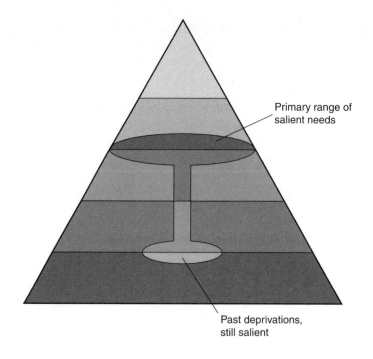

Primary range of salient needs

Past deprivations, still salient

*Figure 2.2* Maslow's theory of fixation

between pleasant and unpleasant moods, situational influences, social comparison, adaptation, adjustment and coping abilities, physiological states and the context of personality, goals and culture (Diener and Lucas, 2000).

From this perspective it becomes easy to understand the linkages between these concepts and tourism. As argued in Chapter 1, holidays possess the potential for cathartic experience, or what Maslow, Diener and others would categorize as 'peak experiences'. As a teacher this author often asks students to write down those things that are the most memorable events that have happened to them on holiday. Almost invariably items emerge from the higher stages of Maslow's hierarchy. Thus one respondent wrote of camping at Meteora in Greece, and remembering a sense of timelessness as he was awoken at dawn by the sound of horns being blown at dawn by monks from one of the monasteries; which noise, in turn, created a cacophony of roosters crowing, donkeys braying and geese cackling. At that moment he had a sense of awe in recollecting that this was probably a scene that had happened each day, unbroken over several centuries. Free from stress, tourists are located in environments that aid spontaneity, encourage social interaction or provide privacy as required, and are in locations that provide differences and challenges to the required level – in short all the requisites for achieving personal self-actualization might be said to be present.

Another explanation for the popularity of concepts derived from the school of humanistic psychology within the leisure and tourism literature might be the nature of human activity that is being considered by researchers. Many theories of psychology relate to neurosis or other facets of dysfunctioning personality wherein emphasis may be laid upon unconscious as well as conscious thoughts. Psychiatric theorizations often relate to situations where the role of drugs is important in shaping human behaviour through influencing the brain and nervous system. On the other hand, leisure and tourism academics are involved in human situations of specified domains of action that are often welcomed by respondents and seen as respites from the everyday world that imposes limits on actions. Recreation, leisure and holidays retain the potential for creative thought and action in a positive sense. Finally, it might also be noted that tourism and leisure researchers may, in part, work with companies who seek product enhancement through a better understanding of client wants, and again, therefore, there is a tendency to look at the more positive motives and components of the holiday experience.

If it is true that travel and tourism are rich providers of meaningful pursuits, then this raises a series of other issues. For example, if meaning is found in tourism, in what ways do these meanings differ from meanings derived from other activities? How important are these separate meanings? What types of meanings are derived from 'escape', and is it an escape *from* society, or an escape *to* what is considered a more meaningful pattern of existence. Do the 'truths' of tourism only possess meaning through comparison with non-touristic life? How does this distinction sit when compared with processes of de-differentiation that mark the late or postmodern world of the early twenty-first century? While tourism and leisure provide opportunities for fun and hedonism, is this the sole purpose for engaging in such activities? Much of the literature that refers to motives for tourism would indicate that pleasure alone is not the main motive (e.g. Havitz and Dimanche, 1990, examine the role of involvement in tourism). Further, Kelly and Kelly (1994) argued that leisure pursuits generated no significantly different searches for meaning than those found in the other domains of family and work life. For his part, Godbey (1994, p. vii) concluded that, 'In our rapidly evolving world, leisure is as much about the search for meaning as it is the search for pleasure. Finding something you love to do, of course, creates both meaning and pleasure. Leisure is ultimately about a search.' From this perspective, Frankl's (1962, 1997) theory on 'Man's Search for Meaning' may have significance for tourism. Frankl suggests that meaning within leisure lies in four dimensions: physical, mental, social and existential or spiritual, and thus there is a pursuit of inner freedom, perceived self-worth, humour, hope, love, striving, significance, inward peace and senses of value, beauty and aesthetics. Thus there exists a 'Paradox of Hedonism' for Frankl (1992) wherein those bent on the search for pleasure and happiness fail to find them because of their concentration upon them. Hedonism will ultimately disappoint. By extension, it can be argued that holidays ultimately satisfy because they are periods of contrast to 'normal life'; if life were a holiday without contrasting activities the consequence would be a sense of failure or boredom on the part of the holiday-maker.

Common linkages between the work of Maslow and Frankl are, therefore, easily identifiable. Both belong to a humanistic, existentialist school of philosophy if not psychology, where the emphasis is placed upon human existence, the nature of humanity, a wish to retain human individuality in an age of growing technological complexities, and to retain an integrity of the human state of being when so many people perceive competing demands associated with the varying roles required of modern living. Within this social construct, holidays as periods of escape to moments of potential self-reassessment are important periods of time. For these, and perhaps other, reasons, theoretical structures derived from the humanistic school of psychology abound in the literature in trying to explain holiday motives.

## TRAITS, DISPOSITIONS AND MOTIVATIONS

The perspective of plurality of expression based on a homogeneity of needs that is adopted in this chapter implies certain assumptions. These include assumptions that people are conscious drivers of their own behaviours, that they are generally motivated to achieve those things that are positive about their own self-conceptualizations and, finally, that holidays are actually special periods of time due to the physical displacement of people from their normal surroundings. As already noted, much of this is consistent with the theories of Allport, Maslow and other psychologists who emphasize the role of motivation with reference to 'normal' adult behaviour. For example, Maslow's hierarchy of needs that ultimately lead to self-actualization emerged from the observation that much of psychology was concerned with abnormal behaviours. If we are to understand psychological health, argued Maslow (1970), it seems pertinent to study those who have mature, healthy personalities. Allport shared this concern, but differed in that he argued that his work was orientated towards empirical problems rather than seeking a methodological unity of theory or construct. For Allport, what people state is important – conscious motivation has value. People are real and possess autonomy. People are not prisoners of unconscious drives, nor are they constructs of factors derived from empirical factor analytic studies. In *Becoming* (1955) he stressed the importance of self and the uniqueness of adult personality. The self, he contended, is an identifiable organization within each individual and accounts for the unity of personality, higher motives and continuity of personal memories. As Allport states: 'Personality *is* something and *does* something ... It is what lies *behind* specific acts and *within* the individual' (1937, p. 48). More formally, personality was defined as 'the dynamic organization within the individual of those psychological systems that determine his unique adjustments to his environment' (*ibid.*).

From the viewpoint of our current concern, what is important about Allport's concepts of personality are the distinctions made later in 1961. Allport then distinguished between common traits and personal dispositions (also known as morphogenic traits), defining the latter as a 'generalized neuropsychic structure (peculiar to the individual) with the capacity to render many stimuli functionally equivalent, and to initiate and guide (equivalent) forms of adaptive and stylistic behavior' (1961, p. 373).

These dispositions are distinguished from attitudes in that they are personal in nature, while attitudes are 'orientations to definite facets of the environment (including people, culture and society)' (1961, p. 348). While personal dispositions may be general, of key importance are the few central dispositions which represent tendencies that are highly characteristic of an individual. Indeed, Allport suggests that they may be as small as five to ten in number. Additionally, these central personal dispositions are both independent and consistent.

How does this help an understanding of tourist motivation and behaviour? The small number of central dispositions that characterize personality, and hence perception and response to an individual's environment, implies that a close relationship exists between attitudes, motivations and traits. Indeed the difference may lie in the constructs adopted by the researcher. Attitudes are expressions of personality when a person considers something in the external environment – Allport argues that attitudes are the concern of social psychology, while traits and dispositions are the concern of those interested in personality. Individual traits help formulate goals, priorities and reactions to the external environment. If morphogenic traits are few, so, too, might be motivations, as is argued by Kelly (1955).

Any reader of the literature of tourism motivation cannot help but be struck by the similarity in findings derived by many researchers. The adjectives and categorizations of tourists based upon motivations may differ in number and type, but recurrent themes emerge. For example, the need to escape from everyday surroundings for purposes of relaxation, and discovering new things, places and people are often alluded to. Holidays, as already noted, may be periods of self-discovery. As Crompton (1979) has also observed, holidays are periods when family bonding can be reinforced (or, as Ryan, 1991 more cynically notes, can be catalysts for divorce), and when adults can regress into childhood in order to play. Other writers have noted the dialectic of tourism as being a tension between the search for and the fear of the new, and the want for either or both social interaction and isolation (e.g. Iso-Ahola, 1982). Yiannakis and Gibson (1992) have identified many types of holiday-makers through cluster analysis based upon three dimensions. These being, first, the need for structure; second, the desire for stimulating or tranquil environments; and, third, the attitude towards strange or familiar circumstances. Using these three dimensions they are able to make distinctions not made by previous researchers. For example, while Wahlers and Etzel (1985, p. 290) described stimulation avoiders as showing 'a preference for activities of lower arousal potential such as a highly structured, traditional package vacation', Yiannakis and Gibson (1992) state:

> it appears that Organised Mass Tourists and other lower stimulation-seeking types ... may not, in fact, be true stimulation avoiders but instead may be low risk takers. That is, lacking the cultural self confidence to foray out on their own, they seek the stimulation and excitement they appear to need in the relative safety of the organised mass circuit. (pp. 295–6)

The research findings of Yiannakis and Gibson are but one among many, with individual researchers using different criteria for an evaluation of motives, and different items in their questionnaires. Hence one problem that Pearce (1993, p. 1) notes is that much of tourism literature is 'fragmented and lacking a firm sense of direction'. He notes a lack of replication in research, an absence of comparative studies and cites, seemingly approvingly, criticisms of errors in published research with reference to methodologies. Whether such criticisms are deserved is a moot point, but it is notable that in the associated area of leisure there are examples of replication of motivational studies that possess implications for an understanding of tourist motivations.

One reason why holidays may be special periods of personality development may lie in the distinction that is made between extrinsic and intrinsic orientation. The areas of humanistic psychology associated with researchers and commentators like Maslow, Csikszentimihalyi and Diener place significant emphasis on states of being wherein the person has a sense of completeness. That sense of completeness retains a sense of independence even while feelings of connectedness can exist. Boggiano and Pittman

(1992) review literature related to learning theory and motivation. It is noted that mastery-oriented children pursue *learning* goals, while the less able pursue *performance* goals, but what emerges clearly from their perspective is that ego-involvement undermines motivation and subsequent motivation. Ego-enhancement-orientated individuals are sensitive to extrinsically determined motives. They write:

> Not only do extrinsic students display a number of cognitive, motivational, and beha-vioural deficits associated with helplessness, but extrinsics also evidence emotional deficits such as depression and a maladaptive attributive style. (Boggiano and Pittman, 1992, p. 270)

However, they also note that in conditions where such people feel possession of control, these tendencies to dependency are inhibited. It can be argued that holidays, by being changes of location, activity and social grouping, actually represent dynamically different places within which people can seek to assert themselves. Holidays are periods where, albeit by perhaps appealing to the hedonistic, the intrinsic motives are triggered and thereby holidays are periods important to the development of healthy personalities. Holidays present opportunities whereby individuals can be free to develop senses of competence, and through a sense of competence the intrinsic motivation that is thought important by writers of humanistic psychology to the development of mature personalities is permitted to flower. While it can be objected that holiday destinations can pose challenges to the 'performance-orientated', it can be counter-argued that even the most psychocentric, familiar destination permits opportunities for the tourist to develop mechanisms of control over their own activities, and thus flow can be generated without a need for excessive challenge. Equally, for the most part, the place of the holiday is one chosen by the holiday-maker; hereby control is exerted from the outset of this period.

In a sense, therefore, such concepts of motive provide theoretical support for the notion of social tourism. Hall (2000, p. 141) defines social tourism as 'the relationships and phenomena in the field of tourism resulting from participation in travel by economically weak or otherwise disadvantaged elements'. Haukeland (1990) has argued that the normative link between social welfare and holiday-taking should be treated as an important indicator of social wellbeing. Therefore, if the argument is accepted whereby holiday periods are potential moments of self-confirmation, then making available holidays to those with the least economic resources becomes an act of confirming the wellbeing of all citizens.

Thus, two facets about motives emerge from this debate. First, holidays are important means that aid personal development through the satisfaction of intrinsic motives that can be orientated towards higher needs. Second, from the pragmatic perspective of product development and enhancement, an understanding of visitor motives permits attraction operators to better understand the nature of the demand that they seek to satisfy. Therefore, given that the nature and types of motives are important because the fulfilment of motives generates either satisfactory or unsatisfactory experiences, it becomes necessary to develop a categorization of motives.

## A categorization of motivations

The context, meanings and experiences of tourism can vary from holiday to holiday, from tourist to tourist. To talk of the 'tourist experience' seems to imply a homogeneity which, in reality, is not always present. Rather, it can be argued that tourists experience competing motives and thus tensions exist between needs that might be, to a greater or lesser extent, mutually incompatible. For example, the adventure tourist who goes sky diving for the first time experiences 'an adrenalin rush' that results from the tension inherent in a drive for survival that competes with a need to test oneself. The tourist exploring in a land whose language is unknown to him or her can suffer frustration from an inability to communicate at a sophisticated level, and a sense of wonderment about different cultures and the way differing beliefs and values are made explicit. From this perspective, the concept of experience is made more difficult, as it lies not in the satisfaction of need, but in the tension between competing needs. Humanistic psychologists seek to tackle this issue through concepts of hierarchies or prioritizations of needs. Ross (1994) lists a number of motives thought by researchers to be important to tourism and includes a partial list of Murray's Classification of Human Needs (see Murray, 1938; pp. 152–226). Unlike many psychologists, Murray's list of motives might be said to include some of the more negative aspects of human behaviour. For example, he includes 'aggression', 'rejection', 'counteraction' (to obliterate a humiliation by resumed action), 'deference' (to admire and support a superior) and exhibitionism. However, like many others, Murray provides a classification and, as Maslow was to do later, writes of a hierarchy of needs. In many senses Murray's conceptualizations of drives and personality is among the more complex in psychological literature as he also clearly sought to show patterns of inter-relationships, fusion and subsidization, while drawing distinctions between *beta press* (the perceptions of the individual) and *alpha press* (the independent existence of the subject of perception). Having drawn our attention to Murray's work, Ross notes that Murray's ideas have had little influence upon theoretical constructions within tourism except for possessing an indirect influence through informing McClelland's concept of a need for achievement (N.Ach). Ross (e.g. 1991) has used this latter concept in his work on motives of employees in the hospitality and tourism industry.

On the other hand, within the leisure literature, and to a lesser extent within tourism, several researchers have adopted the work of Beard and Ragheb (1983), partly because, it is suspected, their classification is congruent with much that has been written about escape and relaxation needs, and, second, because it is consistent with the theories of intrinsic motivation developed by humanistic psychologists. Additionally, their scales have permitted a marriage between the schools of empiricist positivism and the qualitative orientation of humanistic psychology. The former seeks generalization to be derived from quantification while the latter seeks richness of data derived from individual experiences to better understand potentialities inherent in given situations.

Following Beard and Ragheb (1983, p. 225), motives can be classified as fourfold. These are:

(a)   The *intellectual* component, which 'assesses the extent to which individuals are motivated to engage in leisure activities which involve . . . mental activities such as learning, exploring, discovering, thought or imagining';

(b)    The *social* component which 'assesses the extent to which individuals engage in leisure activities for social reasons. This component includes two basic needs ... the need for friendship and interpersonal relationships, while the second is the need for the esteem of others';

(c)    The *competence-mastery* component which assesses the extent to which 'individuals engage in leisure activities in order to achieve, master, challenge, and compete. The activities are usually physical in nature'; and

(d)    The *stimulus-avoidance* component of leisure motivation that 'assesses the drive to escape and get away from over-stimulating life situations. It is the need for some individuals to avoid social contacts, to seek solitude and calm conditions; and for others it is to seek to rest and to unwind themselves.'

These four motivations form the foundation of their Leisure Motivation Scale which has been replicated in other studies, for example by Sefton and Burton (1987) and Loundsbury and Franz (1990). Ragheb and Beard have, in fact, devised three related scales, of which the Leisure Motivation Scale, in 1983, was the last. The two prior scales, the Measurement of Leisure Satisfaction (1980) and Leisure Attitudes (1982) have not proven so reliable. Sefton (1989), in seeking to replicate the Leisure Satisfaction Scale, was only able to confirm three of the original six factors after an initial analysis which identified ten potential factors, some of which were not interpretable. Ragheb and Beard's Leisure Attitude Scale was even less reliable in that Sefton found eight undefinable factors with eigenvalues greater than one. Attempting a six factor explanation still yielded two major undefinable factors accounting for 40 per cent of the variance; a percentage generally regarded as low in the social sciences.

    That the Leisure Motivation Scale can apply to holidays has been shown by various researchers. Ryan and Glendon (1998) applied the scale within the holiday context alone, while Loundsbury and Polik (1992) used the scale to examine the relationship between pre-vacation expressed needs and post-vacation met needs. Many of the studies that utilize the Beard and Ragheb scales apply them to respondents only once, and hence the research of Loundsbury and Hoopes (1988) has importance, for it sought to establish the stability of motivational factors and leisure behaviour. Stability can be assessed in a number of ways, for example by mean scores, rankings and persistence of factor weighting. Loundsbury and Hoopes utilized rankings of factors over a five-year period, including those taken from the Leisure Motivation Scale, and concluded: 'The present results indicate a most encouraging and even surprising level of stability over a five-year period for leisure activity participation as well as, to a lesser extent, the leisure motivation variables studied' (1988, p. 130). Therefore, given these findings, each of the four motives will now be described in a little more detail.

*The intellectual motivation*

The four motivations identified in the Ragheb and Beard Leisure Motivation Scale can be regarded as continua between a high or low level of need. The intellectual needs can be primary drives (a high need), or triggered by a specific event or environment (a low need). For example, a holiday-maker may book a cruise to Greece and Turkey that visits historic sites accompanied by lecturers and in the company of fellow enthusiasts. The need to search for knowledge is, thus, high. On the other hand, a tourist to a beach resort near, for example, Bodrum in Turkey, may know little of the castle located there, other than the fact that its photograph appears in the holiday brochure. However, once there, drawn perhaps by little more than a need for sightseeing as a change from sunbathing, a visit to the castle may prompt a desire to learn more about the Knights Templar and the crusades. Curiosity, in Allport's terms, is a trait common to humans, is individualized in different ways and may be engaged in a social environment so as to be later expressed in an attitude demonstrating interest in a given object.

## *The social motivation*

It is notable that Ragheb and Beard formulate social needs as comprising two components: a need for friendship and a need for the esteem of others. This implies that social interaction is a source of pleasure in its own right, but that it is also important in deriving a sense of self. We know who we are not solely in terms of a sense of personal integrity but in comparison with others, and in the way in which others regard us (or as we perceive and value that evaluation). Writers in tourism have also noted the importance of holidays as ego- and status-enhancing experiences (e.g. Crompton, 1979). Additionally, it would appear that in contemporary society we are not only who we are but also where we have been! Or, to reverse the position, we hold ourselves in higher or lower regard through the places we have visited. For example, it is usually regarded as a compliment to be referred to as 'well-travelled'.

It may be interesting to note that while there exists a sociology (e.g. Urry, 1990 and Rojek, 1993) and psychology (Pearce, 1982) of tourism, it might not be said that there exists a philosophy of tourism. In this concept of self as the sum of places visited, there is an opportunity for tourism to contribute to the philosopher's debate. For Sartre (1957), there is a primacy of *praxis* – individual, free, creative – even though humans are conditioned by social existence. The tension is between sense of self and alienation from society – the dilemma is that while 'I' cannot escape being the object of another's free existence, so too 'I' cannot, if 'I' wish to be free, live the characteristics or situation attributed to me by the other. For tourists seeking a sense of ego and status through an experience of place, and the ascribing of status to those places by others, the sense of 'I' becomes both social and geographical. The social interaction occurs within a place, and the attributes of place subscribe connotations to the sense of self.

It might be thought that this is an abstraction that does not advance an understanding of the tourist experience, but there is evidence to suggest otherwise. In a survey that used the Ragheb and Beard Leisure Motivation Scale, and which was administered to 1127 holiday-makers, Ryan (1994, p. 305) found problems with the item 'to gain a sense of belonging'. Although this is an item within the social dimension of the scale, the item had comparatively low weighting (0.46) and possessed little predictive ability. Analysis of the data permitted cross-checking with data on previous holiday-taking and a gap between importance and perception scores of place visited. It was notable that when assessing importance, the item 'to gain a sense of belonging' had a score of 3.30, and after the holiday the rating of the need being fulfilled rose to 3.69 ($p < 0.001$) on a seven-point Likert-type score, where seven represented the highest rating. It was one of very few items to change this way. Ryan argues that while this item is not overly important, it implies that while on holiday people begin to identify with the place visited. This tendency was higher for those who were more satisfied with their holidays, and for those who had three or more previous visits to the destination. Hence, part of a sense of belonging involves not simply a social identification but also a relationship with geographical place – although it must be recognized that part of the sense of place includes the social interactions, activities and subsequent memories associated with the location.

### Competency and mastery

The original Ragheb and Beard scale contained high-loaded items such as 'to use my physical skills' (0.779) and 'to develop physical skills and abilities' (0.746). In the scale these are associated with competition and keeping fit. But competency and mastery can also be demonstrated in other ways, including intellectual pursuits. For example, earlier in this chapter the work of Frankl (1962, 1992) and Boggiano and Pittman (1992) was referred to, wherein self-worth can be related to feelings of competency and mastery over one's own environment. The purpose of the original research undertaken by Ragheb and Beard was to distinguish between, and measure the importance of, intellectual, social and physical needs. There are obvious inter-relationships between these and relaxation needs. For many, playing sport is a relaxation, even while competency–mastery needs are also being met. Again, an ability to demonstrate mastery in a creative skill such as painting can also meet both needs intrinsic in the exercise of the skill and the obtaining of approval from others.

For tourists the need for a demonstration of mastery in physical activities will vary with the type of holiday. Certainly some holidays exist to enable tourists to develop their physical skills. One such type of holiday is that provided by companies like Sovereign Sailing. This company operated in the 1980s and early 1990s and attracted many keen windsurfers and sailors for whom one of the main pleasures of the holiday was the chance to develop and refine their skills. Continuous practice over fourteen days, with professional tuition at the appropriate level, proved to be very successful with both the holiday-makers and, as a small but profitable part of Sovereign's portfolio, with the then parent company, Owners Abroad. (Subsequently, the Sovereign brand became part of First Choice Holidays plc.) However, market research undertaken in the early 1990s for Sovereign showed that the sailing, while important, was but part of the success of the product. At least two other factors were identified. First, the social interaction with like-minded people sharing a similar experience generated a strong sense of social satisfaction. Secondly, the ethnic nature of many of the Greek and Turkish locations used was a factor that distinguished this company from other sailing holidays in the Mediterranean. This second factor was very popular with large segments of the clientele, although, as some of the resorts grew in size, facilities and popularity with other groups of tourists, this posed a challenge to the company and a need to readjust its promotional material. Nidri in 1996 was very different to Nidri in 1986, and by 1996 the hotel used featured a new swimming-pool, and a greater emphasis was subsequently placed upon the more cosmopolitan nature of the resort before the brand itself was repositioned within a new company structure in the late 1990s. None the less, it can be commented that the original formula still succeeds, as is witnessed, for example, by the Club Vass brand; although in this latter case it might be said the company reinforces the location through promoting the wind conditions, and the sense of 'Greekness' is a supplementary factor providing an environment conducive to sustaining a lifestyle favoured by windsurfers.

For other types of holidays the appeal lies not in physical activity but its very opposite. Physical relaxation may be defined in terms of a lack of exercise, or a physical laziness. On the Ragheb and Beard Leisure Motivation Scale, the item 'to relax physically' had a weighting of 0.66 (1983, p. 224), implying that this item may possess significance in explaining variance in any statistical analysis of behaviour.

*Stimulus avoidance*

Of all reasons for taking a holiday, this is perhaps the most obvious. It is associated with the escape needs identified by many commentators. It is notable that Ragheb and Beard relate this need to a chance 'to rest and unwind'. As shown by the example of windsurfing and sailing holidays, to 'rest and unwind' does not necessarily mean 'to physically relax'. The very action of physical exertion can, itself, be mentally restful even while, paradoxically, the mind is focused upon a specific action. Physical exertion can equate to mental relaxation.

It therefore becomes possible to conceive of a model as shown in Figure 2.3. This indicates that each motive can be represented as a continuum. However, it becomes difficult to locate different tourism products sensibly upon such a figure, as is demonstrated. Table 2.1 illustrates some possible mixes of motives that might be imputed to different types of tourist products, but it is evident that the relationships shown are open to debate. For example, cultural performances might be meeting needs for entertainment and diversion, be high in relaxation and be important as a social occasion for members of a package tour. In short, without more detail as to the specifics of a product, the type of figure or table shown in Figure 2.3 or Table 2.1 has limited usefulness. Thus, as a concept, more is required if researchers are to better understand the nature of the tourist experience through examining motives. Another point to note is that Loundsbury and Polik (1992) found little relationship between pre-holiday expressed needs and post-vacation met needs when using these concepts. They write:

> We suspect that a particular advantage of a vacation over other domains of life experience (e.g. work, family or community life) is that there are so many opportunities to meet one's needs that prior need level does not predict subsequent need gratification. Still, it *cannot* presently be concluded that there is any correspondence between levels of expressed needs and level of met needs. (p. 116)

## THE FLOW EXPERIENCE: THE THEORIES OF CSIKSZENTIMIHALYI

It has been noted that an apparent contradiction exists whereby mental relaxation is accompanied by physical exertion. How can this seeming contradiction be solved? One suggestion is that mental relaxation can occur in physical exercise when the skill of

*Table 2.1* Location of products on motivational products – an allocation

| Tourism product | Social motives | Mastery/competency motives | Intellectual motives | Relaxation motives |
|---|---|---|---|---|
| Adventure | High | High | Medium | Low |
| Cultural | Medium | Low | High | Low |
| Hiking/tramping | Low | Low | Medium | High |
| Sporting | High | High | Low | Low |

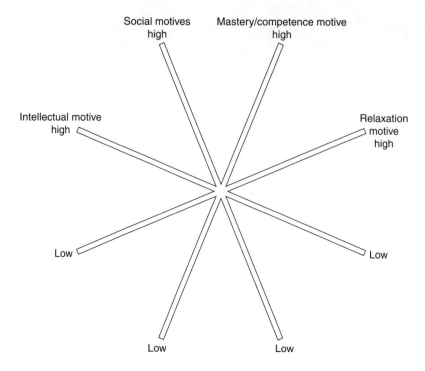

*Figure 2.3* Dimensions of motives

the participant is congruent with the challenge inherent in the situation. Thus the participant can be mentally and physically aroused, focused and engaged, with feedback that is positive in a sense of achieving positive feelings of competency or mastery; or of acquiring new skills. This theory of flow, developed by Csikszentimihalyi (1975) has been pivotal in research of wilderness experiences in North America, and in other recreational activities. For example, Mannell *et al.* (1988) applied the theory to retirees undertaking exercises in Ontario; Priest and Bunting (1993) used it in research into the experience of white water kayaking; and Ryan (1997) used it to analyse the role of guides in white water rafting.

   The theory of flow is often represented in the diagram illustrated in Figure 2.4. The vertical axis represents the level of challenge inherent in any given situation, while the horizontal axis is the level of competence a person possesses. Flow occurs when the level of challenge is not so much that it greatly exceeds a person's competence, or when insufficient challenge exists. Should the level of challenge be insufficient, then people will begin to feel bored, time will hang heavy, and individuals will seek additional stimulation in circumstances where they have control over their environment. On the other hand, should people find themselves in circumstances where the challenge is too great for their levels of competency, frustration can occur, a sense of helplessness may pervade their sense of being and in some circumstances physical or psychological dangers may be present. It is a congruence between challenge and competency that generates a sense of flow where 'behaviour is at once personally satisfying and socially appropriate yet requires neither rehearsal nor correction' (Csikszentimihalyi, 1988, p. 55). Csikszentimihalyi first began to develop the concept of 'flow' through observations

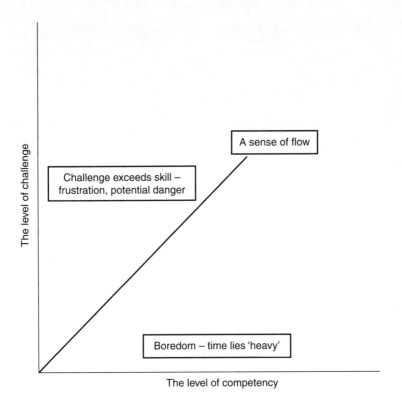

*Figure 2.4* The concept of 'flow'

of artists as part of his doctoral studies. Many years later he was to recall his impressions thus:

> The artists I studied spent hour after hour each day painting or sculpting with great concentration. They obviously enjoyed their work immensely, and thought it was the most important thing in the world. Yet it was quite typical for an artist to lose all interest in the painting he had spent so much time and effort working on as soon as it was finished ...
>
> Few artists expected any of their paintings to make them rich or famous. Why, then, did they work so hard at the easel – as hard as any executive hoping for a raise or a promotion? None of the extrinsic rewards that usually motivate behaviour seemed to be present. (Csikszentimihalyi, 1988, pp. 3–4)

The answer as to why the process so fully caught the attention of the artists lay in intrinsic motivation, but while sharing a common heritage with Maslow, Csikszentimihalyi felt that Maslow's explanations were inadequate. For example, Csikszentimihalyi felt that Maslow had left unanswered such questions as to whether *any* activity could generate 'peak experiences', and did all such experiences feel the same. In short, Csikszentimihalyi was motivated by the question 'What was the quality of subjective experience?'

Csikszentimihalyi (1975, p. 36) came to define the 'flow' experience as 'one of complete involvement of the actor with his activity' and identifies the following seven indicators of its frequency and occurrence:

(a)   the perception that personal skills and challenges posed by an activity are in balance;
(b)   the centring of attention;
(c)   the loss of self-consciousness;
(d)   an unambiguous feedback to a person's actions;
(e)   feelings of control over actions and environment;
(f)   a momentary loss of anxiety and constraint; and
(g)   feelings of enjoyment or pleasure.

(1975, pp. 38–48)

However, for the flow experience to be felt there are four prerequisites:

(a)   participation is voluntary;
(b)   the benefits of participation in an activity are perceived to derive from factors intrinsic to participation in the activity;
(c)   a facilitative level of arousal is experienced during participation in the activity; and
(d)   there is psychological commitment to the activity in which they are participating.

Mannell *et al.* (1988) have noted that these prerequisites impute an importance to expectation and purpose (motivation). They found that there was strong evidence for the prediction that 'higher levels of flow accompany freely chosen activities ... freely chosen activities are not only more likely to be labelled leisure, but to be accompanied by higher levels of flow' (1988, p. 299).

For Csikszentimihalyi the concept of 'flow' was very important in understanding 'the strivings of the self and the quality of individual well-being' (1988, p. 35), and thus essential in the creation of healthy human psyches. In Chapter 1 it was argued that holidays possess the potential to release people from frustrations and are thereby important sources of ensuring healthy, mature personalities that in turn enable people to return to and cope with the patterns of their daily lives. Holidays are a reward for work, a means of enabling people to continue work, a commodification of the periods of rest, leisure and recreation, and, historically, a means of ensuring a primacy of work, albeit one that today is threatened by social processes that de-differentiate between work and non-work. Csikszentimihalyi's concept of flow, it is argued below, has important implications for any overall assessment of the holiday experience.

Additionally, the concept can be seen to work in a number of practical situations that can arise during holidays. For example, Ryan (1997) analysed situations pertaining to white water rafting, as shown in Figure 2.5. First, the potential relationships between competency and challenge are divided into a series of possible relationships that are labelled:

*Devastation and disaster* – which is where the level of challenge is so far in excess of a participant's skill level that the potential for fatal accidents exists.

*Misadventure* – where again the level of challenge exceeds a participant's skill, and where participants may be flung into the river, but without fatal accidents occurring.

*Peak adventure* – where the rafter feels challenged and even endangered, but comes through the experience with an 'adrenalin high' feeling that they have been fully tested.

*Adventure* – where although not feeling endangered, a sense of excitement has been engendered.
*Exploration and experimentation* – where a novice rafter wishes to tentatively experience a sense of rafting but in comparative safety.

However, it now becomes possible to examine the potential role of the rafting guide. At any given level of tourist competency, say OB, then perceived risk or challenge increases given the severity of the river conditions, with the potential for misadventure occurring at risk level OX in Figure 2.5. However, the presence of the rafting guide and the skill that is possessed by the guide has the effect of increasing the 'competency' of the participant from OB to OC, and thus for the condition of the river that generates 'misadventure' at OX, the level of participant competency is increased by YZ, thereby changing the situation from one of 'misadventure' to one of 'peak adventure' for that participant. Such an analysis highlights the importance of the guides' skills and their role, and the model is capable of further extensions to consider, for example, the relationship between the participant's perceptions of guide skills, the confidence that they possess in the guide, and the nature of the experience derived from the trip. Although located within the specific adventure activity of white water rafting the model is applicable to many different forms of holiday experience. The model also illustrates the sometimes arbitrary division of motive and experience. From Csikszentimihalyi's perspective, the role of intrinsic motivation is that the distinction between experience and motive within flow collapses under the integrating nature of a lack of self-

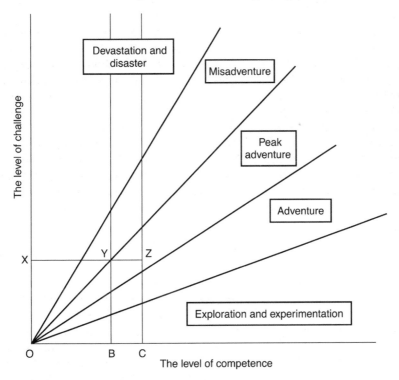

*Figure 2.5* Shifting competencies through intervention

consciousness – motive and experience exist in a dialectical condition whereupon the one continually reinforces the other.

Unlike Maslow, Csikszentimihalyi specifically sought modes of measurement of 'flow'. For example, in *Beyond Boredom and Anxiety* (1975) he investigated rock dance activity as an activity that 'consists of aspects that both increase and decrease the probability of participants' experiencing flow' (p. 108). Based on scores of frequency and intensity of flow statistically significant differences were found between those who did, or did not, experience flow. Csikszentimihalyi notes that the data are limited by the small size of sample, but what remains is that methods of measurement exist whereby 'flow' can be discerned.

## GENDER, FLOW, MOTIVATION AND HOLIDAY EXPERIENCE

Hirschman (1984) has examined whether gender is a factor determining an ability to engage in such focused behaviours, because many of the past applications of the model have been related to male-orientated sporting pursuits. The question she examines is whether feminine traits (conventionally described as nuturance and warmth, and as emotionally expressive and environmentally receptive) score higher on some items used to measure degrees of flow, while other, more masculine, traits, like those of dominance, aggression and control, score higher on items relating to competition and control of environment.

Hirschman first notes that there is a wide agreement that while sex is biologically determined, gender roles are, to some (albeit unknown) but significant extent the result of socialization. Henderson has defined gender as 'a set of socially constructed relationships which are produced and reproduced through people's actions ... [and] a potential analytic framework for the study of women, and the behaviour of females as well as males' (1994, p. 12).

The definition emphasizes that male and female behaviours might only be understood by the relationship between both sexes within existing social structures. Hirschman argues that any analysis based upon sex alone may be problematic because it assumes a congruence or otherwise between gender and psychological sexual identities that can give rise to confirmation of sex type, cross-sexing or androgynous-undifferentiated roles. In a study of 440 adults she reports that sex was not a predictor of an ability to engage in 'absorbing experiences', and was only significant in predicting levels of competitiveness. On the other hand, sexual role, or gender, as measured by the Personal Attributes Questionnaire and Sex Role Inventory, was a predictor in dimensions of the flow experience such as levels of involvement, alertness, competitiveness and attitudes to adventure.

While there are many studies about male and female participation rates in leisure and the nature of constraints that exist, there are few that examine the role of gender in holiday-taking. Davidson (1996, p. 91) notes 'the dearth of literature that explores holiday experiences of women or seeks to determine whether, how or why women's holiday experiences are different from men's. White *et al.* (1992, p. 148) provide one suggestion why such differences might be expected, noting that

> Women's lifestyles can act to prevent them from taking part in informal networks. Many networks are maintained by mixing socially, staying late for a drink or playing sport.

Because of domestic responsibilities, women tend to keep to official working hours. Women are also deliberately excluded from informal systems, because many of the informal network norms are developed in exclusively male territories such as private clubs.

There is evidence to suggest that women, too, have informal networks, but many exist to support them in their domestic roles such as childcare arrangements. Henderson has shown how women adopt different strategies to overcome, cope with or submit to the constraints that might restrict the range of available leisure activities. But it might also be observed that men likewise develop coping strategies, and hence the difference may lie not in the strategy developed but in the circumstances to which it is applied. Some feminists might argue, cynically, that while women 'cope' to adjust to their nurturing responsibilities, men 'cope' to escape them.

If holidays are periods of escape, do women have different expectations of holidays as compared to men, and, if they feel more constrained in 'normal' life, do they gain higher levels of satisfaction from holidays? In a study of life-stage effects upon holiday motivations Ryan (1995b) found mixed evidence that gender was a factor. Table 2.2 shows differences between men and women on items derived from the Ragheb and Beard Leisure Motivation Scale when applied to holiday-taking. It can be noted that very little difference existed between the intellectual, competency and social items, but the relaxation scores differed significantly. For example, on the seven-point scale, where seven represented the maximum score, men rated the item 'relax mentally' at 5.82, while women scored 6.14. Women also scored more highly on the physical relaxation item, and on the item 'to avoid the daily hustle and bustle'.

However, while these results present evidence of sexual differences, the interpretation of the data is made more complex when other factors like life-stage are added. The evidence seemed to show that, in spite of an increasingly complex pattern of family life, an extended conventional life-stage cycle from young independence through marriage and thereafter to solitary survivorship, still retained predictive abilities as to holiday wants. There was found to be little difference between men and women when both were young and employed. The differences shown in Table 2.2 can, to an extent, be explained by life-stage when young children are present, and when women are fulfilling the role of primary care-giver and home-maker. Closer examination of the data also revealed various sub-groups. For example, it can be seen that the item 'to use my physical

*Table 2.2* The impact of gender upon holiday motivations

| Item | Males (N = 523) | Females (N = 490) | t-stat | prob |
|---|---|---|---|---|
| Increase my knowledge | 4.36 | 4.45 | −0.84 | 0.400 |
| Avoid daily hustle and bustle | 5.56 | 5.80 | −2.37 | 0.018 |
| Build friendships with others | 3.51 | 3.46 | 0.45 | 0.653 |
| Challenge my abilities | 2.74 | 2.71 | 0.21 | 0.837 |
| Use my imagination | 3.49 | 3.49 | −0.02 | 0.985 |
| Be in a calm atmosphere | 5.35 | 5.48 | −1.27 | 0.205 |
| Develop close friendships | 2.52 | 2.47 | 0.45 | 0.656 |
| Use my physical abilities | 2.61 | 2.56 | 0.47 | 0.641 |
| Relax physically | 5.28 | 5.73 | −4.18 | 0.000 |
| Gain a feeling of belonging | 2.55 | 3.16 | −3.74 | 0.000 |
| Discover new places and things | 5.84 | 6.05 | −2.55 | 0.011 |
| Relax mentally | 5.82 | 6.14 | −3.44 | 0.001 |
| Be with others | 3.57 | 3.90 | −2.89 | 0.004 |
| Have a 'good time' with friends | 3.83 | 3.87 | −0.38 | 0.705 |

abilities' was comparatively unimportant. However, for a minority, this was an important motivation, and consistent with the hypotheses advanced by Ragheb and Beard (1982, 1983), was found to be closely associated with sporting activities such as windsurfing, mountain climbing, and, to a lesser degree, tramping. For this minority, the interest in the activity was more important than gender difference, for among high scorers, no significant difference existed between men and women. In their study of gender differences based on the Leisure Motivation Scale, Loundsbury and Polik (1992, p. 112) commented that:

> There were no significant differences between men's and women's variance estimates on any of the study variables or on any of the mean scores, with the exception of prevacation intellectual needs, where the mean for women (3.40) was significantly higher than that for men (2.96).

However, some differences existed between the two with reference to links between pre-vacation needs and subsequent satisfaction, but these existed only as to intellectual and mastery/competency needs, and a key determinant was the initial pre-vacation measured need.

The quantitative evidence from these types of studies tends to be supportive of the qualitative work undertaken by researchers like Henderson (1994). In Ryan's (1995b) study respondents were encouraged to provide additional comments, and a female perspective was discernible in responses. Thus, among the responses were comments such as:

> 'One nice thing about this holiday was that I did not have to do the washing up.'
> (respondent on package holiday)

> 'While I enjoyed the holiday, I did find myself tied more to the kitchen than I would have liked. None the less, it was nice to see my husband having time to play with the children.'
> (respondent was on a self-catering holiday)

On the other hand, there were comments made by men such as:

> 'I enjoyed just having time with my wife and the children.'
> 'I did more washing up than normal, but it was a further chance to actually have time with my partner.'

Such comments are revealing, for if gender is a social construct it raises the question as to whether there is a specific sexual female or male experience or perception. It has been argued that women are drawn to nurturing roles and, indeed, one of the issues for feminist writers has been to reinforce the concept that women are able to demand, and have a right to, time for themselves. Such comments as those quoted above indicate an appreciation of a sharing role by some men, although how strong this sense might be is unknown.

These types of findings are supported by researchers like Shaw (1992) and Davidson (1996). Based on a study of diaries, Shaw shows quite clearly that specific differences existed between the sexes as to their interactions with children and perceptions of various household tasks. In her phenomenological study of 24 mothers, Davidson clearly shows that holidays are not periods of an absence of work *per se*, but are times of relaxed frameworks, some work-sharing and less pressurized periods. She argues that, for the mothers, 'getting away' is a respite from the constant pressure of ceaseless routine, and all respondents noted that family holidays required less work and less effort than normal. Also of importance was that holidays were periods of socializing, yet much of this was subject to a limitation, and that was the (self?-)imposed restraint whereby women felt that the role of mother requires manipulating or easing events to ensure that other family members have a happy and successful holiday. Within Davidson's sample, the life-stage of motherhood in relation to young children permitted no *Shirley Valentine* form of escape.

These findings imply a need to distinguish between gender role associated with a sense of feeling female or male on the one hand, and the role of parenthood, whether mother or father, on the other. The issue is complex, and one interpretation of Hirschman's distinction between sexual and gender identities is that psychological and social sexual identity is partly a tautological, or perhaps a definitional, question subsumed by the wider issue of self-perception. For example, women may value competitiveness as a statement of self-value, and its categorization of it being a male trait is simply a secondary consideration.

Another aspect to the argument, and one pertinent to the concerns of the first chapter, is whether there is gender construction of place. Massey (1994) considers this from the perspective that the view of place is one of 'construction of specificities through interrelations rather than through the imposition of boundaries' (Massey, 1994, p. 7), and among these interrelationships are those of gender. Deem (1996) tries to find evidence that supports this contention. Her study was of perceptions of Lancaster in the North West of the United Kingdom, a historic city, complete with castle, that offers access to the Lake District. However, the evidence provided might be described as minimal, Deem observing that of 54 respondents, six were unable to say whether Lancaster was a city, while a further twenty denied that it was a city. Deem does note that perceptions of place were dominated by a consumption of goods and services consumed by women, and in that sense an engendered gaze existed. Additionally, she reinforced the findings reported above wherein women offered contrast between family responsibilities at home and away from home.

It would seem that in many studies of gender, the role of mother has had a significant impact. Yet, if few studies exist about the female gender role on family holidays, the literature on the role of father is almost entirely silent except where it exists as a vague comparison to that of the mother. Feminist researchers have drawn attention to the one but with little to say about the other. That the role of parent in determining holiday experiences is thought, intuitively, to be important, is not a radical thought, but finding evidence for such thoughts, and to further assess how those roles impinge upon and make the holiday experiences different from a subjective perspective proves to be more difficult. At least, the standard sets of abstracts relating to leisure, recreation and tourism (such as those maintained by CAB International) reveal few references. Evidence does exist of behavioural changes. For example, Cantwell and Sanik (1993) provided evidence of decreases in leisure time and in the levels of joint leisure enjoyed by husbands and wives. Osgood and Lee (1993) found a specific curvilinear relationship between age and leisure, with parenthood a key determinant in explaining the nature of the relationship. Verhoef *et al.* (1992) found that parenthood was the single most important determinant of female participation exercise. Yet while objective data exist to changed patterns of leisure, recreation and holiday-taking, little exists as to the quality of those subjective experiences and even less exists as to the role of fatherhood. From an empiricist perspective, in their study of the involvement of couples in family holidays,

Madrigal *et al.* (1992, p. 298) provide some evidence relating to quality of experiences when they write:

> The results also indicate that couples without children were significantly more involved with pleasure-importance than were couples with children residing at home ... Couples in the present study who perceived that their marriage was more egalitarian and less specialised, in terms of domestic and occupational roles, were likely to be more involved in the pleasure and importance components of a family vacation than were more traditional couples.

In short, gender, while a factor, remains a role subject to social and familial construction, and it is the construct of the role as much as matters of sex that is important. The first chapter of this book indicated the importance of signs and symbols. In *Ecce Homo*, Nietzsche wrote:

> To communicate a state, an inward tension of pathos, by means of signs, including the tempo of these signs, this is the meaning of every style, and considering that the multiplicity of inward states is exceptionally large in my case, I have so many stylistic possibilities ... *Good* is any style that really communicates an inward state. (1967, p. 265)

Nietzsche's philosophy of the strong or weak person who fashions a life to establish individuality has been an influence upon postmodernist thinkers. Although out of context, the comment can relate to any individual's experience. Studies may show either a homogeneous or heterogeneous experience of holidaying and leisure for people of either gender. However, of more importance is the nature of experiences created by people regardless of sex. This is not to argue that gender is unimportant; our sexual perception is an inherent part of us, and gender is a socialization process. Indeed, Ryan and Hall (2001) argue that the first exploration undertaken by humans is that of the boundary of body and external environment. But what the literature does provide is evidence of how diverse are the realities, perceptions and reactions of people of both sexes to their social conditions.

Yet, in considering the 'stylistic possibilities' there is no doubt that some 'styles' are more socially approved than others; and that many of the approved styles are conventionally more masculine than feminine in orientation. Thus it has become conventional in turn for academics to note that 'the signs, symbols, myths and fantasies privileged within tourism marketing are invariably male-oriented ... and exclusively heterosexual' (Pritchard and Morgan, 2000, p. 891). It has been noted that holidays are about fun, are perceived to be periods of positive action and are about renewal through optimistic action. The words 'sorrow' and 'sadness' are notably absent in these descriptions. Yet these, too, are important contributors to meaning within human development, and their absence states something about the nature of holidays as a means of human maturation. Greer (1999) specifically argues that sadness is an attribute of women, and writes of the sadness to be had from the realization that a partner engaged in a career can grow away from the home-bound mother; that motherhood is a condition of care and love for children who will also leave home to determine their own independence; of the realization that in the youth, appearance-oriented society that is today's norm, women may feel their age in their mid-thirties, lined by motherhood, while men of that age become 'interesting' to younger women. Such considerations rarely impinge upon the conceptualizations of holiday-making, and concepts like those of Maslow's self-actualization appear to be entirely gender-

*Table 2.3* Masculine and feminized concepts of tourism

|  | Masculine concepts | Feminized concepts |
|---|---|---|
| The tourist | Flâneur | Choraster |
|  | Sightseer | Embodied self |
| The tourist destination | Destination | Chora |
|  | Place | Space |
|  | Object | Interaction |
|  | Image | Social value |
| Tourism | Activity | Experience |
|  | Visit | Process |

*Source:* Wearing and Wearing (1996)

neutral. But if it is accepted that holidays are, in part, social constructs bound by the evolution of society from a modern to a late-modern or postmodernist era, then the changing conditions and perceptions associated with those conditions as they apply to gender roles must have importance. Additionally, any analysis of that which is present in any given situation without reference to that which is absent must remain a partial analysis. Indeed, Wearing and Wearing (1996) strongly argue that social constructs of gender are so powerful as to determine the very concepts of tourism. Commenting upon the popularity in the tourism literature of the concept of the flâneur, the 'man apart from the crowd while being in the crowd' as a means of analysing the temporary status of the tourist in a host society, they cite Wolff (1985, p. 45) in writing:

'There is no question of inventing the flâneuse: the essential point is that such a character was rendered impossible by the sexual divisions of the nineteenth century.' Women could not wander alone in public places. (Wearing and Wearing, 1996, pp. 232–3)

For each masculine characteristic of tourism they submit a feminized counterpart, as demonstrated in Table 2.3. In place of the flâneur they submit the concept of the 'choraster' based upon the 'chora', Plato's space between being and becoming, the space in which place is made possible. Rather than being a place through which an isolated figure strolls, the chora suggests a space occupied by those who give meaning to the space. In their history of tourism, Ryan and Hall (2001) trace the evolution of tourism in terms of generating two liminal figures, tourist and sex worker, as being inherent in the structures of nineteenth-century modernity; thereby implying agreement, to some extent, with Wearing and Wearing that the history of tourism is not gender-neutral. In one sense, though, the distinction between gender and sex is complex, and the masculine sex can operate within female-gendered environments, and vice versa. Indeed, for a feminist commentator like Greer, one of the worst aspects of a feminist tradition is its manipulation by unscrupulous entrepreneurs who purvey 'girl power' as evidenced by magazines like *Bliss*, *Sugar* and *More*, or the UK Channel Four TV show, *The Girlie Show*, which featured 'wanker of the week'. She writes: 'In every colour spread the British girls' press trumpets the triumph of misogyny and the hopelessness of the cause of female pride' (Greer, 1999, p. 319). From this perspective the 'laddettes' occupy a traditional masculine ground of assertive sexuality that has little in common with the female traits listed by Hirschman (1984).

## THE TRAVEL CAREER LADDER

It can be argued, however, that 'stylistic possibilities' are born not only of needs, but also of awareness of what is possible. Such awareness is not created through imagination alone, but is learnt through experience, and, as noted in the previous paragraph, that which is provided by contemporary entrepreneurs. None the less, imagination remains important because each individual perceives different potentialities from what it is they experience. From this perspective travel may be important because it may be the catalyst for change as it takes people away from their normal environment. Philip Pearce's notion of the travel career ladder, derived from the earlier work of Abraham Maslow, is one concept that addresses learning through a tourist experience. Pearce (1988) postulates the existence of a 'travel career ladder' where tourists develop varying motivations of:

(a)   relaxation;
(b)   stimulation;
(c)   relationship;
(d)   self-esteem and development; and
(e)   fulfilment.

The perspective from which Pearce approaches the issue is encapsulated in the definition of a career, that is, quoting Hughes (1937, 409–10), 'the moving perspective in which the person sees his life as whole and interprets the meaning of his various attributes, actions, and things which happen to him' (p. 27). A career is a purposeful and conscious action, to be differentiated from that which is mindless and easily forgotten. In Pearce's model the motivations listed above can be divided into two categories as shown in Figure 2.6. The needs may be self-centred or directed at others. Thus, for example, relaxation may be a solo exercise where the holiday-maker seeks a quiet, restful time alone, or it can be relaxation in the company of others. Pearce has argued, however, that there is a travel career based upon these needs. At a descriptive level it has an obvious appeal. It can be hypothesized that for those undertaking their first overseas trip, their major concerns may be those of wanting relaxation within a safe environment. However, as they become more experienced, so, too, they may become more curious about the culture and history of other places, and possibly even seek a sense of identification either with a place, or establish a sense of self through having knowledge of differences between cultures. They will travel more, and may do so independently. In due course, as they proceed through the 'upper' needs of the motivational hierarchy, their concepts of self and understanding become better formulated in order to become, in Maslow's terminology, more actualized. They engage, increasingly, in more intellectual pursuits, wanting to know about the history and culture of places, perhaps even wanting to learn foreign languages. In the language of Yiannakis and Gibson (1992) they become less risk-averse, and seek more stimulation.

However, there are problems with the concept of the Travel Career Ladder. For example, Pearce argues that stimulation may be understood along a dimension of risk and safety that is expressed by a concern for the safety of self or others. However, it might be argued that there is a real and distinctive difference between these two motivations. To actualize a concern about the safety of others might mean placing one's

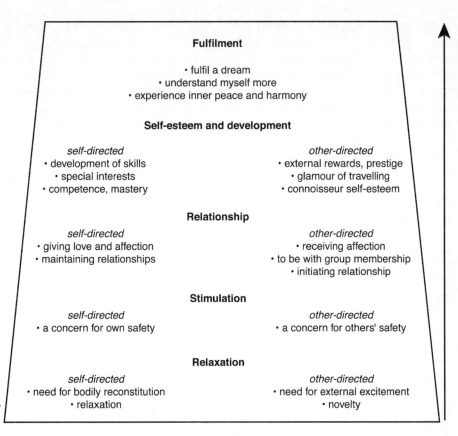

*Figure 2.6* Pearce's motivation model: travel career trajectory

self at physical risk in an attempt to help those who are in danger. The willingness to do this, it can be argued, is a characteristic of those who are certain in their own psychological maturity. Hampden (1971) argues that the 'radical' personality is able to take risks because it is able to conquer its own misgivings. Ryan (1998) also criticized the concept on a number of grounds. First, it is argued that some of the evidence Pearce uses in his original exposition is not particularly strong. It is pointed out that while Pearce quotes Mills' (1985) study of skiers as evidence, the original findings are not without their own problems (as indicated by Ryan, 1994, p. 57).

Secondly, it has been argued that the situation is more complex than the model shown in Figure 2.5 assumes. Iso-Ahola (1982) has noted two motivations for touristic activity: the desire to leave behind an environment, and, second, to seek an intrinsic reward. Like Pearce, he argues that both motivations interact with personal or interpersonal areas of activity, with the result that there exists a dynamic dialectical process as the tourist seeks and avoids push-pull motivations and interaction with others. The nature of this process is that tourists will switch roles while on holiday and that, over time, different needs will arise. Thus a holiday-maker may arrive needing rest, but after a couple of days' relaxation will seek to explore his/her environment. This process of exploration has been shown to be quite rapid. Guy and Curtis (1986) have provided evidence of tourists being able to draw reasonably accurate maps of their environment within five days. Cooper (1981), in his study of holiday-makers on Jersey, provided evidence of an expanding and more diffuse pattern of geographical exploration over a period of a week.

The pattern of learning about places has also been shown to be quite complex, and not a simple accrual of additional information over time. Walmesley and Jenkins (1992) in their study of tourists at Coffs Harbour note that 'the learning process seems to involve an evaluation of what has been learned and a discarding of some information. At various times after the first couple of days, the number of landmarks, paths and districts on the maps actually declines' (p. 278). This is not to imply, necessarily, that there is less knowledge about an area, but rather that tourists may indulge in behaviours that optimize time and space within the short periods they have at a holiday destination, and implicitly accept the opportunity cost of disregarding other areas.

So, too, with behaviour while on holiday. There are two reasons for suspecting behaviour is complex. First, as, within the holiday, initial needs are satisfied, other motivations might emerge. Indeed, it is congruent with Maslow's theories of needs to argue that if, initially, there is a primary need for relaxation while on holiday, the satisfaction of that need will create awareness of other needs such as an exploration of place as a means of acquiring a sense of belonging or to enable processes of self-actualization to take place. Secondly, in the world of the post-tourist, the holiday-maker can indulge in matters of the moment; a ludic involvement with other people, places and activities might occur in an apparent idiosyncratic manner as the tourist knowingly slips from role to role, and redefines place with reference to self. In a different context, that of political philosophy, Murphy Jr describes this process as one

> Where subjectivity reigns, man is not defined in relation to a higher order of reality. No longer seeking certainty in the idea of the good or in human nature, he becomes something in, and for, himself. And rather than being open to the world of social and political and political life, he seeks to subject it to his own image. The self distances itself from experience and then transforms it in thought. The process leads to a selective interpretation of human existence and a restrictive idea of self and its possibilities. (1990, p. 191)

It will be noted that while Murphy Jr rejects the relativity associated with postmodernist thought as being 'restrictive', the point remains that processes of selectivity of needs and opportunities create complex patterns of behaviour. This is partly, perhaps, because the denial of certainty, however 'restricting' in terms of human development it may be, leads to a wider range of behaviours, some frenetic, as in the case of the indulgent, 'irresponsible tourist', others more introspective, as tourists use holidays to seek meaning.

To this pattern of changing motivations (and philosophies) *within* a holiday can be added the scenario of changing needs *between* holidays. Evidence exists (for example, the tourism surveys of the British Tourism Authority/English Tourist Board) of a market sector that takes more than one holiday of four or more nights away from home. Such holiday-makers may well assign specific functions to such holidays. One holiday may be child-centred, the second orientated around a sports activity, a third based on relationships with a partner, and thus, within each holiday, different need patterns for rest and relaxation occur. And, as noted, other factors, like life-stage, have roles to play. The attempt to allocate a developmental pattern of holiday-making based on a maturing personality transformation is thus difficult to sustain.

Some researchers have stressed the adaptive ability of the tourist. Commenting on the work of Phelps in her studies of tourists on Minorca, Ryan (1991) notes:

> The interpretation of the travel experience and the nature of the resort area ... generates both perceptions of gaps between the resort zone and expectations, and governs the nature of interactions with others, but then certain social and psychological skills also come into play in the sense of being able to perceive authenticity, suspend disbelief when required, and conduct positive sets of relationships. These attributes help shape travel and activity patterns which permit the fulfilment of the original or amended expectations and hence create satisfaction. (pp. 47–9)

The thesis that there is a complexity of motivation that renders invalid the maturation process of the travel career has, however, further obstacles to overcome. Pearce is not alone in using the concept. For example, Kim (1994), in a study of Korean tourists to Australia, found that 'those who rated "safety and security" most positively are the least satisfied of tourists. On the other hand, the highly satisfied group was more likely to fulfil higher needs of the travel career ladder' (p. 87). So, too, Pearce shows in his study of visitors to Timbertown (1988, p. 78) that 'repeat visitors show more interest in relationship and self-esteem levels'. In short, the sources of satisfaction differ between more and less experienced tourists within the same milieu, and that greater satisfaction is also experienced by the more experienced (and self-actualized?). Pearce's evidence suggests that mean scores vary from 5.30 to 5.83 on a six-point scale between needs, with the higher needs generating the higher levels of satisfaction. However, the only statistically significant finding would appear to be 'Scheffe post hoc comparison which indicates that the principal difference in the means lies between the self actualization mean and the family and friends [affiliation] mean' (1988, p. 78). It may be pertinent to query why it is expected that satisfaction should be greater for those motivated by self-actualization needs. Satisfaction, it can be argued, is a function of the congruence of need and experience, i.e. a need met by an appropriate experience generates satisfaction. If one seeks social needs and these are met, then presumably the tourist is satisfied. Thus, too, a tourist seeking 'self-actualization' may also succeed in having needs met. Is the second holiday-maker any more satisfied than the first?

Inherent within the Travel Career Ladder concept appear to be three alternative hypotheses:

1. More experienced tourists derive more and better satisfaction than the less experienced because they are further up the travel ladder – that is they are prompted by qualitatively different needs.
2. What is important is the need of the moment; it is immaterial whether it is a social need or one of intellect (self-actualization). Quality of experience is determined by a simple satisfaction of needs that is not related to the quality of needs based on a perceived hierarchy. Satisfaction is derived from the perceived meeting of that need, and the different levels of satisfaction between more or less experienced holiday-makers is simply that the more experienced are more able to meet their needs. Both the experienced and inexperienced are motivated by the same needs.
3. Both experienced and inexperienced tourists are motivated by the same needs – but the more experienced holiday-makers are simply, through experience, more able to meet those needs. However, it is recognized that qualitative differences do exist between needs; that, for example, there are differences between life-enhancing

experiences and others that are needs of convenience. Therefore, more experienced tourists gain more satisfaction and are better able to obtain satisfaction from higher needs.

Pearce's hypothesis assumes a qualitative difference in motivation and satisfaction derived from meeting drives. The experience of the tourist relaxing by the side of the swimming-pool in a safe, familiar environment, while being satisfied, is less satisfying than that derived by the explorer discovering an area previously not known to him. The alternative approach is that inherent in models like the ServQual model of Parasuraman *et al.* (1985, 1988) which argues that satisfaction is a congruence between expectation and perceived meeting of needs. In the latter model there is no ranking of motivations as being higher or lower, or of producing different qualitative results. In the ServQual model any given gap may be associated with different levels of expectation and perception. Perhaps, within the model, it is the ranking of scores that indicates qualitative differences of experience. However, there is no conceptualization that indicates any significant differences in importance between the dimensions of the scale, and it can be concluded that there is a significant difference between the two approaches. While Pearce is concerned with quality of *experience*, Parasuraman *et al.* are primarily concerned with quality of *performance* by service providers. Hence, while the two concepts of ServQual and the Travel Career Ladder offer much to any analysis of tourist behaviour, any comparison between the two is not strictly a contrast between like models. Nor are either without grounds for valid criticism (e.g. Brown *et al.*, 1993; Taylor, 1997, for critiques of ServQual).

In 1998 Ryan again revisited the concept of the Travel Career Ladder in a paper published in *Annals of Tourism Research*. To the above criticisms others were added. These included the argument that, as shown in work published, Pearce and his co-authors were not consistent in their formulation of the model, and that results were not congruent with the authors' own interpretations of the model. Levels of past travel experience seemed to be poorly correlated with measures of self-actualization, and in some instances the theory was being applied to datasets that did not specifically measure a 'travel career' (e.g. the use of the Canadian Pleasure Travel Markets data by Kim *et al.* (1996). Six issues about the concept and its application to tourism were posed, these being:

(a)   Maslow was not concerned with constructing psychometric scales, which is the practice adopted in the travel career ladder approach;

(b)   a definitive listing of items for measuring a developmental process to self-actualisation is not advanced;

(c)   the relationship between open-ended responses, where present, and structured questionnaires is unclear;

(d)   much of the writing on the travel career ladder is isolated from mainstream consumer behaviour research, and there are lessons that can be derived from other research that link ego-involvement and purchase decisions;

(e)   evidence for the travel career ladder is far from clear; and, finally,

(f)   the key problem is that the concept lacks predictive certainty, confuses 'abilities to achieve desired motives with the actual motivations themselves' and perhaps represents a 'wish to obtain quantitative support for what is an emic approach'.

(Ryan, 1998, p. 953)

To these can now be added the issue previously discussed as to whether the concept is gender-neutral.

## MOTIVES, QUALITY OF EXPERIENCE AND LIFE-SATISFACTION

From the viewpoint of studies that relate to the quality of life, for example those of Diener and his associates, there is a realization that while 'peak experiences' (times of strong, positive emotional intensity) are important, they are not necessarily life-defining.

If satisfaction is emotive and judgemental (i.e. it assesses a gap between expectation and perceived reality) it is subjective, may be either positive or negative, and it 'resides in the experience of the individual' (Diener, 1992). Writing of feelings of wellbeing, Diener also argues that these include a global assessment rather than simply a 'narrow assessment of one life domain' (p. 4). Holiday satisfaction, while not possessing global significance in this sense, might contribute to, and be affected by, the personality of the individual holiday-maker. Those who feel good are those who are satisfied because they have a preponderance of positive experiences in their lives and in their holidays. It can be argued that 'positive holiday-makers' exhibit these characteristics. Such holiday-makers were found to score highly in expectation and use of holiday resort facilities, and also as having high levels of satisfaction (Ryan and Glendon, 1998). Those who are less happy would tend 'to appraise a majority of their factors in their life as harmful or as blocking their goals' (Diener, 1992, p. 5).

It has been argued that holidays represent important, positive experiences for people. Does this imply that accumulated positive experiences generate people with positive outlooks upon life, which, in turn, create a predisposition for achieving high satisfaction? And, do the accumulation of positive experiences arise because people have positive outlooks? Diener *et al.* (1991) note that a greater *frequency* of positive experiences do generate higher scores on measures of wellbeing and satisfaction with life, although the *intensity* of the experience seems to add little to the total score. Additionally, intense moments of strong affective emotion seem to follow periods of negative psychological experience, and hence it might be a case of *net* effects (which are small) that are important in establishing long-term effects.

## AN ALTERNATIVE EXPLANATION TO THE TRAVEL CAREER LADDER

This discussion presents some challenges to the concept of the travel career as postulated by Pearce (1988). It might be that the ability to derive self-actualization experiences is not simply a matter of need born of an experience of travel, but a predisposition resulting from, and contributing to, a perception of life-satisfaction, which, combined with an increased experience, makes one more able to meet such needs. It is suggested that while tourists engage in many different behaviours and are multi-motivational, regardless of the number of times they have holidayed, still it can be argued that all tourists have similar types of motivations. Perhaps what Pearce has measured is not a difference of motivation but an ability to better achieve ends on the part of the more experienced tourist. Evidence for this viewpoint has been derived from

*Table 2.4* Intellectual needs and satisfaction by experience

| Number of past visits to a destination | Importance of need Mean score | Satisfaction of need Mean score | Number |
|---|---|---|---|
| never | 3.63 | 2.50 | 472 |
| 1–2 | 3.67 | 3.91 | 294 |
| 3–5 | 3.46 | 4.04 | 164 |
| 6+ | 3.69 | 4.36 | 156 |

a study mentioned earlier of 1127 tourists living in the East Midlands in the UK (Ryan and Glendon, 1998). In this study, holiday-makers were asked to complete a motivational scale based on the Ragheb and Beard scale, and, using various measures of satisfaction, to assess their holiday experience. Additionally, they were asked to indicate how many times they had previously visited the destination and how many times they had previously taken a holiday of that type before. The scale used a seven-point Likert-type scale where seven was the highest score.

Some of the results are shown in Table 2.4. This table relates to the intellectual needs of the tourists, which might be held to be the most akin to the self-actualization motivation of Pearce's Travel Career Ladder. It can be noted that there are no significant differences as to the strength of the motivation between categories of tourist based on the number of past visits to the destination. However, there are significant differences between their abilities to meet these needs, and the more experienced can be seen to be better at fulfilling these drives (F = 102.16, P < 0.001). These findings are consistent with the theory of tourist motivation and behaviour that will be suggested in Chapter 3.

In conclusion, motivations are revealed to be complex phenomena. It has been argued that, essentially, motivations for holiday-taking can be categorized into four main groupings, but, even then, further examination shows close interrelationships between them.

It appears from the above that any discussion of tourist motivation must take into account:

1. the cognitive and affective;
2. the need to distinguish between positive and negative components of the experience as they subsequently shape motivation;
3. the gap between expectation and perceived reality;
4. the possibility that at any one moment reported satisfaction might represent a variation around a baseline of a general sense of satisfaction that a respondent has with themselves and their perception of life in general, i.e. what some researchers have defined as a general sense of wellbeing;
5. that this general sense of wellbeing is itself a determinant of reporting of scores of motivations, expectations and perceptions of satisfaction with any given event;
6. there is the possibility that a motivational, perceptual and evaluative score might reflect a mood of the moment rather than a reflection of the item being examined as befits the 'post-tourist';
7. gender is a socialized process, but while self-image is in part determined by sex and gender, the capability for any given action is also born of individual will, which is both independent of and part of any socialization process; and

8. motivations may be few in type, but give rise to many variants of behaviour. The expression of need is plurivocal, but the needs may be few in number if Allport's categorization of personality based upon few morphogenic traits is adopted. This does not demean individual personality and holiday needs and experiences. Indeed, it perhaps does the opposite in attributing a richness of adaptability by humans to both need and circumstance.

   In Chapter 1 it was stated that the desire of tourists to leave the familiar and to place themselves at risk may appear irrational, and can only be explained by reference to motivation. However, a paradox emerges. Motivations and personality traits are few in number if the concepts of Allport and Ragheb and Beard are adopted, but the diversity of behaviour continues unabated. From this it might be argued that the propositions used in this chapter are themselves insufficient; yet, on the other hand, any model-building is an abstraction from reality. The apparent lack of congruity between the propositions and observable tourist behaviour may mean that the concepts discussed here aid in an understanding of complex behaviour, but are not in themselves 'proof' of the validity of the propositions.

   Yet, if holidays are only rational in the sense of being explicable by reference to motivation, motivations only have meaning with reference to the social environment within which they are formulated. And problems still remain. Why do we assume that holidaying is a rational behaviour; that our motivations for escape, relaxation, discovery, excessive over-indulgence, extra-marital sex, too much drinking and other holiday behaviours are rational? In Chapter 1 the question of 'gaze' was reviewed. The linkages between changes in society, tourist motivation and the translation of motive and expectation into holiday experiences need to be examined further; and this is done in Chapter 3.

# Chapter 3

# From motivation to assessment

*Chris Ryan*

## INTRODUCTION

It has been argued that holiday-taking is understandable as a form of behaviour when motive is taken into account. But, equally, any combination and strengths of the four primary drives described by the Ragheb and Beard Leisure Motivation Model may be involved in an analysis of observed tourist behaviour. In this respect a thesis of holidaying is akin to any theory of human behaviour, and problems abound if the experience of travel is to be understood. For example, does an understanding of motive imply that tourist behaviour is seen to be rational? For rationality to exist, perhaps an act has to be informed and conscious. Also, in themselves, even conscious motives may not be rational, and such a debate further assumes that there is a consensus as to what 'being rational' means. Holiday-makers do irrational things. They burn their skin through too much sunbathing. They get drunk. They indulge in risky sex. To say that the act is 'explainable' by listing motivations of, say, relaxation and social need does not make the act any more 'rational'.

## RATIONALITY OR MINDLESSNESS

Much of holiday-making behaviour may be in a state of 'mindlessness'. Langer and Newman (1979) and Langer and Piper (1987) have argued that there is a predisposition by researchers to attribute to people rational, logical and goal-orientated behaviour in situations where, all too often, actual behaviour is characterized by 'mindlessness'. This is behaviour which is governed by rules and habituation and is opposed to mindful behaviour that is rule-forming, and thus is engaged in creating categories and distinctions. So how much of the memory of lounging by a swimming-pool is retained? What distinguishes one day of such activity on one holiday from that done on another? But perhaps there is a need for such mindlessness? It is a characteristic of relaxation. Why is there a need to recall every detail of the road along which we drive on holiday?

The act of mindlessness is part of a process of optimization of experience; we retain that memory which is sufficient to meet a need.

Thus a picture emerges of holiday behaviour which may or may not be 'mindful', and which may or may not be rational. There may even be a purposeful rejection of the rational. If Urry's ludic post-tourist plays games, what purpose does the game serve? Why is it thought necessary for game-playing to serve a purpose? Fortunately, humans do not proceed all the time in such a confused state. However, an apparently logical process can be based upon a false assumption. It can also be noted that one motivation for travel is the search for the unexpected, for serendipity, the knack of the happy surprise. By definition, therefore, the tourist is unprepared for the experience – it may be hoped for, but unanticipated. Hence a further paradox emerges in describing tourist behaviour, for the occurrence requires factors beyond the control of the tourist, and therein lies the potential for wonder, catharsis or disillusionment.

## DECISION SETS

The opening chapter of this book began a discussion of the cathartic nature of some travel, but the second chapter made little reference to such things in the discussion of motivation. Equally, while in the first chapter much was made of the influence of societal change upon our perspectives of what travel is and what may be gained from it, the second chapter relegated the social context to a vague background through which, possibly, an individual may seek to express themselves.

In this chapter an attempt will be made to bring the variables of wider social factors and individual motivations into a closer relationship. It will do so by extending a conceptual scheme suggested by the author in two previous publications. In *Recreational Tourism* (Ryan, 1991) it was suggested, following the work of writers like Jackson (1983, 1988) and Henderson (1991), that various antecedents existed prior to travel. The diagram used is reproduced in Figure 3.1. Some were inhibitors or constraints upon travel, while others were facilitators. That book followed a conventional pattern where various determinants of the demand for tourism existed. Thus, economic factors were identified as important facilitators in that the level of discretionary income (that is income available for leisure expenditure after meeting the usual costs of living, such as mortgages, rent, travel to work, food etc. had been met) was important in determining the ability not only to go on holiday, but also in identifying the range of destinations and activities available. The model described there (1991, p. 48) also drew upon well-established marketing paradigms. For example, it was partly based upon the work of Howard and Sheth (1969) in an identification of social environmental factors playing a role upon decision-making. Thus, marketing and image projected by the destination was incorporated as an important determinant. In Howard and Sheth's terms, images may be inert, inept or evoked, and of these it is the positive, evoked image that the marketing of destinations seeks to create.

This concept of imagery in marketing was further explored by Crompton (1992) and Crompton and Ankomah (1993). They argue that 'there are finite limits to the capacity of potential tourists to assimilate and process information relating to the large number of alternative vacation destinations from which they can select' (p. 461). They also note that there is a time dimension to be taken into account, and hence a distinction may be

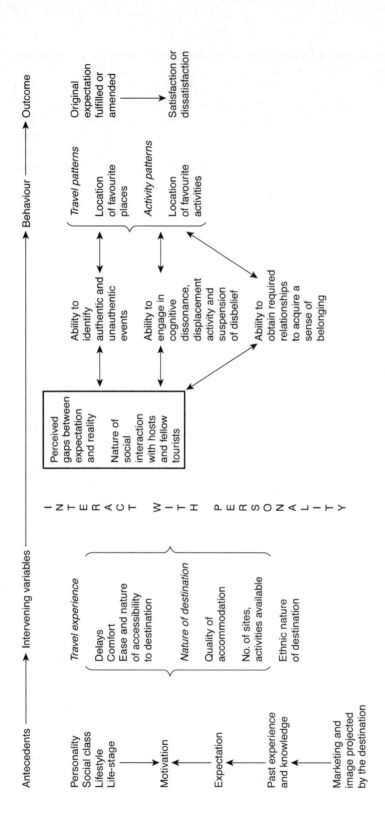

*Figure 3.1* The link between expectation and satisfaction

made between an early and late consideration set. However, there is evidence to suggest that the number of potential destinations considered by holiday-makers in deciding where to take their holidays are few in number. Woodside and Lysonski (1989) report findings which indicate that most tourists consider between two to five destinations. The author, in a study of 1127 UK holiday-makers, found a similar number of destinations being considered, but other factors were also of importance. That is, for some tourists, especially those using package holidays, the destination was secondary to factors such as price, timing, departure airport and other convenience factors when the main needs of sun and 'being away' were met.

## TOURISTS AS PARTICIPANTS

The model shown in Figure 3.1 also incorporated a traditional marketing view by implying a feedback mechanism in that satisfaction derived from the holiday became part of a tourist's knowledge which could be incorporated in the next round of holiday-taking. That feedback was based upon an assessment of whether original expectations were being fulfilled. In short, it was based upon a gap concept akin to the ServQual model of Parasuraman, Zeithaml and Berry (1985, 1988). However, the 'heart' of the model lay in the perception and experience of place, and the interactions that occur at that place. These interactions were with the other players in the formulation of an experience: namely other tourists, the representatives of the tourist industry with whom tourists came into contact and members of the host society.

However, what was thought to be important within this process of interaction was that tourists retain their social skills, and their ability to adapt to conditions that might not have met their original expectation. It is argued that significant differences exist between the situation of a holiday and the type of service encounters that are usually measured with the ServQual model. The service encounter measured by Parasuraman, Zeithaml and Berry is generally one sustained over short periods of time, or, if sustained over a longer time, which consists of a series of encounters. Such an example is that discussed by Cliff and Ryan in their chapter within this book. The tourist, on the other hand, is generally on holiday for a significant length of time, and while the holiday consists of a series of encounters, the totality of the holiday is one of a sustained experience of something that, by definition, is not normal. In Chapter 2 it was noted that ServQual is a measure of performance, or it might be interpreted as a measure of satisfaction with performance of a specific function. The satisfaction derived from a holiday possesses, as Pearce (1982, 1988) has implied, qualitative differences, and, furthermore, it is a satisfaction with both the particular and the whole. This implies that holiday-makers appraise the individual components of a holiday, the contribution that each element gives to a holiday, and perceive the total holiday as a separate entity which is also assessed. While this may be true of other services, one important difference between holidays and other services is the role of the tourist as a participant in the process.

It has long been noted that service encounters lack homogeneity because the client becomes part of the process. In holidaying the tourist is an important decision-maker in the process. The tourist is not simply a passive consumer but a proactive partner. As Getz and Cheyne argue, in their contribution to this book, tourists attending sports events may do so looking for trouble or, to use an old-fashioned UK term, 'a rumble'. The event is chosen with this in mind, and the event fulfils expectation. Any model of tourist behaviour must thus feature the tourist's predisposition to certain actions, as is shown in Figure 3.1. Different tourists possess different abilities to perceive what is, or is not, authentic, have different attitudes towards the importance of authenticity, and have varying responses to initial disappointment. However, all tourists do tend to want successful holidays, however they have defined 'success'. Motivations become goals, and hence behaviours are directed to achieve these goals.

Tourists also operate under time constraints, and hence need to optimize the quality of their experience within these constraints. An initial disappointment might call forth a reaction of wanting to seek redress, but to do so may be time-consuming. The pursuit of financial compensation on holiday becomes a self-defeating act in terms of creating a pleasurable holiday, and thus many might simply adopt alternative behaviours which lead to a more than satisfactory holiday experience.

## MAKING DECISIONS

These themes were more fully explored in a second version of the model, which is shown in Figures 3.2 and 3.3. The schema is a two-stage model and, again, the basic themes of the propositions are based upon marketing paradigms. Central to this is the concept of satisfaction as an evaluation of experience when compared to expectation or that which tourists believe to be important about their holidays. As already noted, this concept, in

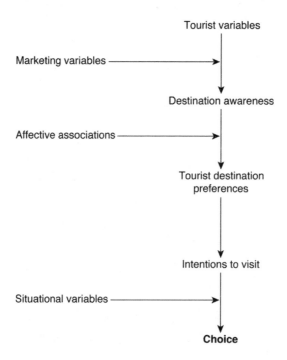

*Figure 3.2* A process of choice

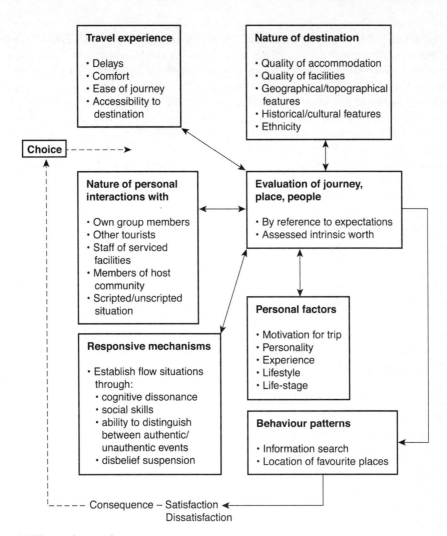

*Figure 3.3* The tourist experience

turn, raises many issues. A learning process is involved. Holiday-makers learn in order to possess an expectation or an ability to evaluate places and events. Part of this learning is their own past experience of holidaying, but they also learn through other intermediaries, both commercial and informal. The creation of expectations requires an identification and evaluation of what is deemed to be important. Importance, too, is a learnt variable, and the evaluative process is shaped by the social context of learning. Thus socio-demographic variables, like social class, occupation and life-stage, are important in shaping the process of conceptualization that each tourist might use.

While these form a backdrop to the decision-making process, specific situational factors can also be of importance. Such variables can relate to life-stage, like the presence of a partner and/or children. Other issues might relate to an ability to have time off work, the price of the holiday and, indeed, the attractiveness of a brochure. The first stage of the model thus takes into account:

1. marketing variables – for example, product design, pricing, advertising/promotion channels;
2. tourist variables – for example, previous destination experience, life-cycle, income, age, lifestyle, value system and motivations;
3. destination awareness – unavailable or considered sets, and whether these sets are inert, inept or evoked;
4. affective associations of destinations – positive or negative;
5. tourist destination preferences; and
6. specific situational variables – for example children's school holidays, partner's holiday entitlement, perceived need for a holiday due to 'overwork'.

These factors lead to forming an intention to take a holiday. The decision is then activated through a booking process which, as Cliff and Ryan describe in the next chapter, is itself an important part in the process of holiday-taking and which is also associated with sets of expectations and assessments.

The second stage is illustrated by Figure 3.3. The stages that lead to a decision about, and subsequent booking of, a holiday, are important in that the holiday becomes an anticipated event. In several senses the experience of a holiday begins before the vacation actually starts. In qualitative work undertaken for this book, which consisted of discussions with two focus groups of adults, one in the United Kingdom and one in New Zealand, each group comprising six adults, this anticipation was evidenced by comments such as:

> I look at the holiday TV programmes. Even though I know I won't go to many of the places shown, it gives me ideas. Collecting the brochures from the agency is part of the fun, and we have family debates about where to go. I guess we form quite a few ideas about places through this, and generally we're not disappointed. (UK female respondent, age 37)

> Well, before we go, we buy the suntan lotion – God knows why – it's not as if we can't get it in Spain! We buy some guidebooks if it's a place we haven't been to before. (UK female respondent, age 28)

> It might be the kids – they keep asking before Christmas – Christmas really means the family get together before we go away – so what with Christmas and everything I guess we are looking ahead to the holidays. (New Zealand male respondent, age 35)

This process of anticipation is possibly a contributing factor to the decision-making process. Marketing texts refer to three types of non-compensatory decision rules, to which Crompton and Ankomah (1993) also refer. The first is the *conjunctive rule*, which is concerned with the negative end of attributes being considered. It might be said to be a choice based on the 'least worst' destination. The second approach is the *disjunctive rule*, which focuses on the positive side, and hence a selection is made on that holiday perceived as the most superior. The third is the *lexicographic rule*, which uses all the attributes in a stepwise fashion. Here all the alternatives are assessed on the most important criterion first. If more than one alternative meets that criterion, then the second rule is used, and so on.

The focus groups seemed to be far less logical than these models, with the processes tending to be a mix, but generally looking at the positive aspects of a destination. The conjunctive rule might be said to apply to pricing, that is some holidays were simply seen as too expensive, but a really attractive destination that was a little more costly than was initially budgeted for might induce the extra expenditure. Also, while final locations might be joint family decisions, some of the earlier parameters might be defined by one or both of the adults, with children perhaps playing a subsequent role in aiding a decision from a selection of places. Thus:

> With three children money is always an issue, and I guess I make a decision when I select the brochures we are going to look at. I don't think it is right at the top of my thinking – perhaps because by now I know the brochures I am going to use – it's more a choice that is made of location from the brochures we use. I just don't use the expensive brands. (UK male respondent, age 38)

Again:

> I guess we work within a budget by looking at a place. If it's cheap, we stay longer; if it's more expensive we just stay a few days less. It's the place (within reason) that attracts. (New Zealand male respondent, age 29)

## GOING ON HOLIDAY

Figure 3.3 illustrates the consequences of choice. By its nature, anticipation implies a consideration of outcomes, and hence in that sense it might be said that an extended Fishbein model of attitude formation is involved (Ryan, 1991). The confirmation of the choice begins with the closing of the door of the family home as holiday-makers set out on their holiday. The travel experience, with its delays, comfort, travel time and ease of accessibility to the destination is important for several reasons. A long, tiring journey can mean that arrival at the site is followed by the first day of the holiday being one of recovery rather than exploration as described by Cooper (1981). On the other hand, a pleasant, relaxing trip can mean, especially if it entails an arrival at not too late an hour at the destination, gaining, effectively, an extra day of holiday, and thus a predisposition to initial favourable impressions.

As already noted, researchers (e.g. Cooper, 1981; Guy and Curtis, 1986; Walmesley and Jenkins, 1992) have found that tourists are quick to learn the key features of a place. The process of learning implies a process of evaluation. It has been seen that Walmesley and Jenkins (1992) report a decline in features marked by tourists as they optimize time by concentrating on that which provides most pleasure. This evaluation of place can be said to involve two criteria: does it meet a need, and does it meet expectation? It might be asked what distinction is being drawn between need and expectation. In this context it can be said that a failure to meet a need represents the absence of some attribute that possesses potential for meeting wants. Failing to meet an expectation, on the other hand, means the presence of a desired attribute, but not of the standard required. Both types of failure would seem to imply potential dissatisfaction.

However, the model in Figure 3.3 continues a theme derived from Figure 3.1, and that is the ability of tourists to adapt to failed expectation. There are many variables in a holiday place – people, culture, topography, scenery, accommodation, service quality – that all have a role to play. As Ashworth and Voogd (1994) have pointed out, holiday destinations are pluralistic in use, and are multi-marketed. Thus, initial disappointment may not lead to a disappointing holiday, as holiday-makers pursue those things that provide satisfaction and avoid those that do not. They are indeed actors in the process; holiday *makers* and not simply holiday *takers*. As Baum points out in Chapter 5, the relationship of the tourist with service providers can be an intense one, and such a relationship can overcome any perceived deficiencies in surroundings. Indeed, a roughness of physical provision combined with friendly interest on the part of the host might meet a tourist's very perception of ethnic authenticity!

The ability to respond appropriately to any disappointment is akin to the concept of flow previously discussed, for it presupposes that the challenge presented by the disappointing environment is not so great that a tourist cannot respond positively. In terms of the Yerkes-Dodson 'Law' (1908), the stimulus is not so great as to produce panic and, finally, inaction through producing too much arousal with which the holiday-maker cannot cope. The 'post-tourist' is also able to respond in ways in which a collection of failures becomes a criterion of success. The broken bed, the non-appearing meal, the beat-up taxi, the worm in the salad, all become trophies for future stories. But again, it is argued, the process is subject to an ability to cope. While many British have come to regard the Costa Brava as a safe, familiar haunt, the façade can be broken by misfortune. A road accident, being arrested by police, falling ill – such incidents place the tourist in a suddenly vulnerable position where, perhaps not speaking the language of the hosts, the familiar becomes replaced by the unfamiliar with the trauma that might occur in such circumstances.

Ryan (1994) uses this model to propose a series of propositions that might be tested and, indeed, provides evidence to support some concepts, and to reject others. For example, evidence emerged to support a gap concept of satisfaction when gaps were correlated with alternative measures of satisfaction derived from tour operators' questionnaires. However, the thesis of search arising from initial disappointment is not sustained by the quantitative research quoted. It is noted that

> What is not supported by the results is the thesis that, given initial disappointment with the holiday destination, higher search activity occurs. There was no evidence that the less satisfied (subsequently) conducted higher levels of exploration activity, indeed the reverse was true – namely those who (initially) explored more had higher scores of satisfaction. (Ryan, 1994, p. 305)

## Those things tourists enjoyed

The research upon which the model was based also included a qualitative component where respondents were encouraged to comment in spaces left for that purpose and, subsequently, as noted, two focus groups have been held. How does the model hold against the stated experiences of holiday-makers? The first thing to note is just how positive holiday-makers tend to be. The questionnaire contained an open-ended question to ask respondents to indicate what experiences they had most enjoyed about their holiday. Of 1127 respondents, only 81 made no response to this item. As might be expected, the very opportunity to relax was the most appreciated aspect of their holidays, with 198 respondents making specific mention of this. Table 3.1 indicates the most frequently mentioned items.

In theories relating to tourist types, Plog (1977, 1990) argues that the continuum between psychocentric holiday-makers (those seeking the familiar) and the allocentric (those who are risk-takers, seeking the unfamiliar) follows a normal distribution. Is there any supporting evidence from this sample? The above table offers some indirect

*Table 3.1* Aspects of the holiday that were enjoyed most

| Item | Number of mentions |
|---|---|
| relaxing/peaceful | 198 |
| a good climate | 153 |
| scenery | 159 |
| exploring/discovering new places | 148 |
| food | 120 |
| being with family/friends | 81 |
| good walking | 64 |
| a sense of freedom/independence | 62 |
| friendly people | 60 |
| good accommodation/good hotel | 59 |
| the history/culture of a place | 54 |
| good beaches | 48 |
| getting away from a stressful job | 46 |
| a chance for physical exertion or sport | 46 |
| the style of living/culture of a place | 35 |
| having company | 34 |
| good facilities for children | 27 |
| entertainment/nightlife | 23 |
| is clean | 17 |
| good facilities | 13 |
| being in a different country | 13 |
| achieving a sense of wellbeing/something new | 12 |
| watching wildlife | 11 |
| isolation | 11 |
| nice swimming-pools | 11 |
| Disney | 7 |

evidence – indirect in the sense that Plog is referring to types of tourists and their activities, while the above refers to most enjoyable experiences. Hence the above table is not a direct measure of Plog's typology. However, while the table indicates only the most frequently mentioned likes, when combined with other items from the research, two extremes can be identified, as shown in Table 3.2.

However, it is very difficult to categorize many of the respondents' descriptions by this method. It would appear that a number of the sources of enjoyment are partially independent of this categorization (for example, an appreciation of scenery could apply across the whole of Plog's spectrum), while most are in the range of mid-centrics, which would be in accordance with Plog's expectation.

Pearce (1982) suggests that most of the enjoyable activities of holidays relate to the higher needs of the Maslow hierarchy of needs, while the dislikes arise from perceived threats to basic needs. Evidence for this view was obtained from the focus groups, and the question arises, Do the lists currently being considered support the notion? A categorization of the ten most frequently mentioned positive items from the sample of 1127 is shown in Table 3.3.

The categorization in Table 3.3 are only 'broad brush' descriptions, and are open to some debate. First, in such a discussion, it might be appropriate to note what Maslow (1970) characterizes as the self-actualized personality – they are realistically orientated, accept themselves, others and the natural world for what they are, have a great deal of spontaneity, are problem-centred rather than self-centred, have an air of detachment and a need for privacy, are autonomous and independent, maintain a fresh appreciation of things, have had profound experiences, identify with mankind, have deep

*Table 3.2* 'Extreme' allocentric and psychocentric experiences

| Experience | No. of mentions |
|---|---|
| **Allocentric likes** | |
| midsummer night in Glencoe, around a camp fire, drinking malt whisky with a few motor-cycling friends | 1 |
| trekking in the jungle | 1 |
| meeting the Burmese Liberation Army | 1 |
| experiencing opera in Verona | 2 |
| watching wildlife | 11 |
| the sense of isolation | 11 |
| achieving a sense of something new | 12 |
| being in a different country | 13 |
| **Psychocentric likes** | |
| good facilities | 13 |
| nice swimming-pools | 11 |
| trip was well organized | 6 |
| a good coach driver | 4 |
| no prior booking for golf required | 3 |
| pub lunches | 2 |
| the flight home | 1 |

*Table 3.3* The most common positive holiday experiences: a categorization

| | |
|---|---|
| relaxing/peaceful | affective to self-actualization |
| a good climate | physiological |
| scenery | self-actualization |
| exploring/discovering new places | self-actualization |
| food | physiological |
| being with family/friends | affective/social |
| good walking | self-actualization |
| a sense of freedom/independence | self-actualization |
| friendly people | affective/social |
| good accommodation/good hotel | physiological |

relationships with a few especially loved ones, possess democratic values, do not confuse means with ends, have a fund of creativeness, resist conformity and are able to transcend the environment. To simply apply the label 'self-actualization' to the above categorization is, hence, crude. Moreover, it must be noted that the above categorization is the result of coding of responses for input into a computer, and the quantification of the qualitative response means that the above count of frequency of mention loses the 'qualitative' feel of the data. There is little doubt that for a number of respondents the feelings expressed are profound. In the case of respondents referring to the affective need of being with their family, there is little doubt about the feelings of affection and, indeed, almost of relief at having holiday time together. This is especially true in the case of children. Statements were made such as: 'a wonderful opportunity to share time with my family'; 'a sadly only too rare a chance to play with my children for any length of time'; and 'a chance to have quiet time with my wife'.

The comments relating to a sense of freedom were also of interest. There are, at a subjective assessment, two aspects to this feeling. One is almost a relief at being away from a stressful job or situation; it is an 'escape' from the daily reality. But also there is a 'pull' factor, as if the holiday situation is seen as the desired way of life, the reality of what a person would like to do or be. Comments that illustrate this include 'the chance to get away from a stressful job', 'a chance to recuperate after difficulties', 'the chance to live as one should, to be independent and feel free', and 'to be able to make my own decisions in my own time'. Some of the comments were combined with other factors. The sense of isolation, being away from it all, was, in a few cases, specifically associated with the feeling of freedom, while in other instances the sense of freedom was combined with either the ability to be with one's family or the opportunity to share in another culture or country for at least a limited period. Whether it was the success of Peter Mayle's bestselling book *A Year in Provence* or something more basic, a number of such comments relating to culture seemed to refer to France.

One aspect often associated with France was that of 'good food', and this item also indicates the difficulty of attributing items to broad headings derived from the Maslow hierarchy of needs. At first sight, the item 'food' would be attributed to physiological needs, but in the case of 'good food' many respondents were linking it with aspects of culture and a way of living, and hence 'good food' and the ambience in which it was enjoyed become much more than the satisfaction of a basic physiological need. On the other hand, 'poor food', which might lead to illness, can be interpreted as a threat to physiological comfort.

In short, within the limited space available on the questionnaire, there was a sense in which the concept of enjoyment being associated with the higher aspects of the Maslow motivation and the characteristics of the 'self-actualization' was evident. Also evident was the real enthusiasm of a number of respondents for their holiday choice. Words such as 'paradise', 'wonderful' and 'enjoyment' indicated the real and deep levels of satisfaction that at least some respondents were getting from their holiday, and there is, therefore, a very real sense in which quantitative measures do not tap this quality of experience.

**Sources of dissatisfaction**

The reverse side is that such expectation can, if disappointed, potentially lead to high levels of dissatisfaction. Sources of dissatisfaction did exist, and these are listed below. The impact of these sources of dissatisfaction can be examined in more detail, but for the moment it might be said that these factors, in many cases, should be viewed as irritants rather than being significant in any final evaluation of a holiday. This was not always the case, but has some substance as a generality. It has been suggested above that there is a very strong motivation to enjoy a holiday, that goals of enjoyment are set, and thus hindrances to that goal are overcome. There are many senses in which this seems to be true.

Of the 1127 respondents, 262 made no comments about sources of dissatisfaction. In total, 319 reasons were identified as causing dissatisfaction. This indicates that the sources of dissatisfaction are far more diverse than the sources of satisfaction, when only 106 reasons were catalogued. Additionally, the number making comments (n = 865) were less than those identifying sources of satisfaction (n = 1046), thus implying that generally satisfaction exceeded dissatisfaction for the sample as a whole. Table 3.4 indicates some of the more frequently voiced sources of dissatisfaction.

In the case of poor weather, the majority of the complaints were from those that had holidayed in the UK. None the less, many were realistic (resigned?) about the nature of

*Table 3.4* Sources of dissatisfaction on holidays

| Item | No. of mentions |
|------|-----------------|
| poor weather | 192 |
| long journey there and back | 68 |
| airport delays | 57 |
| having to go home/back to work | 55 |
| insufficient income/high prices | 42 |
| poor food | 35 |
| insects | 28 |
| cramped/basic accommodation | 24 |
| intrusive noise | 24 |
| being ripped off/hassled | 23 |
| poor hotels/accommodation | 19 |
| long journey back | 17 |
| being rushed/too much to do/see | 16 |
| overcrowding/too many people | 14 |
| long journey there | 13 |
| cramped flight/poor flight | 11 |
| local people not friendly | 11 |
| traffic jams | 11 |
| other British tourists | 10 |
| poor drainage/smells/lack of basic hygiene | 10 |
| lack of children's facilities | 10 |
| having to wash and iron | 9 |
| poor location | 9 |
| flying | 9 |
| poor couriers | 8 |
| lack of variety in entertainment | 8 |
| unfinished building sites | 6 |
| lack of character | 4 |
| car parking problems | 4 |
| French lorry blockade | 3 |
| EuroDisney | 2 |

the British weather in that a large proportion made comments about how the poor weather had not put them off enjoying their holiday. They were the mirror image of those who, when holidaying in the UK and mentioning the good weather, commented to the effect that either they were lucky or that good weather *can* be had in Britain.

The contention made by some authors (e.g. Fussell, 1982) that tourism is not travel, on the basis that the journey is not an important part of the holiday product when compared to the travel of the past, is supported to a degree by the large numbers who comment on the length of the journey. Length is not a matter of distance only, but also of time, and there was no doubt from some of the responses that this was a factor that tired holiday-makers. Also, for some the journey itself was not pleasant, either because of nervousness about flying or the perceived cramped conditions of the flight. A handful were also negatively affected by being near smokers, if they were themselves non-smokers, and were sufficiently inconvenienced by this to make comments, even when the holiday had taken place several months previously.

Pearce's argument that the majority of unsatisfactory experiences occur because of threats to the lower needs of Maslow's hierarchy is sustained by the results shown in Table 3.3. A number of these items can be broadly categorized as threatening physiological comfort or safety. For example, insufficient income, poor food, insect bites, poor accommodation, intrusive noise, being hassled and feeling threatened obviously fall within these categories. Some items threatened other aspects of the need hierarchy. Complaints about the behaviour of other British tourists were sometimes accompanied by the comments that 'it made one ashamed to be British' – implying a threat to self-esteem. The comment about having to return as being the worst aspect of the holiday can be interpreted as a denial of something that permits satisfaction of the higher-order needs.

In some cases, fortunately a small minority, the threats to wellbeing were real. Three tourists had suffered from theft, two had been injured, one had been attacked, two had been caught in a flight from Yugoslavia as the civil war had started, two had been ill and one had been in an earthquake. Self-esteem had also been threatened in other ways. One commented that her holiday had been spoilt by her spouse continually thinking about another person. It was noted that she was separated at the time of completing the questionnaire. Another said continual rows had marred the holiday, and she, too, was recently separated.

Even in 1992 the 'fabled' stories of British tourists being placed in partly built sites by their tour operator were sustained by the sample. One spoke of the 'wonderful view' he had had of a rockface ten feet from his window. Six referred to their hotel being next to, or forming part of, a building site. The petty annoyances of modern travel were also recorded, for example two reported damage to luggage, one bitterly complained about having to leave a hotel bedroom at noon when the flight home was late at night, one complained about his inability to get a decent cup of tea in the United States and five complained about 'the Germans', describing them as arrogant and rude, while three stated that they were embarrassed to be British after witnessing hooligan behaviour by 'young Brits'.

## Focus group evidence

These types of observations were supported by comments made by the UK focus group. Examples of sources of dissatisfaction that obviously incorporated denial of basic motivational drives included:

> 'I had spent all my money and arrived at Calais late. I had to spend the night at the railway station; it was cold and I was hungry.'

> 'While canoeing, I fell in the water. It was colder than I expected, and I had no change of clothing. Nor was it that warm that I could dry out quickly. As a result I had a chill for a few days, and that rather reduced my enjoyment of the holiday.'

One interesting example of psychological security being threatened came from a female respondent who was in her twenties and had been a travel agent. She ruefully described her worst holiday experience as being the realization that she had left her cuddly, fluffy, toy bunny rabbit in a French hotel while taking a motoring holiday through France. She had telephoned the hotel prior to leaving France on the cross-channel ferry, and had been so upset at its loss that she had reported it to the French police. As she commented, what they made of a tearful English female asking them to find her pink, fluffy bunny rabbit she could only guess! She had even taken out an advert in the local French newspaper. She explained she had had this rabbit since the age of 5, and it had been everywhere with her, and it had great sentimental value.

On a happier note, respondents reported many sources of pleasure, and, generally, these occurred at higher levels of the Maslow hierarchy. Over a third referred to the beauty and tranquillity that they had experienced. Quite unprompted, five specifically referred to the experience in terms that were resonant of Maslow's concept of peak experiences. For example, describing a trip to Greece, one respondent stated:

> 'I stood there, and appreciated that this scene had been re-enacted every day from before the time of Homer. It was a link with a distant past, an appreciation of that while an individual's life is but a moment in time, it is part of a chain of time.'

What had prompted these thoughts was the sight of a young boy driving out the goats to the pastures above Corinth in the very early hours of the morning.

In many cases, however, the source of satisfaction could be described in terms of the respondent feeling that, in MacCannell's terms, they had penetrated the 'backstage' because they had established contact with local people that they had found to be particularly satisfying.

Discussions also indicated support for a situation that researchers of satisfaction have identified. This is where holiday-makers derive pleasure from a holiday which, however, is not of the type they would have selected for themselves. For example, in two cases where package holidays had been taken, the source of satisfaction was not the direct experience of the holiday-maker, but a derived enjoyment at being able to provide for children within the family a holiday which they had enjoyed. One divorcee related how she had gone on a holiday with her fifteen-year-old daughter, and thinking that perhaps this might be the last time her daughter would want to go on holiday with her, she (the mother) had gained much pleasure from seeing her daughter enjoy herself so much.

## IMPLICATIONS FOR THE MODEL

Such incidents can be incorporated into deterministic models as outlined above, but is it legitimate to incorporate concepts derived from humanistic psychology into a seemingly deterministic model? When the model was presented as the 'Tourism: State of the Art' conference in 1994, one critic expressed disappointment that the model was of such a nature. In part his criticisms are that the model seeks to reduce what can be strongly emotional events to a series of stages and steps. Certainly, Skinnerian thought may be described as the proposition that observable behaviour can be explained in terms of contingent environmental stimuli, and the process whereby the rate of response is brought under the control of consequent stimuli (reinforcers and punishments). As a deterministic model, however, the suggested explanation lacks many components. For example, it does not indicate the nature of reinforcement schedules, and is relativistic in its approach. It incorporates a plurality of paradigms. On the one hand, while primarily arguing that the holiday experience, by its nature, uniquely meets a series of needs (for example, escape and fulfilment needs) and consists of extended learning behaviours, it accords a role to routinized procedures where, arguably, Skinnerian approaches are apt descriptors.

Yet, on the other hand, the model also ascribes to internal, cognitive processes, important functions as motivators for holidays. These processes are described as a means of adjustment to, initially, less than satisfactory scenarios resulting in subsequent satisfaction with the holiday. These internalized processes are important, for a basic premise is that neither like motivations or holiday settings are sufficient to predict either behaviour or quality of experience.

It must also be noted that the model is, at best, only a partial concept. The final outcome with which it is concerned is a measure of satisfaction, not a prediction of behaviour. Ryan (1994, p. 303) notes that

> The link between satisfaction and behaviour is viewed as a reiterative process. That is, where performance meets or exceeds expectation, satisfaction is deemed to be an outcome. Where performance is inferior to expectation, then it is expected that adaptive behaviour results to achieve satisfaction because the motivation for satisfaction of wants is high within the holiday context. Where it is not possible to achieve those initial wants, alternative wants are substituted, behaviour changes, and again the goal is the satisfaction of those alternative wants.

It should be noted that the consequences of achieving satisfaction from one holiday for future holiday behaviour is a complex relationship. This is because there are reasons for believing that the linkages between one holiday and another may be either indirect or weak. Pearce's theory of the travel ladder assumes a developmental relationship – tourists progress from one holiday to another type. Laing (1987) has argued that holidaying is a matter of habit. Ryan (1994) has implied that future holidays are the consequence of learning and, hence, after a time, holiday-makers cease to experiment in order to optimize time and money by repeating experiences known to create satisfaction, subject to personality traits. It is also argued that tourists are pluriactive and multi-motivated in that they might use the same holiday for fulfilling several different roles.

Pearce (1988) also confronts criticisms that the setting out of properties of a social situation in a series of steps is both 'static and arid ... [and inappropriate as it] ignores the subjective understandings of actors in social settings.' He continues, commenting, 'This point of view is poorly thought out, as it contains a limited vision of the ways in which the structural properties of tourist situations can be combined and deployed to understand the full and rich character of observable tourist-guide behaviour' (p. 37).

To argue that processes are complex is not to state that chains of events cannot be discerned. It might none the less be argued that the conceptual scheme being suggested highlights the importance of a process, namely that of the adaptive abilities of the tourist, without explaining the processes. A number of concepts apply that might aid understanding. Festinger (1957) has suggested that if people have difficulty in fitting information into a preconceived mental model, then one way of achieving a fit is to devalue the source of contrary information. A similar process might occur here. If, for example, hotel accommodation does not meet expectation, then the tourist might rationalize this as being unimportant because little time will be spent in the room. That is, those things that are seen as sources of discomfort are revalued as being unimportant. Of course, the opposite might also happen, where a trivial item assumes significance for the holiday-maker.

Pearce (1988) refers to the work of Argyle *et al.* (1981) who categorized eight features of social situations. These are:

*goals* – purposes or ends of social behaviour
*rules* – shared beliefs that regulate behaviour

*roles* – duties and obligations attending social positions people occupy
*repertoire of elements* – sum of behaviours appropriate to a situation
*sequences* – ordering of the repertoire of behaviours
*concepts and social cognitive structure* – shared definitions and understandings needed to
   operate situations
*environmental setting* – props, spaces, barriers, modifiers that influence the situation
*language and speech* – the codes of speech inherent in language

From this perspective adaptive behaviour can be viewed as determined by goals – holiday-makers make their vacations work for them to achieve fulfilment of needs. It might be deemed by the rules of the group that complaint is not sanctioned – hence complaining is an inappropriate behaviour. Complaints in a foreign language may be difficult to pursue. On the other hand, complaints might be pursued because ill-feeling is shared among many, for example a coach-tour party might express dissatisfaction about something to a courier or a driver which brings about a change in itinerary planning. The identification of structures in itself does not postulate any specific outcome while the importance and strength of the variables are unknown.

## THE ROLE OF ACCIDENT AND ILLNESS

One feature that is often overlooked in the tourist literature is not only the irrational but also the accidental. If serendipity is dependent upon events outside the control of the tourist, how much more is accident and illness? The first question is, to what extent is the unexpected beyond the tourist's control? The concepts outlined in Figure 3.3 imply that the tourist as actor can choose from a series of alternative strategies. An extended Fishbein model (see Ryan, 1991) implies that the tourist can select from alternative behaviours by a consideration of probabilistic outcomes. Thus, if the holiday-maker enjoys the surprise of, for example, meeting local people in their 'backstage' (to use MacCannell's terminology, which implies the acquisition of 'authenticity'), then relaxing by the side of the swimming-pool in the tourist complex is not the type of behaviour which would create the required meeting. Independent travel becomes one way of increasing the probabilities of success. Each mode of behaviour has an associated series of possible outcomes, and this is implicitly recognized in the models postulated by various writers. Thus, in Pearce's writing, the search for self-actualization implies sustaining action with greater degrees of risk. Thus, the unexpected event is still unforeseen, but in hindsight it might be 'explained' as a logical consequence of actions taken. In truth, it might be one of a series of alternative outcomes, but the fact of occurrence generates its own logic in the mind of the tourist. There has been little work done on the role of hindsight in tourism, but given such strong goals to enjoy the holiday, hindsight must be a factor. Thus Kierkegaard surmised, 'Life is lived forwards, but understood backwards.' Myers (1990, p. 18) has noted:

> One problem with commonsense explanations is that we tend to invoke them *after* we know
> the facts. Events are far more 'obvious' and predictable in hindsight than beforehand ...
> [Researchers] have demonstrated many times that when people are told the outcome of an
> experiment, the outcome suddenly seems unsurprising – certainly less surprising than it is to

people who are simply told the experimental procedure and its possible outcomes. People overestimate their ability to have foreseen the result.

Indeed, Myers calls the process 'The I-Knew-It-All-Along' Phenomenon. So, too, it may be with tourist behaviour: 'I did $x$ and $y$ happened.'

But might there be a continuum between, on the one hand, the logical outcome of an action and, on the other, the totally unforeseen result? Accidents might possess this characteristic. In hindsight, an accident or illness might be seen as a logical outcome of an event, or it might be the result of a number of coincidental events occurring together.

How often do such unanticipated accidents occur? In a study of 785 tourists in Malta, Clark *et al.* (1993) found that 1.1 per cent had an accident. No data are indicated about the nature of the accidents, but research from other sources would imply that in most cases these are generally quite minor. Page and Meyer (1995) analysed overseas tourist claims for Accident Compensation in New Zealand and found that 0.6 per cent of such tourists made a claim (which was less than the total rate for domestic claims (2.34 per cent)). Of a total of 424 claims registered and paid to overseas visitors, 75 arose from injuries sustained while driving, with the majority of claimants being aged between 20 and 39.

In a study of students as tourists, Ryan and Robertson (1996) found that of 360 respondents, 2.3 per cent had an accident on holiday. Among the accidents listed were a sore knee from falls, a hook in the hand when fishing, a sprained ankle, a skiing accident, a cut finger through cooking, a fall down stairs, and a splinter which infected a finger.

Unfortunately, more serious accidents do occur. For example, drownings occur, tourists are killed in scenic helicopter trips, kidnapped or beaten to death by muggers or terrorists (Ryan, 1991, 1993; Aziz, 1995). However, it would seem from the evidence that while each individual case is, of course, extremely serious, in total less than 0.001 per cent of all tourists are so affected.

That accidents can be related to tourist behaviour is confirmed by both observation and some data. Dawood (1993, p. 281) argues that

> Accidents abroad tend to follow a depressingly repetitive pattern. Injuries from moped accidents are especially common in young visitors to island resorts for example. Renting a moped is cheaper than renting a car, and public transport is often poor; if it is hot, protective clothing and a helmet will be unattractive, even if they are available at all ... Motorists who wear seatbelts at home, use child seats for their children, observe speed limits and drink-drive laws, seem less inclined to do so abroad.

In 1995, reports emerged from the European ski fields not only of the usual number of broken legs, but also of snow-boarders who lost their lives through deliberately flouting regulations as to safe ski areas and seeking to 'surf' falling snow which caused avalanches (various Reuters reports). Behaviour also contributes to illness. In their study of students as tourists, Ryan and Robertson (1996) found evidence not only of increased drinking leading to hangovers, but also of the presence of a small but specific cluster categorized as 'boozy bedders' – a group of predominately young males accounting for about 16 per cent of the sample, who were characterized by above-average incidences of drinking and having sex. Often the two activities were linked together – as one respondent wrote tersely, 'Got drunk, got in back seat of car, had sex'.

Cartwright (1996) provides evidence of how the very choice of holiday location might be a determinant of the incidence of travellers' diarrhoea. Quoting the work of Pitzinger *et al.* (1991) he notes how patterns of a greater incidence of diarrhoea is associated with travel to North Africa and the tropics, and also the greater incidence among those under the age of 30. He notes that 'this probably reflects the different life styles of the younger adults who tend to be more adventurous in their eating and drinking habits'.

The relationship between sex and tourism has been well documented, and it obviously brings its risks. Kinder and Ryan (1995) conservatively estimated that the sex industry catering for tourists in Auckland, New Zealand, was worth approximately NZ$4 million. A feature of the massage parlours in Fort Street that has grown over recent years has been the number offering 'Asian Girls'. In a study of 163 female Thai sex workers at the Auckland Sexual Health Clinic, Shrew and Chaimongkol (1993) estimated that 58 per cent had at least one sexually transmitted disease. While condom usage was high with clients, 50 per cent had regular partners in New Zealand with whom condoms were not used. The potential for the transmission of sexual diseases was thus higher for this group than for others.

## CONCLUSION

Some tourist behaviour has been categorized as irresponsible in that it steps beyond the normal conventions and is often characterized by short-term self-indulgence. Thus, it appears that some aspects of tourist behaviour are characterized by little anticipation of possible consequences. This observation implies that the categorization of tourist behaviours and experiences undertaken by various commentators like Pearce (1982) and Yiannakis and Gibson (1992), based upon motivation alone, may provide an insufficient explanation of consequent behaviour, as it is not known if the holiday-maker has considered consequences, has acted rationally or is the best judge of perceived need.

It has been noted that holiday motivations can be categorized as needs of relaxation, social contact, mastery and intellectual needs. It has also been noted that such a categorization applies to all forms of leisure. This locates tourism as being a subset of leisure, and that travel is akin to many other forms of recreation in that it is a means of meeting these needs. It is debatable whether the fact of travel, and meeting needs in new environments, alone make tourism conceptually and specifically different from other forms of leisure experience to the extent that it requires a totally separate conceptualization from that of other leisure activities. In part, it depends upon the emphasis of the researcher. It cannot be denied that the process of being 'away' has a special appeal, that many do not feel they have had a holiday unless they have travelled away from home. For the researcher concerned with spatial patterns, then, arguably, tourism is a very specific set of activities. However, from the viewpoint of behaviour and motivations, the position is less 'clear cut'.

'Being away' does create potentials for behaviour that would not occur at home. It has been noted that holidays are significant temporal margins (Cohen, 1982; Rojek, 1993; Ryan and Kinder, 1996), and that margins assume significance because of their ability to explain unquestioned assumptions and conventions (Shields, 1991). Part of the marginality of holidays is that they represent opportunities for the 'abnormal' to occur. Holidays are thus very different from other forms of leisure. Does this mean that the motivations used to explain leisure are no longer pertinent? This is not necessarily the case. For example, Ryan and Kinder (1996) take the motivations used by Crompton (1979) to explain holidaying and apply them to tourists visiting prostitutes. For example, they argue that the evidence supports Crompton's (1979) comment that holidays provided family-bonding situations. Thus, it is a conventional argument advanced by sex workers that their services can mean that spouses are provided with coping mechanisms that overcome differences in libido between partners.

It has been noted that core motivations are few in number, but the expression of need is multiple. Both Crompton (1979) and Pearce (1982) have commented that it is not possible either to have a single theory of motivation or to credit motivation as a sole determinant of holiday behaviour. It is certainly true that, put bluntly, high income permits travel. But income *per se* is not an explanatory variable when discussing the type of holiday to be taken, or where the tourist will travel to. Nor do social or economic variables alone explain holiday behaviours. Psychological factors are thus obviously important, but it is also possible to over-emphasize their importance. As the proposed concept outlined in Figure 3.3 shows, the individual acts within a physical, as well as a social and psychological, environment. Hence it is important to discuss at least some components of these different environments. Thus, the next chapter will consider the role of the travel agent as a factor that creates its own sets of expectations and evaluations, while subsequent chapters will take some examples of the social and physical environments to further the analysis.

## Chapter 4

# Vital encounters: When tourists contact travel agents

*Andrew Cliff and Chris Ryan*

## INTRODUCTION

> When we arrived in Hawaii we found the hotel bookings had not been made in time so the hotel didn't have any rooms for us. The travel agent initially did not respond to the Hawaiian Hotel's requests so we had to make alternative arrangements ourselves and ring personally from Hawaii to get the problems sorted out. On our return we made very little headway with the agent when trying to resolve the matter. We were disgusted with the service and won't use them again.

This comment, taken from a survey of travel agency customers, illustrates how a tourist is likely to feel when the results of these vital encounters between the tourist and a travel agent have an adverse effect on the travel experience. In this example it is not possible to identify the exact nature of the problem nor its cause. However, it is clear that the actions of the travel agent, in the view of this tourist, caused unnecessary problems that affected the client's level of enjoyment of the holiday. This kind of experience is the exception rather than the norm, but it does highlight the importance of the role of the travel agent in organizing travel arrangements for tourists.

The travel agent works at the interface between the tourist and the travel and tourism operators. Agencies act as the retailer in the tourism distribution chain, marketing services to customers on behalf of wholesalers and other tourism suppliers.

This chapter will explore the relationship between the tourist and the travel agent and its contribution to the 'tourist experience'. This will involve analysing the nature of the relationship, the roles a travel agent can play for the tourist, the stages of the service encounter, tourists' expectations and their evaluations of travel agencies' service quality. The conceptual basis for this analysis is that the relationship between the tourist and the travel agent develops as a result of the service encounters they engage in. A service encounter has been defined as 'a period of time in which a consumer directly interacts with a service' (Shostack, 1985, p. 243). Other writers (Normann, 1984; Carlzon, 1987; Gronroos, 1990) have termed these encounters the 'moments of truth', because it is what happens during these encounters, when the consumer is interacting with the service provider, that forms the basis for how consumers will judge the business. The outcome of this evaluation will largely determine whether the holiday-maker will continue dealing with the same travel agent or switch to a competitor. In a wider context, as discussed in Chapter 3, the outcome also plays a role in developing expectations about future holidays. For a tourist, the service encounter encompasses all the time they spend interacting with the agency, not just the time spent with the travel agent. From this perspective, the receptionist answering a customer's telephone call, time spent waiting before an agent is free and receiving a welcome home note from the agent are all examples of 'moments of truth' in a service encounter. The evaluation of these encounters extends beyond the personal contact to include its physical or tangible elements and the outcomes of the service process.

## A RANGE OF RELATIONSHIPS

Just as there are a large number of different types of tourist, so there are many different types of relationships that can evolve between the tourist and a travel agent. These can range from a one-off telephone call to arrange tickets, to a long-term relationship in which the agent becomes a trusted friend and guide as the tourist expands the boundaries of his/her travel experiences. The relationship, while essentially a business one between buyer and seller, can become a personal relationship. If the tourist is satisfied by the service provided by the agent, the tourist is more likely to return to that agent the next time travel arrangements are being planned. The more frequent the need to use a travel agent, the more likely the tourist will develop a loyal relationship with a specific travel agent, even to the extent of following an agent from one agency to another.

Typically, tourists contact travel agents during the planning stage of their travel. The nature of the tourist/travel agent encounter will depend largely on the needs of the tourist. The arrangements may only require one contact, or a series of service encounters, depending on the tourist's planning prior to contact, past experiences and the complexity of the arrangements to be made. Some tourists may be very well prepared, having definite plans, and only requiring the agent to make the necessary bookings. Others may only have the desire to go on holiday and need assistance in selecting their destination, their travel provider, their accommodation and a range of activities, as well as making the bookings. The outcomes of these encounters can have effects throughout the many different stages of the travel experience.

A number of writers have commented on the roles a travel agent could play for the tourist. Bitner and Booms (1982) noted that one role of a travel agent is to counsel travellers. Using their greater knowledge of the travel market, the agent can offer a number of options to the client, and then assist them in making a decision. From the agency's perspective, during this encounter, the agent should be acting as a marketer, collecting information on the tourist's motivations and desires, developing a package to meet those needs and then selling the package. How well the agent performs this role depends on a number of factors including his or her ability to listen to the client, knowledge of the travel market, responsiveness to the client, ability to match needs with available products, the provision of information in an accurate and timely manner, and how the sale is closed. This process may be completed during one meeting, yet often it involves a number of encounters as both parties may require time to find information and/or consider available options. These encounters are generally face-to-face but all other communications between the client and the agent, including telephone calls and written correspondence, including e-mail, should also be seen as vital engagements. They are all vital because at any one of these the tourist may be given information which later causes a problem, or may decide that the agent is not meeting his needs, so requiring a change of agency. The reliability of the service provided by the travel agency, which includes performing the service right first time, honouring promises, the accuracy of information provided and the records kept, has been identified as the most important determinant of travel agency customers' evaluation of service quality (Cliff and Ryan, 1994).

A new feature of growing importance is the role of the internet. This is particularly important for travel agents because it increasingly allows direct contact between the principals in the tourism industry and the client. Indeed, for 'no frills' airlines direct booking via the internet is an important means of controlling costs, as such bookings omit the travel agent and the commissions traditionally associated with airline bookings. For a market that is increasingly confident about making seat-only bookings, such bookings are increasingly common as shown by varying surveys and the increasing popularity of internet websites like expedia.com. Given this situation, in many countries the number of retail travel outlets has been declining. The response being made by the industry has been one of embracing the new technologies as a means of providing better service to its clients. Equally, the varying trade associations have sought to ensure that their membership is fully acquainted with the net and its issues. For example, in June 2001 the Association of British Travel Agents (ABTA) ran a seminar that included discussion and advice on topics that included The Data Protection Act, Contracting/ selling on the internet, Setting up links – your responsibilities, Advertising law infringements, Delivering a premium service and Low-cost acquisition of customers. The range of topics also highlights the legal issues that surround the use of the internet, and provides in part a rationale as to why good travel agencies still retain a function in the days of the World Wide Web. Not only have many travel agencies installed their own web-based systems but also business associations have done the same. For example, ABTA operates a web page as a portal for members, and it is then possible to identify separate agencies and the services they offer. However, it would be fair to state that in June 2001 the quality of a number of these sites was variable, and the clichés of marketing still remain true. For example, Alford (2000) noted that a major failing of many tourism websites was the failure to respond, or very slow response by companies to reply to the queries of potential clients that were posted through the use of e-mail. As e-mail promises an immediacy not associated with conventional 'snail mail', the client has been found to have expectations of same-day replies, and a failure to meet that expectation is perceived as 'poor' service by a potential customer.

THE AGENT AS A BOOKING CLERK

The importance of the travel agent's reliability to the tourist highlights another role the agent must perform, that is as a booking clerk. One possible cause of the problems encountered by the tourist in Hawaii, mentioned at the beginning of this chapter, could have been an oversight on behalf of the agent to make the hotel booking, to make it in time or in the correct manner to ensure a reservation for the tourist.

Obviously errors or oversights in performing this booking role can have serious consequences for the traveller and result in adverse evaluations of the travel agent. Another role identified by Middleton (1988) is to receive and assist with complaints from customers. These complaints may relate to the travel agency or to a travel or accommodation provider booked through the agency. How well these complaints are handled also has a significant outcome on the customer's evaluation of the travel agency as well as the other provider. Bitner *et al.* (1990) argue that these 'critical incidents' present opportunities to retrieve client goodwill that may otherwise be lost due to the failure of technical delivery systems or for other reasons.

When the tourist requires more than a simple transport booking, the number of possible options can rapidly escalate into a series of complex travel decisions. Many tourists expect the agent to simplify this process by developing an acceptable itinerary within their constraints of time and money. This process of simplifying the travel arrangements can also extend to providing assistance with passport or visa applications, advice on inoculations, and arranging medical insurance and traveller's cheques. To be able to perform these services efficiently and effectively for the traveller, the travel agency must have an appropriate network of commercial links to other service providers and an information system capable of providing the correct information when it is required.

## THE DYNAMICS OF THE SERVICE ENCOUNTER

### The process

One way to explore the dynamics of service encounters between tourists and travel agents is to divide an encounter into its typical stages. Bitran and Lojo (1993) developed a framework for analysing service encounters consisting of six stages, arguing that while every service encounter will be unique for both client and service provider, such encounters tend to possess the common themes identified in Figure 4.1. However, the length and the nature of the interaction at each stage can vary considerably. This framework can be used to analyse a single service encounter or a series of encounters, as often happens between a tourist and an agent. Thus the following text adopts this framework to discuss the ways in which expectations, perceptions and evaluations are formed by the holiday-maker of the service provided by the travel agent.

*Figure 4.1* Typical stages of a service encounter

## Access to the agent

Before a tourist and a travel agent can conduct business, the tourist must have access to the agent. This is the first stage of the service encounter. If access is difficult then the tourist may decide not to proceed and may take his business elsewhere. The access stage encompasses any means the tourist uses to make initial contact with an agent. This includes making a personal visit to the agency, a telephone call, sending a fax, and using e-mail or letter of inquiry. If the agency is not open when the tourist wants to visit or call, if all the staff are too busy to greet him or answer the telephone, or a reply is not received in time, then the difficulties encountered in accessing a travel agent to meet travel needs become a problem. This may result in the tourist going to another agency that has easier access. The more accessible the travel agent, the more likely it is that the tourist will progress to subsequent stages of the service encounter. A number of factors influence this accessibility. These include the opening hours of the agency, whether it provides any after-hours service and the physical location of the agency. Being on the ground floor rather than the first floor, or providing customer car-parking spaces, could be factors that initially influence a tourist to make contact with a particular agency rather than another. The number of telephone lines, telecommunication systems and procedures used by an agency will impact on the amount of time a potential customer spends waiting before establishing contact with an agent. Again, the longer the delays, the more likely the service encounter will be terminated without any business being transacted. Once the tourist has gained access to the agency the next stage, the check-in, begins.

## The check-in stage

The check-in stage involves tourists identifying themselves to the agency staff, generally by giving their names, and commencing an interaction between the tourist and the agency that establishes the nature of the service they require. For example, the tourist might tell the receptionist that she would like to make a booking. During this period it is important for the agent to make prompt personal contact with the customer, make her feel welcome and advise her of what action will be initiated to meet her requirements. For first-time customers it is important that the agency's physical appearance and atmosphere reassure customers that they have made a good decision to use a particular agency. For established customers, greeting them by their names can help to enforce the impression that they are valued clients. During this stage, agency staff must be skilled in forming good interpersonal relations, be able to establish the purpose of the encounter and be knowledgeable as to how the agency can best meet the customer's needs. In terms of internet usage, the design of the web page and ease of search facilities become determinants of success. If it is known that there will be any delays between the time that the enquiry is dealt with by the initial contact person and whoever eventually handles the client's requirements, the customer should be advised of the extent of the likely delay. The check-in stage is normally longer and more critical to first-time customers than to those who have a long relationship with an agency. The next stage in the service encounter is the diagnosis stage.

**The diagnosis stage**

During this diagnosis stage, the travel agent meets or communicates with the tourist by phone or e-mail to establish her requirements. The diagnostic stage usually takes more time in the initial planning phase of a new travel experience, for, on most occasions, when the client contacts the agent, there is a need to identify why the customer has made contact. It is during this stage that the tourist conveys her travel needs and expectations to the agent. It is the responsibility of the agent to identify clearly those needs so that appropriate arrangements can be made. The better an agent gets to understand the tourist's travel needs the better able they are to meet those requirements and make suggestions. If a member of the agency staff is asked to perform a service for a customer for which he has not been adequately trained, then the staff member should refer the client to someone with the appropriate training. It is better to prevent mistakes, errors or omissions than have a customer complain and to have to rectify the situation later. In the case of a holiday, the actions required to resolve problems may involve several different parties spanning around the world, as was the case in our earlier example of the tourist in Hawaii.

Good communication skills are critical to this stage. If the agent is not a good listener, it is unlikely that they will fully understand the tourist's demands. The agent should clarify the requirements by reflective responses, then inform the client of what can be offered and how to proceed. Once the tourist's requirements have been identified, the process of service delivery can commence with the agent developing a travel package to meet the tourist's requirements.

**Service delivery**

This next step of service delivery may be completed during one meeting, but for many transactions this stage may be spread over a series of encounters. Often, after an initial encounter, where the agent has presented some possible alternatives, the tourist will require time to consider the options. Similarly, an agent may have to obtain further information before being able to meet the tourist's requirements. Although all six stages of the service encounter can influence tourist behaviour and the final evaluation of the service provided, this service delivery stage is the most crucial. This is when the agent is directly concerned with meeting customer requirements. If the agent's knowledge base is inadequate, if the agent's interpersonal skills or service attitude cause difficulties with the client, if the travel agency's information systems are slow, unreliable and inaccurate, or if the agency's network of suppliers is inadequate to meet the plans of the tourist, then the service delivered to the client would generally be considered less than satisfactory.

**Disengagement**

The check-out or disengagement stage closes the service encounter. During this stage the agent can check that both parties know what is to happen next. Previous misunderstandings can be identified and corrected while personal contact is still maintained. While first impressions are important, so, too, are last impressions. It is this stage that leaves the client with his final view of the service encounter. If the travel arrangements have involved a series of service encounters, the last encounter before the tourist departs on his travel is the one most concerned with this process of check-out. The most often neglected stage of the service encounter is the follow-up. For tourists, this stage takes place usually after they have returned from their travels. However, it can occur at other times, particularly if there are gaps between service encounters and if the agent is unsure whether the client still wants to proceed with arrangements. During this stage, reasons why clients have not completed their arrangements with the agent can be identified. These reasons might include the customer's perception that the agent has not followed up items the customer believes to be important, or has not adhered to promised schedules.

**Follow-up**

The follow-up stage is usually initiated by the travel agent. It can be a 'welcome home' letter that also includes a request for feedback of the service provided, or a more formal questionnaire. It could be a telephone call or e-mail to the holiday-maker seeking some feedback or even a follow-up appointment. This stage should identify any unsatisfied clients and their reasons for being dissatisfied. If anything can still be done to satisfy the client at this stage it should be initiated. If the cause of the dissatisfaction is something that is likely to reoccur, then action should be taken to prevent it happening again.

The six stages described here are progressive. It is the cumulative effect that will ultimately determine the tourist's overall evaluation of the service quality provided by a travel agency. All stages should create a positive impression. If mistakes occur or problems arise they should be dealt with promptly during the period in which they occur. It is usually harder and more expensive to rectify problems later than to prevent them, so the emphasis should be on delivering the travel service required by the tourist that meets his needs adequately the first time.

## THE TOURIST'S EXPECTATIONS

What do tourists expect of travel agencies? Tourists' expectations of travel agents are often unclear. This is partially due to the intangible nature of the service, the complexity of the arrangements and the inherent variability in human interaction. One factor which distinguishes the tourist–travel agency transaction from many others is that the tourist, as the customer, is not fully aware of the price he is paying for the travel agency's service. This is because the price paid for any arrangements includes an undisclosed amount for commission. Therefore, the ability of the tourist to evaluate whether he received value for money from his travel agent is less clear than might otherwise be the case. This may mean that factors other than price become more important to the tourist when evaluating the quality of service being provided by a travel agency. One complicating variable is that the client may develop a perception of service based on total cost being paid. For example, a client paying for a holiday that costs £4000 might expect more than one that costs, say, £2000. Yet the difference in commission, in these days of variable commission rates, might mean that the agency does not receive twice the figure associated with the lower-cost holiday. Equally, assuming a once traditional 10 per cent commission, the client might be expecting a £2000 or £4000 'quality service' from a provider that is actually receiving £200 to £400. In short, evaluation may be based on a comparison between the tourist's expectations of the travel agency's service and their perception of the service they received, based in part on what they expect for any given payment. Although the emphasis might vary during the various stages of the service encounter, and between different tourists, it is possible to discuss some generic expectations of travel agency service quality.

In a study conducted by Le Blanc (1992), six significant determinants of travel agency service quality were identified. These were: corporate image, competitiveness, courtesy, responsiveness, accessibility and competence. Although the names of the determinants are different they have similarities to the generic determinants of service quality proposed by Parasuraman *et al.* (1988), which were tangibles, reliability, responsiveness, assurance and empathy. The content of these dimensions, as described by Parasuraman *et al.*, are shown in Figure 4.2. Various researchers have questioned whether the data actually support the distinctions made by these factors, and in a study of travel agency customers Ryan and Cliff (1997) argue that the responsiveness, assurance and empathy dimensions consolidate into one factor that was labelled 'reassurance'. However defined, for each of these determinants it can be contended that tourists develop a set of expectations based on previous experience, personal needs, promotional material and word-of-mouth references.

To answer the question What do tourists expect of travel agencies? it can be noted, first, that tourists develop one set of expectations relating to the tangible aspects of a travel agency. They expect the physical facilities and staff of an agency to have a neat appearance, consistent with the overall impression the agency wants to portray in the marketplace. All the promotional material, such as travel brochures and documentation provided as part of the service, should be visually appealing and, again, consistent with the overall image of the travel agency. However, while these positive appearances can be achieved, Ryan and Cliff (1996, 1997) found that customers appear to be aware that appearance is not always a good guide to the service actually provided when gaps between expectation and perception were analysed.

## THE IMPORTANCE OF RELIABLE SERVICE

Ryan and Cliff (1997) argue that during the service encounter one of the more important sets of expectations formed by clients relates to the provision of information and the components that form the factor of reliability. Indeed, the reliability of the information and staff is even more crucial to the tourist than the reassurance gained

| | |
|---|---|
| **Tangibles** | physical facilities, equipment and appearance of personnel |
| **Reliability** | ability to perform the promised service dependably and accurately |
| **Responsiveness** | willingness to help customers and provide prompt service |
| **Assurance** | knowledge and courtesy of employees and their ability to inspire trust and confidence |
| **Empathy** | caring, individualized attention the firm provides its customers |

*Figure 4.2* Parasuraman *et al*'s five dimensions of service quality

from the nature of the interactions involved. This means that to meet or exceed those expectations travel agencies must develop reliable systems to provide accurate information, train staff on how to complete all necessary processes correctly and motivate staff to perform all aspects of their jobs correctly the first time, every time, in a courteous manner.

Hence, the basis of reliability lies in speedy, accurate responses to any questions or inquiries the client may have. This requires the travel agent to develop a knowledge-base covering destinations, transport links and many other facets of the travel industry. As it is impossible for any agent to know everything in such a complex and rapidly changing field, the agent must have the ability to locate any required information quickly and accurately. This requires the development of information-retrieval skills, increasingly from electronic networks. Moreover, as a true impression of a destination or hotel cannot be gained from a brochure or even from a video, holiday-makers value the knowledge gained by a travel agent who has actually 'been there'. It is contended that this still remains largely true, even though clients might be able to access images of the place through the internet. This knowledge gained from experience can greatly enhance the service encounter, especially if it provides useful tips or added attractions to the holiday of which the tourist would otherwise have been unaware. A determinant of reliability can be how recent was the agent's visit. For example, an agent may have enjoyed food served in a particular hotel during a stay five years ago. Hence, knowing that a client has a passion for good food the agent may recommend the hotel. Unfortunately, if the standard of food at the hotel has not been maintained during the intervening period, the recommendation will lead to dissatisfaction on the part of the client. In short, the information has ceased to be reliable. Again, however, both agent and client are able to check such information through services being provided by 'switched on' operators that not only maintain up-to-date websites, but also maintain newsletters that incorporate users' comments. Additionally, companies like Lonely Planet also have websites that incorporate travellers' experiences. These can be accessed by knowledgeable agencies that provide the service of time and knowing what websites are available to travellers.

## TIME MANAGEMENT

Ideally, holiday-makers would like their enquiries answered instantly, but appreciate that, in reality, this is not always possible. Tourists, like other customers, generally find waiting frustrating. The amount of frustration significantly increases if they consider the amount of time spent waiting is excessive. Agency clients can experience two types of waiting. The first is waiting to be served. If this is too long, then the agency needs to improve its reception, appointment scheduling or staffing procedures. The second type of waiting occurs during the process. This may be only a matter of minutes but could be days, depending on the reason for the delay. A common reason is waiting for additional information. Often in these situations the travel agent will make a promise to get back to the client in an hour or by the end of next week, for example. Based on these promises tourists develop expectation deadlines. If this deadline is exceeded and the agent has not gotten back to the client, the amount of frustration and ultimately dissatisfaction with the service provided by the travel agent increases dramatically. In their survey of travel agency customers Ryan and Cliff (1997) identified that the biggest gap between the client's expectations and the agent's performance was on honouring these promises to do something by a certain time. The nature of these expectations require the travel agent to have excellent time-management skills, to be able to find information quickly and efficiently and, above all, make honest predictions about when they can have a response for the client. If circumstances change after the time of making the deadline promise which will prevent that promise being honoured, then the agent should advise the client promptly of a revised deadline and the reasons for the delay. This will alter expectations and mitigate the effect of any delay.

The reliability of information systems and the agent's ability to use them is crucial. An agent who proves to be unreliable or who provides unreliable information is less likely to have customers return and more likely to have adverse word-of-mouth comments passed around the network of potential clients. This is because the agent has failed to meet this most basic and yet most important of the clients' needs – a reliable service.

## PROBLEM HANDLING

Should a problem occur, whether it is the fault of the agency or one of the travel suppliers, clients expect the travel agent to resolve the problem satisfactorily. The ability of the agent to do this is dependent on the agent's willingness to address the problem, their knowledge of the situation and systems which have led to the problem occurring, and the amount of discretionary responsibility they have to be able to initiate actions which would satisfy the client and recover his goodwill. Once again, keeping the client informed is vital. The client expects to be informed about what has happened, what can be done and whether his needs or requests can be accommodated, and, if not, why. The lack of a suitable response or an uncertainty as to what actions are being taken only serve to increase the client's dissatisfaction with the agency he has dealt with. Often tourists only become aware of any problems when they are on their travels, and so the inconvenience, anxiety and frustration are heightened by the distance from the travel agent who may then be expected to solve the problem. From the agent's perspective, the distance and time factors also complicate the recovery process and generally increase the associated costs. This reinforces the point that for both parties – tourist and travel agent – the service system should focus on providing what the client wants, on time and accurately, every time. Prevention is indeed better than cure when seeking to generate tourist satisfaction with an agent's services.

With particular regard to the interpersonal interaction of the service encounter between a tourist and a travel agent, tourists develop another set of expectations with which to evaluate the service provided by the travel agent. Tourists not only expect travel agents to be able to help them with the travel arrangements, they also expect them to be willing to help. This willingness to help is conveyed to the tourist by how promptly they receive attention, the language used during an encounter and the agent's general behaviour. As well as being willing to help, tourists expect agents to be responsive to their needs. This requires agents to be skilful, empathetic communicators who can identify those needs and respond in an appropriate way. The client should never gain the impression that what they are asking is too difficult, that the agent would rather be doing something else, or that the agent is too busy to be concerned with clients' special needs. Tourists expect to be treated in a courteous respectful manner, appropriate to the type of relationship that has developed between the agent and themselves. They expect individualized treatment and can become resentful if they feel that the agent is not responsive to their particular needs and is more interested in fitting them into a ready-made package. Holiday-makers also expect that their dealings with the agent will be treated with confidentiality and that they can trust the agency. Any factor that endangers this feeling of trust also threatens the completion of the transaction, and can result in loss of monies to perhaps both parties. Equally, it might be argued that to receive such a quality of service imposes a requirement upon the customer to exercise both honesty and reasonableness. Unfortunately, many retail agents can provide stories where this has not always been present, as is occasionally evidenced by the pages of the *Travel Trade Gazette* in the United Kingdom and, probably, the trade press of other countries.

## EVALUATING THE EXPERIENCE

Expectations have been shown to be important in determining satisfaction, as has been discussed in the literature relating to, amongst other concepts, the ServQual model postulated by Parasuraman *et al.* (For example, see the special issue of the *Journal of Retailing*, spring 1993.) From our perspective there are two components involved: the satisfaction with the service provided by the agent *per se*, and secondly how that service, in turn, formulates expectations about the holiday. In the discussion of the various stages of the interaction between client and agent, it was argued that an evaluation of the process occurs along the dimensions of the ServQual model (Parasuraman *et al.*, 1985, 1988). It is thus possible, using the ServQual scale, to measure satisfaction with the performance of the travel agent, and the contentions made were derived in part from the data shown in Table 4.1. From this it can be seen that clients are generally satisfied with the tangible components of the service and the personal skills of employees, but are less satisfied about reliability. For example, no significant difference existed between perceptions and expectations relating to the materials and appearance of travel agencies. On the other hand, as measured by the t-test, which measures the significance of the gap formed by the difference in perceptions and expectations, significant differences existed on the other dimensions of reliability and reassurance (Cliff and Ryan, 1994).

It is also possible to use the same dimensions to establish whether holiday-makers booking holidays through travel agencies establish distinctions between different agencies on these criteria, or whether travel agencies are seen as a homogeneous group of retail outlets. Cliff and Ryan (1994) analysed these questions by the use of analysis of variance (ANOVA) for six different agencies and found differences for eighteen items on the expectations and evaluation scales of the ServQual instrument. Differences between expectations and the clients' evaluations lay in promptness of service, understanding needs and the promptness and individual attention paid to clients. In other words, the differences lay in the dimensions of empathy and responsiveness. Perceptions of performance, however, tended to lay in more diverse areas, and in single items across dimensions (namely 'adhering to promises of delivery', 'not being too busy', 'having up-to-date equipment' and 'having the best interest of the client in mind').

*Table 4.1* ServQual scores for New Zealand travel agents

|  | Expectation | Perception | Gap | t-test |
|---|---|---|---|---|
| When a travel agency promise to do something by a certain time, it will do it. | 6.83 | 5.95 | 0.88 | 8.74*** |
| When customers have a problem, the travel agency will show a sincere interest in solving it. | 6.79 | 6.15 | 0.64 | 7.77*** |
| The travel agency will provide its services at the time it promises to do so. | 6.76 | 6.07 | 0.68 | 7.06*** |
| Employees of the travel agency will always be willing to help customers. | 6.65 | 6.21 | 0.43 | 6.06*** |
| Customers of the travel agency will feel safe in their transactions. | 6.63 | 6.16 | 0.47 | 4.79*** |
| The travel agency will have the customer's best interests at heart. | 6.59 | 5.98 | 0.61 | 7.58*** |
| Employees of the travel agency will be consistently courteous with customers. | 6.50 | 6.37 | 0.13 | 1.84 |
| The travel agency will perform the service right first time. | 6.50 | 5.87 | 0.63 | 5.87*** |
| Employees of the travel agency will have the knowledge to answer customer questions. | 6.48 | 6.04 | 0.43 | 4.84*** |
| Employees of the travel agency will give prompt service to customers. | 6.48 | 5.97 | 0.51 | 5.49*** |
| The travel agency will insist on error free records. | 6.48 | 5.71 | 0.77 | 8.07*** |
| The behaviour of employees of the travel agency will instil confidence in customers. | 6.46 | 6.02 | 0.44 | 5.19*** |
| The travel agency will give customers individual attention. | 6.43 | 6.28 | 0.14 | 2.03* |
| The employees of the travel agency will understand the specific needs of their customers. | 6.40 | 6.01 | 0.39 | 4.76*** |
| Employees of the travel agency will tell customers exactly when services will be performed. | 6.37 | 5.98 | 0.40 | 4.32*** |
| The travel agency will have employees who give customers personal attention. | 6.30 | 6.25 | 0.05 | 0.66 |
| The travel agency will have up-to-date equipment and technology. | 6.18 | 5.94 | 0.24 | 2.51* |
| Employees of the travel agency will never be too busy to respond to customer requests. | 6.12 | 5.58 | 0.54 | 5.25*** |
| Employees of the travel agency will be well dressed and of neat appearance. | 5.75 | 6.01 | −0.27 | −3.11** |
| The travel agency will have operating hours convenient to all their customers. | 5.71 | 5.51 | 0.19 | 1.74 |
| Materials associated with the travel agency's service (such as pamphlets or quotations) will be visually appealing. | 5.58 | 5.55 | 0.03 | 0.29 |
| The physical facilities at the travel agency will be visually appealing. | 5.12 | 5.14 | −0.01 | −0.13 |

*Key:* * p < 0.05, ** p < 0.01, *** p < 0.001

Hence it can be argued that the dimensions of the ServQual scale can show differential performance between companies – differences that have implications for marketing practice. However, the results need to be interpreted with caution because the number of studies relating to travel agencies available in the public sector are limited (the industry itself monitors customer satisfaction, but generally does not publish results for reasons of commercial sensitivity). Additionally, as already noted, identifying the gap between expectation and perception with client satisfaction requires further examination in situations like those of travel agents, for final holiday satisfaction may create a hindsight which changes perception of what might otherwise have been little more than simply 'competent' performance by a travel agent, however this may have been defined (see Myers, 1990, p. 18). Indeed, examination of the literature raises many issues pertinent to this analysis, such as how do clients generate expectations? For example, are expectations formulated against 'optimal' performance levels, or does the customer undertake a process of 'satisficing' based on what is perceived to be a tolerable level of experience?

However, it can be argued that the client's experience with the travel agent is to a large degree shaped by the actual holiday experience. Thus, an 'adequate' performance by the travel agency is sufficient if the actual holiday experience meets the needs of the holiday-maker. From this perspective the 'travel agency experience' becomes both an antecedent of final satisfaction as discussed in Chapter 3 and an outcome of the holiday experience. Appropriate performance by a travel agent is not in itself a sufficient condition of holiday satisfaction, but can be a determinant of a failure to achieve a satisfactory holiday. Equally, a successful holiday can create a sense of satisfaction with the performance of the travel agent, even if by other criteria that performance might have been judged as being little more than 'competent'. Travel agencies are in the position of being both a determinant of demand and a beneficiary of derived demand and successful performance by other holiday service providers. This means that agencies derive their business from the promotional activities of tour operators, airlines and other components of the tourism industry, but can subsequently shape the demand of the client once the client establishes contact with the agent. In terms of the literature relating to 'selling', poor agencies are 'order takers', good agencies are 'demand-makers'. From a research perspective, however, assessment of a travel agency's performance without reference to the satisfaction generated by the actual travel experience might be said to represent only a partial study.

## THEORETICAL CONSIDERATIONS

Such considerations are quite consistent with advances being made in the theoretical constructs that have been developed in the period since 1994 with reference to ServQual. The model developed by Parasuraman *et al.* (1985, 1988) was one that attracted significant attention in the literature relating to services marketing generally, and the hospitality and tourism literature specifically. In the light of comments and critiques, Parasuraman *et al.* reviewed their original model and in 1994 introduced a measurement of a 'zone of tolerance'. In some senses this was a recognition of an earlier literature. In 1963 the American sociologist Rodman had described, first, a satisfaction gain – a gap between what one can tolerate and what one expects; secondly, a concept of reconciliation as the gap between what were achievable and non-achievable goals;

and, thirdly, a 'value stretch' – the sum of these two gaps denoting a gap between minimum needs and the absolute quality of goals. In one of the first pieces that appeared in the tourism literature that made reference to ServQual, Saleh and Ryan (1992, p. 115) had noted that 'If customer tolerance of some deviation from expectation exists, and thus a level of service less than ideal does not generate dissatisfaction, this implies that the boundary between that which is acceptable and that which is not is "fuzzy".' They suggested that 'the just noticeable difference was not only a factor of past consumer experience, but also a structural component within the service delivery process' (*ibid.*, p. 115) while drawing attention to a habituation effect in the formation of expectations and perceptions of service quality. Thus one issue was: what was the gap actually measuring? Indeed, what was ServQual measuring – was it client satisfaction or service quality? What were the linkages between these two variables?

Bearing in mind the above discussion on travel agencies it is of interest to note that more recent literature has sought to develop a feedback mechanism within the modelling whereby satisfaction is not simply an outcome, but also an input. Extending the argument from solely a consideration of travel agency situations and applying it to the issue of tourist satisfaction more generally, the holistic and reiterative processes of client satisfaction are increasingly being modelled in other than linear ways. Following Bolton and Drew (1991) and Boulding *et al.* (1993) it can be argued that customer satisfaction and service attributes are determinants of both service quality and customer behaviour; that is, the formulation can be rewritten as:

Purchase + b Perceived Quality = a + c Expected Quality + d Gap + e Satisfaction Intention

Statistically such representation presents problems of interdependence of variables; the prime condition of regression analysis that the variables are independent is obviously broken (e.g. see Sincich, 1992). However, an alternative approach is to view the variables as being moderating, interventionist or acting as antecedents. For example, in 1993 Oliver suggested that while service quality is formed by a comparison between ideals and perceptions of performance on quality dimensions, satisfaction is a function of the disconfirmation of the predictive expectations regarding both quality dimensions and non-quality dimensions. Thus perceived service quality is, partially, an antecedent to satisfaction. This is akin to the view of Taylor and Baker (1994) that disconfirmation moderates the quality-purchase intention relationship, implying a reiterative process as shown in the above formula.

It is possible to define and model the quality of tourist experience and resultant satisfactions in the terminology of amended confirmation/disconfirmation paradigms. Following Taylor (1997) the purchase intention towards a given holiday can be derived whereby the relationship between quality and intention, and between satisfaction and intention are both of a higher order and are fully interactive. Such a quadratic relationship would take the form:

$$Y = a + b_1X + b_2Z + b_3X^2 + b_4Z^2 + b_5XZ + b_6XZ^2 + b_7X^2Z + b_8X^2Z^2 + e$$

where  $Y$ = purchase intention
  $X$ = quality perception
  $Z$ = satisfaction judgement
  $a$ = intercept and $b_1 \ldots b_8$ coefficients to be established empirically

and the confirmation/disconfirmation paradigm is included by the satisfaction judgement being assessed by questions such as 'I would generally characterize this holiday as being ...... than expected' with the value being selected from a Likert-type scale.

However, a debate exists as to whether such global, as against transaction-specific, forms of quality perceptions and satisfaction judgements are valid. It may be that $X = \Sigma x_1, x_2, x_3 \ldots x_n$ and likewise with $Z$. Iacobucci (1995) argue that consumers do not make this type of distinction when assessing a consumer experience, while Ryan and Glendon (1998) report that tourists had little difficulty in undertaking a global assessment of their holiday experience when assessing levels of satisfaction. However, in the same article Ryan and Glendon (pp. 170–1) note that

> The relationship between motivation, performance and resultant satisfaction invites consideration of a number of variables. From a psycho-sociological perspective, following concepts of involvement ... the perceived importance of an activity in terms of self-development, self-enhancement, ego, role fulfillment, and responding to perceived requirements of significant others, can be argued to be important variables determining motivation, behaviour and derived satisfaction.

Taken as a whole, this represents a view of the nature of the holiday experience different to that of the linear relationship of the attention, information-seeking, decision and evaluation marketing models. It emphasizes the nature of involvement and issues of status and ego enhancement in holiday-taking as both determinants and outcomes. What the simple confirmation/disconfirmation model does not do, unless it is explicitly extended, as done by Suh *et al.* (1997), is to specifically elicit these types of consideration.

## CONCLUSION

To return to the specific issues of the tourist–travel agent interaction, the willingness to respond to client needs, courteous individualized treatment and the development of trust all act to reassure the client that the travel agent they are entrusting their business to will not let them down. Although the reliability of the travel agent is considered the most important factor contributing to the ultimate satisfaction of the client, the reliability of the travel agent's service cannot be fully determined until after the tourist has completed the travel experience organized by the agent. However, the client can and does make continual evaluation of the reassurance aspects of the service throughout the service encounters with the agent. If, at anytime, an agent does not meet the client's reassurance expectations, the client is less likely to complete the arrangements with that agent.

Therefore, the different dimensions of the service quality provided by travel agents have different impacts. If the agency does not meet or exceed the customer's tangible expectations, the customer is not likely to commence the service encounter. If the agent falls short of the reassurance expectations, then the customer is not likely to complete the travel arrangements with the agent, and if after the customer has travelled they feel the service was not reliable, they are less likely to use the same agent again.

The encounters between a tourist and a travel agent should be considered vital encounters by both parties, especially when these encounters lay the foundation for, and shape, the future travel experience. They are vital because the tourist relies on the agent for information and the ability to make the necessary arrangements correctly. In turn, the agent relies on the tourist to generate sales, now and in the future, while tour operators rely on agents to generate future business. A process of mutual interest exists, characterized by encounters and 'moments of truth'. During the encounter expectations are being created, not only relating to the travel agency's service, but also relating to the travel experience itself, and the subsequent level of satisfaction felt by the tourist. In many cases it can be argued that the travel agency acts as a 'sign poster' and 'gate keeper', identifying and opening the portals to the far-off land. The information provided becomes part of the information that determines a holiday-maker's expectations. The travel agent possesses the means to create the antecedents of success or failure of the holiday. A poor selection of a hotel, or misinformation as to prices, vaccinations needed or the weather, can cause subsequent problems. On the other hand, insightful 'tips', e.g. information on how to gain 'value for money', might engender, for the tourist, a feeling of already being 'in the know', an 'insider', and hence may enhance the quality of the holiday experience. Travel agents thus fulfil an important role in that although a tourist's final assessment of their holiday will owe much to many factors beyond the travel agency's control, the travel agency possesses an influence to significantly mar a holiday through poor performance.

*Chapter 5*

# Making or breaking the tourist experience: the role of human resource management

*Tom Baum*

## INTRODUCTION

The experience of the guest or consumer, within the tourism industry, is both highly intense and intimate in the interaction that takes place with those providing the services. This intensity and intimacy are only matched in a few other personal service sectors and then rarely do they occur over the same timespan and in such unfamiliar environments as within tourism. Furthermore, for most tourists, their interactive experience is with the tourism industry's front-line staff, generally those who have the lowest status and are the least trained and poorest-paid employees of the company. The management of the guest–employee encounter remains one of the most difficult and contentious areas within the development and enhancement of tourism operational and service standards worldwide. It is an encounter that is laden with meaning that varies according to historical, geographical and economic context. This chapter will explore aspects of the historical origins of the relationship between guest and server and consider some of the implications of attempting to manage the encounter in differing contexts.

## THE CONCEPT OF SOCIAL DISTANCE: A HISTORICAL PERSPECTIVE

The nature of guest–employee interaction in the contemporary international tourism industry is linked closely to the historical origins of tourism and its development from elitist to mass-participation during approximately the past 300 years. In many developing countries, the nature of this interaction also has a strong relationship to colonial history and perceptions of the neocolonialism that modern tourism can be seen to represent. In order to understand the nature of guest–employee interaction today it is necessary to undertake a brief historical scan.

Tourism evolved as a highly elitist activity, the prerogative of a small number of, generally, aristocrats for whom travel was closely linked to education and cultural refinement. The 'Grand Tour', which flourished between the sixteenth and nineteenth centuries, albeit in evolving form, is described by Towner (1985, p. 301) as 'a tour of certain cities in western Europe undertaken primarily, but not exclusively, for education and pleasure'. The original conception of the Grand Tour, and related journeying to fashionable resorts and spas of the eighteenth century, was very much an extension to the normal pattern of aristocratic living, and this is reflected in the employment structure that existed in support of travel at this time. Essentially, the rich and well-bred travelled with all or part of their normal retinue of servants. In the case of domestic travel to Bath, Deauville or Weymouth, this could well have comprised much of the household. Accompaniment on the Grand Tour was, generally, on a rather more modest scale but would probably include a tutor plus one or more personal servants. During the early days of the tour, accommodation was found in the great houses of families of the same class and background and only on rare occasions would commercial establishments be frequented during travel. Thus the employment impact of travel at this time was very limited and it is not possible to identify tourism-related jobs with any certainty. Furthermore, whatever contact there was between guest and those serving was on the same basis as the established master–servant relationship of the time.

While the Grand Tour had its heyday in the eighteenth century, one significant feature of its evolution is the timespan committed to the experience, which fell from an average of 40 months in the mid-sixteenth century to just four months in the 1830s, at the dawn of railway travel (Towner, 1985, p. 316). This propensity to shorten the travel experience over time is a characteristic of the development of tourism generally and continues to be an important feature in market trends today. It reflects changes in lifestyle, social, economic and working conditions and the impact of improved transport and other technologies but, probably most significantly, the popularization of the travel experience from selective to relative mass-participation (Urry, 1990). As we shall see, this process, in turn, has had significant implications for the characteristics of the guest–tourism employee encounter. Buzzard, rightly, argues that industrialization in Europe provided the main focus for this change from elite to mass-participation status, in that modern tourism arose 'as a broadly accessible form of leisure travel no longer based in the overt class and gender prerogatives of the Grand Tour' (1993, p. 18). This link between industrialization and the development of mass tourism accounts for the importance of Britain in the development of tourism as an industry. According to Feifer (1985), by 1820 about 150,000 British travellers a year were visiting Europe and this was prior to the impact of rail transportation. This level of participation represents considerable growth from the mid-eighteenth century, the period that has been described by Poon (1993) as the 'golden age' of the Grand Tour. Essentially, the growing middle classes were adopting the travel model developed by the aristocracy and popularizing it on a much larger scale, part of a process of what Steinecke (1993) calls 'imitation-segregation' and which has been referred to elsewhere as 'replication' (Baum, 1995). This process sees tourism destinations and trends developing in response to demand from an elite few travellers but expanding through replication to attract much larger numbers of socially 'inferior' status. In turn, the original group abandon the destination and move elsewhere, generally further afield. This process of change also attracted the first attempts to package tourism in a commercial manner, through the efforts of Thomas Cook and others.

Changes in the pattern and structure of the tourism industry and, in particular, its commercial packaging had inevitable consequences for the nature of work in the industry and, as a result, for the guest–employee encounter. As already noted, supporting the travel of the aristocratic rich, whether while in transit or at a temporary destination was, in reality, an extension of many aspects of the home routine for the travellers and their retinue, little different from the movement between, for example, London, Bath and the country estate to reflect the social seasons of Georgian England. Thus, those employed were the normal serving staff of the travellers and/or their hosts and the nature of work as well as the relationship between the travellers and those that served them derived from existing conventions of the great aristocratic homes, underscored by mutually held Malthusian assumptions about respective status and roles.

The advent of travel by the middle classes or the bourgeoisie initiated significant changes in these conventions because, first, these new travellers were not able to avail of the hospitality of their social peers in the resorts and cities that they visited and thus were required to utilize commercial accommodation premises as well as public transportation. Secondly, they did not have the retinue of serving staff to allow the transfer of whole households to new locations and, as a result, the employment of local assistance was required in order to support the tourism industry. Finally, the new travellers did not have the leisure time traditionally available to the aristocratic rich. As commercially driven, business or professional families, leisure provided a limited change, of maybe two to three weeks, from the normal working routine and thus the impracticality of moving the full household was further underscored.

The circumstances of employment in support of the fledgling commercial tourism industry may have changed as a result of widening participation but consumer expectations were rather slower to evolve. The relationship between guest and employee continued to reflect its origins in master/mistress–servant roles within the growing tourism industry of the nineteenth century and, indeed, beyond. Tourism was by no means a democratic activity but one largely confined to a relatively small (if growing) minority of the population in most European countries and North America. Further, the nature of work and the relationships that existed within tourism reflected this elitism through what can be described as high 'social distance' between the two parties involved, the guest and those providing the services. Changes in the underlying premises behind the guest–employee relationship, arguably only partial in many countries, have only evolved in response to the growing level of popular participation in tourism.

Over the last 50 years, tourism in the developed world has become a mass-participation industry, with an increasing trend towards the creation of a workforce which mirrors its consumer market in terms of its demographic, social and economic profile. This is particularly true of North America and increasingly so in Europe. The growth of the industry and, particularly, of seasonal, part-time and temporary working opportunities in most sectors of tourism provides many young people and those returning to the workforce after a period of absence with opportunities for employment. At the same time, these employees are, frequently, relatively seasoned tourists in their own right at both domestic and international levels. Thus, in contrast to earlier years of tourism development, there exist tourism employees who have experienced tourism from 'the other side of the fence' and who have a first-hand understanding of the needs of their customers; as a consequence, the 'social distance' between the guest and employee is likely to be much narrower. Experience of work in hospitality and tourism at some point in people's employment profile, generally at an early stage, is increasingly common and this further contributes to the decline in social distance. Schlosser (2001, p. 4) notes that 'an estimated one out of every eight workers in the United States has at some time been employed by McDonalds'. Therefore, many of us, as consumers, have also experienced life on the other side of the counter. This, inevitably, colours our attitude to the service encounter.

Indeed, the evolution of tourism to an industry of mass-participation and the consequences that this has had for the nature of work in the sector would not have been feasible had the basis of the guest–employee relationship remained the same as it was during the early periods of tourism development. Much of the tourism industry in the developed world now operates on the basis of relative social and economic equality between visitors and those working in the industry to meet their needs. This reduced level of 'social distance' is widely evident in large resorts such as Benidorm, Blackpool, Las Vegas and Orlando, but is also present within farmhouses providing agri-tourism opportunities, and within most international airlines.

However, 'social distance' remains widely in evidence within the tourism industries of the developing world. The basis is frequently economic in origin in that levels of remuneration are such that similar opportunities for participation in tourism to those experienced by guests are not available to those working in the industry in these countries. In some parts of the world this 'social distance' is further compounded by the complex issue of former colonial relationships between the tourist-originating countries and the destinations and perceptions that modern, mass tourism contribute to neo-colonial attitudes and behaviour.

The nature of hospitality and tourism work is also a factor in relation to this issue of social distance in developing countries. There is a widely held assumption in western countries that work in the sector, particularly the hospitality industry, is dominated by a low-skills profile (Wood, 1997). This is, in part, what makes such work so readily accessible to a high proportion of the population, as already suggested by Schlosser. Hospitality work is widely characterized both in the popular press and in research-based academic sources as dominated by a low-skills profile (Wood, 1997) or, as Shaw and Williams (1994, p. 142) rather brutally and, probably, unfairly put it, 'uneducated, unmotivated, untrained, unskilled and unproductive'. However, Burns (1997) questions the basis for categorizing hospitality employment into 'skilled' and 'unskilled' categories, arguing the postmodernist case that this separation is something of a social construct that is rooted in, first, manpower planning paradigms for the manufacturing sector and, secondly, in the traditional power of trade unions to control entry into the workplace through lengthy apprenticeships. Burns bases this argument on a useful consideration of the definition of skills in hospitality, noting that

> the different sectors that comprise tourism-as-industry take different approaches to their human resources, and that some of these differences ... are due to whether or not the employees have a history of being 'organised' (either in terms of trade unions or staff associations with formalised communication procedures). (Burns, 1997, p. 240)

This strong internal labour market analysis leads Burns to argue that skills within 'organized' sectors such as airlines and hotel companies with clearly defined staff relationship structures, such as Sheraton, are recognized and valued. By contrast, catering and fast food 'operate within a business culture where labour is seen in terms of costs which must be kept at the lowest possible level' (Burns, 1997, p. 240) and where skills, therefore, are not valued or developed. Burns's definition of hospitality skills seeks to go beyond the purely technical capabilities that those using 'unskilled' or 'low skills' descriptors assume. He draws upon Ritzer's (1993) drama analogy for the service workplace to argue that

> Working in such an environment requires more than an ability to operate a cash register; emotional demands are made of employees to constantly be in a positive, joyful and even playful mood. An ability to cope with such demands must be recognised as a 'skill' *par excellence*. (Burns, 1997, p. 240)

Burns's emphasis on 'emotional demands' as an additional dimension of hospitality skills has been developed in the work of Seymour (2000). Seymour considers the contribution of what she calls 'emotional labour' to work in fast food and traditional areas of service work and concludes that both areas demand considerable emotional elements in addition to overt technical skills.

Burns rightly argues that the low-skills perspective of hospitality is context-specific and is drawn from a western-centric view of hospitality work. He cites the inappropriateness of these assumptions when applied to environments such as the Soloman Islands, Sri Lanka and the Cook Islands. Likewise, Baum (1996) questions the validity of claims that hospitality is a work area of low skills. His argument is based on the cultural assumptions that lie behind employment in westernized, international hospitality work whereby technical skills are defined in terms of a relatively seamless progression from domestic and consumer life into the hospitality workplace. In the developing world, such assumptions cannot be made as employees join hospitality businesses without western acculturation; without knowledge of the implements and ingredients of western cookery, for example. Learning at a technical level, therefore, is considerably more demanding than it might be in western communities. Social and interpersonal skills also demand considerably more by way of prior learning, whether this pertains to language skills (English is a widespread prerequisite for hospitality work in countries such as Thailand) or wider cultural communications. On the basis of this argument, Baum contends that work that may be unskilled in Europe and the USA requires significant investment in terms of education and training elsewhere and cannot, therefore, be universally described as low-skilled. This issue is one that is beginning to assume significance in western Europe as a combination of service sector labour shortages and growing immigration from the countries of eastern Europe and elsewhere means that skills assumptions in hospitality can no longer be taken for granted. This issue of the skills and skills status of hospitality and tourism work is one that has considerable significance in our consideration of social distance and the service encounter.

The master–servant relationship, at the root of wide 'social distance' in tourism, has much less potency today than in the past in most parts of the developed world. Vestiges do remain in some sectors of the industry, particularly in the environmental trappings of some businesses such as cruise liners, hotels and restaurants, where the service ritual may give the appearance of encouraging notions of servility. However, democratization is now much more widespread than in the past. The Ritz Carlton motto that 'We are Ladies and Gentlemen serving Ladies and Gentlemen' is a good illustration of this change in practice. Likewise, the Austrian airline Lauda Air contributed to this when they redesigned their cabin staff uniforms to match the normal attire of their business customers, which includes casual wear such as jeans, to 'create an environment that is casual but polite and leads to a more personal contact with customers' (Churchill, 1994).

In many respects, these examples should bring us to the opposite end of a spectrum which started at a point at which traveller and employee were totally detached in social, economic and cultural terms. What is more, both parties, during tourism's early development, fully accepted this 'social distance', tacitly buying into the Malthusian notion that divisions in society were part of the natural order of things and each person had their place and role. The democratization of tourism in many countries, supported by legislation to regulate the worst excesses within the working environment, has created a climate where, in theory at least, employee and guest are equal. Critical to this process has been the exposure of many tourism employees in the developed world to travel and international guest status in their own right, something unthinkable even 50 years ago. At the same time, the distance between guest and employee in developing countries frequently remains much greater, primarily as a consequence of economic rather than social status disparity. This gap can only realistically close through rising economic prosperity and the resultant opportunities for outbound travel and tourism which this provides, as the experience of countries such as Singapore and Taiwan has demonstrated in recent years.

## 'MOMENTS OF TRUTH' AND THE GUEST–EMPLOYEE RELATIONSHIP

The importance of front-line staff to the delivery of quality service and, ultimately, customer satisfaction is widely accepted (e.g. Mahesh, 1988). Perhaps the most effective conceptualization of ideas relating to the role of front-line staff can be attributed to Jan Carlzon, past president of Scandinavian Airline Systems (SAS). Carlzon introduced the concept of the 'moment of truth' into the service vocabulary (Carlzon, 1987). Carlzon described a 'moment of truth' as every point of contact between the customer and front-line staff of the company, thus applying it to every contact, however seemingly trivial, that a customer has with a staff member or agent of the company in question. In SAS terms, Carlzon estimated that perhaps 50,000 'moments of truth' occurred each operating day. Although in themselves relatively small incidents, 'moments of truth' are make-or-break occasions when a company has the opportunity to disappoint the customer by failing to meet expectations, get it right by matching those expectations, or excel by exceeding expectations. From an organizational perspective, while it may be gratifying to exceed expectations, the key objective in the management of the front-line zone must be consistency in meeting customer expectations and minimization of the occasions when customers are disappointed.

As argued elsewhere (Baum, 1995; Ryan, 1996), the tourism industry presents particular challenges in the management of 'moments of truth' because of the fragmentation of the experience for many customers. Take, for example, the experience of a customer purchasing the typical package holiday in order to illustrate this point. From the purchaser's perspective, the client is buying from one company and yet the reality is that the 'moments of truth' which contribute to the experience may well occur through contact with a wide range of intermediaries over which the principal agent company, usually the tour operator, has varying levels of control. These intermediaries may include:

- the retail travel agent;
- insurance companies;
- ground transport to and from the airport;
- at least two sets of airport handling agents (outbound and return);
- airport services (shops, food and beverage outlets; bureaux de change) (outbound and return);
- the airline on all legs of the journey;
- immigration and customs services;
- local ground transportation;
- the hotel or apartment;
- tour services at the destination;
- companies and individuals selling a diversity of goods and services at the destination (retail, food and beverage, entertainment, cultural and heritage, financial etc.);
- emergency services at the destination (medical, police, legal); and
- service providers on return (photography processing, medical etc.).

Many of these companies, organizations and individuals are, of course, beyond the control of the tour operator and most customers would not directly attribute problems with them to the company through which they made their original vacation booking. However, good or bad experiences or 'moments of truth' with, for example, the local police, beach vendors, timeshare salespersons and taxi companies will colour the visitor's perceptions of the total tourist experience in a way that does not really apply to the purchase of other goods and services. Tour operators as principal agents, of course, are legally responsible under consumer protection legislation in many European and other countries for the satisfactory delivery of many of the components within the package tour experience, but such liability cannot include the full range of intermediaries listed above. One response from the tourism industry is to reduce the risk of inconsistent or unmanaged 'moments of truth' faced by guests within the holiday experience by maintaining close regulation and control over as many of the intermediaries as is possible. This may be achieved through vertical integration of a number of the key service providers within the tourism chain.

Such integration may result in tour operators acquiring their own retail travel agents and airlines as well as hotels and ground tour operators at the destination. There are potential financial and other benefits from such integrative practices but perhaps the most significant benefit lies in the increased control and consistency in the delivery of service which it gives through effective management of as many 'moments of truth' within the guest experience as possible. Integration, in this sense, may involve outright ownership of the various components or intermediaries or, alternatively, the establishment of a network of partners, all of which operate to agreed standards and systems and may even adopt the sponsoring company's branding.

Similar strategies include isolating the guest from contact with many of the uncontrolled intermediaries, and thus unmanaged 'moments of truth', at the holiday destination. 'Sanitizing' the guest–employee encounter, while not the only motivating factor, is at the heart of experiences offered to tourists by 'old-style' holiday camps (such as Butlins in the UK) as well as Club Méditerranée, the increasing range of all-inclusive products that are available on the market (for example, Sandals in the

Caribbean) and the growing cruise ship sector. Within this model, the guest will, typically, only come into contact with employees selected and trained by the sponsoring company for most of the activities that they may wish to undertake, and will thus be insulated from the uncertainty of unmanaged 'moments of truth' through contact with a diversity of local providers.

This level of control and standardization of service is not feasible with respect to many tourism destinations, nor, indeed, is it desirable for many visitors themselves. The local encounter is a central attraction within the vacation experience, whether it is in a bar in Connemara in the west of Ireland, a Parisian nightclub, a train journey through India, or on safari in Kenya. In this context we cannot anticipate the nature or outcome of the 'moments of truth' which the guest will experience, nor, realistically, can or should they be managed by the tour operator or travel agent through which the tourist originally booked.

In a very real sense, then, the range of 'moments of truth' which the tourist will encounter can involve much of the total population of the tourist destination locality and not just those specifically involved in working to meet guest needs. The welcome and assistance that the visitor receives from the community as a whole becomes an important factor in ensuring an extended or return visit to the locality or in helping to decide that 'once is enough'. In many communities, there is a certain ambivalence to visitors, who can create congestion on roads; saturate facilities such as shops and theatres; contribute to inflating prices charged to locals for goods and services; behave in ways that are not compatible with local custom and practice; or exhibit high levels of 'social distance' through demonstration of conspicuous affluence unattainable within the host location. A major challenge for the tourism industry is to support the education of the local community about tourism and tourists so as to ensure a welcome or at least to avoid outright hostility. At the same time, it is arguable that tour operators have the responsibility to encourage sensitivity to local customs and culture among their clients. Tourism awareness programmes, at community and national levels, have become widespread, designed to enhance the welcome that visitors receive from the whole community within which they are staying. Likewise, responsible tour operators do provide information and briefings for visitors on the locations they are visiting as well as on behaviour that is and is not acceptable. These strategies will all contribute to ensuring that the uncontrolled variables within the guest–employee encounter or 'moments of truth' cycle are more likely to be positive in their outcomes and do not negatively affect the overall perception that visitors derive from their visit.

It is evident, therefore, that the concept of the 'moment of truth' within the guest–employee encounter has applicability throughout the three main parts of what Leiper (1990) calls the tourism system, as shown in Figure 5.1. Although conventional studies of service tend to focus on the transit and destination regions within the system, there are important elements of interaction prior to departure and upon return within the guest-originating region. Furthermore, as we have seen, the wider political, social, cultural and economic environments all have a bearing upon the nature of the guest–employee encounter in its broadest interpretation and can influence the quality of 'moments of truth' that take place as a result. The extent to which 'social distance' is an issue, as well as the influence of political and religious environment, cannot be disregarded when considering the management of the tourist's encounters with the local community, whether in a working or informal context.

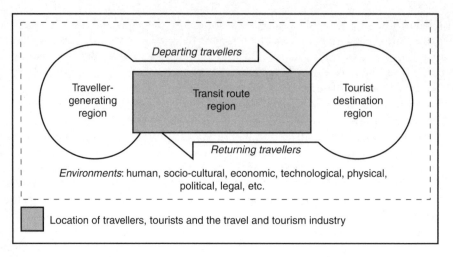

*Figure 5.1* The tourism system

If we take Leiper's system as the horizontal representation of the tourist's experience, we can attempt to scale the intensity of likely guest–employee interaction through 'moments of truth' in order to provide an albeit crude complementary vertical axis. This recognizes that 'moments of truth', in relation to the wide range of organizations that go to make up the tourism system, need not be of equal 'weighting' or status or have the same intensity in so far as the guest is concerned, and a positive or negative experience in one area may elicit a very different response to a similar experience elsewhere in the guest cycle. Figure 5.2 provides an example of this two-dimensional model. Clearly, the detail will vary according to the nature of the tourist package that the customer purchases. What the model does allow is for those managing the total tourism experience, generally the principal agents, to attempt a prediction of those areas within the tourism system where the potential intensity of guest–employee interaction is high and where, as a consequence, particular care must be given to the management of 'moments of truth'. It will also assist to identify those areas of guest–employee interaction where the principal agent has little or no control but where risks are also high and where responsibility lies with other authorities. This recognition may initiate representation or liaison with the relevant public or private sector authorities within whatever sector of the tourism system they are located.

Plotting 'moments of truth' against the guest cycle in this way provides those responsible for the management of the total guest experience with the opportunity to attempt to exert some control over what has hitherto been left very much to chance and fortune. What this means in practice is considered in the next section of this chapter.

## MANAGING THE GUEST–EMPLOYEE ENCOUNTER

We have considered the importance of every 'moment of truth' to the total guest experience. It is a central feature within the achievement of quality service, the main outcome that is sought from the guest–employee encounter. Management of the 'moments of truth' cycle is a critical process and, according to Albrecht and Zemke

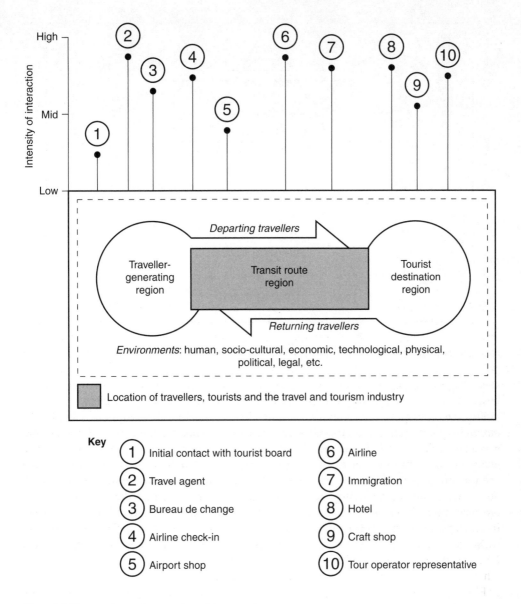

*Figure 5.2* The travel experience and tourist encounters

(1985, p. 31), requires a fundamental mind shift from traditional control-based supervision and management: 'When the moments of truth go un-managed, the quality of service regresses to mediocrity.' The traditional approach to managing relationships within a company can be seen to operate on a hierarchical basis, as depicted in Figure 5.3.

What is important in this model is that the decision-making process flows from the base of the pyramid to its apex, the senior management level. The customer contact zone is figuratively and, frequently, literally adrift at the bottom. A caricature of this model at work, which has more than a touch of reality in it, is the situation where staff

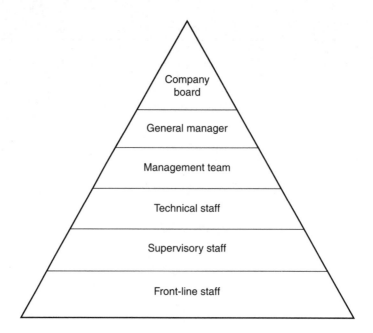

*Figure 5.3* Traditional management hierarchy

in a busy hotel restaurant swarm to serve the general manager when he arrives for lunch, and, in doing so, neglect the needs of paying guests. Staff at each level, in this model, are primarily concerned with satisfying their immediate superiors within the hierarchy, even if this means neglecting the real customers of the business. Figure 5.4, by contrast, shows what Blanchard calls the inverted service triangle, a philosophical inversion of traditional management hierarchies (Mahesh, 1994).

This simple reversal of the triangle has major ramifications for the management of the guest–employee encounter within tourism businesses. The energy flow remains upwards but is the complete reverse of that which operates within the traditional model. In this approach the customer contact zone becomes the most important component within the management of the organization. Everything else is subservient to that aspect of the service process. Carlzon saw the relationship between front-line staff, those responsible for handling the many thousands of 'moments of truth' on a daily basis, and the technical, supervisory and management functions as one of service, with the back-of-house team existing primarily to facilitate the critical work of those at the front line. As Carlzon (1987) put it, 'if you're not serving the guest, your job is to serve those who are'. Disney's application of this principle is to consider all employees as cast members, with those at the front-line sharp edge as 'on stage' and those working behind the scenes as 'off stage'.

The inverted triangle demands an approach to management that is not control-based but is designed to facilitate the work of operational staff. Management are there to assist their front-line colleagues to provide a better service to guests at the point of contact. By providing this superior service, of course, a tourism company is enhancing its competitive position and increasing the likelihood that repeat custom will be generated.

*Figure 5.4* The inverted service triangle
*Source*: Adapted from Mahesh (1994)

Cook Johnson (1991) clearly demonstrates, within the hotel sector in North America, the link between perceived superior service and management style. In her study, establishments were rated by guests and employees on the basis of their service, and three groups resulted from this rating analysis. They were:

- service leaders: the group of hotels where, on average, 92 per cent of employees and customers rated these organizations as consistently very good in their service – the top quartile;
- service average: the group of hotels where 79 per cent of employees and customers rated service as consistently very good – the middle two quartiles; and
- service problems: the group of hotels where only 62 per cent of employees and customers rated service as consistently 'good' – the bottom quartile.

Cook Johnson then used this classification in order to look at the ways in which superior service is delivered by front-line staff and management. She notes that the good service leader group of companies have attributes which clearly point to the importance of the relationship between those delivering the service and those providing support to enable them to do so. Service leader companies

- are highly focused and consistent in everything they do and say in relation to employees;
- have managers who communicate with employees;
- facilitate, rather than regulate, their employees' responses to customers;
- solicit employee feedback about how they can do things better;

- stress the importance of teamwork at each level of the organization; and
- plan carefully the organization's recruitment and training needs.

Cook Johnson concludes her analysis by summarizing the characteristics of service leaders in the following terms. Service leader companies are those which are recognized for

- their unfailing commitment to service principles;
- their investment in people to ensure staffing competence;
- a management philosophy which stresses communication, a proactive orientation and employee feedback; and
- a dedication to teamwork.

(Cook Johnson, 1991)

The link between service quality at the point of the encounter between front-line staff and the guest and the management environment within companies is one that is also considered by Mansfield (1990). She identifies four key principles in the development of customer care within tourism companies. These are:

- Customer care starts at the top, meaning that commitment to the principle of customer care must emanate from senior management levels within an organization. Successful management is not only about the right management style but also an attitude, ethos or culture of the organization which overrides the management techniques used, such that in the absence of other instructions these values will dictate how an employee will behave.

- Customer care involves everyone within the organization. It is not just about front-line staff. In keeping with Carlzon's argument, Mansfield contends that the contrary view only serves to reinforce the technicians' or administrators' opinion that the standard of service they give in support of front-line staff is not important. How can cleaners do the right job unless they fully appreciate the customers' needs and the importance of their role? High standards of customer care cannot be achieved by ignoring seasonal, part-time or voluntary staff who represent the face of the business to many customers.

(Mansfield, 1990, A68)

- Care for your staff and they will care for your customers. Too often organizations look first to the customer, whereas the emphasis should be placed on the staff.
- Improving the experience of the staff encourages a better service and a better experience for customers. More customers are obtained, thereby improving the climate in which management and staff work. Investment and greater professionalism follow success and the cycle of achievement is reinforced.

- It's a continuous process, meaning that customer care is not a quick fix project but a long-term plan.

(Mansfield, 1990, A69)

Mansfield's analysis places considerable emphasis on what Lewis and Chambers (1989) call the internal marketing process. Internal marketing can be defined as applying the philosophies and practices of marketing to people who serve the external customers so that (a) the best people can be employed and retained and (b) they will do the best possible work (Berry, 1980, cited in Lewis and Chambers, 1989, pp. 51–2).

Service quality, therefore, is much more likely to be delivered within a supervising and managing culture that conforms to what has been described elsewhere as the sustainable human resource development model (Baum, 1995). This model seeks to identify the human resource conditions necessary to overcome tourism's key issues such as high labour attrition, poor career commitment and the image of the industry from an employment perspective. Foster (1991) highlights this distinction clearly in relation to British Airways (BA). She discusses the change, within BA, from a traditional management environment to one where managers recognize the power and importance of internal marketing and its benefits to customer service standards:

> In the early 1980s, before the changes began, BA was a very hierarchical organisation. Decisions could only be made at the top, and were often the result of protracted committee meetings. Managers and employees at more junior levels felt powerless to achieve change. Employees believed that they were cogs in the big BA machine and often felt their concerns were unheard or unanswered.
>
> BA management has since become much more participative, caring and involved. We believe that a company's management style must be consistent with the way in which it expects its staff to treat its customer: if we want our crew to be always attentive and ready to help with the passengers, then they have the right to expect that their managers will always be attentive and ready to help when they require assistance. (p. 223)

The concept of internal marketing and the application of a supportive management culture which enables the delivery of quality service lead to the notion of empowerment of front-line staff, which, in recent years, is a concept that has gained considerable currency within service-focused companies. It is also a concept which, as Figure 5.5 demonstrates, is used to market what companies see as the competitive advantage of service excellence.

Empowerment means enabling and encouraging front-line staff to make decisions that will help solve customers' problems or meet their needs, without reference to an interminable management hierarchy. As such, it is at the heart of the guest–employee encounter. The ability to deal professionally and competently with immediate queries, problems and complaints is an attribute that is rated very highly among customers of tourism organizations and makes a major contribution to effective relationship marketing (Bitner *et al.* 1990; Ryan, 1996). One common recognition of this is the 'no-quibble goods-return' policy that is adopted by many retailers. Customers purchase with greater confidence but front-line staff are also in a position where they can contribute to overcoming customer problems and complaints by immediate refund or replacement. This is not total empowerment but rather a recognition, by management, that the customer-care zone requires clear operating guidelines within which staff work.

Similar absolute policies are more difficult to apply when the purchase is less tangible than a purchase in a shop; for example, a restaurant meal, theme park ride or transportation arrangement. It is not possible to replace an unsatisfactory hotel experience, although the establishment can attempt to recover its position through a full or partial refund or the offer of a future complimentary stay. Thus front-line staff need to be able to assess and evaluate each particular situation with confidence and authority and have to be empowered to provide a solution insofar as one is available. Guidelines are clearly important so as to enable front-line staff to respond in a consistent manner.

*Figure 5.5* Marriott Hong Kong advertisement: empowerment
Reproduced with the kind permission of Marriott Hotels and Resorts, London.

In some cases, relatively standard provision may be acceptable; for example a complimentary meal for delayed airline passengers and compensation, within specified scales, for those offloaded due to overbooking. However, generally speaking, effective empowerment is 'ring-fenced' insofar as financial decisions are concerned, so that staff have the authority to act up to a specified level without reference to supervisory or management authority. The American Ritz Carlton company permits all employees to change anything, on behalf of guests, up to a value of $2000. Rather greater freedom may be available if no direct financial consequences are involved. Novotel, part of the French Accor group, use the word 'subsidiarity' to describe their approach to empowerment. Serge Ravailhe, formerly managing director of Novotel UK, interviewed in 1993, described the concept in the following terms:

> 'Subsidiarity' is another way of saying that employees should be encouraged to take responsibility for decisions. Whatever decisions employees make, at least they have made them. If they can't make a decision on a problem then they pass it to the next person above them and they try to make it. It's like carrying the ball instead of passing it all the time. (*Caterer and Hotelkeeper*, 1993)

Ravailhe accepted that from time to time 'subsidiarity' would lead to employees making the wrong decision but argued that it was important that they had made the decision for themselves and learned from mistakes. Of course, such a system requires the total absence of a punitive environment when mistakes are made or employees will avoid making decisions of any consequence.

Customers, undoubtedly, greatly value the effects of empowerment. Albrecht and Zemke (l985) relate the case of a British Airways survey into what customers considered

Plate 6.1 Disneyland – an integral part of Hannigan's Fantasy City

Plate 6.2 Apartment complex in San Francisco

Plate 6.3 Disneyland

Plate 6.4 Fisherman's Wharf, San Francisco

Plate 6.5 The Shambles in York

Plate 6.6 'Fingerpoints' black and gold signposts in Canterbury, England

to be important in their flying experiences, and this supports the approach which Novotel has adopted. Four factors stood out as of paramount importance:

- care and concern;
- spontaneity;
- problem-solving;
- recovery.

Albrecht and Zemke quote the response of Donald Porter of BA to these findings:

> Care and concern are fairly clear, I think, says Porter. We weren't surprised to find this a key factor, although I think we'd have to confess that we couldn't claim a very high level of performance on it.
>
> Spontaneity made us stop and scratch our heads a bit. Customers were saying 'We want to know that your frontline people are authorised to think. When a problem comes up that doesn't fit in the procedure book, can the service person use some discretion – find a way to jockey the system on the customer's behalf? Or does he or she simply shrug shoulders and brush the customer off?'
>
> Problem solving was pretty clear, we felt. Customers thought our people should be skilled at working out the intricacies of problematical travel schedules, handling complicated logistics, and in general getting them on their way.
>
> The fourth factor sort of threw us. It had never really occurred to us in any concrete way. 'Recovery' was the term we coined to describe a very frequently repeated concern: if something goes wrong, as it often does, will anybody make a special effort to set it right? Will someone go out of his or her way to make amends to the customer? Does anyone make an effort to offset the negative effects of a screw-up? Does anyone even know how to deliver a simple apology?
>
> We were struck by a rather chilling thought: if two of these four primary evaluation factors were things we had never consciously considered, what were the chances that our people in the service areas were paying attention to them? For the first time, we were really beginning to understand and come to terms with the real motivational factors that are embedded in our customer's nervous system. (Albrecht and Zemke, 1985, p. 34)

Empowerment, as the Cook Johnson study clearly suggests, also implies trust and confidence by management in the front-line workforce. For example, many traditional service organizations, where empowerment is not a concept that is fully adopted, restrict access to annual capital budgets and operating plans to management ranks only and on a 'need to know' basis. By contrast, the Disney Corporation provides operational personnel with full access to these tools, entrusting them to translate the strategic plan from the boardroom to the point of action within the theme parks (Johnson, 1991, p. 42).

Real empowerment of staff, however, is not something that takes place as a result of a head office circular and attached guidelines. Empowerment is a direct factor of, on the one hand, effective human resource development policies which give staff the skills and confidence to act autonomously and, on the other, a supervisory and management culture that is based on trust and partnership and not control and censure. Thus front-line staff will only be able to act outside prescribed boundaries if they are equipped with the information and skills to do so but, more importantly, they know that their managers will support whatever action they decide upon and will not penalize or undermine such decisions.

Empowerment is, therefore, the result of a combination of corporate and senior management commitment with appropriate training and support at all levels. Sparrowe

(1994), in an empirical study of the factors which contribute to the fostering of empowerment, identified two such factors:

> First, the relationship employees have with their immediate superiors appears to be a significant element in the development of empowerment. To the extent that supervisors are unable to develop positive exchange relationships with employees because of job demands, frequent shift rotation, or burnout, those employees are less likely to enjoy meaning, choice, impact, and competence in their work activities. Policies and procedures that enable supervisors and employees to establish effective relationships over time would function to support empowerment efforts.
>
> Second, the importance of culture in efforts to foster empowerment ... Constructive norms and shared behavioral expectations appear to facilitate employees' experience of meaningfulness, impact, choice, and competence at work. (p. 69)

The effects of the genuine empowerment of front-line staff can also have a significant effect upon reducing the social distance between customers and those providing the tourism services. When management demonstrates, in a public way, that all their staff have autonomy and the full trust of the company, they are demonstrating their own evaluation of these staff, both as employees and as people. Guests, in the presence of this attitude, are much more likely to respond to those serving them on the basis of equality. Mahesh (1994) argues cogently for a trust in the better side of human nature and this attitude is at the root of effective empowerment. The issue of social distance or the service/servitude conundrum is one that we have already reflected upon in earlier discussion. Real empowerment of the kind espoused by the Ritz Carlton organization in the USA, where guests and staff are seen as social equals temporarily undertaking different roles, can make a real contribution to overcoming problems in this area, providing that macro-social and -economic conditions permit. Thus the effects will be far greater within developed economies than, for example, within the countries of eastern Europe.

The case for empowerment is by no means conclusive. Lashley (1997) provides a balanced analysis of empowerment from a western-centric perspective but, essentially, concludes by supporting its value against its limitations. The arguments put forward by Ritzer (1993), through the notion of 'McDonaldization' as well as the earlier concept of segmentalism, which Kanter (1983) proposed, point to the potency of forces which are seeking to move in a very different direction. The processes, which they discuss, seek to reduce the human input to service delivery to an absolute and well-controlled minimum as well as denying the employees a perspective on the total production or service delivery system. Control of the workforce is a central tenet within successful fast-food businesses and others in the tourism sector. Control is incompatible with empowerment in its true sense because empowerment means relinquishing control while at the same time ensuring that front-line staff have the skills and confidence to represent the company to customers and help to meet their needs in the best possible way.

## CONCLUSION

In this chapter, an attempt has been made to address aspects of the guest–employee encounter and, in particular, problems which arise in the management of this interaction. The starting point for this analysis was the historical context of work in the tourism industry and its origins within the domestic master–servant relationship. The key concept of 'moments of truth' was then considered as providing the structure for the management of the guest–employee encounter within what is a highly fragmented industry. Clearly, as in any other field of human relations and interaction, the issues can be considered from a far broader perspective and a wide variety of additional dimensions could legitimately feature in a chapter bearing this heading. The focus here has been on the management of the encounter and little consideration has been given to the perspective of the guest. This omitted area would merit further research and consideration.

This chapter considers a field where new approaches and analyses continue to emerge, enhancing understanding of a complex relationship environment. One of the most intriguing of these themes considers the aesthetics of customer–guest relations in terms of the characteristics of employees and the theme or concept represented by the bar, club or restaurant in which they work. The work on aesthetic labour in Glasgow which has been undertaken by Warhurst *et al.* (2000) points to the expectation of a social dimension to the relationship that has not been considered hitherto. This emerging theme is one that requires exploration in other contexts. What it illustrates, however, is the dynamism of this topic and the need for researchers and practitioners alike to remain abreast of developments in a truly dynamic area.

# Chapter 6

# Urban tourism: Evaluating tourists' experience of urban places

*Stephen J. Page*

## INTRODUCTION

Urbanization is a major force contributing to the development of towns and cities, where people live, work and shop (see Johnston *et al.*, 1994 for a definition of the term urbanization). Towns and cities function as places where the population concentrates in a defined area, and economic activities locate in the same area or nearby to provide the opportunity for the production and consumption of goods and services in capitalist societies. Consequently, towns and cities provide the context for a diverse range of social, cultural and economic activities in which the population engages, and where tourism leisure and entertainment form major service activities. These environments also function as meeting-places, major tourist gateways, accommodation and transportation hubs, and as central places to service the needs of visitors. Most tourist trips will contain some experience of an urban area; for example, when an urban dweller departs from a major gateway in a city, arrives at a gateway in another city-region and stays in accommodation in an urban area. Therefore, most tourists will experience urban tourism in some form during their holiday, visit to friends and relatives, business trip or visit for other reasons (for example, a pilgrimage to a religious shrine such as Lourdes in an urban area). Yet urban tourism has largely been neglected in academic research with a number of notable exceptions (Ashworth, 1989; Law, 1993, 1996; Page, 1995). This chapter examines the concept of urban tourism, reviewing the principal contributions towards its recognition as a tourism phenomenon worthy of study, and it also emphasizes the scope and range of environments classified as urban destinations together with some of the approaches towards its analysis. The chapter then considers a framework for the analysis of the tourist's experience of urban tourism, followed by a discussion of key aspects of urban tourist behaviour: Where do urban tourists go in urban areas, what activities do they undertake, how do they perceive these places, learn about the spatial attributes of the locality and how is this reflected in their patterns of behaviour? Having reviewed these features, the chapter concludes with a discussion of service quality issues for urban tourism.

## URBAN TOURISM: UNDERSTANDING ITS NEGLECT BY RESEARCHERS

Ashworth's (1989) seminal study of urban tourism acknowledges that

> a double neglect has occurred. Those interested in the study of tourism have tended to neglect the urban context in which much of it is set, while those interested in urban studies ... have been equally neglectful of the importance of the tourist function cities. (p. 33)

While more recent tourism textbooks (Shaw and Williams, 1994) have expanded upon earlier syntheses of urban tourism research in a spatial context (see Pearce, 1987), it still remains a comparatively under-researched area despite the growing interest in the relationship between urban regeneration and tourism (see Law, 1992) for a detailed review of the relationship of tourism and urban regeneration. The apparent reluctance of researchers to investigate urban tourism can be traced to the pioneering study by Stansfield (1964) that notes the reluctance of American recreational researchers to examine urban areas due to the complexity of disaggregating the tourist/recreational and non-tourist/recreational function of cities; a view reiterated by subsequent researchers (see Vetter, 1985; Page and Sinclair, 1989). Despite this problem, which is more a function of perceived rather than real difficulties in understanding urban tourism phenomena, a range of studies now provide evidence of a growing body of literature on the topic (see Vetter, 1985; Ashworth, 1989, 1992; Ashworth and Tunbridge, 1990, 2000; and Page, 1995). But even though more publications are now appearing in the academic literature (see Page, 2000 and Hall and Page, 2002 for a more detailed review of the literature) this does not imply that urban tourism is recognized as a distinct and notable area of research in tourism studies. One reason is the tendency for urban tourism research to be based on descriptive and empirical case studies that do not contribute to a greater theoretical or methodological understanding of urban tourism. This is in spite of a proliferation of edited books and texts on the subject in the late 1990s (e.g. Law, 1996; Murphy, 1997; Mazanec, 1997; Tyler *et al.,* 1998). In fact, such an approach is perpetuated by certain disciplines which contribute to the study of tourism, where the case study method of approach does little more than describe each situation and fails to relate the case to wider issues to derive generalizations and test hypotheses and assumptions within the academic literature (see Yin, 1994 for a discussion of case study method in social science research). In this respect, the limited understanding is a function of the lack of methodological sophistication in tourism research noted in recent critiques of tourism research (Pearce and Butler, 1993; Faulkner and Ryan, 2000).

According to Ashworth (1992), urban tourism has not emerged as a distinct research focus; rather, research is focused on tourism in cities. This strange paradox can be explained by the failure by planners, commercial interests and residents to recognize tourism as one of the main economic rationales for cities. Tourism is often seen as an adjunct or necessary evil to generate additional revenue, while the main economic activities of the locality are not perceived as tourism-related. Such negative views of urban tourism have meant that the public and private sectors have used the temporary, seasonal and ephemeral nature of tourism to neglect serious research on this theme (see Butler and Mao, 1997, for a useful review of seasonality in urban tourism).

Consequently, a vicious circle exists: the absence of public and private sector research makes access to research data difficult and the large-scale funding necessary for primary data-collection that uses social survey techniques is rarely available to break this circle. The absence of large-scale funding for urban tourism research reflects the prevailing consensus of the 1980s that such studies were unnecessary. However, with the pressure posed by tourists in many European tourist cities in the new millennium this perception is changing now that the public and private sectors are belatedly acknowledging the necessity of visitor management. For examples of this as a mechanism to enhance, manage and improve the tourists' experience of towns and places to visit, see van der Borg *et al.*'s (1997) review of Venice and publications of the English Tourist Board/ Employment Department (1991). Nevertheless, as Ashworth (1992, p. 5) argues:

> Urban tourism requires the development of a coherent body of theories, concepts, techniques and methods of analysis which allow comparable studies to contribute towards some common goal of understanding of either the particular role of cities within tourism or the place of tourism in the form and function of cities.

One way of assessing progress towards these objectives is to review the main approaches developed within the tourism literature.

## URBAN TOURISM AS A DISTINCT RESEARCH AREA IN TOURISM STUDIES

The international literature on urban tourism can be reviewed under a number of headings: theory and conceptual developments; demand and supply issues; tourist behaviour; management, planning and policy; and modelling and forecasting. In terms of theoretical developments, the literature has not advanced significantly in the last decade or developed theoretical perspectives since Ashworth's (1989) seminal study. However, developments in social theory have had some impact on the research approach adopted towards urban areas as locations producing tourist experiences and as places that have been consumed for pleasure. A notable study which focuses on the globalization of the postmodern metropolis is Hannigan's (1998) *Fantasy City*, with the city as an entertainment hub. Such studies have adopted earlier theoretical developments in social science pertaining to postmodernity and the city. Similarly, the contribution made by other critical debates on the processes shaping urban economies and the role of tourism as integral elements of the economic base are certainly leading a limited number of researchers to rethink their approach to urban tourism. In the journal literature, many of the articles published in the 1980s and 1990s have been concerned with demand (e.g. Buckley and Witt, 1989) or supply, particularly in terms of development (e.g. Oppermann *et al.*, 1996; Hall and Hamon, 1996; Timothy and Wall, 1995; Cockerell, 1997; Bramwell, 1998; Pearce, 1998; Heung and Qu, 1998; Hughes, 1998).

In terms of the modelling and forecasting for urban destinations, this has remained the domain of a small number of specialist economic forecasters, reviewed by Mazanec (1997) in the most comprehensive review of the field to date. The complexity of disaggregating urban tourism systems and their interrelationship from other economic activities still remains a major obstacle to the modelling and forecasting activities that would sit firmly in the practitioner contribution. But inadequate data sources and information still precludes detailed analysis for many destinations. Therefore, how does one approach the study of urban tourism?

## APPROACHES TO URBAN TOURISM

To understand how research on urban tourism has developed distinctive approaches and methodologies, one needs to recognize why tourists seek urban tourism experiences. Shaw and Williams (1994) argue that urban areas offer a geographical concentration of facilities and attractions conveniently located to meet both visitor and resident needs alike. But the diversity and variety among urban tourist destinations has led researchers to examine the extent to which they display unique and similar features. Shaw and Williams (1994) identify three approaches:

1. the diversity of urban areas means that their size, function, location and history contribute to their uniqueness;
2. towns and cities are multifunctional areas, meaning that they simultaneously provide various functions for different groups of users; and
3. the tourist functions of towns and cities are rarely produced or consumed solely by tourists, given the variety of user groups in urban areas.

Ashworth (1992) conceptualizes urban tourism by identifying three approaches of analysis:

1. The supply of tourism facilities in urban areas, involving inventories (for example, the spatial distribution of accommodation, entertainment complexes and tourist-related services), where urban ecological models have been used. In addition, the facility approach has been used to identify the tourism product offered by destinations.
2. The demand generated by urban tourists, to examine how many people visit urban areas, why they choose to visit and their patterns of behaviour, perception and expectations in relation to their visit.
3. Perspectives of urban tourism policy, where the public sector (for example, planners) and private sector agencies have undertaken or commissioned research to investigate specific issues of interest to their own interests for urban tourism.

More recently, attempts to theoretically interpret urban tourism have been developed by Mullins (1991) and Roche (1992). Whilst these studies do not have a direct bearing on attempts to influence or affect the tourist experience of towns and cities, their importance should not be neglected in wider reviews of urban tourism: they offer explanations of the sudden desire of many former towns and cities with an industrial base to now look towards service sector activities such as tourism. Both studies examine urban tourism in the context of changes in post-industrial society and structural changes in the mode of capitalist production. In other words, both studies question the types of process now shaping the operation and development of tourism in post-industrial cities, and the implications for public sector tourism and leisure policy. One outcome of such research is that it highlights the role of the state, especially local government, in seeking to develop service industries based on tourism and leisure production and consumption in urban areas, as a response to the restructuring of capitalism which has often led to employment loss in the locality. Mullins' (1991) concept of tourism urbanization is also useful as it assists in developing the following typology of urban tourist destination:

- capital cities;
- metropolitan centres, walled historic cities and small fortress cities;
- large historic cities;
- inner-city areas;
- revitalized waterfront areas;
- industrial cities;
- seaside resorts and winter sport resorts;
- purpose-built integrated tourist resorts;
- tourist-entertainment complexes;
- specialized tourist service centres;
- cultural/art cities.

(after Page, 1995, p. 17)

This classification illustrates the diversity of destinations which provide an urban context for tourist visits and highlights the problem of deriving generalizations from individual case studies without a suitable conceptual framework. For this reason, it is pertinent to focus on the theoretical issues which have emerged in the last decade on the conceptualization of the city as a place for tourism. This is followed by a concept of the 'tourist experience of urban tourism' as a framework to assess some of the experiential aspects of this phenomenon.

## THEORIZING THE CITY AS A PLACE FOR TOURISM: THE POSTMODERNIST CRITIQUE

The development of urban tourism in the period since the late 1970s has to be viewed against long-term economic and structural change in the nature of capitalism. This has resulted in a transformation from an industrial to an information technology-based, post-industrial (sometimes called post-fordist) form of capitalism which is now very evident in the nature of urban places. At the same time, globalization has produced an increasingly transnational, multi-polarized, interactive and highly interdependent world economic system since the 1980s. The significance of these macro-economic processes for urban places is reflected in the declining economic autonomy of the individual city and, arguably, the nation-state.

Whilst urban tourism *per se* is not a new activity for cities, towns and coastal resorts that exhibit urban characteristics (i.e. the agglomeration of people, services and infrastructure), it is the nature of what Roche (1992) calls the 'new urban tourism' based on the consumption of places in a post-industrial society that assumes so much significance. Indeed, urban tourism may be a parody of modern-day society and a reflection of the way in which the supposed 'leisured society' spends and consumes its affluence and time. For example, Meethan (1996, p. 324) recognized that

> tourism involves the visual consumption of signs and, increasingly, simulacra and staged events in which urban townscapes are transformed into aestheticised spaces of entertainment and pleasure ... Within these places of consumption ... a variety of

activities can be pursued, such as promenading, eating, drinking, watching staged events and street entertainment and visually appreciating heritage and culture of place.

It is this preoccupation with consumption, such as the purchase of tangible services and souvenirs, that is embodied in the new urban tourism where places seek the economic and cultural advantage and has led critics such as Hewison (1987) to challenge the basic tenets of heritage interpretation that places have been commodified in pursuit of a populist appeal.

The postmodernists emphasize the cultural dynamics of society by utilizing theoretical constructs that characterize postmodern society as fast-moving and technologically sophisticated, where vast amounts of information are available and knowledge is a prerequisite for accessing information, employment and wealth. Society is also characterized by a fascination with consumerism, where consumer goods and media images play a major role in the everyday life of urbanites. The mass consumption of goods gives way in postmodern society to hierarchies of taste (niche markets), where reality and simulation blur and are characterized as a stage in late capitalism. Mansfeld (1999) highlighted three underlying processes which characterize postmodernism and the fascination with consumption, commodification, social division and new forms of everyday life.

In Urry's (1995, pp. 1–2) analysis of places as sites for consumption, he concurs with much of the literature on the postmodern city in that

> First places are increasingly being restructured as centres for consumption, as providing the context within which goods and services are compared, evaluated, purchased and used. Second, places themselves are in a sense consumed, particularly visually. Especially important in this is the provision of various kinds of consumer services for both visitors and locals. Third, places can be literally consumed: what people take to be significant about a place ... is over time depleted, devoured, or exhausted by use. Fourth, it is possible for localities to consume one's identity so that places become almost literally all-consuming.

What the sociologists highlight in the debates on the postmodern city, is the significance of the economic basis of cultural transformations that have occurred between the modern and postmodern epoch. It is both the spatiality of these cultural transformations and the impact on the urban dweller and visitor which attract a great deal of interest. Most notably, it is the creation of cultural industries that embody the arts, leisure and tourism as complex and diverse postmodern phenomena to be consumed in the city which characterize the 'new urban tourism'.

Geographical research by Dear and Flusty (1998), based on an analysis of the Los Angeles urban agglomeration, devised a range of theoretical propositions that were mirroring wider urban changes in the socio-geographic composition and space of U.S. cities. Whilst Soja (1989) recognized Los Angeles embodied the spatial fragmentation inherent in post-fordism, with a flexible, disorganized regime of capital accumulation, more wide-ranging postmodern series of changes were occurring.

Within a growing postmodern literature on urbanism, a new range of buzzwords have been coined to describe elements of the urban landscape based on the Los Angeles experience within which tourism is embedded, including:

- *privatopia*, the 'quintessential edge-city residential form ... a private housing development based in common-interest development' (Dear and Flusty, 1998, p. 55);

- *cultures of heteropolis*, based on the cultural diversity arising from ethnicity and minority populations (see Caffyn and Lutz, 1999 for a tourism perspective) and a socio-economic polarization reflected in racism, inequality, homelessness and social unrest;
- *the city as a theme park*, a feature epitomized in Hannigan's (1998) *Fantasy City* (see Plate 6.1);
- *the fortified city*, with residents' preoccupation with security and safety where 'fortified cells of affluence' are juxtaposed with 'places of terror' where the police attempt to control crime (see Plate 6.2);
- *interdictory space*, where spaces in the postmodern city are designed to exclude certain people and activities through their design.

Historical geographies of restructuring on which the L.A. schools have focused in order to understand de-industrialization and re-industrialization are located within the information economy and globalization–localization debates of the region. Soja (1996) identified six types of restructuring that affected the L.A. metropolis 1925–92 including:

*Exopolis*, where hyper-reality based on theme parks such as Disneyland (see Plate 6.3) create a copy of an original that never existed in reality; it is an image.

*Flexicities*, with the growing flexibility of capital and de-industrialization that coincides with the rise of the information economy.

*Cosmopolis*, referring to the globalization of Los Angeles and the region's emergence as a world-city. This is accompanied by not only the multicultural diversity of the city, but also an urban restructuring that generated three specific geographic forms:

- *the splintered labyrinth*, where the social, economic and political polarization are a dominant characteristic of the postmodern city;
- *the carceral city*, where there exists a new 'incendiary urban geography brought about by the amalgam of violence and police surveillance' (Dear and Flusty, 1998, p. 58); and
- *Simcities*, which are new ways of seeing the Los Angeles urban form.

What Dear and Flusty (1998) identified was a Keno capitalism to describe the process whereby urbanization is a random set of opportunities for capital. A more parcelled approach to land development without reference to the urban core in evolving patterns of consumption spaces has developed. What results in Dear and Flusty's (1998) model of Keno capitalism and postmodern urban structure is a 'noncontiguous collage of parcelized, consumption-oriented landscapes devoid of conventional centres yet wired into electronic propinquity and nominally unified by mythologies of the disinformation superhighway' (Dear and Flusty, 1998, p. 66). As a result, their analysis of the post-modern city proposed four broad and overlapping themes:

1. the World city concept and globalization;
2. the dual city where social polarization is a dominant element;
3. altered spaces, with urban change and the reconfiguration of communities and space and new cultural space in the city; and
4. the cybercity.

Dear and Flusty (1998, p. 67) also acknowledge that none of these overlapping themes adequately explains the urban outcomes that one observes in the postmodern city.

What is apparent is that the processes of urbanization, with its postmodern forms, is itself a power element that directly shapes tourism and leisure spaces in cities and a greater theorizing is needed to understand it in a global and comparative context.

Aside from the production of services and experiences, the city is a patchwork of symbols and opportunities for consumption. As Murphy (1999, p. 302) remarked,

> While consumption is significant within the postmodern city, it needs to be remembered that the places or sites of consumption are manufactured or created spaces. Shopping malls, hypermarkets, multiplexes, planned communities, waterfront spaces, museums and cybercafés are all products of service, property and entertainment industries. Indeed it has been argued that the new urbanism is akin to a giant theme park.

But what needs to be emphasized in a consumption context is that many of the urban landscapes in postmodern cities can only be consumed by those who have the means to do so.

## THE TOURIST EXPERIENCE OF URBAN TOURISM

There is a growing literature on tourist satisfaction (see Ryan, 1995d), and what constitutes the experiential aspects of a tourist visit to a locality. In the context of urban tourism, the innovative research by Graefe and Vaske (1987) offers a number of important insights as well as a useful framework. Graefe and Vaske (1987) acknowledge that the 'tourist experience' is a useful term to identify the experience of an individual which may be affected 'by individual, environmental, situational and personality-related factors as well as the degree of communication with other people. It is the outcome which researchers and the tourism industry constantly evaluate to establish if the actual experience met the tourist's expectations' (cited by Page, 1995, p. 24). Operationalizing such a concept may prove difficult in view of the complex array of factors which may affect the visitor experience (Figure 6.1). For example, where overcrowding occurs at major tourist sites (for example, Canterbury, Venice, St Paul's Cathedral, London and the Tower of London), this can have a negative effect on visitors who have a low tolerance threshold for overcrowding at major tourist sites. Yet, conversely, other visitors may be less affected by use levels, thereby illustrating the problem within tourism motivation research – predicting tourist behaviour and their responses to particular situations. In fact Graefe and Vaske (1987, p. 394) argue that 'the effects of increasing use levels on the recreation/tourist experience can be explained only partially ... as a function of use level'. Therefore, the individual tourist's ability to tolerate the behaviour of other people, level of use, the social situation and the context of the activity are all-important determinants of the actual outcome. Thus, evaluating the quality of the tourist experience is a complex process which may require a careful consideration of the factors motivating a visit (i.e. how the tourist's perception of urban areas makes him predisposed to visit particular places), his actual patterns of activity and the extent to which his expectations associated with his perceptions are matched in reality (Page, 1995, p. 25). For this reason, attention now turns to some of the experiential aspects of urban tourists' visits and the significance of behavioural issues influencing visitor satisfaction. In view of the diversity of tourists visiting urban areas, it is useful to define the market for urban tourism.

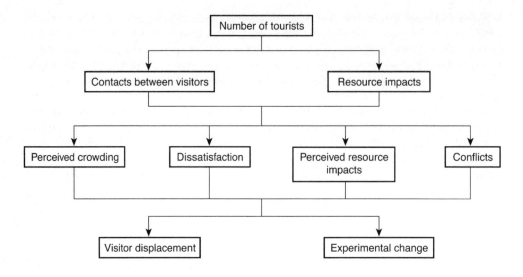

*Figure 6.1* Factors affecting the urban tourist experience

## THE URBAN TOURISM MARKET: DATA SOURCES

Identifying the scale, volume and different markets for urban tourism remains a perennial problem for researchers. Urban visits and tourist use of towns and cities are multi-faceted and structured around different motives: they are complementary and yet compete. In other words, a tourist may seek to visit a number of towns and cities as part of an integrated itinerary or circuit where the wider urban experience is being sold. Yet the various elements (i.e. places) that compose this experience are also competing with each other to gain a share of the market and visitor spend in the wider context of tourist travel patterns and the experience of tourism.

Cockerell (1997) pointed to the only pan-European data source – *The European Travel Monitor* (ETM) which has information on demand issues. The section on city trips only refers to the holiday sector, ignoring business and VFR travel and only including international trips involving a minimum stay of one night. A number of other data sources, including academic studies (e.g. Mazanec, 1997) and research institutes such as the Institute National pour la Recherche dans les Transports et leur Sécurité (INRETS) in Paris and the Venice based Centro Internazionale di Studi sull'Economica Turistica (CISET), have generated research data on urban tourism demand. Yet, internationally, most sources of data are destination-specific rather than country- or region-specific.

### The European Travel Monitor and urban tourism

In 1996, the ETM found that Europeans made 33 million city trips abroad; 23 million of the trips were long holidays of four nights or more and 10 million trips were short breaks of one to three nights in duration. Although nearly 30 per cent of city trips were short breaks, this appeared to be the most significant type of European short break, reflected in the wide range of packaged and unpackaged options. In the late 1990s, this phenomenon was given an artificial boost by the establishment of low-cost airlines in Europe, particularly those in the UK such as Go Easy, EasyJet, Virgin and discounted fares offered by established carriers such as RyanAir, British Midland and KLMUK. Many of the additional trips generated by low-cost airlines and new infrastructure options such as the Channel Tunnel and Eurostar Service have been short-break-oriented, leisure-based and targeted at key urban centres in secondary destinations which complement the established primary tourist cities (e.g. London, Paris, Amsterdam, Geneva, Brussels and Madrid).

The fact is that many urban holiday trips are secondary trips, complementing the traditional summer-long annual holidays which are coastal-based. In attempting to explain the factors behind the rise of secondary urban trips (excluding the attraction of cheap, low-cost airfares), a number of structural changes among the European travelling population may be identified, including:

(a)  increased holiday and leave entitlements;
(b)  the availability of public and national holidays which encourage 'long weekends' that are ideal for short breaks;
(c)  rising prosperity from double income families with greater disposable income;
(d)  changing perceptions of travel with relative reductions in price convenience and the availability of transport options, making it a social, psychological and recreational necessity; and
(e)  time–space compression, where improvements in transport technology (e.g. the advent of the high-speed trains and the development of regional air services outside of the main national gateway) have made access to destinations for short breaks a reality, avoiding multiple-travel options to national airports.

In terms of the main outbound markets, the ETM found that five origin markets generated 54 per cent of all trips, with almost 25 per cent generated by Germany. This is shown in Table 6.1 where the market potential of Germany is still to be fully realized.

*Table 6.1* Hotel arrivals and bednights in some of Europe's favourite cities, 1995 (mn)

| City | Arrivals | Bednights |
|---|---|---|
| London[a] | 23.7 | 100.0 |
| Paris | 11.3 | 24.8 |
| Rome | 5.4 | 12.8 |
| Prague[b] | 5.2 | Na |
| Madrid | 4.3 | 8.4 |
| Munich | 3.1 | 6.1 |
| Florence[c] | 2.6 | 5.9 |
| Barcelona | 3.1 | 5.7 |
| Vienna | 2.0 | 5.0 |
| Brussels[d] | Na | 3.3 |
| Copenhagen | Na | 3.1 |
| Budapest | 1.2 | 3.0 |
| Oslo | Na | 2.0 |
| Frankfurt | 1.0 | 1.8 |
| Geneva | 0.7 | 1.6 |

[a] Figures from the London Tourist Board are not strictly comparable as they include arrivals in all other forms of accommodation as well as hotels. [b] Based on actual figures for January–September. [c] Based on actual figures for January–June. [d] (1994 data)

Cockerell (1997) supported this assertion, referring to a survey in early 1997 by Urlaub and Reisen which indicated that at least 17 per cent of the German population took at least one city break in 1996 (in Germany and overseas). In a French context, the former annual survey of urban travel conducted by the Institute National de la Statique et des Etudes Economiques (INSEE) found that between 1981 and 1992 urban leisure travel doubled. The proportion of short-break travel increased from 35 per cent to 50 per cent of the total in the same period. In 1994, INRETS analysis of transport and urban tourism estimated the total volume of city trips (of at least one night) at 124 million a year, generating 370 million nights, of which 60 per cent were short breaks. The INRETS survey was unique because it analysed all forms of travel and found that VFR accounted for 35 per cent of trips, business travel 10 per cent and holiday trips 33 per cent, while special events and shopping each accounted for 6 per cent (see Hall and Hamon (1996) for a discussion of casinos as urban tourist entertainment, and Heung and Qu's (1998) study of tourist shopping and a wider conceptualization of tourist entertainment in Hughes (1998, 2000)). Of these trips, 73 per cent were undertaken by car and 21 per cent involved hotel accommodation.

Table 6.2 illustrates the dominant destinations for city trips, where Paris is a key element in the pattern. German cities followed by the UK and Italy were the principal destinations in 1995. The major weakness with Table 6.2 is that it only enumerates tourists of European origin and does not consider other visitors. When one refers to accommodation for selected tourist cities in Europe in 1995, these statistics provide an indication of how difficult it is to harmonize urban tourism statistics and to establish acceptable measures.

According to Wöber (1997, p. 26),

> research in [sic] tourism is usually based on accommodation statistics, results from sample surveys of guests, accommodation providers or other experts, or estimates achieved by grossing up procedures using other statistical sources. Even elementary tourism data like

*Table 6.2* European city trips[a] by leading markets, 1995

| Market | Total trips | Per cent of market share | Per cent booked through trade |
|---|---|---|---|
| Germany | 8.1 | 26 | 51 |
| CIS[b] | 2.5 | 8 | 28 |
| UK | 2.2 | 7 | 67 |
| Italy | 2.1 | 7 | 57 |
| France | 1.9 | 6 | 59 |
| Spain | 1.6 | 5 | 61 |
| Switzerland | 1.5 | 5 | 46 |
| Belgium/Luxembourg | 1.4 | 5 | 32 |
| Netherlands | 1.3 | 4 | 56 |
| Poland | 1.2 | 4 | 31 |
| Austria | 1.0 | 3 | 48 |
| Sweden | 1.0 | 3 | 57 |
| Finland | 0.8 | 3 | 76 |
| Denmark | 0.5 | 2 | 61 |
| Norway | 0.5 | 2 | 64 |
| **Total** (incl. others) | 31.0 | 100 | 52 |

[a]   Estimates of holiday trips only – excludes business travel and visits to friends and relations (VFR)
[b]   Russia, Belarus and Ukraine
*Source*: European Travel Monitor (ETM), cited in Cockerell (1997, p. 49)
© Travel and Tourism Intelligence

nights, arrivals, number of beds, number of accommodation establishments, occupancy rates or length of stay may vary significantly between cities.

Therefore, to derive data on international patterns of urban tourism requires cities to conduct research using identical surveys and methodologies, while standardizing the terminology such as city, tourist, hotel, expenditure and trip. Since the reality of the situation is a multiplicity of different research studies and data lacking consistency, one has to work within the confines of what is available.

In the mid-1990s, Wöber was commissioned by the Federation of European Cities Tourist Offices (FECTO) to examine the harmonization of city tourism statistics (Wöber, 2000). This represents one of the major methodological breakthroughs in attempting to harmonize urban tourism data in Europe which is shown in Table 6.3.

*Table 6.3* Domestic and international visitor arrivals and bednights in selected urban tourism destinations in 1995 based on FECTO data

| Destination | Visitor arrivals | Bednights | Duration of stay |
| --- | --- | --- | --- |
| Aachen | 270,000 | 707,000 | 2.6 |
| Aix-en-Provence | m-d | 1,336,000 | m-d |
| Amsterdam | m-d | 6,584,300 | m-d |
| Athens | 2,057,479 | 4,689,178 | 2.3 |
| Augsburg | 263,000 | 416,000 | 1.6 |
| Baden-Baden | 244,000 | 771,000 | 3.2 |
| Barcelona | 3,090,000 | 5,674,580 | 1.8 |
| Basel | 314,457 | 606,080 | 1.9 |
| Berlin | 3,166,000 | 7,529,639 | 2.4 |
| Bern | 235,903 | 448,839 | 1.9 |
| Bonn | 491,245 | 1,037,372 | 2.1 |
| Bordeaux | m-d | 913,295 | m-d |
| Bratislava | 353,851 | 724,878 | 2.0 |
| Bregenz | 119,242 | 223,017 | 1.9 |
| Bremen | 484,753 | 896,212 | 1.8 |
| Brussels | m-d | 3,302,099 | m-d |
| Budapest | 1,636,909 | 4,327,671 | 2.6 |
| Cagliari | 129,000 | 290,000 | 2.2 |
| Cologne | 1,362,255 | 2,622,685 | 1.9 |
| Copenhagen | m-d | 3,080,000 | m-d |
| Dijon | 526,655 | 750,953 | 1.4 |
| Dublin | m-d | m-d | m-d |
| Dubrovnik | m-d | m-d | m-d |
| Dusseldorf | 1,088,768 | 2,163,253 | 2.0 |
| Edinburgh | 2,190,000 | 9,700,000 | 4.4 |
| Eisenstadt | 16,336 | 30,069 | 1.8 |
| Florence | 2,512,459 | 6,455,060 | 2.6 |
| Frankfurt | 1,794,636 | 3,174,009 | 1.8 |
| Freiburg | 330,024 | 623,426 | 1.9 |
| Geneva | 292,835 | 2,119,892 | 2.3 |
| Genoa | 432,941 | 1,058,200 | 2.4 |
| Gent | 211,000 | 404,000 | 1.9 |
| Glasgow | 1,500,000 | 6,900,000 | 4.6 |
| Graz | 246,420 | 479,439 | 1.9 |
| Hamburg | 2,271,694 | 4,164,533 | 1.8 |
| Heidelberg | 488,720 | 781,469 | 1.6 |
| Helsinki | 1,106,840 | 1,914,561 | 1.7 |
| Innsbruck | 598,277 | 1,005,526 | 1.7 |
| Karlsruhe | 260,854 | 501,678 | 1.9 |
| Klagenfurt | 140,703 | 327,575 | 2.3 |
| Lausanne | 260,000 | 623,000 | 2.4 |

| Destination | Visitor arrivals | Bednights | Duration of stay |
|---|---|---|---|
| Leipzig | 434,008 | 1,042,568 | 2.4 |
| Linz | 295,000 | 542,000 | 1.8 |
| Lisbon | 1,477,784 | 3,267,760 | 2.2 |
| Ljubljana | 140,950 | 313,192 | 2.2 |
| London | 22,611,000 | 103,300,000 | 4.6 |
| Lubeck | 357,837 | 825,370 | 2.3 |
| Lucerne | m-d | m-d | m-d |
| Luxembourg City | 308,948 | 683,043 | 2.2 |
| Lyon | 1,558,038 | 2,375,675 | 1.5 |
| Madrid | 4,281,000 | 8,371,630 | 2.0 |
| Malta | 1,115,000 | 10,919,000 | 9.8 |
| Manchester | 3,300,000 | 11,000,000 | 3.3 |
| Mannheim | m-d | m-d | m-d |
| Marseille | m-d | m-d | m-d |
| Milan | 2,532,402 | 6,004,656 | 2.4 |
| Moscow | 991,577 | 5,439,358 | 5.5 |
| Munich | 3,080,923 | 6,126,930 | 2.0 |
| Munster | 357,373 | 1,169,385 | 3.3 |
| Nice | m-d | m-d | m-d |
| Olomouc | 107,507 | 171,942 | 1.6 |
| Oslo | 1,300,839 | 2,101,578 | 1.6 |
| Padua | 377,500 | 825,500 | 2.2 |
| Paris | 11,345,751 | 24,813,248 | 2.2 |
| Prague | 1,805,286 | 5,104,409 | 2.8 |
| Regensburg | 251,084 | 485,041 | 1.9 |
| Rome | 554,849 | 13,346,206 | 2.4 |
| Rostock | 288,648 | 724,247 | 2.5 |
| Salzburg | 831,000 | 1,570,000 | 1.9 |
| San Sebastian | m-d | m-d | m-d |
| Zaragoza | 648,219 | 1,164,283 | 1.8 |
| Sintra | 71,640 | 189,580 | 2.6 |
| St Etienne | m-d | m-d | m-d |
| St Gallen | 77,000 | 181,000 | 2.4 |
| St Polten | 43,239 | 87,946 | 2.0 |
| Stockholm | m-d | m-d | m-d |
| Stuttgart | 807,323 | 1,554,000 | 1.9 |
| Tarragona | 233,010 | 349,550 | 1.5 |
| Toulon | m-d | m-d | m-d |
| Trier | 447,200 | 447,258 | 1.0 |
| Venice | 1,355,361 | 2,944,329 | 2.2 |
| Verona | m-d | m-d | m-d |
| Vicenza | 135,882 | 409,064 | 3.0 |
| Vienna | 2,806,057 | 7,049,710 | 2.5 |
| Warsaw | 1,341,000 | 2,048,000 | 1.5 |
| Wurzburg | 337,866 | 586,127 | 1.7 |
| Zagreb | 259,936 | 642,148 | 2.5 |
| Zurich | 938,149 | 1,791,000 | 1.9 |

*Note*: m-d = missing data; see Wöber (2000) for a discussion of the statistical generation of missing values for destinations. *Source*: Modified from FECTO (2000)

As Table 6.3 suggests, urban tourism is a major economic activity in many of Europe's capital cities but identifying the tourism markets in each area is problematic. In countries where the majority of accommodation is urban-based, such statistics may provide a preliminary source of data for research. While this may be relevant for certain categories of tourist (for example, business travellers and holiday-makers), those visitors staying with friends and relatives within an urban environment would not be included in the statistics. Even where statistics can be used, they only provide a preliminary assessment of scale and volume, and more detailed sources are needed to assess specific markets for urban tourism. For example, Page (1995) reviews the different market segmentation techniques used by marketing researchers to analyse the tourism market for urban areas to better understand the types of visitors and motives for visiting urban destinations (also see Kotler *et al.*, 1993).

Jansen-Verbeke (1986) points to the methodological problem of distinguishing between the different users of the tourist city and Burtenshaw *et al.* (1991) discuss the concept of functional areas within the city, where different visitors seek certain attributes from their city visit (for example, the historic city, the culture city, the nightlife city, the shopping city and the tourist city), where no one group has a monopoly over its use. In other words, residents of the city and its hinterland, visitors and workers all use the resources within the tourist city, but some user groups identify with certain areas more than others. Thus the tourist city is a multifunctional area which complicates attempts to identify a definitive classification of users and the areas/facilities they visit.

Ashworth and Tunbridge (1990) prefer to approach the market for urban tourism from the perspective of the consumers' motives, focusing on the purchasing intent of users, their attitudes, opinions and interests for specific urban tourism products. The most important distinction they make is between use/non-use of tourism resources, leading them to identify: (a) intentional users (who are motivated by the character of the city), and (b) incidental users (who view the character of the city as irrelevant to their use). This twofold typology is then used by Ashworth and Tunbridge (1990) to identify four specific types of users:

- intentional users from outside the city-region (e.g. holiday-makers and heritage tourists);
- intentional users from inside the city-region (e.g. those using recreational and entertainment facilities – leisure seeking residents);
- incidental users from outside the city-region (e.g. business and conference/exhibition tourists and those on family visits – non-leisure visitors); and
- incidental users from inside the city-region (e.g. residents going about their daily activities – non-recreational residents).

Such an approach recognizes the significance of attitudes and the use made of the city and services rather than the geographical origin of the visitor as the starting point for analysis. Although the practical problem with such an approach is that tourists tend to cite one main motive for visiting a city, any destination is likely to have a variety of user groups in line with Ashworth and Haan's (1986) examination of users of the tourist-historic city of Norwich. Their methodology involved tourists self-allocating the most important motives for visiting Norwich. While 50 per cent of holiday-makers were intentional users of the historic city, significant variations occurred in the remaining markets using the historic city. But this does confirm the multi-use hypothesis advanced by Ashworth and Tunbridge (1990) which was subsequently developed in a geographical context by Getz (1993). In fact, a range of studies, such as Oppermann *et al.* (1996), Timothy and Wall (1995) and Pearce (1998) have extended spatial descriptions of urban hotel locations and the resulting land-use patterns based on the initial arguments presented by Ashworth (1989). Having outlined some of the methodological issues associated with assessing the market for urban tourism, attention now turns to the behavioural issues associated with the analysis of tourist visits to urban areas.

## URBAN TOURISM: BEHAVIOURAL ISSUES

Any assessment of urban tourist activities, patterns and perceptions of urban locations will be influenced by the supply of services, attractions and facilities in each location. Recent research has argued that one needs to understand the operation and organization of tourism in terms of the *production* of tourism services and the ways in which tourists *consume* the products in relation to the locality, their reasons for consumption, what they consume and possible explanations of the consumption outcome as visitor behaviour. As Law (1993) argues:

> tourism is the geography of consumption outside the home area; it is about how and why people travel to consume ... on the production side it is concerned to understand where tourism activities develop and on what scale. It is concerned with the process or processes whereby some cities are able to create tourism resources and a tourism industry. (p. 14)

One framework developed in The Netherlands by Jansen-Verbeke (1986) to accommodate the analysis of tourism consumption and production in urban areas is that of the 'leisure product' (Figure 6.2). As Figure 6.2 shows, the facilities in an urban environment can be divided into the 'primary elements', 'secondary elements' and 'additional elements' (see Jansen-Verbeke, 1986 for a more detailed discussion of this approach). To distinguish between user groups, Jansen-Verbeke (1986) identified tourists' and recreationalists' first and second reasons for visiting three Dutch towns (Deneter, Kampen and Zwolle), where the inner-city environment provides a leisure function for various visitors regardless of the prime motivation for visiting. As Jansen-Verbeke (1986, pp. 88–9) suggests:

> On an average day, the proportion of visitors coming from beyond the city-region (tourists) is about one-third of all visitors. A distinction needs to be made between week days, market days and Sundays. Weather conditions proved to be important ... the hypothesis that inner cities have a role to play as a leisure substitute on a rainy day could not be supported.

Among the different user groups, tourists tend to stay longer, with a strong correlation with 'taking a day out sightseeing and visiting a museum' as the main motivation to visit. Nevertheless, leisure shopping was also a major 'pull factor' for recreationalists and tourists, though it is of greater significance for the recreationalists. Using a scaling technique, Jansen-Verbeke (1986) asked visitors to evaluate how important different elements of the leisure product were to their visit. The results indicate that there is not a great degree of difference between tourists' and recreationalists' rating of elements and characteristics of the city's leisure product. Thus, 'the conceptual approach to the system of inner-city tourism is inspired by common features of the inner-city environment, tourists' behaviour and appreciation and promotion activities' (Jansen-Verbeke, 1986, p.97). Such findings illustrate the value of relating empirical results to a conceptual framework for the analysis and replication of similar studies in other urban environments to test the validity of the hypothesis, framework and interpretation of urban tourists' visitor behaviour. But how do tourists and other visitors to urban areas learn about, find their way around and perceive the tourism environment?

| PRIMARY ELEMENTS | | SECONDARY ELEMENTS |
|---|---|---|
| **Activity place** | **Leisure setting** | • Hotel and catering facilities<br>• Markets<br>• Shopping facilities |
| *Cultural facilities*<br>• Concert halls<br>• Cinemas<br>• Exhibitions<br>• Museums and art galleries<br>• Theatres | *Physical characteristics*<br>• Ancient monuments and statues<br>• Ecclesiastical buildings<br>• Harbours<br>• Historical street pattern<br>• Interesting buildings<br>• Parks and green areas<br>• Water, canals and river fronts | |
| *Sports facilities*<br>• Indoor and outdoor | | |
| *Amusement facilities*<br>• Bingo halls<br>• Casinos<br>• Festivities<br>• Night-clubs<br>• Organized events | *Socio-cultural features*<br>• Folklore<br>• Friendliness<br>• Language<br>• Liveliness and ambience of the place<br>• Local customs and costumes<br>• Security | **ADDITIONAL ELEMENTS**<br><br>• Accessibility and parking facilities<br>• Tourist facilities: information offices, signposts, guides, maps and leaflets |

*Figure 6.2* Categorization of the leisure product

## TOURIST PERCEPTION AND COGNITION OF THE URBAN ENVIRONMENT

How individual tourists interact and acquire information about the urban environment remains a relatively poorly researched area in tourism studies, particularly in relation to towns and cities. This area of research is traditionally seen as the forte of social psychologists with an interest in tourism, though much of the research by social psychologists has focused on motivation (for example, see Guy and Curtis (1986) on the development of perceptual maps). Reviews of the social psychology of tourism indicate that there has been a paucity of studies of tourist behaviour and adaptation to new environments they visit. This is somewhat surprising since 'tourists are people who temporarily visit areas less familiar to them than their home area' (Walmesley and Jenkins, 1992, p. 269). Therefore, one needs to consider a number of fundamental questions related to

1. How well do tourists know the areas they visit?
2. How do they find their way around unfamiliar environments?
3. What features in the urban environment are used to structure their learning process in unfamiliar environments? and
4. What type of mental maps and images do they develop?

These issues are important in a tourism planning context since the facilities which tourists use and the opportunities they seek will be conditioned by their environmental awareness. This may also affect the commercial operation of attractions and facilities, since a lack of awareness of the urban environment and the attractions within it may

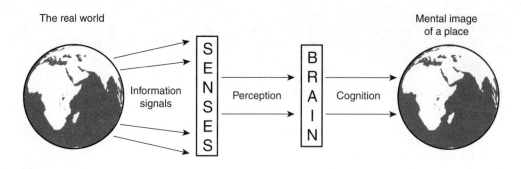

*Figure 6.3* Perceptions of place

mean tourists fail to visit them. Understanding how tourists interact with the environment to create an image of the real world has been the focus of research into social psychology and behavioural geography (see Walmesley and Lewis, 1993, pp. 95–126). Geographers have developed a growing interest in the geographic space perception of all types of individuals (Downs, 1970), without explicitly considering tourists in most instances. Behavioural geographers emphasize the need to examine how people store spatial information and 'their choice of different activities and locations within the environment' (Walmesley and Lewis, 1993, p. 95). The process through which individuals perceive the urban environment is shown in Figure 6.3.

Whilst this is a simplification, Haynes (1980) notes that no two individuals will have an identical image of the urban environment because the information they receive is subject to mental processing. This is conditioned by the information signals received through one's senses (e.g. sight, hearing, smell, taste and touch) and this part of the process is known as *perception*. As our senses may only comprehend a small proportion of the total information received, the human brain sorts the information and relates it to the knowledge, values and attitudes of the individual through the process of *cognition* (Page, 1995, p. 222). The final outcome of the perception and cognition process is the formation of a mental image of a place. These images are an individual's own view of reality, but they are important to the individual and group when making decisions about their experience of a destination, whether to visit again, and their feelings in relation to the tourist experience of place.

As Walmesley and Lewis (1993, p. 96) suggest,

> the distinction between perception and cognition is, however, a heuristic device rather than a fundamental dichotomy because, in many senses, the latter subsumes the former and both are mediated by experience, beliefs, values, attitudes and personality such that, in interacting with their environment, humans only see what they want to see.

Consequently, individual tourists' knowledge of the environment is created in their mind as they interact with the unfamiliar environment (or familiar environment on a return visit) they are visiting.

According to Powell (1978, pp. 17–18) an image of the environment comprises ten key features which include:

1. a spatial component accounting for an individual's location in the world;
2. a personal component relating the individual to other people and organizations;

3. a temporal component concerned with the flow of time;
4. a relational component concerned with the individual's picture of the universe as a system of regularities;
5. conscious, subconscious, and unconscious elements;
6. a blend of certainty and uncertainty;
7. a mixture of reality and unreality;
8. a public and private component expressing the degree to which an image is shared;
9. a value component that orders parts of the image according to whether they are good or bad; and
10. an affectional component whereby the image is imbued with feeling.

Among geographers, the spatial component to behavioural research has attracted most interest, and they derive much of their inspiration from the pioneering research by Lynch (1960). Lynch's research asked respondents in north American cities to sketch maps of their individual cities, and by simplifying the sketches, derived images of the city. According to Hollis and Burgess (1977, p. 155):

> Lynch developed a specific technique to measure people's urban images [where respondents drew] a map of the centre of the city from memory, marking on it the streets, parks, buildings, districts and features they considered important ... Lynch found many common elements in these mental maps that appeared to be of fundamental importance to the way people collect information about the city.

Lynch (1960) identified five important elements from the resulting maps. These were:

1. paths which are the channels along which individuals move;
2. edges which are barriers (e.g. rivers) or lines separating one region from another;
3. districts which are medium-to-large sections of the city with an identifiable character;
4. nodes which are the strategic points in a city which the individual can enter and which serve as foci for travel; and
5. landmarks which are points of reference used in navigation and way-finding (see Plates 6.4 and 6.5).

The significance of such research for the tourist and visitor to the urban environment is that the information they collect during a visit will shape their image of the place, influencing their feelings and impressions of a place. Furthermore, this imageability of a place is closely related to the legibility of place, defined by Walmesley and Lewis (1993, p. 98) as

> the extent to which parts of the city can be recognised and interpreted by an individual as belonging to a coherent pattern. Thus, a legible city would be one where the paths, edges, districts, nodes and landmarks are both clearly identifiable and clearly positioned relative to each other.

Although there may sometimes be confusion among individuals regarding recognition of Lynchean urban landscape elements, it does help researchers to understand how individuals perceive the environment. Even so, Walmesley and Lewis (1993) review many of the issues associated with the methodology of imagery research and raise a range of concerns about deriving generalizations from such results. Such studies do have a role to play in understanding how people view, understand and synthesize the complexity of urban landscapes into images of the environment. Nevertheless, criticisms of spatial research of individual imagery of the environment are that it imports methodologies and concepts from other disciplines. In a tourism context, Walmesley and Jenkins (1992) observe that tourism cognitive mapping may offer a number of useful insights into how tourists learn about new environments and for this reason it is pertinent to consider how visitor behaviour may be influenced by the ability to acquire spatial knowledge and synthesize it into meaningful images of the destination to assist them in finding their away around the area or region.

## TOURISM COGNITIVE MAPPING

Walmesley and Lewis (1993, p. 214) review the factors that affect visitor behaviour in terms of five interrelated factors which may initially shape the decision to visit an urban environment. These are:

1. antecedent conditions;
2. user aspirations;
3. intervening variables;
4. user satisfaction; and
5. real benefits.

These factors will, with experience, raise or reduce the individual's desire for recreational (and tourism) activity. The opportunities and constraints on visitors' behaviour are affected by income, disposable time available and a host of other socio-economic factors. Research by Stabler (1990) introduces the concept of 'opportunity sets' where the individual or family's knowledge of tourism opportunities is conditioned by their experience and the constraints on available time to partake in leisure and tourism activities. Thus, once the decision is taken to visit an urban environment, the tourist faces the problem of familiarity/unfamiliarity of the location. It is the latter which tends to characterize most urban tourist trips, though visitors are often less hesitant about visiting urban destinations if they live in a town or city environment.

Pearce (1977) produced one of the pioneering studies of cognitive maps of tourists. Using data from sketch maps from first-time visitors to Oxford, England, the role of landmarks, paths and districts were examined. The conclusion drawn indicated that visitors were quick to develop cognitive maps, often by the second day of the visit. The interesting feature of the study is that there is evidence of an environmental learning process at work. Walmesley and Jenkins' (1992, p. 272) critique of Pearce's (1977) findings note that:

(a) the number of landmarks, paths and districts increased over time;
(b) the number of landmarks identified increased over a period of 2–6 days, while recognition of the number of districts increased from 2 to 3; and
(c) the resulting sketch maps were complex with no one element dominating them.

A further study by Pearce (1981) examined how tourists came to know a route in Northern Queensland (a 340 km strip from Townsville to Cairns). The study indicated that experiential variables are a major influence upon cognitive maps. For example, drivers had a better knowledge than passengers, while age and prior use of the route were important conditioning factors. But as Walmesley and Jenkins (1992, p. 273) argue, 'very little concern has been shown for the cognitive maps of tourists' except for the work by Aldskogius (1977) in Sweden. For this reason it is interesting to examine the findings of one of the most up-to-date studies of tourism cognitive mapping: that of Walmesley and Jenkins (1992) relating to Coffs Harbour, Australia.

## COFFS HARBOUR: TOURISM COGNITIVE MAPPING OF AN UNFAMILIAR ENVIRONMENT

Coffs Harbour on the mid-north coast of New South Wales, with a population of 18,074 (1986), developed its tourism industry during the 1980s, with the northern coast providing a nearby resort area. While the area has traditionally depended on the domestic tourism industry, Coffs Harbour's development of tourist facilities has led to the evolution of an urban environment, where some degree of 'way-finding' problems exist for visitors. Using a sample of 115 tourists, the study sampled visitors at their accommodation centre, followed by a second stage sample at Coffs Harbour city mall in the town's central business district. Using a random sampling technique, the survey sought to gain some insight of the learning process associated with tourism cognitive mapping among the visitors to the region each year. Respondents were asked to draw a map of Coffs Harbour, and interviewers made no attempt to indicate the type of features to include. A random sample of 30 residents was also selected to aid comparison of the results to assess their learning experience relative to the visitors who were less familiar with the urban environment. A detailed questionnaire also sought to elicit information on the tourists' experience of cognitive mapping, their length of stay in Coffs Harbour and other salient data.

The results found that 48 landmarks and 30 different districts emerged. Visitors appear to learn about their new environment very quickly, with visitors staying an average of 4.36 days and reproducing maps with between 50–66 per cent of the features identified by residents. Those respondents who were car-drivers out-performed those respondents without a licence in terms of the accuracy and number of features included in the sketch maps. In addition, those respondents from 'capital cities included more landmarks, paths and districts than do respondents from country towns and rural areas' (Walmesley and Jenkins, 1992, p. 278). Thus, respondents from complex urban environments appear to learn more about other urban areas with ease, since they have experienced unfamiliar areas in their home region. This may also indicate that tourists from large cities think in terms of landmarks, paths and districts compared to those from rural areas.

One notable feature which Walmesley and Jenkins (1992, p. 279) observe is that:

> landmarks are the most important feature in the first several days immediately after arrival. The number of landmarks, paths, and distinct places known to the individual tourist in fact increases sharply for about 3 days. There appears to be a period of revaluation when the prominence of both landmarks and paths declines. For a time, then, districts feature strongly in tourist interpretation of the environment.

Thus, routes learnt in the early stage of a stay may be discarded later in favour of those which offer a less congested and shorter route based on the acquisition of new geographical knowledge. In other words, the tourists' learning experience of places is a constant process of revaluation, adjustment and development which fails to readily fit any existing models or theory.

Yet, as Walmesley and Jenkins (1992, p. 283) conclude, 'tourist maps are idiosyncratic, partial, and distorted versions of reality. The idiosyncratic nature is to be expected and is probably inevitable, given that individual tourists encounter and interpret the environment in a unique way.' Although their research points to the incomplete nature of some maps, implying a lack of knowledge of what attractions and facilities the city has to offer, it implies potential lost opportunities for the tourism industry as mentioned earlier. Their study also suggests that tourism marketing and publicity material needs to provide accurate rather than schematic maps of the urban environment which locate attractions and facilities. Such maps need to relate the location of tourism attractions and facilities to the structure of the city, and in this context brochures and materials (such as city A to Zs and tourist brochures which also guide tourists to attractions) are important to the visitor experience and ability to navigate around the city (see Lawton and Page, 1997 for an example of the value of tourist brochures in a city context). Where maps and diagrams fail to develop this important feature, visitors will find it difficult to locate and visit the attractions unless exceptionally good signposting is in place (see Plate 6.6). A follow-up study to Walmesley and Jenkins (1992) might pursue this issue a stage further by investigating how tourism facilities are cartographically represented (e.g. maps in guidebooks, pamphlets and leaflets) and the extent to which representations may lead to distortion or greater recognition of tourism districts and areas in relation to the overall structure of the city. For example, does a schematic map of the city's principal tourist attractions, which emphasizes landmarks and nodes, aid the tourist cognition process or does it actually have the opposite effect? Such research would have an important contribution to make to the tourism industry in view of the vast investment in glossy publicity and marketing literature. If research findings indicate that tourist perception and cognition is being adversely affected by inadequate maps and diagrams, they may be mis-representing the tourism structure of the city. It is possible that the tourists' image and cognition processes are being adversely affected by maps that neglect to relate services and facilities to features the visitor can readily identify during the early stages of a visit. Although there are obvious weaknesses in the cognitive mapping methodology (e.g. it relies on an individual's artistic and graphic skills), research methods which use visual elements and auditory stimuli may also offer a starting point for a more comprehensive assessment of how other environmental stimuli may influence a tourist's perception and image of a destination (see Burgess and Hollis, 1977 for a more detailed discussion of how to assess the quality of urban experience). Despite these criticisms, 'cognitive mapping provides major insights into tourist behaviour, not least by helping develop understanding [sic] of how previously unfamiliar environments are learned, interpreted, and subsequently used' (Walmesley and Jenkins, 1992, p. 284) by urban tourists. This has important implications for the quality of experience which destinations provide for urban tourists since the 'imageability' of the city and the ease with which a visitor can travel around the environment may be a major determinant of satisfaction. For this reason, attention now turns to issues of tourist satisfaction and service quality associated with urban tourism.

## SERVICE QUALITY ISSUES IN URBAN TOURISM

The competitive nature of urban tourism is increasingly being reflected in the growth in marketing and promotion efforts by towns and cities as they compete for a share of international and domestic tourism markets. Such competition has led to tourists' demands for higher standards of service provision and improved quality in the tourist experience. As Clewer *et al.* (1992) note, certain urban tourists (e.g. the German market) have higher expectations of service quality than others. But developing an appropriate definition or concept of urban tourism quality is difficult due to the intangible nature of services as products that are purchased and consumed. In the context of urban tourism, three key issues need to be addressed. First, place-marketing generates an image of a destination that may not be met in reality due to the problems of promoting places as tourist products (see recent studies by Gold and Ward, 1994; Gold and Gold, 1995; Tyler *et al.*, 1998; Ward, 1998). The image promoted through place-marketing may not necessarily be matched in reality through the services and goods which the tourism industry delivers (see Bramwell, 1998). As a result, the gap between the customer's perception of a destination and the bundle of products they consume is reflected in his or her actual tourist experience, which has important implications for their assessment of quality in their experience. Secondly, the urban tourism product is largely produced by the private sector either as a package or as a series of elements that are not easily controlled or influenced by the place-marketer. Thirdly, there are a large range of associated factors that affect a tourist's image of a destination, including less-tangible elements like the environment and the ambience of the city, that may shape the outcome of a tourist's experience. As a result, the customer's evaluation of the quality of the services and products provided is a function of the difference (Gap) between expected and perceived service. It is in this context that the concept of service quality is important for urban tourism. Gilbert and Joshi (1992) presented an excellent review of the then existent literature, including many of the concepts associated with service quality. In the case of urban tourism, it is the practical management of the 'gap' between the expected and the perceived service that requires attention by urban managers and the tourism industry. In reviewing Parasuraman *et al.*'s (1985) service quality model, Gilbert and Joshi (1992, p. 155) identify five gaps that exist between

1. the expected service and the management's perceptions of the consumer experience (i.e. what they think the tourist wants) (Gap 1);
2. the management's perception of the tourist needs and the translation of those needs into service quality specifications (Gap 2);
3. the quality specifications and the actual delivery of the service (Gap 3);
4. the service delivery stage and the organization/providers' communication with the consumer (Gap 4); and
5. the consumer's perception of the service they received and experienced, and their initial expectations of the service (Gap 5).

Gilbert and Joshi (1992) argue that the effective utilization of market research techniques could help to bridge some of the gaps. For:

Gap 1 – by encouraging providers to elicit detailed information from consumers on what they require;

Gap 2 – the management's ability to specify the service provided needs to be realistic and guided by clear quality standards;

Gap 3 – the ability of employees to deliver the service according to the specification needs to be closely monitored and staff training and development is essential: a service is only as good as the staff it employs;

Gap 4 – the promises made by service providers in their marketing and promotional messages need to reflect the actual quality offered. Therefore, if a city's promotional literature promises a warm welcome, human resource managers responsible for employees in front-line establishments need to ensure that this message is conveyed to its customers (see Chapter 5); and

Gap 5 – the major gap between the perceived service and delivered service should be reduced over time through progressive improvements in the appropriate image which is marketed to visitors, and the private sector's ability to deliver the expected service in an efficient and professional manner.

Such an approach to service quality can be applied to urban tourism as it emphasizes the importance of the marketing process in communicating and dealing with tourists. To obtain a better understanding of the service quality issues associated with the urban tourist's experience of urban tourism, Haywood and Muller (1988) identify a methodology for evaluating the quality of the urban tourism experience. This involves collecting data on visitors' expectations prior to, and after, their city-visit by examining a range of variables (see Page, 1995, for a fuller discussion). Such an approach may be costly to operationalize, but it does provide a better appreciation of the visitation process and they argue that cameras may also provide the day-to-day monitoring of city experiences. At a city-wide level, north American and European cities have responded to the problem of large visitor numbers and the consequences of mass tourism for the tourist experience by introducing:

1. *Town centre management schemes* (see Page, 1994a and Page and Hardyman, 1996 for further detail of this issue); and
2. *Visitor management schemes* (see Page, 1995 and Page *et al.*, 2001 for more detail on the development and application of such schemes).

Whilst there is insufficient space here to review these new management tools to combat the unwieldy and damaging effect of mass tourism on key tourist centres in developed and developing countries, it is notable that many small historic cities in Europe are taking steps to manage, modify and, in some cases, deter tourist activities. Yet before such measures can be taken, to improve the tourist experience of urban tourism in different localities, Graefe and Vaske (1987) argue that the development of a management strategy is necessary to

1. deal with problem conditions which may impact on the tourist experience;
2. identify causes of such problems; and
3. select appropriate management strategies to deal with problems (see Graefe and Vaske, 1987 for more detail on operationalizing this approach to improving the tourist experience).

## CONCLUSION

Tourism's development in urban areas is not a new phenomenon. But its recognition as a significant activity to study in its own right is only belatedly gaining the status it deserves within Tourism Studies. The reasons why tourists visit urban environments, to consume a bundle of tourism products, continue to be overlooked by the private sector that often neglects the fundamental issue – cities are multifunctional places. Despite the growing interest in urban tourism research, the failure of many large and small cities which promote tourism to understand the reasons why people visit, the links between the various motivations and the deeper reasons why people are attracted to cities remains a fertile area for theoretically informed and methodologically sound research. The continued problem for researchers is that the theoretically informed research on urbanization has not been adequately synthesized, integrated and embedded in the research studies of urban tourism in the last fifteen years. At a more practical level, even where cities are beginning to recognize the importance of monitoring visitor perceptions and satisfaction and the activity patterns and behaviour of tourists, all too often the surveys have been superficial, naive and devoid of any real understanding of urban tourism, even if such studies may have provided rich pickings for market research companies. For the public and private sector planners and managers with an interest, involvement or stake in urban tourism, the main concern continues to be the potential for harnessing the all-year-round appeal of urban tourism activity, despite the often short-stay nature of such visitors.

Where special events are harnessed as a mechanism to develop the urban tourism potential of a destination and its wider appeal to a range of visitors, research has only belatedly begun to move beyond a preoccupation with economic analyses to consider the wider consequences of urban tourism for both the tourist and host. The host experience of urban tourism has not been examined in this chapter, although a number of useful studies exist which address this growing issue. What is a common theme between the tourist and host experience of urban tourism is how such activity may also impact upon the social framework and community in which it is situated. This is accentuated during special events (see Barker *et al.*, forthcoming) such as the recent hosting of the America's Cup in Auckland, New Zealand and the effect on crime within the city for both visitors and residents.

The tourist experience of urban tourism, like the tourist experience *per se* is a complex phenomenon, a frame of mind, a way of being and, above all, more complex to researchers than a simple series of constructs which can be measured, quantified and analysed quantitatively. Why people like urban areas for tourist experiences is a perplexing and enduring question for researchers to answer and to begin approaching it – an interdisciplinary perspective, as engendered in this book, is a first starting point to cross into the realms of geography, planning, economics, social psychology and other social science subjects that help shed light on what it is that makes urban areas an attractive proposition for tourist experiences.

Ensuring that the urban tourist stay is part of a high-quality experience, where visitor expectations are met realistically through well-researched, targeted and innovative products, continues to stimulate interest among tour operators and other stakeholders in urban tourism provision. Yet, as the research reported in this chapter suggests, the urban tourism industry, which is so often fragmented and poorly co-ordinated, rarely understands many of the complex issues of visitor behaviour, the spatial learning process which tourists experience and implications for making their visit as stress free as possible. If researchers are still grappling with this topic, one can feel sure that the tourism industry does not have any unique proposition which universally appeals to the urban visitor.

These concerns should force cities seeking to develop an urban tourism economy to consider the feasibility of pursuing a strategy to revitalize the city-region through tourism-led regeneration. All too often, both the private and public sectors have moved headlong into economic regeneration strategies for urban areas, seeking a tourism component as a likely backup for property and commercial redevelopment (e.g. Lutz and Ryan, 1995). The implications here are that tourism issues are not given the serious treatment they deserve. Where the visitors' needs and spatial behaviour are poorly understood and neglected in the decision-making process, it affects the planning, development and eventual outcome – the urban tourism environment. Although the experience of waterfront areas in large cities has not been reviewed in this chapter, recent research which reviews the ambitious schemes to market tourism in such locales has seen a continued series of missed business opportunities and a range of business failures (see Page, 1994b for further discussion of this issue). Yet there are also some resounding success stories, and what continues to ensure viability is the production of clusters and a threshold of tourist activity in a geographically defined area that the visitor can grasp and within which he can feel comfortable, particularly with concerns of safety and security within urban areas. Therefore, tourist behaviour, the tourism system and its constituent components need to be evaluated in the context of future growth in urban tourism to understand the visitor as a central component in the visitor experience. Managing the different elements of this experience in a realistic manner is requiring more attention among those towns and cities competing aggressively for visitors, using the quality experience approach as a new-found marketing tool. Future research needs to focus on the behaviour, attitudes and needs of existing and prospective urban tourists to reduce the gap between their expectations and the service delivered. But ensuring that the tourism system within cities can deliver the service and experience marketed through promotional literature in a sensitive and meaningful way is now one of the major challenges for urban tourism managers. The approach adopted by the tourism industry needs to be more proactive in its pursuit of high-quality visitor experiences rather than reactive towards individual problems that arise as a result of tourist dissatisfaction after a visit. Research has a vital role to play in understanding the increasingly complex reasons why tourists continue to visit urban environments and the factors which influence their behaviour and spatial activity patterns. While urban tourism continues to be a recognized and established form of tourism activity, research by the academic community and private sector has really only paid lip service to what is a central feature of the tourism system in most developed and developing countries.

# Chapter 7

---

# Special event motives and behaviour
*Donald Getz and Joanne Cheyne*

## INTRODUCTION

Special events, from the visitor's perspective, provide opportunities for leisure, social or cultural experiences outside the normal range of choices or beyond everyday experience (Getz, 1991, 1997). By implication, travel motivated by events should be centred on attaining unique benefits and should involve unusual behaviour.

Better knowledge of the event experience, and the ways in which customers buy or develop event-related packages, will enhance event marketing and event tourism. Some of the key questions include: What motivates specific event tourist segments? Who attends events, and under what circumstances? What constitutes an attractive event travel package? What messages or promised benefits work best to attract target markets? Do people feel and behave differently at special events, and if so, what are the implications for the planning and marketing of events?

Research on motivation to attend events and related event behaviour has expanded considerably over the past decade, although many questions remain only partially answered. In particular, as will be seen in the following literature review, more work is required to differentiate event motives and behaviour by locals as opposed to event tourists. Accordingly, this chapter summarizes related literature and, assisted by some qualitative research conducted in New Zealand, raises new questions. Progress in this field allows formulation of a framework or model for assessing event motives and behaviour, and this is presented in the chapter's conclusions.

To define 'motive' we defer to Iso-Ahola (1982, p. 230) who said: 'A motive is an internal factor that arouses, directs and integrates a person's behavior.' The event-goer wants to satisfy one or more needs through attendance or participation in the event, so event-related motivational studies must address not merely the reasons given for being at an event but also the underlying benefits sought. 'Behaviour' in this context refers to more than superficial activities at events; it refers also to the meanings attached to those actions. For example, having a party is generally fun, but is also likely to involve social bonding or cultural celebration.

In the ensuing sections a number of perspectives on events are taken, with a literature review incorporated in each. We start with an anthropological and sociological examination of events, and particularly of festivals.

## ANTHROPOLOGICAL AND SOCIOLOGICAL PERSPECTIVES

### Symbols of fun

Festivals, celebrations, and other 'cultural performances' are rich in meaning and provide a 'text' by which much can be learned of the host culture and community. As explained by Manning (1983), celebration is performance: 'it is, or entails, the dramatic presentation of cultural symbols'. Celebration is public, with no social exclusion, is entertainment for the fun of it, and is participatory – actively involving the celebrant who takes time out of ordinary routine, and 'does so openly, consciously and with the general aim of aesthetic, sensual and social gratification'.

Festivals are themed, public celebrations (Getz, 1991) and have become one of the most common forms of modern special events. To Falassi (1987) the festival is unique:

> At festival times, people do something they normally do not; they abstain from something they normally do; they carry to the extreme behaviours that are usually regulated by measure; they invert patterns of daily social life. Reversal, intensification, trespassing, and abstinence are the four cardinal points of festival behaviour.

MacAloon (1984) emphasized that 'Festival demands engaged participation, leaving little room for dispassionate behaviour ... Festival means being there; there is no festival at a distance.' Festivals provide their own energy source, according to Abrahams (1987), in the form of role playing, confrontations, noise, spectacle, movement, costumes, entertainment, games, contests and nonsense. Carnival (and Mardi Gras) are special types of celebration which Turner (1983) called a form of play embodying rituals of reversal. The term 'carnival' has come to be associated with partying and licence, whereas 'festival', in most instances, is associated with a more sedate atmosphere. Accordingly, the name of the event can potentially influence motives and behaviour.

### Festivals as celebration

While many special events are true celebrations, or entail a celebratory component, many fall into the less complex realm of entertainment and spectacle. In essence, these events do not require or permit engagement by the audience; they are to be viewed or passively experienced. MacAloon (1984) argued that spectacle and festival are in opposition to each other. He further demonstrated through an analysis of the Olympics how events can embody a number of genres at once: spectacle (larger-than-life, visual performance); festival (celebration and a feeling of joy); ritual (invoking sacred forces to effect social and spiritual transformations) and games (play, humour, and competition).

Festivals and celebrations that are true cultural performances display common elements, or building blocks. Falassi (1987) observed that festivals begin with a 'valorization' (or 'sacralization') of the setting, a ritual which modifies the usual and daily function of the place. Any number of rites will follow, including rites of purification, of passage, ritual dramas, rites of exchange and competitions. When the event is over, a 'devalorization' ritual is commonly performed. Thus the festival-goer is tangibly and emotionally 'freed' from routine and enters willingly and with anticipation into a temporally and spatially special environment. Special event programmers know very well how to accomplish this through ceremonies and well-designed ambience.

Some festivals are constructed as tourist attractions that should lure tourists to destinations. For example, in Fiji today the Hibiscus Festival in Suva, the Sugar Festival in Lautoka, the Bula Festival in Nadi and various other festivals have become natural parts of the national culture. However, when the festivals were started, they were constructed as tourist attractions to lure tourists to Fiji (Bossen, 2000).

## Benefits of participation

The benefits obtained by participation in special events are diverse and complex. True festivals and celebrations involve the event-goer in social and cultural processes that might be invisible and subtle, such as community-building and reinforcement of values, all of which might be seen as 'belonging and sharing'. More visibly, the celebration engages people in settings and times that are clearly out of the ordinary, foster a sense of joy and often permit and even encourage licence in terms of behaviour. Other special events, however, emphasize spectating and passive entertainment. They, too, are attractive for being out of the ordinary, but their form and meanings are much less complex.

Formica and Uysal (1998) examined cultural authenticity as a motivator to attend the Spoleto Festival, and other events that combined cultural and historical elements. Ethnic events have been associated with cultural identity, pride and promotion (Carlson, 1998). Similarly, gay and lesbian event-related travel has been linked to the need for group identity and bonding (Pitts, 1999). Specific to sport events, Bale (1989) suggested that travel to mega-events was symbolic, or 'collective rituals', like a pilgrimage. Green and Chalip (1998, p. 277) concluded from a study of a women's sport event that participants valued the opportunity 'to come together to celebrate the subculture they share as women football players'.

## Unruly behaviour

Festivals, and in particular carnivals, engage the participant in an emotional experience – even to the point of fostering unruly behaviour. Event organizers and community authorities often tolerate a 'party atmosphere' and a degree of licence during special events, but, unfortunately, they occasionally get out of control. In a well-documented case, Cunneen and Lynch (1988) evaluated an annual series of riots in Australia in the 1980s at a motorcycle race event. They concluded that the riots inverted, temporarily, the established power relationships between youth and police in a highly symbolic and institutionalized manner. Alcohol consumption figured prominently in the conflicts.

But as police restrictions increased, the play element of the event was diminished and the seriousness of the conflict increased – thus controls became counterproductive.

The Province of British Columbia, Canada, undertook a major investigation of riots and other undesirable behaviour at a number of community festivals and events (Province of British Columbia, 1992). Alcohol, and the failure of authorities to adequately police its sale and consumption, was blamed for much of the problem. It was noted, however, that some events gained such a reputation for behavioural licence that young people would travel to the events for the purpose of unruly behaviour, rather than for the event programme itself. Cancelling one event could lead to the problem shifting elsewhere.

A similar phenomenon is the 'sports hooligan', the subject of much research and debate. While sports fixtures share much with other types of special events, there are important differences. Many of the problems at sports events stems from fan behaviour – fans being more emotionally involved than mere spectators. Competitions often bring together fans of opposing teams and place them in settings which foster antagonism. Moreover, the heavily committed and aggressive fan is likely to possess quite different socio-demographic characteristics from other spectators, being, typically, male, young and from lower-income or social classes (Pooley, 1979; Centre for Leisure Research, 1984).

The nature of many sports as ritualized conflict (e.g. football, hockey, basketball) make them inherently different from festivals, which stress belonging and sharing, and other sports which are forms of entertainment or spectacle (e.g. swimming, track and field) or are individualistic in nature (e.g. golf). The behaviour of athletes, officials and coaches can also contribute to rising emotion and antagonism. Research into crowd or collective behaviour in general sheds light on the subject. As summarized by Pooley: 'Individuals who join large groups anticipate a relaxation of "normal" controls and a tolerance for usually prohibited behaviours. Accordingly, an apparent gain of freedom may be associated with increased conflict' (1979, p. 9). Getz (1991) discussed strategies for dealing with events that go bad: change of name, theme or venue; de-marketing or re-targeting to new segments; changing the sponsors or even the organizers; moving the time; programme alterations (e.g. banning alcohol). For the most part, festivals and other special events can easily avoid the more common problems of unruly behaviour among sports fans. Even where alcohol consumption and a party atmosphere are features of the event, attention to atmosphere, target marketing, security and management of crowd flows will usually ensure better behaviour.

## LEISURE THEORY

Attendance at events is, for most people, a leisure experience; that is freely chosen for its intrinsic rewards. Several leisure theories or constructs can be applied effectively to the event experience and related motives.

'Leisure' as a construct involves a number of dimensions (Horna, 1994, p. 41) which can clearly be realized at events: absorption or concentration on the ongoing experience; lessening of focus on the self; feelings of freedom or lack of constraint; enriched perception of objects and events; increased intensity of emotions; increased sensitivity to feelings; and decreased awareness of the passage of time. Closely related is the concept of 'flow', which was described by Csikszentimihalyi (1975) as being achieved whenever a person is in optimal interaction with the environment. It is a positive feeling, related to play, which Smith (1990, p. 41) described as 'the experience of total, intrinsically satisfying involvement in an activity in which an individual's skills are in balance with the challenges posed by the activity'. Participation in sports and hobbies can result in 'flow', and so, too, can work.

While it is generally conceded that people 'need' play and leisure, can it be argued that people need festivals and special events? Given the ancient history of festivals, sports and cultural events of all kinds, it might easily be concluded that they form an inherent and irreplaceable part of civilization – and, consequently, are 'needed'.

Maslow's (1970) hierarchy of needs offers a theoretical framework for examining event-related motives and benefits. As with other forms of leisure, events can motivate or satisfy people on different levels: basic physical needs (providing exercise, relaxation, food, sexual gratification, earning a living); interpersonal or social needs, including self-esteem and the esteem of others (being with and meeting people, access to cultural traditions, celebration, belonging and sharing, competing and volunteering); and personal needs, including aesthetics and self-actualization (education, appreciation of the arts, discovery, participation and learning). However, research has not been undertaken to link types of events and event experiences with fulfilment of the various levels of need, and other scholars like Iso-Ahola have rejected the notion of a needs hierarchy (Crompton and McKay, 1997).

A widely accepted leisure theory with direct bearing on travel motives was developed by Iso-Ahola (1982). This 'seeking and escaping' model suggests that people are simultaneously motivated to seek rewards and to escape from their routine, both on personal and interpersonal dimensions. Thus an event provides the opportunity for achieving an optimal level of arousal, but the motive to attend also depends on the potential customer's environment, needs and preferences. Some events will be more successful in certain environments because of the 'push' or 'escape' factors, even when the programme is identical.

Ajzen and Driver's (1992) theory of planned behaviour is also relevant. It is used to predict leisure intentions and behaviour, suggesting that intentions to perform activities (e.g. event attendance and behaviour) can be predicted from attitudes, subjective norms and perceived behavioural control with respect to the activities. One of the major conclusions of the application of the theory to leisure choice was that people seem to evaluate a leisure behaviour in terms of its instrumental costs and benefits as well as in terms of the positive or negative feelings it engenders.

## TRAVEL AND TOURISM MOTIVES

Pleasure travel is a form of leisure entailing a special set of motives and rewards. Tourism demand and, accordingly, event attendance are the outcome of tourists' motives, as well as marketing, destination features and contingency factors such as money, health and time relating to the traveller's choice of behaviour (Morrison, 1989).

Gray (1970) identified two basic reasons for pleasure travel: 'wanderlust' (essentially a push factor) and 'sunlust' (a pull factor). Crompton (1979) presented nine motives influencing selection of types of pleasure vacations and destinations, each of which were further divided into being either socio-psychological (push) or cultural (pull) factors. Krippendorf (1989, p. 16), like Crompton and Gray, presented a relatively simple approach to travel motivation, seeing it as a search for balance. He even suggested that 'everyday life is bearable in the long run only if there is a chance to get away'.

Moving away from descriptive approaches to travel motivation, Dann (1977) reinforced motivational concepts of Maslow's hierarchy of needs, but still emphasized the 'push' factors associated with travel (Pearce, 1982). One of the first to take a psychological approach to tourist behaviour and motivation was Pearce (1982), and as Mansfield (1992) observed, with this approach, the larger the number of motivators influencing travel behaviour, the more difficult it becomes to distinguish each separate motive, to evaluate its relative importance as a trip generator and, hence, to predict any future travel behaviour as its basis.

To Horna (1994, p. 188) the compulsion to visit certain attractions and events with tradition and high profile is like a pilgrimage. Related to this notion is the theory that modern tourists seek 'authenticity' in their travels (MacCannell, 1976), that is, the genuine experience of a different culture or way of life. Events provide tangible access to culture in ways that many built attractions cannot, especially through direct host–guest interaction. Accordingly, some tourists will seek out events in which cross-cultural contacts are high. Also, attending some events will entail the feeling of a 'must see', or 'once-in-a-lifetime authentic experience'.

Building on earlier psychological work (Pearce, 1982), and again using Maslow's hierarchy of needs, Pearce and Caltabiano (1983) designed a descriptive tool to combine biological and social/psychological motives within one framework. It was argued that there exists a motivational career in travel, with more experienced travellers emphasizing higher needs than less experienced travellers (Kim, 1994). Pearce (1988) concluded that the Travel Career Ladder model contains five hierarchical steps affecting tourist behaviour (see Figure 2.1). People at the lower level emphasize basic services and enjoy a sense of escape, whereas people at the higher levels are concerned with developing their skills, knowledge, abilities and special interests. Tourists at a certain stage of their travel career seek to satisfy specific needs, so that different satisfaction levels depend on their travel career level (Kim, 1994).

Applied to events, the travel career ladder might suggest either that events should cater to all levels, or that events can be targeted to segments defined by stages in the ladder. A related approach was suggested by Getz (1991) in which essential services (required by all), generic benefits (sought by all) and targeted benefits (aimed at specific segments) form a comprehensive event offering. Furthermore, as market segments mature, the products themselves might have to change to conform with a demand-based life-cycle based on higher-order needs.

Ryan (1994) argues that a strong tourist motivation to derive enjoyment from the holiday experience becomes a determinant of behaviour. He suggests that two viewpoints of holiday career can be said to exist. First, the developmental viewpoint argued by Pearce, where holiday-makers learn and so progress along the hierarchy towards higher needs, and, secondly, the process of early habits becoming ingrained, whereby tourists repeat that process found to be satisfactory on earlier trips. Both viewpoints stress the importance of the holiday experience as a determinant of future behaviour. If both extreme viewpoints are seen as simplistic, then the process of development or confirmation of behaviour arises from the satisfaction gained from the holiday trip. The process of confirmation of development, therefore, is a function of (a) actual experience, (b) perception of the experience as satisfactory or unsatisfactory and (c) personality in terms of whether that experience is a trigger for returning to the destination, or for exploring new places (Ryan, 1994).

## RESEARCH ON TRAVEL MOTIVES FOR EVENTS

A growing number of event patron studies have been reported in the tourism and event management literature. However, many have not compared or separated traveller and resident motives or behaviour adequately. The ensuing review first looks at festival-related studies, then sports.

Backman *et al.* (1995) analysed data from the 1985 National Travel Survey (USA), focusing on a sub-sample of respondents who had attended a festival or special event, or had taken a trip to an exhibition. Motivational dimensions identified for this sub-sample were: excitement; external; family; socializing and relaxation (explaining, together, about 66 per cent of variance). Family size and income did not explain motivational differences, but older respondents were less interested in excitement.

Uysal *et al.* (1993) examined the Travellers' Rest County Corn Festival in South Carolina and Mohr *et al.* (1993) studied the Freedom Weekend Aloft hot-air balloon festival in Greenville, South Carolina. Both studies employed the seeking–escaping theory of leisure and travel motivation of Iso-Ahola. The Uysal *et al.* study identified five dimensions through factor analysis, all of which explained 63 per cent of variance: escape; excitement and thrills; event novelty; socialization; and family togetherness. Demographic variables did not explain motivational differences, except for marital status related to 'family togetherness'. Although not statistically significant, the analysis suggested that older respondents placed greater emphasis on event novelty and that 'excitement and thrills' were less important to higher-income visitors. Repeat visitors did demonstrate significant differences from first-timers, as they were more interested in event novelty and socialization factors. There were also significant differences between weekday and weekend visitors.

The research by Mohr *et al.* (1993) also found that demographic variables did not explain motivational differences. Results of factor analysis yielded similar dimensions, although the order was somewhat different – socialization ranked highest, not escape. They did find that repeat visitors to the festival, who did not attend other events, were very loyal and motivated most by excitement, and least by event novelty. Again, it was found that different types of visitors, with different motives, attended on different days of the week. Weekday visitors were wealthier and travelled further. Significant differences were also found between visitor types and their level of satisfaction with the event, with the highest satisfaction scores coming from repeat visitors to the festival.

Research by Saleh and Ryan (1993) on a Canadian jazz festival revealed that a portion of the event-goers were dedicated event tourists who travelled specifically because of their special interests. One implication was that the greater the distance travelled, the more concerned people were about programme quality. Other studies have also focused on situation-specific motives. Gitelson, Kerstetter and Kiernan (1995) examined motives for attending an educationally themed festival and found that most respondents sought benefits related to the exhibits. Scott (1996) compared motives across three types of festival and uncovered six dimensions: nature appreciation; event excitement; sociability; family togetherness; escape; and curiosity. He concluded that the type of festival is the best predictor of motives.

Crompton and McKay (1997) evaluated motives for attending Fiesta San Antonio, with a sampling of mainly residents. They concluded that prestige or status was relevant in motivating pleasure travel, but not for residents attending festivals. Also, 'escape' factors were less important than 'seeking' factors. Patrons attending food events were found to be much less interested in cultural exploration and significantly more likely to be motivated by the 'novelty/regression' factor. Most festival-goers 'were eager to engage in cultural exploration, but they wanted to do so in the company of familiar faces' (p. 437). Crompton and McKay did not incorporate a 'family togetherness' domain in their motivational statements, but concluded that it was important for festivals. These researchers also stressed that multiple motives are likely to apply when people attend events, and recommended that festival motivation studies should include six dimensions: cultural exploration, novelty/regression, recover equilibrium, known-group socialization, external interaction/socialization and gregariousness.

Kerstetter and Mowrer (1998) examined patrons' reasons for attending a First Night festival. Most respondents were residents and repeaters. Despite the alcohol-free theme, that dimension was only moderately important. The 'family fun' factor displayed the highest overall mean scores, but none of the motivational dimensions they tested were really strong. The researchers speculated that this occurred because little was invested or at risk in attending the festival.

Formica and Uysal (1998) reported on research from the Spoleto Festival, with emphasis on the cultural authenticity of this event. Spoleto's main appeal to travellers was its combination of culture and history. They argued, from their findings, that some events are so unique that they attract enthusiasts, whereas community or rural festivals typically attract more people looking for 'family togetherness' benefits and short getaway trips. Formica and Murrmann (1998) also reported on Spoleto, specifically examining the relationship between social groups and motives for attending. Their analysis found that factors named 'socialization' and 'entertainment' explained almost half of the variance. This reflected the dominance of family-and-friend groups at the event. However, the main motives of couples could not be isolated, but the evidence suggested that they did not enjoy the festival as much as others.

Carlson (1998) wrote about the growth of ethnic festivals in the USA, particularly Cinco De Maya celebrations. These events are linked to increasing immigration and pluralism in American society and offer participants the opportunity to either party or express cultural pride. Carlson said (p. 14): 'the festival has become a means whereby all ethnic groups are able to maintain a sense of self-identity and promotion within their community'.

Research by Light (1996) studied historical enactments as events in South Wales. The characteristics of visitors on event and non-event days were compared and it was apparent that the events were particularly appealing to local residents and were successful at encouraging repeat visits. It was also concluded that visitors to events stayed longer than average and considered that they had learned something from their visit. However, Light also concluded that there was no evidence that events were broadening the market, as socio-demographic characteristics of visitors on event days were similar to those on non-event days.

Turning to sport events, Nogawa, Yamaguchi and Hagi (1996) studied two 'sport for all' events in Japan, where the emphasis was on the joy of participation and health or fitness, not on winning. They found that, regardless of travel duration, the 'health/ fitness' and 'challenge' motivators were paramount among participants.

Gillis and Ditton (1998) compared tournament and non-tournament recreational bill-fish anglers as to their motives. This sport attracts mostly the wealthy elite and they are highly sought-after tourists. The researchers found the respondents to be mostly interested in the challenge of sport fishing, and the experience of catching large specimens. Raybould (1998) also studied motives for participating in a fishing event, this one a week long in a remote, Australian location. His research found that 'social stimulation' and 'escaping' motives were rated highest. Most respondents were male, and 'family togetherness' ranked lowest. The statement 'because the event was unique' achieved the highest individual mean response, and it was included in the 'social stimulation' factor. The researcher concluded that organizers should emphasize the social and relaxation benefits and make less of the extrinsic rewards (i.e. prizes) and competitive elements.

The Travel Industry Association of America (1999) produced a report called *Travelscape Profile of Travelers Who Attend Sport Events*. About 40 per cent of American adults are sport event tourists, including more men than women. Women have a higher preference for amateur, compared to professional, sports, in large part reflecting their children's activities. This research found that the sport event itself motivated 76 per cent of organized sport event travellers, while 13 per cent said the event was a secondary reason for the trip and another 11 per cent said it was just a trip activity. Of all the sport event trips recorded (the most recent ones taken), 84 per cent were for spectating, 16 per cent were for participating and some did both. Travelling to watch a child or grandchild play a sport is popular.

## QUALITATIVE RESEARCH ON EVENT MOTIVES AND BEHAVIOUR

There are limitations to survey-based research at events. The questions are pre-determined and respondents are not allowed to modify the statements, nor add to the list. There is the risk both of forcing responses in the direction of confirming the underlying theory and of missing important dimensions. Furthermore, only visitors are covered, so that results apply only to the particular segments attending. General market research (such as omnibus surveys) is needed, but traditionally large-scale surveys have not isolated specific types of festival and event visits, so that focused analysis has not yet been possible. Also, qualitative research methods will be useful in conjunction with, or prior to, surveys when exploring event motivation. Techniques such as focus groups and interviews, along with observational methods, are even more important when exploring actual behaviour at events.

A small-scale qualitative study was undertaken specifically to assist in preparation of this chapter in the first edition of this book. The purpose was to delve more deeply into general motives to attend events (especially to travel to them), consumers' perceptions of benefits, behaviour at events and how choices are made. Two small convenience samples were selected for combined group and individual interviews: one consisting of university students, the second comprising university staff and faculty members. Each session lasted about 60 minutes and consisted of three parts: (1) completion of a short, individual questionnaire on leisure pursuits and preferences; (2) a group discussion; and (3) short, individual interviews on the subject of a recent event-related trip.

The self-completion questionnaire was intended to get respondents thinking about how special events fit into their lifestyle and leisure behaviour. It also created a good introduction for the round of individual interviews which followed group discussions. Group discussion followed a prepared set of questions and prompts. As each respondent had already indicated their general leisure and travel behaviour and preferences on the questionnaire, the purpose of the open group discussion was mainly to generate possible benefits of attending events, a range of event-travel and event-attendance behaviours, and ideas on how choices were made about attending events versus other pursuits, and among events. Each respondent started the individual interviews by re-examining or revising their initial questionnaire responses. Most of the interview involved the profiling of a recent event experience.

This qualitative approach does not prove or disprove any existing theory about event motivation, behaviour or benefits obtained through attendance at events. Rather, it allows researchers to gain potentially new insights based on actual experiences and freely expressed attitudes, as opposed to the usual practice of leading respondents with predetermined, categorized questions.

**Work, leisure and event attendance**

Six participants were students, two of whom also held a job, four were lecturers in business studies, and the remaining five held staff positions in the university (one of whom was also a student). Only three of the fifteen respondents said that their work or study involved any recreational activities. Of those answering in the affirmative, one indicated a connection with tourism studies and one listed social outings. Three tourism students (two of whom answered 'no') noted a potential connection between work and leisure either through field trips or studies of resorts. One sport management student also replied in the affirmative. The connection between travel, events and pursuit of knowledge came up several times in the group discussions, with respondents suggesting that it might be the social environment, rather than simply the nature of work, that led to related leisure activities.

There is a potential connection between almost any hobby or leisure pursuit and special events, as virtually every interest group has associated events. This is particularly true for sports, and when asked to list their main leisure/recreational interests ten of fifteen respondents mentioned at least one sport. It is also true for music and the arts in general, which were also mentioned by ten (including crafts, theatre, movies, singing, concerts, festivals, art exhibitions, listening to music, tapestry). Of greater interest, four respondents were interested in events (namely theatre, festivals, concerts and art exhibitions). There is a possible response bias here, as the theme of the focus groups was apparent in the questionnaire, and the respondents might not be representative of the population as a whole. But there is certainly no inconsistency with the types of leisure pursuits mentioned or the subsequent discussion, suggesting that events do figure prominently in some people's leisure lifestyles. When asked what it was that they did most frequently when travelling for pleasure, four of fifteen listed events:

sports events; festivals; attending shows; going to special events. Group discussion suggested that many respondents felt that events were not a strong reason to engage in pleasure travel (although the number of event trips generated appears to be high), but that events were something to do for socializing and while travelling. Consequently, many of the pleasure travel motives, such as the frequently mentioned visiting friends or relatives (six respondents), could easily result in an event excursion. Similarly, those who indicated an interest in museums and art galleries (three respondents) might find a special exhibition provides the extra incentive for a trip.

## Patterns and preferences of event attendance

The questionnaire asked 'When was the last time you attended a festival or special event, and what exactly was it (name or type of event)?' Fourteen of fifteen listed a specific event and ten of these gave actual dates within the previous three months, showing a very high level of event attendance. It is most unlikely that any unusual exogenous factors influenced this level of event attendance. The interviews were held in spring, while most New Zealand events are held in summer, and the host city does not have a particularly well-developed event calendar.

The types of events mentioned are most interesting in that they were not at all prompted; respondents were essentially asked to self-define festivals and special events. The list included five festivals (flowers, gardens, wine/food and film themes); two musical shows; two lifestyle shows/expos; and one each of motor show, sports meet, consumer expo, conference, farm show and horse show. In part, this list will reflect the opportunities available to these particular respondents, but the list does demonstrate a considerable breadth. Perhaps surprisingly, given the higher level of interests in sports demonstrated in previous and subsequent answers, sports were only mentioned once. This could suggest that many sports events were not considered to be 'special'.

Four of the five festivals mentioned were attended by females, suggesting the possibility of gender preferences. Their events included three flower or garden festivals (springtime favourites in New Zealand). It is well-established in the literature that arts in general attract more females than males, so this might apply as well to certain types of festivals. The emphasis respondents placed overall on socializing at events, however, suggests that mixed-gender groups of families and friends are the norm at festivals and many other special events. Sports might be an exception, as males typically dominate certain sports crowds.

When asked what types of events they enjoyed, most respondents listed two or more, of which sports were the most frequent (ten of fifteen), followed by shows of various types (six mentions) and festivals (five, of which one was implicit). No-one left this question unanswered, although at least one participant clearly was not an event-goer.

## What makes events special?

Respondents were asked on the questionnaire: 'What do you think makes an event special compared to regular events?' Responses can be grouped into three categories:

*1. Uniqueness – not-usually-available opportunity*

- out-of-the-ordinary type of attraction
- rarity
- something unique
- different activities
- novelty

These terms might all be synonymous, or further exploration might have revealed subtle but closely interrelated differences. For example, 'novelty' might imply a personal evaluation of the event related to one's past experiences, while 'out of the ordinary' might imply bizarre or weird. 'Rarity' clearly pertains to frequency of availability, but 'something unique' might encompass frequency and types of experiences.

*2. Atmosphere*

This was only listed once, but based on other answers and group discussion it is likely to be more important than this single response suggests. The emphasis placed by respondents on socializing at events, for example, suggests strongly that the right atmosphere is a necessary prerequisite to group enjoyment. So, too, does the mention of people-watching, variety and other elements related to atmosphere.

*3. Quality*

- well-presented and run
- reputation
- calibre of the participants; best in their field
- size
- international scope; from around the world
- presence of stars or very important persons

Interestingly, the presence of stars or international-calibre persons was applicable to both sports and arts/music events. This might be related to the remoteness of New Zealand, and its small size, but it definitely helps separate regular sports fixtures from 'special' sports events, so it could be universal in its applicability. Quality, therefore, is a factor relating to both the management of the event and who is featured in it. 'Reputation' might apply both to the event (or to the organizers) and to the persons featured. 'Size' is another universal criterion, but obviously relative to the population base of the host area and to the size of the regular range of events. 'Big' is associated with 'special'. To a degree, the presence of international or world-calibre stars is covered by the above elements, but it could be that their presence could imply 'specialness' in the absence of large-scale or 'calibre'. Thus an event promoting itself as being international in scope – without big names – could be perceived as being 'special'.

**Motives and benefits**

The group discussion was opened by asking respondents if there were a lot of festivals and special events in New Zealand to choose from. The predominant answer was no, there were not as many events as there could be, especially when compared with other countries. Also, there was a feeling that within New Zealand most festivals and special events take place in the main centres, Auckland and Wellington. Some of the respondents answered that there were a lot of special events to choose from, but they were mainly sports. There was a suggestion that perhaps there may be a lot of events, but people may not know about them.

Time, cost, social factors and life interests came through strongly in response to the question 'How does one decide which festivals and special events to attend?' The time taken to get to an event and how the event fits into other plans, especially holiday plans, were important and were mentioned first by both focus groups. Obviously, distance comes into the time factor, as does cost, which also came through strongly in impacting on decisions. The other two factors which respondents mentioned often as being important in deciding which events to attend were, first, what friends, family and workmates were doing and, second, that decisions were dependent upon one's interests. It was said that people go to the events that relate to things in which they are interested.

Another factor which was mentioned several times was that respondents would go to festivals or special events with 'rarity value', such as major musical shows or one-off exhibitions. Social factors were important, for example, when decisions about events depend on decisions made by friends and family. Also, some respondents said they might go to an event because 'everyone else is going', even though they may not be interested in the event theme or type of sport. One was also more likely to go to an event if an acquaintance or family member was involved in it, and one might decide to go to an event as 'an excuse' to get out of town or as a break from routine.

When discussing the benefits gained from attending events, the two benefits mentioned most often were: (a) socializing with friends and (b) the chance to get away and to do something different. Associated with the first benefit were comments on meeting new people and seeing different sides of friends through being in different situations. Associated with the second main benefit were: the chance to gain new experiences and knowledge; the chance to experience different cultures; enjoyment; entertainment and excitement.

### Event behaviour

The question 'What unique things do people do at festivals and special events?' prompted a strong feeling that people are more relaxed at events, and this feeling provides opportunities for getting to know friends better. Meeting new people was also suggested as a unique thing done at festivals. It was also noted that people get drawn into 'crowd behaviour', and might even get patriotic, especially at international sporting events. Finally, there was some discussion of people using more senses at events, as in generating a heightened emotional state. It was also felt by most of the group members that event attendance can be an excuse for intoxication.

### Selecting from choices

When asked which of four specified events they would specifically want to attend and why, responses were obtained from each member of the group. These are shown in

*Table 7.1* Focus group findings

| Event | Number choosing this event (groups 1 and 2 combined, number out of a possible 15) | Reasons for choosing |
|---|---|---|
| Sydney's 2000 Summer Olympics (Australia) | 10 | • An opportunity to go to Sydney – to see the other attractions of Sydney<br>• Interested in the Olympics/sport<br>• Once-in-a-lifetime opportunity – proximity to NZ |
| Calgary Stampede (Calgary, Canada) | 4 | • To go to Calgary<br>• Heard/read about event<br>• To see culture of country<br>• Something different<br>• Because family want to go |
| A wine and food festival in New Zealand (there are many) | 7 | • To learn more about NZ and about wines<br>• Because of the wine and food<br>• Because of a special interest in wine<br>• A fun thing to do |
| Festival of the Arts (Wellington, New Zealand) | 6 | • Interested in art<br>• Something different<br>• Because of the international nature of the performers<br>• Chance to see artists not seen often |

Table 7.1. The most popular event was the 2000 Summer Olympics, held in Sydney. The most common reason was that it was seen as a once-in-a-lifetime opportunity, being especially convenient for New Zealanders. Also, some said they would go to the Olympics because it was a chance to go to Sydney.

When asked to identify any other events that they were looking forward to attending, and why, the responses indicated they would attend events that reflect their own interests. Someone interested in cars and racing would go to a car race, for example the Nissan Mobil 500, held in Wellington, and someone interested in basketball would like to go to an NBA game in the USA. It would seem that when thinking of events that they would like to attend, people select those related to existing interests, but they are likely to attend others that their friends are attending or which are perceived as unique.

**Recent event experiences**

In the third part of the research, respondents were asked to individually profile a recent event experience of their choice. Most respondents were able to give details of a recent experience that was still fresh in their minds. Of the profiles obtained (from seven males and seven females), eight pertained to out-of-town trips and five were local experiences. The remaining event was experienced abroad, during an extended visit. The local events included one sport match, one festival, a ballet performance, lifestyle show and home show. Trips were made to three festivals, two sport matches, two concerts and a museum exhibit. Analysis concentrated on identifying major insights on decision-making and event experience packages.

It was again revealed that socializing is both a powerful motive and recognized benefit of event attendance. The average group size was described as between two and four persons. Many decisions in this sample were actually made by others, or in deference to the preferences of significant others (such as making a birthday gift out of an event-related trip). Sports, however, are a type of event that some people do not mind attending alone.

Some of the events, namely concerts and sports, offered less opportunity for generating unusual experiences. They were local, did not require special travel arrangements and involved mostly spectating. However, learning was identified as an important motive, and local events can equally offer this benefit.

This group of respondents revealed that trying something new was important, and that taking photographs, watching people, eating and drinking, shopping, and socializing were in different ways associated with event experiences. The nature of event experiences were said to be dependent on a number of variables, including the venue, crowd, the group one is with, weather and the attitude or expectations one attends with.

One very important observation made in this research is that event experiences can easily be substituted. When the event is perceived to be an excuse for a trip, a social outing or an opportunity to try something new, the exact nature of the event matters less. This places events squarely in a competitive environment where marketing-mix decisions will be very important in drawing customers. Indeed, respondents revealed that both word-of-mouth and advertisements were influential in some of their decisions.

## SUMMARY AND CONCLUSIONS

This chapter has addressed the problem of understanding event-related motives, especially as they stimulate travel, and the related topic of behaviour at special events. Increased theoretical knowledge and market research in these areas will undoubtedly aid event producers to better cater to the needs and preferences of their target audiences, and should improve the tourism attractiveness of events.

Event-specific research on motives and behaviour has revealed that traditional socio-economic and demographic variables often do not explain differences between consumers. Results tended to confirm the seeking–escaping model, with key dimensions being: escape; excitement and thrills; novelty; socializing; and family togetherness. Differences between first-time and repeat visitors were confirmed. However, visitor surveys are limited in their scope, and qualitative techniques must be further developed to explore these issues. In addition to generic motives and benefits, there are many who seek event-specific benefits stemming from the theme, sport or programme.

In the exploratory qualitative research conducted for this chapter, a number of important observations were made. The centrality of social motives and behaviour at events were highlighted, including the fact that decisions to attend events might often be made for reasons other than direct interest in the event product. Getting away is a common motive, but events have to compete with many other attractions and activities;

hence, events can be packaged and substituted. However, the social benefits of attending events in groups are well recognized by consumers, and this provides a strong competitive advantage when compared to other attractions. Insights were gained on how people define 'special' events, under the headings of uniqueness, atmosphere and quality. Several unique dimensions of event behaviour and emotions were revealed, stressing relaxation, trying new things, socializing in different ways, watching people, eating and drinking, photo-taking and shopping. The nature of the event experience was shown to be dependent on venue, weather, the crowd, who the consumer comes with and their expectations or attitudes. Thus, what people bring to events might be as important as what they find there.

This study did not permit detailed analysis of a potentially interesting question: Are there packages of leisure interests that predispose some individuals to attend events, or types of events, more than others? It could be hypothesized that life interests, say in sports, arts or culture, are more likely to include event trips than life interests in individual hobbies like gardening, sightseeing, reading, watching television and so on. Given the high incidence of event-going demonstrated by the study sample, however, it seems more likely that life interests are connected more to the types of events attended, and possibly frequency of attendance.

Motives for attending events seem to follow closely general theories on motivation for leisure and travel. One of the major conclusions of Ajzen and Driver's theory of planned behaviour to leisure choice was that people seem to evaluate a leisure behaviour in terms of its instrumental costs and benefits as well as in terms of the positive or negative feelings it engenders. It was observed in the current research that events were not always seen as being a reason for travelling, but how events fit in with holiday plans was important in any decision to attend events; often events were seen as a chance to get away, and provided something to do while on holiday. This relationship needs to be explored in more detail.

**Theoretical framework**

Figure 7.1 provides a general framework for evaluating and researching motives to attend events. It is clear from research findings that multiple motives may apply to any given event visit, so the overlapping circles represent possible combinations. First, generic leisure and travel motives incorporate the related theories of seeking-escaping (Iso-Ahola) and needs fulfilment (Maslow). Seeking-escaping embodies personal and interpersonal dimensions. For event-related travel, escaping might be the precondition even if respondents fail to identify its importance. Residents are less likely to be motivated primarily by escape, with the novelty of events and their unique, targeted benefits (the so-called 'pull' forces) being predominant. The hypothesis that events can satisfy all levels of the needs hierarchy remains untested.

Event-specific motives stem from the inherent uniqueness of events (every one is a different mix of people, management and setting) and targeted benefits related to the theme and programme. For example, festivals can attract cultural tourists, art lovers and history buffs. Sports attract fans of particular teams and games. These can be built on top of generic appeals in order to grow the event's audience, although it is necessary to consider the risk of attracting incompatible groups.

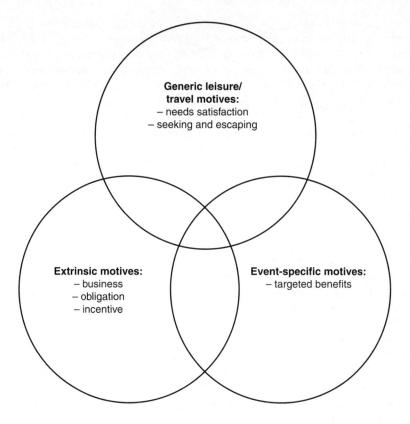

*Figure 7.1* Framework for evaluating event motives and behaviour

Finally, there are a number of extrinsic motives that can apply, that is, unrelated to any specific appeal of the event itself. Some might attend out of obligation (e.g. because friends or family want to go), others for work-related purposes. Incentives might be offered to induce people to attend who do not really have an interest in the event, or they might receive an event package as a reward. These people might very well end up enjoying the event, though they came for a completely different set of reasons.

A case can also be made for a fourth generic category of motives consisting of 'accidental tourists' or 'casual bystanders'. That is, some people might simply find themselves being caught up in an event, and they could prove to be a significant component of event audiences in popular tourist areas or places where residents gather frequently. However, their original motives are independent of the event, and marketing to them is akin to encouraging spontaneous purchases.

Figure 7.2 covers the special problem of separating tourists from residents. Those who travel for events must have an underlying set of generic travel motives that apply to everyone who leaves home for pleasure or work, and so the 'escape' motives are more important. Tourists search for cultural authenticity when attending events away from home, and this is different from residents' motives. More prosaically, tourists might simply follow the crowd of other tourists or residents when attending events, on the assumption that the others know what is interesting. Finally, many visitors are taken to events by friends and relatives, and this introduces extrinsic motives.

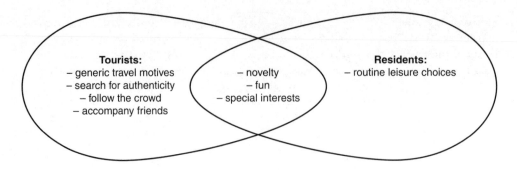

*Figure 7.2* A framework for evaluating event motives by residents and tourists

Tourists and residents share a number of motives, especially those related to event-specific motives such as the theme and programme. Special interests abound, and so a mix of tourists and residents can be expected at most events (conferences and meetings, however, might appeal exclusively or mainly to travellers). Novelty and fun are also generic motives shared by residents and tourists, although when respondents say they are looking for fun they do have underlying needs to meet.

Residents' decisions to attend events might be motivated by routine leisure choices, rather than any desire to experience something new or unique. An event might simply be a way to spend time with friends and family or a substitute for another routine form of recreation. In this context, socializing is the predominant generic motive for most forms of public leisure pursuits, so it is deserving of special consideration.

**Future research**

Considerable potential exists for qualitative research to build on the understanding of event motives and behaviour. First, direct observation of event behaviour is necessary to codify and explain several key factors that shape the event experience, for example:

- social groups (types, sizes, malleability, actions);
- interactions between visitors with other visitors, with the setting, and with the staff and management system;
- mechanisms by which behaviour can be influenced (towards management's aims and away from unruly activities);
- differences between event types, settings and management systems in explaining behaviour.

International comparisons are strongly suggested. The type of qualitative research described herein can be refined and adapted to provide insights on how different cultural groups perceive and consume events, and how event production and tourism marketing can be improved accordingly. Results of qualitative research can form the basis of subsequent quantitative testing, or be fed directly into the planning and marketing process.

More research effort is needed to compare tourist and resident motives in a way that will yield practical marketing implications. In a tourism context, not only must needs, motives and benefits be better understood, but destination and event attractiveness, marketing efforts, barriers and personal contingency factors will also shape decisions to travel. Some events can succeed on the basis of their authenticity, while others are so unique as to foster a must-see, once-in-a-lifetime attitude.

# Chapter 8

# Memories of the beach

*Chris Ryan*

## IS-LAND OR IN-LAND: A FURTHER MARGIN

There is little doubt that for many tourists the beach remains a popular destination. For centuries coastlines have fascinated human beings. For many centuries the beach represented the fringe between the known and the, often frighteningly, unknown. For Lencek and Bosker (1998), in their history of the beach, the beach is a history of paradise on earth. Today, few are perplexed by the question of what lies beyond the horizon, but humans are still drawn. Perhaps it is an unconscious genetic memory of the origins of life, or a wish for the comfort of the liquids of the womb. Whatever the reasons, coastlines in the modern period have exerted an attraction for tourists that has resulted in millions of people travelling to the coast for holidays each year. From a historical perspective it was not always so. While comfortable Romans may have built villas by the side of the sea, the 'seaside' as a tourist attraction is comparatively modern. Initially, as Jarvis (1993) among other historians has discussed, the seaside was a place of medical recuperation – a rather specific form of re-creation. It was a place one went in order to obtain benefit – a process that conforms to the sanctions of behaviour that, as noted in Chapter 1, Rojek (1993) discerns in his explanation of the history of tourism. That today it is seen as a form of pilgrimage for millions does indeed imply a distinctive change of 'gaze', whereby the tourist views the beach as a place of relaxation, fun and idleness. If the beach does 'good', it is in a far more self-indulgent way than was considered by early eighteenth-century medical practitioners.

Beaches have thus changed their function, but also retain an ambivalence. Our Victorian forbears were aware of that ambivalence. At one time it was common to bathe nude, but with the greater use of the beach came the bathing-hut and the bathing-costume. But historians have noted that as attempts were made to protect Victorian proprieties, so, at the same time, the questions of sex were being highlighted. Beaches are marginal littoral strips neither of land nor sea; a site of rest and relaxation, which while, in part, private, are also places of bodily disclosure where both sexes can stare and imagine fulfilling the sexual adventure of their 'beachtime' books and papers.

Much has been written of holidays as compressed time-space experiences of fantasy and escape – realms that lie outside of 'normal' daily experience, and it is within this discourse that the appeal of beaches can be found, and it is that which makes islands and shores unique holiday destinations (Urry, 1990; Rojek, 1993). Ryan (1995) has postulated that differences exist between the coastlines of the mainland, and those of islands.

It is noted that islands are attractive tourist destinations but although having a commonality, upon closer examination the homogeneity dissolves. Islands that are successful holiday destinations are not characterized by common size, climate or even coastline. There are significant differences between the islands of the Mediterranean and those of more temperate zones, such as the Chathams, the Hebrides or the Orkneys. Yet these groups of islands attract tourists. Ryan argues that the one constant factor is a concept of culture of an island; that the differences are not simply geographical, but rather lie in the 'gaze' of the tourist. Thus he notes that

> Islands are, for tourists, 'is lands'; lands of the immediate present freed from concerns of future mortgages and pensions; locations of beaches that skirt and contain the land safely from an appealing but uncertain sea. Perhaps, in using rational techniques it is not possible to assess the uniqueness of the island as a tourist destination – all that is identified is variation upon variation, but nonetheless a variation without a theme. It is in this consumer perception of 'is-lands' of geographically confined space and historical/cultural strangeness that the unifying theme of the island might be found – an irrationality not sensitive to empirical exploration. (Ryan, 1995, p. 8)

Thus a distinction is drawn between the 'is-land' and the 'in-land'. On the mainland the tourist can leave the beach at the end of the day and retire to the haven of home, away from both the promise and the uncertainty of the sea, whereas upon islands the sea is a continuous presence. The island represents an escape wherein the person can attempt to find themselves. Indeed, some holidays are based explicitly upon this very notion. One of the foremost examples is that of the Skyros Experience, a holistic holiday where participants can meditate, engage in the arts and experience a social communion with like-minded people.

## BEACHES AND FUN

As both geographical and psychological margins, beaches are one of the few areas where it is socially tolerated for adults to have fun as distinct from leisure. The literature of leisure studies and recreation has observed a growing industrialization of leisure. Leisure is had in leisure centres. Facilities are booked in advance. Leisure has become high-tech, with carbon-fibre masts for wind-surfers, the use of air bubbles in sports shoes to absorb impact, and Goretex and Lycra to make the participant look good while they sweat. Leisure is encouraged by companies to aid workers' efficiency and thereby make profit. So, ask commentators like Podilchak (1991), what has happened to the simply spontaneous and silly? For Podilchak fun has four dimensions; it is

1.  doing things on the surface, being silly, laughing;
2.  as growing out of an activity, being purposeless;
3.  exciting, exhilarating – unique, not everyday; and
4.  a shared experience with others who are also open, relaxed and carefree.

By comparison, leisure and recreation are more premeditated, involving a choice from alternative behaviours. This is illustrated by Hendersen and Bialeschki (1994) in their analysis of women and their participation in leisure. Various coping behaviours are identified which lead to different typologies of female participants in leisure. These are the 'achievers', 'attempters', 'compromisers', 'dabblers' and 'quitters/defaulters', depending upon their ability to overcome responsibilities and other perceived constraints upon leisure. Such a categorization might also apply to males, albeit that the nature of the constraints and the attitudes displayed by males may vary.

None the less, in such an analysis of leisure, as requiring pre-planning, there is much to support Gunn's point when he notes that:

> As it was formalized and institutionalized, recreation became whatever the proponents and agencies created as policy. Some recreational professionals draw a strong distinction between that which is an end in itself and that which is purposeful, claiming that the former is negative whereas the latter is positive. Leisure, engaged in for its own sake, provides no focus; those recreational activities accepted by society as wholesome, creative and uplifting are worthy of public support. (1988, p. 13)

On the other hand, both Crompton (1979) and Cohen (1979) have observed that tourism offers opportunities as a 'sanctioned escape route' and a 'regression into childhood'. Nowhere, perhaps, is that better illustrated than by behaviour on the beach. Fathers, who perhaps rarely exercise, play cricket or throw frisbees on the beach with their children, parents throw youngsters into and over the waves. Sand gets into the sandwiches, adults eat childish foods with relish and no-one cares. Yet here, too, gender and age differences can be observed. Teenage females will play beach volleyball with their male counterparts, but mothers tend to sit watching over the children. Teenagers use the beach as a meeting-place with those of the opposite sex. The body is exposed, in some nudist beaches totally, and the healthy and the shrivelled are on full view.

This quick review raises many issues. First, is the beach totally free from the industrialization of leisure? Secondly, what are the motivations of beach users? Thirdly, why does the beach have this air of freedom that is denied to many other aspects of both leisure and tourism?

## THE INDUSTRIALIZATION OF THE BEACH

So far the beach has been presented as the epitome of spontaneity. The word 'spontaneity' is often used as implying not simply carefree but also active, involving movement. That, of course, is not always the case in the way in which tourists use the beach. It is a place of idleness, of feeling the warmth of the sun upon the skin, even to the point of possibly risking skin cancers. Certainly, incidents of sunburn rate high on lists of 'minor' health complaints identified by holiday-makers (see Ryan and Robertson, 1997). Leisure and recreation in the sense described by Gunn, however, denies this idleness of the beach. Leisure, almost by definition, means 'doing something'. Thus the planners move upon the beach!

Some beaches are now highly organized. A tour through the internet will reveal some excellent examples, some of which are specifically orientated towards certain markets.

Three examples will be used. First, the Daytona Spring Break '95 describes the break as follows:

> Spring Break in Daytona Beach is hot. Twenty-three miles of wide, smooth, sandy beaches. Driving directly on the beach. Great accommodations. Outrageous clubs. Concerts. Exhibitions. Free stuff. And thousands of college students from every corner of the continent ... But whatever, don't blow it. Break with the rest of the world at the Spring Break capital of the universe. Daytona Beach. During Spring Break, there are many exhibits and activities on the beach. The competition is friendly and there are loads of freebies from companies marketing their products. There are many activities available including surfing, skimming, surf fishing, volleyball, jet skiing and more. Best of all, you'll be surrounded by students from all across the continent who are eager to soak up the sun and meet new people. Spring Break offers one concert after another.
> (http://www.america.com/mall/store/springbreak/kids.gif: June 1995)

The beach includes such attractions as the *Sports Illustrated* Beach Club, which includes diverse sports like the bungee jump, sumo wrestling and jousting. And the page includes answers to the ten most asked questions about Spring Break, including 'Why will my parents want me to go to Daytona Beach?' The answer is that along with the hottest nightclubs and the 200–400,000 students, there is also a Career Fair.

Many of these beach events have a long history. For example, in 1995 the 44th Annual Sun Fun Festival was held at Myrtle Beach, South Carolina. Here, highlights included a 'Little Olympics', a 'Miss Sun Fun Pageant', a 'Beach Run', a 'Sun Fun Air Show', a 'Watermelon Eating Contest' and a 'Sandcastle Building Contest' (Myrtle Beach Area Chamber of Commerce, 1995). This example indicates not only the long history of organized beach leisure, but also a difference of emphasis – in this case an emphasis upon shared family activities.

The very size, milieu and organization of beaches can be contrasted. For example, the internet page on Pacific Grove commences:

> In 1875, a Methodist summer retreat set up their tents on the edge of Monterey Bay near Lover's Point. In time, the tents became small board and batten cottages. Then beautiful churches and grand Victorians sprung up throughout the village. In 1889 Pacific Grove was incorporated. Since then it has maintained its quiet comfort and charm. People came from all over to taste and smell the sea air and to walk the trails lined with lilac and wind blown cypress ...
> That natural beauty still exists today ... Awaiting you are great seasonal celebrations, parks and playgrounds, gourmet restaurants, unique shops and galleries, scuba diving, kayaking, golf, surfing or just cruising the shoreline recreation trail and soaking up all the beauty that is Pacific Grove. (http://www.montereybay.com/pgdir2/pg-page1.html, 2001)

However, from being carefree places, beaches are increasingly managed places. And managed places are measured places. Perhaps the clearest indication of this are the criteria for the Blue Flag scheme that is operated by the European Union under the Bathing Water Directive (76/160/EEC). At the time of writing (June, 2001), this is under review, but not yet amended due to the expectation that the World Health Organisation will announce guidelines for safe environmental and recreational waters. However, in 2000 the European Commission issued a communication notifying member states that new criteria were to be established. Currently the criteria number 27 for beaches and sixteen for marina, and are classified under four main headings, namely water quality, environmental education and information, environmental management, and safety and services. A key concern has been the bathing water quality and the two

*Table 8.1* Microbiological and physiochemical criteria for bathing water quality

Microbiological parameters:

| Parameter | Guideline values | Accepted % test results higher than guideline value | Imperative values | Accepted % test results higher than imperative values |
|---|---|---|---|---|
| *Total colibacteria* | 500/100 ml | 20 % | 10,000/100 ml | 5 % |
| *Faecal colibacteria* | 100/100 ml | 20 % | 2,000/100 ml | 5 % |
| *Faecal streptococci* | 100/100 ml | 10 % | – | – |

Physicochemical parameters:

| Parameter | Guideline values | Accepted % test results higher than guideline value | Imperative values | Accepted % test results higher than imperative values |
|---|---|---|---|---|
| *pH* | 6 to 9 | 5 % | | |
| *Colour* | No abnormal change | 5 % | | |
| *Mineral oils* | *Water*: No film visible on the surface and no odour *Land*: The beach must be monitored for such pollution, and emergency plans should cover response in case of oil pollution (see criterion 3). Municipal land-side sources must also be identified and managed | 5 % | | |
| *Surface active substances* | No lasting foam | 5 % | < 0.3 mg/L | 10 % |
| *Phenols* | No specific odour | 5 % | | |
| *Transparency* | Secchi depth > 1 m or 'No abnormal decrease' when > 1 m cannot be respected for geographical reasons | 5 % | Secchi depth > 2 m | 10 % |
| *Tarry residues and floating materials such as wood, plastic articles, bottles, containers of glass, plastic, rubber or any other substances* | Absence of sewage solids both in water and on land | 5 % | Absence of any of the mentioned items in the water and on land | 10 % |

main sets of parameters, the microbiological and physiochemical, which are set out in Table 8.1. One important issue relates to coliform content in that it is possible (but increasingly unlikely) that a beach may gain a Blue Flag where coliform content is not counted if such counts are not part of a national policy. However, a state must first provide evidence as to why such a policy is thought proper, and, secondly, if a beach is affected by any sewage-related or land waste run-off, then remedial action must be undertaken as soon as is possible. There are equally important requirements for action where waters are affected by tarry substances.

The regulations also state that a beach must have at least one sampling site but, more importantly, the number and location of sampling sites must reflect the concentration of bathers along the beach as well as sources potentially affecting the water quality at the beach.

The sampling must first of all be done where the concentration of bathers is highest. Quoting directly from the website www.blueflag.org/frameset/criteria.htm (as at June, 2001) the regulations proceed to state that the location of sampling sites must also reflect the location of potential sources of pollution. Samples must be taken near where streams, rivers or other inlets enter the beach in order to provide documentation that such inflows do not affect bathing water quality. Alternatively, the inflowing water must have been analysed at source, documenting that it meets the Blue Flag bathing water quality criteria. Similarly, in the case of inland waters, where the water is supplemented by outside sources during dry periods, the water quality of that outside source must meet the Blue Flag bathing water quality criteria. Additionally, samples should be taken 30 cm below water surface, except for the mineral oil samples, which should be taken at surface level. An independent person officially authorized and trained for the task must collect samples and an independent laboratory must carry out analysis of bathing water quality. The laboratory must be nationally or internationally accredited to carry out microbiological and physicochemical analyses. In addition, the laboratory must be authorized for the task of collecting and analysing the bathing water by the authority responsible for the implementation of the national regulation on bathing water quality and monitoring. The sampling has to be undertaken, first, within the fortnight before the beginning of the official bathing season, and during the bathing season sampling must be carried out at least fortnightly. The last sampling of the season must be taken within one fortnight of the last date of the bathing season. Additional regulations relate to the levels of treatment to which all waste water should be subject before it is discharged into the sea, and these criteria are summarized in Table 8.2.

This period of the bathing season has been one that has been significantly criticized, especially by organizations that represent all-year-round users. For example, Surfers Against Sewage have led active campaigns in general on issues pertaining to water quality, and specifically against water authorities like those of South West England, when they considered that water authorities would deliberately utilize the off-season for the discharge of poorly or non-treated sewage.

As environmental groups have generated more political awareness and harnessed public support for their concerns relating to the environment, so, too, the legislative authorities have begun to adopt more proactive stances over poor performance. This was made evident in January and May 2001 when the European Commission decided to proceed to the Court of Justice against Denmark for the non-respect of the Bathing Water Quality Directive. With regard to Belgium, the Commission has decided to take the first steps in the procedure to enforce an earlier judgment of the Court. Commenting on the decision, Environment Commissioner Margot Wallström said: 'I would urge both Denmark and Belgium to put the compliance of their bathing waters with Community standards at the top of their agenda for 2001' (www.waternunc.com/gb/dg11en47.htm, June 1st, 2001).

There exists good reason for such concerns. From around the world there are reports of the health of swimmers and other recreational water users being put at risk. For example, McBride *et al.* (1998) conducted interviews of over 3800 beach users at seven New Zealand beaches, combined with tests for water quality at these beaches. They reported that:

*Table 8.2* Guidelines for water discharge treatment

| Size of settlement (p.e.): Type of area: | < 2,000 | 2,000–10,000 | 10,000–15,000 | 10,000–150,000 |
|---|---|---|---|---|
| *Freshwater +* *estuary – sensitive* | appropriate treatment (by 31.12.2005) | secondary (by 31.12.2005) | stricter than secondary | stricter than secondary |
| *Coastal – sensitive* | appropriate treatment (by 31.12.2005) | appropriate treatment (by 31.12.2005) | stricter than secondary | stricter than secondary |
| *Freshwater +* *estuary* | appropriate treatment (by 31.12.2005) | secondary (by 31.12.2005) | secondary (by 31.12.2005) | secondary (by 31.12.2005) |
| *Coastal* | appropriate treatment (by 31.12.2005) | appropriate treatment (by 31.12.2005) | secondary (by 31.12.2005) | secondary |
| *Coastal – less* *sensitive* | – | – | at least primary | at least primary |
| *Estuary – less* *sensitive* | – | at least primary | secondary (by 31.12.2005) | secondary (by 31.12.2005) |

> Log-linear modeling showed that enterococci was most strongly and consistently associated with illness risk for the exposed groups, particularly for respiratory illness among paddlers and long-duration swimmers. Crude risk differences for these 2 groups were 7 and 33 per 1000 individuals, rising to 62 and 87 per 1000 individuals for the highest enterococci quartile. (McBride *et al.*, 1998, p. 173)

In short, while not overly serious, for specific groups of beach users, poor water quality adversely impacted on health at statistically significant levels. Such results are being reported from all over the world. To provide but two more examples: first, in a study of a sample of 18,741 beach-goers in Hong Kong, Holmes and Kay (1997) found risks associated with swimming and a specific correlation between water quality and health risks. They concluded that pollution control authorities would be judged by their ability not to meet specific standards of water quality *per se*, but whether they were actually attempting to improve water quality at minimum cost. A Swiss study by Chamot (1998), of 153 swimmers at four Lake Leman beaches, found 555 reported probable cercarial dermatitis at follow-up, of whom about half had had recourse to drug treatment. They concluded that past history of skin complaints, time spent in water, hour of the day, barometric pressure, maximum daily temperature and time spent in the water were all predictors of disease occurrence at given levels of water pollution.

There is a growing awareness that good water quality is an important selling point for beaches and each year, as more beaches gain ratings as to their water quality, so tourism and governmental bodies proclaim the news in attempts to retain or attract more beachgoers and their money. It is thus being recognized that beaches, as part of a water and tourism system, have financial value, are assets and, like many assets in capitalistic systems, require investment. Thus, for example, in the United Kingdom a £600 million investment was announced in November 1999 by the Director General of Water Services as part of a £7.4 billion water industry package for water improvements. By March 2005, the government intends that (a) all significant sewage discharges will receive at least secondary level treatment, and that even higher levels of treatment are provided where necessary to protect bathing or shellfish waters, (b) over 3800 unsatisfactory storm outflow pipes will be improved, and (c) bathing water standards will improve so that they reach at least 97 per cent compliance against normal EU standards – and help more resorts to gain Blue Flag status.

That beaches are increasingly subject to management in terms of ensuring that the waters are free from pollution is understandable not only in terms of human health, but also for the maintenance of natural environments and aesthetics. Yet the industrialization of the beach in the sense of it being managed for human consumption is beginning to go beyond these concerns. Increasingly, not only are beaches being groomed daily as required, for example, to obtain a Seaside Award from the Keep Britain Tidy Group, but also they are being costed and measured in many terms including aesthetics and facilities. Morgan (1999) describes a detailed system of beach assessment that includes nature of the beach (e.g. shingle, sand), amounts of noise, availability of showers and other items. Interestingly, he notes that '13% of beach users interviewed stated a preference for visiting beaches without any commercial facilities. It seems that many beach users in the area surveyed did not desire beaches to be "improved" either in terms of supplementation of facilities . . . or in terms of resort/area infrastructure development to ease access' (Morgan, 1999, p. 409). From another perspective, Smith *et al.* (1997) found that beach users in the United States would be tolerant of charges to clear what they perceived as significant levels of beach debris.

## BEACHES, CARNIVAL AND THE GAZE OF GENDER

It has already been noted that differences exist between males and females, albeit influenced by the family life-cycle and other socio- and psychological variables. Over a decade ago, Monk (1992) argued that the observation of any landscape was not a neutral, objective process, but one dependent upon the context of a specific 'gaze'. As Rose (1993) notes:

> They interpret landscape not as a material consequence of interactions between a society and an environment, observable in the field by the more-or-less objective gaze of the geographer, but rather as a gaze which itself helps to make sense of a particular relationship between society and land. (p. 87)

So it is, too, with the seashore. If any landscape creates images and meanings, it is the beach – from the paintings of Victorians who noted Raleigh's gaze to the postcards of Donald McGill. Also, as several tourists visiting Mediterranean countries will know, many postcards are primarily illustrated from a male, heterosexual view. Naked or near-naked women are portrayed as either objects to be admired/desired by males or, in some cases, as suggestive of promised sexual delight. The women so posed are young, nubile, sensual and akin to those shown by magazines like *Playboy*. While there are male counterparts, for example of Hawaiian windsurfers, more of their male counterparts are shown as engaged in action shots. In some ways these postcards of women continue a tradition derived from more conventional art. Theweleit (1987) notes the derivation of the myths of the South Seas when the image of the South Sea Maiden 'began to construct the body that would constitute a mysterious goal for men whose desires were armed for an imminent voyage, a body that was more enticing than all the world put together' (1987, p. 296), while Rose draws attention to the 'sexual, fertile, silent and mysterious Woman with a gorgeous, generous, lush Nature' (1993, p. 94) painted by the artist Gauguin in his representation of Tahitian women.

For feminist writers like Rose, geographers have failed to understand or recognize the 'sensual topography of land and skin' which is mapped by a mainly white, male, heterogeneous gaze. Mention has already been made of the males who looked upon the Victorian bathing-huts wherein females changed. This form of very literal gazing has been the butt of jokes, exemplified by postcards of the period. Ryan (1995d, p. 115) uses a late example of one such postcard in which the question is posed, Who is the figure of fun – the bather or the male? The same question applies to earlier postcards. Shields (1991) reproduces postcards of the 1850s, including one of the 'Gentlemen! Who pass the morning near the ladies bathing machines', which show a line of otherwise respectable males complete with eye-glasses and binoculars. Again, however, it is the males who, while active and intruders upon privacy, are themselves the figure of fun. It is, arguably, a genre of cards designed by males for males because it is the males who recognize the situation and behaviour.

## THE BEACH AS CARNIVAL

But the significance of the gaze for the onlooker is sharpened by a knowledge that if the males are portrayed as oglers of female flesh, then also there were, and are, women who fulfil the roles. The paradox of the caricature of the McGill postcard is that the comic is a form of satire where the irony is defused, and made acceptable and safe by the tolerated humour. 'Office girls' did go, and continue to go, to meet young males. And not only the female office workers. In July 1994, one of the British Sunday tabloid papers ran an article on the prostitutes who work the seaside resorts of Blackpool and Brighton. The Daytona Beach Spring Break, previously outlined, is also concerned with an opportunity for sex amidst the carnival.

Carnival is a concept used by many writers in examining leisure (for example, Bakhtin, 1984; Rojek, 1985, 1993; Shields, 1991). It not only implies fun, but in its lewdness, its chaotic, unruly character, its concern with farts, copulation and confusion, it also represents a challenge to the ordered world of norms and ethics. The beach has often been analysed as a place of display and impulse, and examples such as 'Muscle Beach' at Los Angeles, California illustrate this well. Within New Zealand, with its past tradition of being 'a good mate', an interesting aside is the popularity of summer beachside campsites running competitions whereby males parade as female bathing beauties – a practice that still exists today at some summer locations like Waihi. But, equally, particularly at locations where the funfair is present, like Blackpool, Niagara Falls or Coney Beach, the 'other world', which lifts the curtain upon suppressed profanities, continues to lurk. However, what is of interest is how, in a place like Blackpool, the tourist turns his back upon the beach, so strong is the pull of the funfair.

## A REJECTION OF THE BEACH

The turning of the back upon the beach is further demonstrated in the period from 1945 to the present by the British Holiday Camp. Ward and Hardy (1986) show how even many of the earliest camps, such as those run by 'Maddy' Maddieson before the Second World War, were located by the seaside. Interesting parallels exist between the holiday camp and the beach. Initially, the beach was used for medicinal purposes, and, initially, the camps were inspired by idealists seeking social improvement. Ward and Hardy cite *Ladbrokes Life* when they write of the Caister Socialist Holiday Camp of 1906:

> The campers slept under canvas and sang around the camp-fire within sound of the waves. The camp committee, many of them trade union leaders, organised socials, dances, lectures and debates. Every Sunday there was a lecture in the afternoon, and for many of the campers this was one of the most exciting moments in the week. (1986, p. 16)

The disciplines noted in Chapter 1 of a Baden-Powell were not restricted to the Boy Scout movement alone, and thus a specific gaze of the period might be discerned as transcending political differences. This was a period of earnest pleasure, consistent with Rojek's concept of policing leisure. But the cynic might ask, for just how many was the lecture the highlight of the week? Like the beach, the holiday camp by the seaside was to go through a transition to become a burlesque which was, itself, to be parodied by a later generation with disappearing but fond memories of the carnivalesque holiday camp in the British TV series *Hi-Di-Hi*.

By 1955, a *News of the World* reporter (Jones, 1985) noted that:

> Our revelations on the hi-de-high old time for staff came as no shock to Butlin bosses who commentated that 'People are motivated to work here for a variety of reasons apart from nipping into a chalet with the nearest girl. There's a certain camaraderie about the place, a special atmosphere.'

Ward and Hardy note that few casual employees felt loyalty to the organization, and saw customers as people 'to be "conned" into providing drinks, snacks, petting and sex – and a job at the end of the season' (1986, p. 88). From the reports of the author's students who were placed with holiday camps for periods of work experience, these norms continued to be exercised into the 1990s. But to concentrate upon follies is to ignore the very real pleasures that these camps provided by the sea for older people and for those with young families. Knobbly knee competitions, pillow fights over the swimming-pool, talent contests – all offered the opportunity to 'star', and, in doing so, to reconfirm an experience of solidarity within a framework where there was no need to 'pretend'.

## THE DECLINE OF BURLESQUE

It is also interesting to note that the carnival of the summer was a transient period, a temporal margin; and that in the off-season the camps would return to their more serious origins. They would often be booked by Christian groups prior to Easter, or by charitable and other similar organizations, in an attempt by the camp operators to diversify business and maintain revenues. Finally, by the 1990s, the margin changed again, as the new holiday camps that were created by groups like Center Parcs turned their back upon the carnival and the beach to establish not camps but Holiday Centres within forests and parkland settings. Today, it might be argued that the true successor of the carnival is still to be found on the beach, but the beaches of Mediterranean islands, where companies meet the needs of the 18–30 holiday-maker. The scandals of sex noted in the holiday camp were true of only part of the clientele, and, indeed, not for all camps or for all of their history. Indeed, many camps refused to accept bookings from single-sex parties in order to protect what was seen as the core of the business, namely couples with young families and older people. What, possibly, has happened is that certain groups of the young are being divorced from other age groups, and so the carnival changes from a burlesque, and harmless activity, to one with potential for more violent undertones (e.g. see Getz and Cheyne in Chapter 7).


## THE MOTIVATIONS FOR USE

What has emerged from this review is that there is a coherent body of literature which regards the beach as a temporal, spatial, experiential yet managed margin as, for example, described by Cohen (1982). This literature tends to be drawn to the social rather than the psychological. The analyses advanced by writers like Rojek and Shields are attractive because they link the beach into other aspects of leisure, tourism and social action. However, what has also been shown is that the beach is used and experienced in many different ways by various ages and groups. It is used by children, families, teenagers, nudists, dune buggy riders, fishermen, introverts and extroverts to mention but a few categories. To reiterate that the beach is a margin, while useful, is but a partial analysis, and it is necessary to disaggregate further what is meant by the 'beach experience'.

One way in which this can be done is to refer to the motivations of the beach user. Backman *et al.* (1986) note ten basic motives and benefits sought. These are: 'diversion', 'family togetherness', 'experiencing nature', 'outdoor activities', 'solitude', 'physical fitness', 'affiliation', 'beach activities', 'self-awareness' and 'status'. Using a scale derived from Driver (1977), Backman *et al.* distinguish three factors that combine such motives. The first was composed of variables concerned with: 'being with and observing others, chance of a thrill, being with others who enjoy doing the same things I do, and a chance to be active' (p. 57). Two themes thus emerge from this factor, and they are social and physical activity. In Chapter 2 a discussion of holiday motives argued that four main motives existed derived from the Ragheb and Beard Leisure Motivation Scale. Ryan (1993) argued that, based upon these four motivations and research findings, various clusters of holiday-makers emerge, none of which, however, combined these two main motivations alone. Yet there were groups which exhibited some of these variables. These included a minority group, 'the active relaxers', which accounted for only 2 per cent of the sample, and tended to be male and higher-income groups, very much into sports, and a larger group constituting 11 per cent of the sample, the 'positive holiday-makers', who, however, tended to score highly on most items of the scale.

The second factor was composed of 'benefits concerned with safety, being there for children, being with others who are considerate and being with people of similar values' (Backman *et al.*, 1986, p. 57). This factor, Backman *et al.* found, tended to be important for those with young children. These sentiments were generally endorsed by a convenience sample of those found on Foxton Beach, New Zealand, one fine day in autumn 1995. Foxton Beach is used by many with young children because, unlike other beaches in the area, during the summer, cars are not permitted to be driven along the beach. A primary motive for respondents there was because it was safe for their children to play. Other motives were also present which reinforced the issue of safety. The beach is patrolled by surf guards during the summer, and during the weekends of spring and autumn.

The items, 'being there with others who are considerate' and 'being there with people of similar values' also emerged. In one case, for example, the parents of a lone child explained that one nice aspect about the beach was that they could take their young son there, and often he would find other children with whom to play. This meant that he had a 'good time' while they could relax.

The third factor was composed of being close to the sea, being able to relax and to enjoy the natural scenery. This factor is a mix of relaxation and self-awareness attributes which were again identified by Ryan (1993). In a sample of 1127 holiday-takers, 12 per cent formed the relaxed discoverers who combined high scores on the relaxation and intellectual components of the Ragheb and Beard Leisure Motivation Scale. This group was found to be primarily middle-aged, which partially fits the data provided by Backman *et al.* (1986).

## PATTERNS OF BEACH USAGE

The reason why the data only partially fit is because of a further variable – the nature of the beach. While the beach is a margin between land and sea, it can assume many different forms. From the length of Ninety Mile Beach at the top of New Zealand to Brandy Cove (a small cove once reputedly used by smugglers) on the Gower coastline, beaches can vary in length, sand and immediate environment. Are they surrounded by coastal marsh, or by towering cliffs? To these natural variations can be added man-made characteristics. Some are almost inaccessible; others have car parks built by their side. Others have clean water, others are a danger to swim in, due to sewage outfalls.

One result of such physical variations is that usage patterns of beaches can be very different, and thus give rise to different sets of expectations, perceptions and satisfactions. Also, within any one beach, there may be groupings of usage. For example, reference has been made to Foxton Beach on the west coast of the southern part of the North Island of New Zealand. This part of the country is bordered by a long strip of sandy beach interrupted by a few river mouths, with no rocky outcrops until the southern part of the Kapiti coast is reached just north of Wellington. It is, in many respects, an undistinguished beach, although on clear days Kapiti Island and the north coast of South Island, New Zealand, can be discerned in the distance. It is used because of the proximity of Foxton, located by the side of the river, and thus, historically, a place of human settlement. It is accessible by road, and a car park is located right above the beach. Hence those with young families come, and most sit within 100 metres of the car park. However, at the northern end of the car park is located the surf rescue headquarters, and this is a centre for teenagers who, around the surf rescue operations, and especially during the summer, congregate around this immediate area. Spatially, a clear pattern of distinct social usage of the beach can be discerned, based upon factors of accessibility and provision of facilities.

Backman *et al.* (1986) also observe the same phenomenon. Studying four Texas beaches during the spring and summer they note significantly different socio-demographic patterns between the beach users. For example, at Mustang Island Beach during the spring, the beach was primarily used by older people motivated by environmental benefits, whereas at Padre Balli in the spring,

> Visitors ... participated in activities that provided social as well as environmental benefits. Spring visitors had a mean age that was significantly different (lower) from the mean age of spring visitors to other beaches ... These visitors can be described as fun loving sun seekers, with a low income, reflecting their student status. (p. 58)

A detailed study of the usage of beach spaces is provided by Preston-Whyte (2001) of Durban, South Africa. In such an instance the use of space is made more complex by a past history of apartheid and Preston-Whyte notes that 'With the exception of North Beach, Bay of Plenty Beach, and Battery Beach, attendance at the beaches appears to be racially biased' (p. 588). However, later in his article it emerges that racial tensions exist with the 'exceptions', with race and activity being intermingled. Thus, the white users of these beaches tend to be middle-class, young, white surfers, while the other users, it is stated, are working-class Indian males who use the piers for fishing. Preston-Whyte (2001, p. 592) observes that:

> Competition for the use of these scarce and valued spaces has led to intense hostility and conflict between surfers and fishers.
>   The resolution of the conflict between the groups is complicated by the history of discrimination between racial groups, the nature of each activity, and the relative size of each stakeholder lobby.

Other factors also emerge from his analysis, including the observations that surfers themselves are divided into various categories depending upon age and experience, while wave and sea conditions are also important in determining usage patterns.

Ryan (1995) argues that such findings have significant implications for the planning of beaches. The usage of beaches, and the experiences gained, can be changed by planning decisions based upon factors such as the control of accessibility. A beach with a car park located by its side, and with café and restaurant facilities, will produce a very different usage pattern from one where access is through a wooded walk a kilometre or more from the nearest car park. Additionally, these combinations of natural and physical controls produce different sets of expectations.

Elsewhere in this book reference is made to the gap analysis of Parasuraman *et al.* There is little point in repeating the basis of the analysis here, other than to extend the concept as the authors have done in 1994. Parasuraman *et al.* now argue that service provision needs to be measured on two dimensions – and thus:

> ServQual's structure was modified ... to capture not only the discrepancy between perceived service and desired service – labelled as *measure of service superiority* (or MSS) – but also the discrepancy between perceived and adequate service – labelled as *measure of service adequacy* (or MSA). (1994, p. 6, italics are authors' original emphasis)

## EXPECTATION AND PERCEPTION OF THE BEACH

There exists within the customer's perception of expected service, a zone of tolerance between the desired and the adequate levels of service. So, too, arguably, it is with the holiday-makers' experience of the beach. The literature on carrying capacities has long recognized that there exists a psychological dimension to the concept, and, equally, that there is a 'zone of tolerance'. This is implicit in more recent thinking that has sought to recognize the difficulties of impact studies that incorporate both scientific and social evidence leading to specific outcomes. Rather, therefore, a concept of 'discernible differences' has come to the fore.

The pleasure of the beach partially depends upon expectations. Those seeking solitude will be disappointed if a group of young people are found on the beach having a barbecue. However, this group may melt into the atmosphere of a beach, and be tolerated. On the other hand, if loud music is being played, then the isolation seeker's zone of tolerance will be exceeded, and the experience will be unsatisfactory.

In Chapter 3 it was argued that holiday-making is a goal-driven activity whereby the goal to 'have a good time' is often achieved where expectations are initially disappointed by processes of cognitive dissonance and social readjustment/coping mechanisms. The same applies to the beach. Adams (1973) undertook a study of the effects of uncertainty about the weather for beach usage. The problem is this. If a family decide to visit the beach, and then learn that the weather forecast is unfavourable, what should they do? They can cancel the trip, and so be disappointed, or revalue the source of the information about the possibility of poor weather, and still make the trip. This latter course of action retains the possibility of disappointment if it rains.

What Adams found was that there were distinct differences between those committed to going to the beach, and those less committed, as to how they evaluated a weather forecast of a 60 per cent chance of rain. Of those committed to a beach trip, 16 per cent interpreted the weather forecast as meaning that it was 'almost certain to rain', as against 46 per cent of those not having that commitment. Adams concludes that the desire for travel can cause a potential traveller to distort his perceptions of a weather forecast – in short, in the terms of the model of Chapter 3, the goal of holiday satisfaction in itself distorts environmental information. Thus, one explanation of the apparent irrationality of holiday-taking previously discussed is that the behaviours are logical, but based upon faulty supposition. However, this explanation is only partial in that it does not explain why, in this case, the appeal of the beach is so strong as to overturn what, in other circumstances, people would assume to be the case. In other words, if the subject of potential behaviour was not beachgoing, but, say, shopping for groceries, would the distortion of environmental information be so strong?

## CONCLUSION

Beaches are margins of experience. This marginality is not simply one of geography, but is also social and psychological. Additionally, as social and psychological experiences, then, as society changes, so, too, does the meaning and use of the beach. The beach has been associated in the past with a carnival of freedom, and thus like many margins becomes meaningful as an analysis of the constraints of 'mainstream' society. In the Victorian period, it was a place of flesh and bodily exposure not generally tolerated elsewhere. Today, as contemporary norms are more accepting of skimpiness of dress elsewhere, the beach retains a different marginality. As the Daytona Spring Break illustrates, the beach provides opportunities for the young to pass through rites of passages without the presence of the older and younger generations.

Beaches also enable different experiences by reason of different geographies, both natural and man-made. As such, the experience of the beach can be analysed in terms of expectations, desires and zones of tolerance, and, like other tourist products, they are plural in their uses and imagery. However, as shown by the work of Adams, potential plurality of use and strength of attraction are distinctly different variables. Hence, to analyse the expectational and perceptual components of the beach, a complex model of attitude measurement based upon an extended Fishbein (1967) multi-attribute concept may be required. In addition to the assessment of the importance of attributes ($\Sigma b_i$) and an evaluation of the attributes possessed by any beach ($\Sigma e_i$), must be added the evaluation of potential consequences and outcomes ($\Sigma o_i$). Thus:

$$\text{Strength of conviction} = \sum_{i=1}^{n} B_i \, a_i + \sum_{i=1}^{m} b_i \, e_i$$

where
$B_i$ = strength of belief $i$ about beach $j$
$a_i$ = evaluative aspect of belief
$n$ = number of beliefs
$b_i$ = the belief that action will lead to consequence $i$
$e_i$ = the evaluation of consequence $i$
$m$ = the number of salient consequences

An additional variable that might also have to be taken into account is that normally, around any island or coastline, alternative beaches exist, each competing with others. Thus the formulation can be extended so that:

$$BI_{ij} = A_{ij} = \sum_{j=1}^{m} \sum_{k=1}^{n} (B_{ijk} \, V_{ik})$$

where
$i$ = holiday-maker
$j$ = beach
$k$ = attributes of beach
$n$ = number of attributes
$m$ = number of alternative beaches
$BI_{ij}$ = holiday-maker $i$'s behavioural intention towards beach $j$
$A_{ij}$ = a unidimensional measure of holiday-maker $i$'s attitude toward beach $j$
$B_{ijk}$ = the strength of holiday-maker $i$'s belief that attribute $k$ is possessed by beach $j$
$V_{ik}$ = the degree to which attribute k is desired by holiday-maker $i$

This statement of the intricacy of the beach is not to be interpreted as a substitution of the quantitative for the qualitative as a means of analysis, but rather as an alternative and complementary mode of expression of the complexity of the beach. Like many aspects of human behaviour, paradoxes abound. At one level the pleasures of the beach are simple and unaffected – they are venues of spontaneity. On another level they imply profound questions: Why is that spontaneity not found in the same profusion in the behaviour of adults? Examples might be found, say, at parks, but the beach experience is often longer in duration. Beaches are also pluriactive in the use that is made of them and can vary temporally. Hence within the simplicity of use lie shades of meaning, but seeking to understand the holiday-maker's 'gaze' upon the beach by complicating the analysis is to lose the meaning of the experience. While holiday-makers can be sophisticated 'post-tourists', they also retain the ability to be simple-minded in their pursuits. The pleasure of the beach is that it affords such simple-mindedness.

# Chapter 9

# Playing with the past: Heritage tourism under the tyrannies of postmodern discourse

*Keith Hollinshead*

## INTRODUCTION

This chapter explores the fundamental nature of history that managers and operators of heritage-tourism sites work with in conceiving of and developing their storylines. It starts from the premise that 'history' and 'heritage' are social constructs: they are truths that are held to be 'known' about the past, by a given population or within a given society or culture. In this sense, the chapter thereby works from the premise that the managers and operators in tourism are usually second-storey players, in that they work with given versions of the past that have been generated or handed on to them by other first-storey players, who (often being many in number acting over count-less generations) have authorized, validated or merely participated in the general legitimation of particular or revered storylines about the past. Yet, in positing 'history' and 'heritage' as social truth, or as a set of aggregated social narratives, this chapter also works from the premise that the past is subject to much subtle and not so subtle doctoring, and has always been so treated and re-treated since primordial times. To that end, therefore, this chapter seeks to explore the degree to which the past that heritage-tourism practitioners work with is being re-aligned or re-cooked under 'postmodernity', an era or 'condition' of prodigious change for our received identities and imagined affinities of time and place.

It is important to consider the possible effect postmodernity has (or, rather, postmodern imperatives and impulses have) on history and heritage for a number of reasons. The postmodern moment is a period (or as some would prefer to state it, the postmodern mood is a *condition*) during which thoroughgoing and asystemic changes are taking place. The postmodernization of things is thus held by many commentators on life and society to constitute an admixing of processes at which an amalgam of forces from the very physical and substantive to the very sensual and cerebral co-mingle: as they co-mingle, they are held to thereby challenge outlooks about all sorts of things and claiming reactions about all sorts of beliefs. Thus, postmodern understandings compose a revised and refreshed field of insight, a new and often radical realm of discourse of and about the world. And, to repeat, this reconfigured discourse arises not only from *material changes in the world* but also from *changes in the way we learn to look at the world*.

*Table 9.1* The transformation of the personal and the public world: some different and powerful ideas associated with the postmodern condition

❏ **A moment of dislocation**

To commentators like Baudrillard (1981), postmodernity is a period of nihilistic disruption where meanings are divorced from images and reality from representations of it. Under such postmodern dislocations, knowledge of and about things is no longer restricted to bodies and institutions whom we used to regard as being properly powerful in that respect: under the postmodern predicament, even the state cannot so readily define and demarcate things.

*Application for heritage: Under such de-alignments, for instance, it is harder for a national government to dictate what the received history of a country ought to be, and it is harder for an established group of (for instance) white, male academics to rule the roost over other interest groups in the declaration of what is or is not 'appropriate' heritage.*

❏ **A mood of fusion**

To commentators like Bauman (1993), the world has become much more bricolaged under postmodern impulses where fusion reigns, and where 'messiness' much more frequently results in the order of things. To observers like Bauman, it is harder for individuals to spot or to relate to any set of core values to things. Under the abandonments of postmodernity, individuals have to juggle and perm a variety of traditional identities with artificial ones, and juggle and accommodate a variety of longstanding/hallowed affiliations with the new sets of emergent/ersatz interests.

*Application for heritage: Under such mix and match impulses, the postmonauts of the postmodern world learn to pool their heritage values as they pool almost all other things. It is harder for them to accept single or normal interpretations to history/heritage at (variously) school, in the museum, or on film: the received relationship between what was deemed to be 'high culture' heritage and 'popular culture' heritage blurs considerably in such 'rainbow' heritage permutations of the postmodern moment.*

❏ **A mood of unpredictability**

To commentators like Crook *et al.* (1992), the de-alignments and re-alignments of postmodernity produce an uncertainty in things where the general directionality of those things are unclear. Hence postmodern society has become (or as some would prefer it, *is*) much more unpredictable than modern society was (*is*). As lifeworlds become more segmented or pluralized, it is harder for key societal institutions to realistically project how their society is or has been *different* from others.

*Application for heritage: Under such breakdowns in held unity and felt integration, it is much more difficult for any institution to do more than barely pattern the narratives of the past it wishes to broadcast, for under the postmodern mood, all of the individuals within that society are much less likely to respond to the self-same values or to the self-same cultural vocabularies as each other.*

❏ **A multidinity of signs**

To commentators like Lash and Urry (1994), postmodern society has become, or *is*, a society of images and signs where style and the power of projection dominate every aspect of our lives. To Baudrillard (1993) the resultant age of *hyperreality* constitutes a moment where this myriad of signed images increasingly supplants reality itself.

*Application for heritage: Under the hyperreal realm of constant communication and infinitous representation, it is hard for any single narrative about history or heritage to gain universal acceptance or absolute validity. There is just so much competing signification for people to digest and react to. Even 'heritage' itself becomes a style, that is, a passing image to reveal about oneself, or an attractive veneer to project about one's house or current identity.*

❏ **A moment of manumission**

To commentators like Gibbins and Reimer (1995), those who have a postmodern value orientation are individuals who endure the fewest 'first-order' categorical imperatives (or lifestyle/lifecourse rules), and are thereby able to exhibit considerable freedom of choice in the way they live. Such postmonauts generally believe that each person ought to be able to think, to believe and 'to be' in ways of their own choosing. Hence, their lifestyles and their selves can be continuously remade and restyled as they are 'culturally released' under the postmodern condition.

*Application for heritage: Under the so-called 'cultural release' of postmodernity, the postmodern self of individuals is less tightly fixed than its predecessors in terms of received history and bounded heritage. Under the abandonments of postmodernity, the individual can much more readily escape, for instance, a nation state's capacity and will to control interpretations of the past, to live within a more personalized and pluralized complex intersection of storylines and inheritances from yesteryear.*

---

❑ **A mood of expressivism**

To commentators like Ewen (1998), the postmodern era is a perpetual field of vision and understanding where no meanings have a half-life, and where there are no enduring ideas or questions. The image-gripped culture of postmodernity has thereby cultivated a mood where the projection of new significations is indeed everything, and where new ephemeral ways of acting and feeling continually evolve. To Gibbins and Reimer (1999), the resultant postmodern temper is one of *expressivism*. Individuals are much more frequently 'expressivist', and, therefore, more open, reflexive and fleeting in their desire to project themselves and their experiences. They have a greater will and capacity to actualize self-constructions or to actualize highly imaginative self-identities of and for themselves.

*Application for heritage: Under this added expressivism, history and heritage may be (within the postmodern mood) produced, reproduced and consumed in forms of creative self-articulation that had hitherto been unimaginable. A given person's felt past/held inheritances are just one source through which the self can be enlarged and projected, as it is freed from traditional confines, and as it absorbs all sorts of fragmentary sources and scattered storylines in that act of proud self-expression.*

---

❑ **A myriad of new relationships**

To commentators like Crouch and Marquand (1995), the postmodern predicament is one where the local/territorial/bounded market place of ideas and connectivities is replaced by a larger, global, and more fluid field of knowledge and communication. Accordingly, while people still behave as social beings, their lives are more heterogeneous than before, and they take their ideas and connectivities from a far wider range of alternative sources and reflexive relationships. Hence the knowledges, the communications and the networks which structure everyday life become increasingly complex.

*Application for heritage: Under this increasing reflexive multidimensionality of social space, the predicaments of postmodernity constitute a more aqueous milieu where people shift between an increasing number of 'thinking' and 'communicating' domains frequently, and where they become more exposed to a wider pool of interpretations about the past: they do not just gain new outlooks on present-day life, they gain it on times of yore and on things from yesteryear.*

---

❑ **A moment of performance**

To commentators like Butler (1997), the enhanced expressivism of the postmodern condition is a highly charged performative and (thereby) political activity, in the sense that it makes claims about lifestyle and social ways, and it legitimizes not only things in the present, but things in the past and future, too. The performative power of governments, corporations and special interest groups increasingly involve themselves in performative 'battles' to articulate alluring visions of difference and attractive projections of what is civil, deserved, and attainable.

*Application for heritage: Under these new performative incitements of lifestyle and civility, existing statist (i.e. governmental) and capitalist (i.e. corporate) versions of history and heritage will be increasingly conjoined by versions of the past which emanate from 'interest groups'. While postmodern impulses reign, heritage is and will be increasingly harnessed in the new performative and pluralized games to re-envision the world. Under the predicaments of postmodernity, history and heritage are or will be tools by which contesting interest groups will continually seek to articulate their preferred habitus.*

---

Table 9.1 presents a list of the critical ways in which commentators on postmodernity consider how our views of the world have changed, or are changing, under the postmodern mood or condition. The table is meant to be illustrative rather than comprehensive, which (that is, the absence of total or absolute intent) is perhaps a postmodern impulse in and of itself! So what does Table 9.1 reveal about the changed/changing profile and importances of heritage? It suggests that under the postmodern predicament:

1. as the institutions of the world and the received ideography of the world have conceivably been de- and/or re-aligned, new spectrums of heritage narratives are being peddled and projected by a different array of interest groups and powerful organizations across society;

2. as cultural spaces become increasingly pluralistic, multidimensional and complex, heritage storylines become an increasingly blurred mix of supposedly esteemed 'traditional'/'established' accounts and 'budding'/'fabricated' accounts that have less seeming historical association with the people or the place in question;
3. as societies, in the west predominantly, are under increasing pressure to change and to reinvent themselves, the continuity and predictability of received versions of history/heritage become ever-difficult to sustain;
4. as the large collectivities of old suffer in their power to differentiate themselves, an increasing proportion of individuals under postmodernity now seek to affiliate themselves (and thereby support the history/heritage) of smaller identity groups with which they have a more personal/particular relative or reflexive association;
5. as traditional and hierarchical bonds across society loosen, individuals increasingly want to take their own responsibility for what they themselves do in their lives, and for the sorts of inheritances they wish to revere;
6. as nations and large collectives gradually lose the capacity and will to socialize and regularize the culture of their citizenry, it is increasingly possible for individuals in that citizenry to be self-directive and self-creative about the styles of heritage they wish to uphold or articulate;
7. as the value orientations of individuals become much more self-invoked, individuals will use preferred versions of history/heritage to blend together (with other preferred attitudes and affiliations) a less exclusive outlook on life; and
8. as traditional loyalties to macro and territorial groups may diminish, expressed heritage may become a resource by which individuals can performatively articulate new special interest attachments and new personalized lifestyle preferences.

Hence, under the postmodern predicament, postmodern thought suggests that new kinds of less territorial but more embracing global city-zenships that characterize the world will melt embedded cultural ties, and will steadily replace them or conjoin them with a new plural, differential and eclectic mix of affinities, and a new plural, differential, eclectic mix of identities. These processes and proclamations of differentiation will conceivably become complex, as everyday life for individuals becomes more heterogeneous than before and as they have a much larger range of alternative histories/alternative heritages to associate with. Over time, the crisis in contemporary/postmodern representation (and, more importantly, the liberation in and of self-production) means, as postmodern thought has it, that it will become increasingly futile to try and classify individuals by strictly binary or tightly categorical understandings about historical affiliation or heritage association. But, of course, the very act on anyone's part to draw up replacement postmodern classifications is itself a political activity; it is an attempt to project a certain vision of how the world is, and was.

The value of postmodern insights clarified, this chapter is now offered as a transdisciplinary critique of such forms of postmodern social engineering of the past via the following steps:

1. the literature of history will be examined to identify the degree to which history and heritage are nowadays seen to be fabricated entities;
2. the concept of postmodernity, itself, is distilled, serving for some as a 'mood', during which the re-manufacture and re-concoction of the past has been notably

accelerated here and there. Here a particular effort will be made to introduce a number of key thinkers on and about the kind of postmodern imperatives which are helping us reassess our understanding of our received inheritances and (particularly here) our celebrated pasts;

3. the dynamic of the relationship between postmodern thought and history/heritage will be inspected to gauge whether what is known about the past is substantially changing under the believed experiences and the felt exposures of postmodernity. In turn, this affects what is available for promotion and packaging in and through tourism.

4. a particularly pungent analysis of the postmodern invention of history, namely that of Fjellman's (1992) critique of Walt Disney World's presentation of history and heritage in Florida, USA, will be reviewed to see if any important lessons can be gleaned from it for tourism researchers about the manner in which well-positioned, well-connected or well-financed power-players in tourism (such as the Disney Corporation) can, and indeed do, decorate or lubricate the past under the enabling autarky of the postmodern moment;

5. finally, a short critique will be given as to some of the problematics that are involved with postmodern modes of analysis. In that regard, a number of significant difficulties in and of postmodern forms of analysis will be outlined. They constitute a number of felt tyrannies, which those who are uncomfortable with postmodern critiques of truth maintain typify postmodern outlooks on and over the world, and thereby reduce the usefulness of postmodern distillations of things.

Such a process will illustrate the essential political nature of past-making under the postmodern predicament, whether it be of history/heritage passed on for presentation in tourism, or of novel history/heritage stories which have been borne through tourism exhibitory.

## POWER AND TRUTH IN THE DISCOURSE OF HISTORY AND HERITAGE

As Lowenthal (1985) evinces, today the past is everywhere: the lineaments and images of bygone times are omnipresent. The 1970s, especially, saw an immense expansion of interest in heritage and history (Cleere, 1989a, p. 15), and in Britain the literature records 'an extraordinary growth in "history and heritage" in the public imagination' over recent decades (Bagguley *et al.*, 1990, p. 156). When the history of a place is presented to tourists or the heritage of a people is otherwise projected afar, choices have to be made about what ought to be exhibited. No interpreted site or designated monument can include all the possible interpretations, nor all the involved themes and subjects, even if they could each be identified. The presentations of history and heritage are presentations of choice and bias. Judgements cannot be avoided in the telling of the past, or in the promotion of inheritance, because of the manifold heroes and heroines, sites, scenes, and causes and consequences that are possible. And if one accepts a Foucauldian interpretation of the order of things in the world, while much of the ongoing and everyday decision-making in the world is or will be consciously taken, many other quotidian decisions will be enacted subconsciously within privileged institutional parameters, in seemingly petty but in actually quite significant *cumulative* fashion. In historical map production, for instance, 'the interpretation of history (importantly) resides in the (seemingly incidental) choice of spreads' (Wallerstein, 1980, p. 156). How such choices are made, and why people are attached to certain pasts, is a complicated matter. The sense of belonging to a place or to a tradition has not been probed for long, and it appears to be 'so ill-formulated in the minds of most individuals that it is difficult to draw any valid analytical conclusions' (Cleere, 1989a, p. 6).

A review of the contemporary literature on history and heritage reveals that historical truth is a problematic concept, and at least ten outlooks on the health and place of history and heritage can be discerned. These are listed below.

## The slow growth of the notion of truth in historical presentation

Scholars in history have only lately begun to plumb the attitudes of populations to the past (Wallace, 1981), and have only recently begun to explore *which* segments of a given population support which truths and *why* they do so. In so doing, a revolution has taken place as history has and is changing from the study of history 'as an accumulation of *events* of all kinds which have happened in the past (to becoming) *the science of human communities*' (the dictum of Fustel de Coulanges; cited in Bloch, 1949, p. 110, emphasis added). This switch of focus, which was initiated by Bloch and Febvre, was a shift from history and heritage built as a playground for the *homme isolé*, to history and heritage conceived as an arena for the *homme en groupe* where each individual is inescapably part of local influences and wider social connections (Würstermeyer, 1967). Barraclough (1978, pp. 41–2) comments poignantly upon this revolution:

> History which starts and ends with the individual, which takes individual action as its measure may not need to be, may not even be capable of being [sic!], scientific; the history of man is of man in society, and cannot be otherwise. Its closest affiliations are with sociology. Bloch professed more than once to see no real difference between history and sociology.

Thus, historians who have followed Bloch and Febvre to 'new history' tend to no longer be satisfied with the methods of traditional investigation. As historians and theorists on heritage have adopted stronger skeletal frames for their works, they have inevitably been drawn to more rigorous investigations of the truths that communities hold, and that groups act by. Though not just referring to matters of human history *per se*, Swiecimski (1989) produced a useful typology of truth in heritage presentation, as shown in Table 9.2.

In this paper, Swiecimski considered the normative role of museums, as lead institutions in the presentation of heritage, in the conveyance of truth. The presumed *ought* for museumologists is that *they should represent 'the truth'*: the transmission of *untruths* is assumed to be contrary to their scientific and historical purpose. But Swiecimski questions whether truth can ever be communicated at heritage sites in a *pure* form: to him, 'it is probable that every exhibit unavoidably transmits some untruth' (1989, p. 203). These untruths have not only to be neutralized in content and meaning by the visitor, but also (first) to be recognized as such.

To Swiecimski, the perceived truth of a heritage project can emanate from:

(a)   its intrinsic, observable physicality;

*Table 9.2* Truths in heritage presentation: the unavoidable transmission of untruths

---

Swiecimski's categories of truth in museum exhibitions

**Group A: the transmission of truths of scientific or artistic value**

1  **Truth connected with the entity,** or with the state of being, of exhibitions.
   Here the truths revealed are largely concerned with the exhibit's physical existence, where one can distinguish the object's intrinsic truth for information (i.e. other truths) ascribed to it.

2  **Truth connected with a priori norms** or definitions formulated for exhibitions, or for the objects being exhibited, whether real or conceptual [the latter occurs when objects are presented not for themselves but as symbols of general classes or types].
   Here the truths revealed are largely concerned with a set of conventionally selected features or by 'its origin'; thus only some objects are selected as 'true', the rest are 'untrue'.

3  **Truth connected with the content and value of assertions** about particular objects or classes of objects.
   Here the features of an exhibit may be heterogeneous in origin, perhaps some 'physical/inherent' and some 'added' to communicate a scientific concept, class of objects or notion. The truth then depends upon the satisfactory concordance of the highlighted features with the notions they are illustrating, a perspectival matter.

4  **Truth connected with the artistic concept** of exhibition design, in particular with the expression of an exhibition as a whole, with its own or added meaning.
   Here an exhibit may offer a heterogeneous communication where the design or placement of it becomes (itself) and expression of the scientific message. In this way, the design may convey information which is not programmed in the exhibit's original or intended script.

5  **Truth connected with the [placement] appearance** or exhibits and their [*in situ*] aesthetics.
   Here exhibit conditions may affect the appearance of objects and thereby disturb the quality of the truths/untruths being conveyed, particularly where a heritage object is removed from its natural surroundings to a different exhibition milieu.

**Group B: the didactic transmission of truth as elementary knowledge**

1  Where the truth of an exhibition (or exhibited objects) is **independent of any set of consciousness**.
   Here the truth is intended to be elemental and unconnected, i.e. in terms of the evaluation of the exhibition's content or meaning with respect to its 'pure' or 'fundamental' truthfulness.

2  Where the truth of the exhibition (or exhibit) is evidently a product of **acts of cognition** and their expression.
   Here, again, the truth is intended to be 'unconnected'; it is assumed that the reader, viewer or visitor can neutralize any variant or unwanted shifts in content or meaning that have arisen from the placement or the design of the heritage presentation, and develop their own cognitive understandings.

---

*Source*: Adapted from Swiecimski, 1989, pp. 203–11.

(b)    its perceived representativity of a larger class, age or type; where either:

   (i)   its truth value is identified with its authenticity;

   (ii)  its truth is deemed to be a value independent of the objects' authenticity (e.g. when the materiality of an object can be replaced by a non-authentic physical entity);

(c)    the assertions made about it:

   (i)   where the object or site presented is 'untouched' and stands as an unaltered representation of a class, an idea or a process in history;

   (ii)  where the object or site presented may be altered in material substance or in its objective structure in order to better convey a visualized account of a class, an idea or a process;

   (iii) where the object or site present may be altered through the significant use of artifacts materially and structurally different from the documentary material upon which they are based;

(d)   the qualities of the design used to project the heritage features; and

(e)   the conditions of the site, particularly the new or relocated site to which a heritage entity is moved, for natural or built surroundings have their own forms of influence on the 'truths' conveyed.

Given such a helpful typology as is provided by Swiecimski's ideas in Table 9.2, it is relatively easy to understand how untruths can axiomatically be transmitted from almost each historical tourism interpretation and every heritage presentation. For each of the above five types of perceived truths, the following untruths may be accordant where they may arise:

(a)   accidentally, when an unintended defect is taken to convey an object's identity;

(b)   because the *a priori* classification is arbitrary, simplistic or otherwise weakly conceived;

(c)   through disinformation, for instance in the provision of a depictive artwork which is 'too detailed';

(d)   where the visitor is not able to distinguish exhibit convention and infers an unintended truth from the schematic arrangements adapted, or otherwise from the surrealisms utilized;

(e)   from the juxtaposition of the heritage object in a relocated, an artificial or even a contemporatory setting where all manner of aesthetics pertaining to the new site unpredictably cross-fertilize with the object of presentation. (1989, pp. 203–11)

The work of Swiecimski is critical to the development of insight on historical and heritage tourism. It pointedly illustrates that historians' (or rather heritage interpreters') knowledge of truth is maturing. But it also underscores the fact that, with the best will in the world, the normative intentions towards the transmission of truth will always inexorably be interfered with by the dictates of the given aesthetic setting.

**The alteration of the past is inflexible**

This second outlook on truth and power (in the shaping of history and heritage) further elaborates an issue touched upon at the end of the previous point: the telling of every history inevitably involves the conveyance of untruths. Lowenthal (1985, p. 412) made the point in the culminatory observation of his magnum opus, *The Past is a Foreign Country*:

> Some preservers [of bygone times and places] believe that they can save the real past *by preventing it from being made over*. But we cannot avoid remaking our heritage, for *every act of recognition alters what survives*. We can use the past fruitfully only when we realise that *to inherit is also to transform*. (emphasis added)

Tourism historians, heritage interpreters, and Swiecimskian museologists inescapably put 'real history' and 'proper heritage' under the scalpel. History simply cannot be faithfully 'photocopied' so that it is absolutely preserved in all of its senses and dimensions: every act of interpretation of the past taints the past. And such particularly occurs when historians, heritage interpreters and museologists, let alone state bureaucrats and national politicians in tourism, do not recognize their own teleological intent. Where and whenever such teleology is present, violence is done to history and to heritage. Interpretations become assumptive and circular, or, in Foucault's terms, the charting of history and heritage becomes carceral (Merquior, 1985, p. 107) where the articulated narratives are determined by or imprisoned within a particular regime of truths, validities and certainties which are held to be 'just so' by that believing age or community.

For Lowenthal, neither history nor heritage can ever just be conserved when being retold, it is always narration to a purpose:

> What our predecessors have left us deserves respect, but a patrimony [Sic!] simply preserved becomes an intolerable burden; the past is best used by being domesticated, and by accepting and rejoicing that we do so.
> The past remains integral to us all, individually and collectively. We must concede the ancients their place ... But their place is not simply back there, in a separate and foreign country; it is assimilated in ourselves, and resurrected into an ever-changing present. (1985, p. 412)

So, there we have it. It is either a case of history and heritage to-be-altered-inflexibly, *or* history and heritage to-be-altered-inflexibly-for-some-felt-positive.

**History cosmetized**

Frequently, historians report that the population of a given contemporary age alters history and/or its projected inheritances because something within it/them mortifies or humiliates that population. In Britain, Laslett (1965, p. 170) considers that the attitudes, practices and relationships from past political and historical ages have often so completely vanished from modern society that they encumber the present day British in the same way that 'the huge crumbling ruins of the buildings of the late Roman Empire embarrassed the Goths and the Saxons'. Hence the incongruous physical signs of past shames have to be cleverly explained away.

To Lowenthal (1989, p. 215) the embarrassments of a people's history or the baggage of a population's heritage can prove unshakable: they then become its *domnosa hereditas*, viz., the legacy that a population is stuck with and would rather not have, but must accept because it is deemed to be an integral part of the place or of the people. One such example of the beautification of a toady or rum past concerns the creation of the 'notion' of Romania; an example of how a European nation-state is conceived and cut from an old dynastic empire: such is not an unusual occurrence. In the case of Romania, a national and enduring literary language 'appeared', a traditional and evergreen 'economy' of crafts and industry was found, a durable architecture was seen to be 'typical', and all sorts of triumphant deeds were recorded as having been performed in the perjuring resistance against the Ottomans (Horne, 1986, pp. 8–10). While the newly ascribed glories of 'Romania' were predominantly moulded by nineteenth-century intellectuals, they have also proven to be invaluable for succeeding ruling groups:

> This concept of 'Romania' became reinterpretable, shifting in functions and meanings. One of the greatest creations of Romanian cultural nationalism was a painting by Nicolae Grigorescu; it showed a woman in a pure white kerchief, wise and trusting with steady eyes and smooth skin. The *Peasant Girl of Musecel* has served them all; merchants and nobility, racketeers and idealists, King Carol, the Iron Guard, President Ceausescu. (Horne, 1986, p. 11)

## History as a reactionary revival

Illusion in the narratives of history and heritage is as old as history itself, but nowadays illusion-of-and-about-the-past has become a very profitable commodity (Breitbart, 1981, p. 116). Hewison (1989) records that an explosion of interest in nostalgia has occurred during the 1980s with, for instance, Japan building 500 museums in fifteen years, and every city in Europe and North America creating new museums or converting old ones.

Analysis of the recent and vast expansion of the heritage tourism industry in Britain by contemporary social historians suggests that the growth in museums and promoted historical sites is inversely related to current levels of national confidence: 'Imaginatively deprived in the present [The British] turn to images of the past, either in reactionary revivalism, or in a spirit of ironic quotation that emphasises the distance between the source and its recycled imagery' (Hewison, 1989, p. 113). Such cultist presentations, moreover, can be seen to constitute a tribute to an history that is actually over. Dislike of the conditions of the present and fear of the future are felt to orientate the British people back towards their past, and such backward orientations can stifle.

## The past as ideological messenger

The telling of history and the account of heritage have always been a confrontation zone for contesting cultures or lineaments. Oppositional forces martial their truths in order to uncover, discover, recover and/or to over-cover storylines. And such modification exercises upon history are no intellectual pastime alone. They deal in legacy, they ruffle critical meanings and they rouse lasting passions. They divide or unite whole populations at single rulings or via single symbolic revelations (Lowenthal, 1985).

In a nutshell, the past is generally acquired by the ruling and possessing classes of privilegentia, at the sufferance of the common fold and the artisan classes, an actuality well-recorded through the centuries (Plumb, 1970).

One rider must be placed against this view that the ruling classes usually steal control of the past. This caveat is that the oppositional uses of history and heritage are less well known. In the USA, the American history profession has generally neglected 'subordinate histories', or what might be called 'people's histories'. Narratives pertaining to open and democratic history and to open, alternative heritage have tended to come from pressure groups beyond academic circles, and may therefore lack the place and prominence of orthodox, mainstream works (Benson *et al.*, 1981). 'People's Histories' have certainly to overcome 'the manifest structural biases of conventional scholarship' (Frisch, 1981, p. 9).

**Historical truth as sedative for the populace**

Historians around the world acknowledge that history and heritage are used by dominant institutions and groups in communities to reaffirm their power bases: 'various social modalities – family, peers, neighbourhood, ethnicity, state – validate various pasts, their custodial roles waxing or waning' (Lowenthal, 1985, p. 41). Lynch (1972, p. 40) notes that while 'many symbolic and historic locations in a city are rarely visited by its inhabitants ... the survival of these unvisited, hearsay settings conveys a sense of security and continuity'. And in similar vein, it is recorded that when the German Nazis plundered old Warsaw to destroy the pluck of the Polish people, the latter immediately set out to reconstruct the medieval township precisely as it had been before the Nazi demolition work; they felt they had a duty to rebuild the old centres and rekindle the ancient tradition (Lorentz, 1974, pp. 46–7). In many senses, a population's history and its heritage are its identity. The past can be an inherited (i.e. a believed in) or a constructed, that is, an imposed, sedative; as either a counterpoint to ongoing social change or a counterpoint to other rival truths. Hence, in Britain, for example, an esteemed and well-positioned semi-public agency like the National Trust can become 'an ethereal kind of holding company for the dead [but not gone] spirit of the nation' (Wright, 1985, p. 56).

In Britain, even industrial heritage is now officially sanctioned for public consumption (West, 1988, p. 42). But the conveyance of urban-industrial culture has been fraught with complexities in England as elsewhere (pp. 55–6):

> The town of Ironbridge [in Staffordshire] is one of those [uncertain] places, like Hebden Bridge in West Yorkshire, that is caught in the contradiction between serving the local community, with its transmuted bourgeois needs and the transient expectations of visitors. Just over ten years ago the overall feel of the place was one of dereliction, but the museum has changed all that and not entirely for the better. Post office, greengrocers, butchers, chemists, and small supermarkets, all antique shops, and endless knick-knack emporiums that all sell the very same glitzy junk. Added to this, cafes, 'tea shoppes', and restaurants that come and go like speculative butterflies, puffed up on the golden rays of summer when the visitors flit and cash registers chatter, only to spend the winter in fitful hibernation. Some die off, some return, others metamorphose into different dreams of an 'independent living'. (West, 1988, pp. 55–6)

In such places, history/heritage as sedative, guide and teacher can become swamped by history/heritage as sedative, profit-source and ideal playground. At Ironbridge and at Hebden Bridge, the industrial inheritance is proffered as show, not as substance, something that Gramsci had warned against, for 'Folklore should ... be studied as a "conception of the world and life" implicit to a large degree in determinate (in time and space) strata of society, and [it should be studied] in opposition to "official" conceptions of the world' (Gramsci, cited in Bennett, 1988, p. 63).

The point Gramsci makes is that, while even the heritage of subordinate classes may be used for sedative purposes, they may also be used for reasons of high seriousness. The problem is that such endeavours have only recently begun to happen with consistency and commitment. In Britain, once more, there remains a shortfall in such critical approaches to the projection of industrial history (West, 1988). Sanctioned history remains tilted to the storylines of the privileged: in practice, that is perhaps history, by definition.

So while it was learnt from this review of the literatures of history and heritage that academic historians have tended to relatively neglect what Foucault would call 'the investigation of counter-memory' (Hartsock, 1987, p. 202), now we learn that the promoters and manufacturers of 'the historical moment' have also been inclined to under-service 'counter-memory'.

## The reciprocity of versions of the past and the present: pastmodernization

The past is inevitably treated in the present, whether that be through enlargement or diminishment, embellishment or purification. The past is always tinged with present colours (Lowenthal, 1985, p. 362). The present pre-selects its own eminent advice for the past. It is not just any old happenstance history that is allowed to unfold. It is 'specific pasts' and 'rewritten pasts' that are permitted to unfurl. An unwatched past, an unpunctuated legacy, could easily prove to be an unchecked and paralysing anachronism for present-day rulers and leaders of society (Hughes, 1971). In such ways, history and heritage are rendered not only comprehensible for the present, but also apposite for the present. To coin a verb for such preparation of the past and for such therapy for tradition, one could coin the verb 'to pastmodernize', whereby history is tenderized and heritage is marinated for a wider or fresher mix of contemporary uses and contemporary consumptions.

What the term 'pastmodernization' deals in is the double equation that the local or national past of a place is a political past, is a modern past. 'Pastmodernization' as the favouring of accounts of the past to suit the motley present has seemingly long been occurring in certain heritage centres of the USA. Certain periods of US history have been notably strong in their efforts to postmodernize. First, the 1890s witnessed an unparalleled expansion in the numbers of patrician ancestral societies willing and able to turn history over to give it a proud but self-reflexive airing, and then the 1950s brought a vibrant Corporate Roots movement which channelled unparalleled amounts of iron, steel, textile, farming and other industry dollars into appropriate 'traditional/ patriotic' shrines. To reiterate, under such eras of enthusiasm in history and heritage, the output is always closely connected to broader sociopolitical concerns. Past-modernized presentations are projects which mediate the past, whomever are the conceptual architects.

## Media deflections of history

According to the emergent literature on legend and myth, the media is inclined to confuse history and lore. It mixes fiction with fact, and it has strong 'natural' preferences toward some storylines rather than to others. But, of the media, it is television that has conceivably had most effect upon remodelled, late twentieth-century conceptions of the history and the heritage of peoples and races. Indeed, 'the small screen has become a veritable history machine, spewing forth dozens of re-creations of historical, semi-historical, and pseudo-historical events in dramatic form' (Breitbart, 1981, p. 117). With its continuity, its ubiquity and its repetitivity, television is held to be the quintessential vehicle for many prime postmodern values: 'The flatness, the depthlessness, the superficiality of [inherited and] contemporary culture is expressed by these networked pictures with their constantly shifting collage of images and points of view' (Hewison, 1989, p. 135).

To Strong (cited in Lumley, 1988, p. 21), television equals the negation of culture. Strong (a museum executive) suggests that television is replacing museum visitation, being an idle and inert pursuit that does little to develop the thinking capacity of the viewer. Hence, many observers like Strong condemn the effect of the television monitor on culture because it is only able to provide closed and contained rather than open and participatory experiences.

Critical theorists warn how indelible can be the etching of stellar images of history and heritage as projected upon the popular imagination by programmes of the ilk of *Upstairs, Downstairs* (Higgs, 1986) from Britain. But how does the medium of television so heavily reinforce such trenchant imagery of the past? The literature on history and heritage indicates that the following are four of the paramount reasons:

1. its ease of watching. Consequently, 'the conception of history that my [history and heritage] students have now comes from television, [or] to some extent from the movies ...' (Foner, cited in Breitbart, 1981, p. 120);
2. its enticing reproducibility; while theatre depends upon the conventions of formalized illusion and can only 'stage' reality (Lasch, 1979), television is a much more direct medium: it dispenses with many of the established artistic conventions of the presentation drama and appears to always provide reality itself (Breitbart, 1981);
3. its strong conveyance of interpersonal drama; television lends itself to rich and resonant drama with full dialogue, readily definable characters, a componential storyline, and a climax, et cetera (Wolper, 1980, p. 87);
4. its constant support of 'reduced' images; the ubiquity of television (and its need to cater principally for the mass market) forces television producers into broadcasting rather narrowcasting strategies. And broadcasting feeds upon stereotyped images. It is all fine for those audiences who just do not want to know the facts, or who, appreciably, think they are getting the facts. Television appears to invent new truths and reconveys hackneyed truths just that bit better than anything else.

**The rights to history and heritage**

Historical sites and built interpretive heritage centres can be loaded with contesting meanings and identifications. In 1972 the National Parks Service in the USA attempted to solve these kinds of problems by producing a National Master Plan by which all of its existing historic sites would be classified, and from which gaps in thematic provision would be identified. The plan became a taxonomic nightmare. Nine major themes (for example, #6: Westward Expansion) were first subdivided into 43 subthemes and then classified into six broad types of work (for example, #D: Transport and Communication). These subthemes were then broken down into 'facets' (e.g. #7: Scientific Exploration). The result was rather simplistic and grossly arbitrary. The Statue of Liberty, for example, was categorized as 9A1, viz., 9 = 'American Way of Life'/A1 = 'Melting Pot' (Foresta, 1984).

The National Parks Service in the USA has experienced an immense amount of difficulty over the contested nature of its historical claims, and on account of the sheer elasticity of the 'historical significance' with which it deals. It has received considerable condemnation over the decades for submitting to pressure from contemporary social forces and for nominating sites for 'civil rights', for 'black history' and for 'women's rights' (*ibid.*) Its staff have also been virulently attacked for concerning themselves in trite and banal 'living history' representations for visitors of the prosaic rather than the national. Foresta considers that the National Parks Service will never ever be able to put a widely accepted programme of heritage management into place because, unlike experts on the environment (who tend to meet among themselves on common ecological grounds), expert historians and heritage buffs remain specialists only for specific localities or only for specific eras. Hence, consensus on questions of significance, issues of priority rights and matters of standards-of-provision, are each notoriously difficult to attain across the telling or representation of plural pasts.

## History as authorship

The final important contemporary outlook on the meaning and/or function of the past from the literatures of history and heritage concerns questions of authorship of history. The purpose here is to contrast Foucault's archaeological accounts of the past with orthodox accounts of the past from academic history.

Foucault claims that his archaeology of the past may be clearly distinguished from the history of ideas since:

1. it pursues the structure of documented discourse on itself, not individual themes and ideas;
2. it explores each discourse regardless as to what precedes or follows, not necessarily being concerned in tracing the full run of history and the origin of ideas;
3. it does not look for psychological or sociological causes of intellectual events, unlike academic history; and
4. unlike orthodox study, it does not highlight ineffable moments of origin in history (see Foucault, 1972, pp. 138–40).

While Foucault tends to stress impersonality, and is prone to emphasizing the regularities and discontinuities in discourse of and about the past, academic historians are inclined to focus upon authors, upon novelty. While Foucault looks for the play of abstract rules that govern what is appropriate in the writing of history in a given place, for a given society, at a given juncture, historians of ideas tend to look for the human subject within historical action and heritage signification. Foucault, after all, does not claim to be an historian. He did not claim to produce 'normal history' (*ibid.*, p. 144). His accounts are philosophical, almost nihilistic and heavily Nietzschean. But through his structuralist style of thinking we can, perhaps, understand the importance of all other historians-of-ideas just that much better. Foucault's outlook on the past and its telling may have been non-restrictive, indulgent and imprecise, yet it reveals how cohorts of 'normal' and revered historians are conceivably over-restricted by social truth, constrained by professional rule and precisely predictable. Foucault's 'failed project' has been good for our collective awareness of and about the way our inheritances are interpreted differentially, i.e. good for the health of history: historians are much more readily able to identify and are willing to confront their own time-bound and language-bound discursivity.

## HISTORY AND HERITAGE UNDER POSTMODERNITY

According to many social science observers, the so-called advanced societies of the west are currently undergoing a period of radical change as capitalism disintegrates, as markets globalize, as classes differentiate, as states are dismantled and/or are re-politicized, as culture fragments, and as time-space distantiations reduce (Lash and Urry, 1987; Harvey, 1989; Crook *et al.*, 1992). Such is the supposed age or the mood of postmodernity, a condition under which many established aspects or strong elements of the culture of the so-styled advanced societies have conceivably collapsed into a potpourri of packaged styles. And while there are many innumerable debates about the nature of postmodernity, one might (for present purposes) simply suggest that under the transformations of the era of postmodernity, many established theories on social change no longer appear to be so relevant as they once appeared to be.

Clearly there is a considerable range of opinion as to what the postmodern condition is, and thereby what its critical tendencies and components are. In summarizing that range, Hebdige (1986, p. 78) notes that postmodernity has been styled as the following 'things' or 'happenings', among others:

- an anti-teleological tendency within epistemology;
- a general attenuation of feeling;
- the predicament of reflexivity;
- a new phase of commodity fetishism;
- a fascination for images, codes and styles;
- a process of cultural, political or existential fragmentation and/or crisis;
- the decentring of the subject;
- an incredulity towards meta-narratives;
- replacement of unitary power axes by a pluralism of power/discourse formations;
- the implosion of meaning;
- the collapse of cultural hierarchies;
- a broad set of societal and economic shifts where features of life take on a 'media', 'consumer' or 'multinational' dominated hue; and
- a generalized substitution of spatial for temporal co-ordinates.

Rather than attempt to neatly extract, at this stage, a singular, all-purpose definition for postmodernity, an endeavour will be made to identify the critical components of postmodernity that are believed to have an effect upon the construction of culture. It is possible to identify twenty commonly attributed aspects of postmodernity and to note briefly the relevance of each to the 'production' of history and to the 'manufacture' of heritage. These are:

1. That single historical accounts are likely to be superseded by multiple, different accounts;
2. That grand master-narratives of the history and heritage of peoples/places are likely to be increasingly questioned;

3.  That the worth of each and every tradition is now contestable;
4.  That considerable latitude exists over the degree to which imaginative and hybridized simulations of historical events can be provided for today's visiting public;
5.  That considerable latitude exists over the type and style of images that may be harnessed to depict history and/or heritage;
6.  That existing accounts of history and heritage may be modified by the kinds of rhetoric and image which are well adapted to the technicized communication of the age;
7.  That different versions of history and heritage will, over time, beget novel and differentially connected symbols and images with which to characterize that account;
8.  That secure and longstanding presentations of history and heritage will compete with what, originally, purists would regard as miscellaneous and promiscuous depictions of history;
9.  That the proportion of 'untouched' accounts of history and heritage in currency will fall *vis-à-vis* both 'masked versions' and 'pure simulacrum';
10. That the proportion of 'vernacular', 'local' and 'populist' accounts of history and heritage in currency will rise *vis-à-vis* standard elitist accounts;
11. That 'old' history/'old' heritage is being increasingly 'infused' with new lexical descriptions and conceptual treatments arising from liberated academic, media and previously subjugated parties;
12. That the uniformity of the designation of eras and epochs in the history and the heritage of peoples and places is diminishing;
13. That at macro-levels of analysis the number of leading centres of legitimacy for 'authentic' history and heritage is rising for given states, regions and nations;
14. That the range of forms and diversity of avenues is rising, by which capitalist practice is involved in the interpretation and presentation of history and heritage;
15. That the certainty of understanding and the depth of affiliation/association with which a population identifies with given celebrated persons, places and events from its past can change considerably in scale and scope over time;
16. That support is declining in the western world for notions of linear progress within historical accounts of given regions;
17. That the extant range of 'alternative'/'adversarial' critiques of the past of states, regions and nations (which are distinguishable from mainstream versions of those areas' history and heritage) is increasing;
18. That the proportion of new and synthesized interpretations of history and heritage among emergent 'alternative'/'adversarial' interest groups is increasing *vis-à-vis* mainstream versions of the past;
19. That the supremacy of 'western'/'Eurocentric' master explanations for global history, and for the worldwide human heritage, is declining *vis-à-vis* 'non-western'/'non-Eurocentric' interpretations;
20. That the range of aesthetic treatments commonly utilized within the interpretation of history and heritage is increasing.

Table 9.3 now provides a short critique of some of the key conceptualists on the subject of postmodernity. The table seeks to familiarize readers with the distinct and

*Table 9.3* Key thinkers of and about postmodernity: heritage tourism in the light of 'post'-thought

| |
|---|
| **Lyotard**<br>To many, Lyotard was the first philosopher to make a cogent case for postmodern understanding. His late 1970s work *The Postmodern Condition* (1984) is a strong polemical dismissal of the tenets of modernity. Anti-foundationalist in spirit, Lyotard famously offers an incredulity towards metanarratives, as he condemns the manner in which (under modernity) the great ideological narratives of western knowledge (such as the Enlightenment, Marxist history and Freudian theory) have been violent and despotic in their promulgation of totalized understandings. Consonantly, Lyotard is disrespectful of all claims to proof or truth, and calls for the use of locally-situated knowledge to explain things. Under his version of postmodernity, usable knowledge can only ever be partial, fragmented and incomplete. Like Baudrillard, Foucault and Deleuze and Guattari (who each follow below), Lyotard is a French litero-philosopher. |
| **Baudrillard**<br>Absorbing a motley mix of ideas from Marxism, cybernetics, psychoanalysis and communications theory, Baudrillard bemoans the degree to which industrial capitalism regulates the world (under high modernity) via the ubiquitous political economy of the sign. To Baudrillard, signs themselves act as commodities, signifying a world of simulation (where the image and the model become more real than 'the real'), and heralding a world of *hyperreality* (where the distinctions between things and representations-of-them dissolve, leaving only *simulacra*). For Baudrillard (1988), the United States is a particularly distasteful and alienated world of simulacra – a world without much need of concrete referents, and a world where (under postmodernity) meanings have generally imploded, notably in and via the fast-consolidating transnational media. In terms of tourism and heritage, Baudrillard had much to say about how super techno-companies like the Walt Disney Corporation were regularly engaged in the commodification and decontextualization of culture and heritage. |
| **Foucault**<br>Although Foucault constantly maintained that he was not a postmodernist *per se*, his criticisms of Enlightenment rationality and his condemnations of 'history' and 'society' as over-unified wholes do give his writing a pungent postmodern colouration. Principally examining the way all forms of experience are regulated through the quotidian discourse and praxis of institutional domains, Foucault probes the systematic construction of the held knowledges and the held practices of associative bodies. In this light, Foucault shows how understanding of and about things is orchestrated (largely under-suspectingly) through the regimes of power-knowledge which course through those institutions/those domains. In this way, Foucault inspects the technologies of truth which run in capillary and opaque fashion through such institutional regimes. He maintains that such everyday truth-in-currency forms things as 'subjects' and people as 'subjects' (or, rather, helps people to form themselves as 'subjects'!). He suggests the petty talk (discourse) and the petty deeds (praxis) of singular organizations/specialist agencies carcerally discipline those who come into contact with them. Such 'governance', or such eye-of-power *surveillance*, may be metered out by the given body or the presiding institution as it ordinarily conducts its routine affairs over its assumed specialism. In Foucault's judgement, such 'governmentality' over the order of things can help normalize not only those who work for the said mainstreaming body, but also those who are attended to (i.e. 'regulated by') its power-knowledge (Foucault, 1980). While Urry loosely took a Foucauldian line in his book *The Tourist Gaze* (1990), Hollinshead (1993, 1999) has attempted to more explicitly translate Foucault's thinking on the eye-of-power to the quotidian governmentality of things in tourism and heritage. |
| **Deleuze and Guattari**<br>Drawing heavily on psychoanalytic ideas, Deleuze and Guattari deliver a potent poststructuralist assault on the repressive mechanisms of modernity which they posit as a monstrous era of normalizing institutions, structures and discourses. In *Anti-Oedipus* (1972), they show how all sorts of collective/communal edifices work to prevent individual and collective desires from attaining fruition: in it, they call for a postmodern liberation of desire where craving/nomadic individuals can play with plural and multiple identities in a constant round of becoming and transformation. Later, in *A Thousand Plateaus* they further call for the liberation of those sorts of differences and intensities which have been and are tightly held in the grip of machineries of the state. Again, they condemn fixed identities to and for things, and they decidedly celebrate decentred, dispersed and multiple being (Deleuze and Guattari, 1980). Clearly, the relevance of the work of Deleuze and Guattari for tourism and travel is strong, even if it has not yet been regularly or significantly drawn into the literature of Tourism Studies. |

## Bell

A US sociologist with a long background in journalism and socialist politics, Bell theorized that contemporary/postmodern society was highly disjunctive. To him, the lack of a moral belief system (or 'transcendental ethic') in post-industrial society has generated increasing decadence within things which (in turn) has yielded a widening disjunction between 'the culture' and 'the social structure'. For Bell, the resultant postmodern culture of the 1960s (and beyond) was scarcely radical or revolutionary: it merely constituted a counterfeit arena and atmosphere which produced little culture, *ipso facto*, and actually countered nothing (Bell, 1976). In Bell's view the cultural consequences of capitalism were the undermining of bourgeois morality by the adversarial forces of both modernity and postmodernity. To him, the market-focus processes of capitalism generated a postmodern 'pornotopia', and thereby gave rise to all sorts of tasteless and discordant hedonistic lifestyles. The scarcity of over-the-years and multi-site *longitudinal* work in Tourism Studies has meant that few (if any) researchers have attempted to inspect Bellian relations between production and consumption in heritage tourism/cultural tourism *per se*.

## Jameson

A literary critic in the USA, Jameson's interest in postmodernism propelled him, over time, into a much wider engagement with the emergent field of cultural studies. In his view, postmodernism was not just a new aesthetic or cultural style, it was a periodizing concept which housed a whole new type of social life and economic order (Jameson, 1983). Indeed, to Jameson, postmodernism composed the particular and powerful cultural logic of contemporary multinational capitalism. In this sense, Jameson sees the realm of postmodernism as a frenzied sphere of commodity production, driven by the unquenchable drive in and across society for the production of new novel goods after new novel goods, and continually at faster and faster rates of productivity. All of this intense capitalist activity brought about a deep disintegration of people, in his view. And in culture it yielded a new depthlessness to things, where mere *pastiche* became the presidential style, thereby giving a sad weakening in and of the very received or adjudged historicity of things. Perhaps Buck's (1993) study of the effect of tourism on the heritage of Hawaii mirrors some of Jameson's thinking on the form/power of the new capitalistic order of the late twentieth century: Buck herself, however, maintains that her observations on the influence of tourism on the history and politics of culture owe an ideological debt to continental (European) philosophers Althusser and Foucault, rather than to the North American Jameson.

## Thinkers on feminism

Like postmodernism, feminism is a pluralist exercise, and a number of leading feminist ideologists like Haraway have embraced postmodernist thought on account of its capacity to challenge *essentialist* (and particularly gender-essentialist) identities. Such feminists tend to welcome the degree to which postmodernism opens up the fluid of boundaries around things (Haraway, 1990), the degree to which it challenges the solid assumptions of the heavily-masculine Cartesian universe, and the degree to which it demonstrates the dominance – rendering and subjugation – moulding powers of language. Other feminists, however, tend to find the impulses behind postmodernism, particularly of its lead French litero-philosophers Derrida, Lacan, and Foucault, to be resonantly patriarchal. In this light, Brodribb (1993) worries that the postmodernist framing of difference in fact displaces 'the other sex' and strategically depoliticizes women. To such sceptical thinkers in feminist thought, the lack of coverage of 'real' social structures in postmodernist analyses (allied to the sustained preoccupation with 'text' and 'authorship' of such postmodernist accounts) far too regularly channels attention away from the crippling political realities of the day; to many feminists, the concerns of leading postmodernists simply attend insufficiently to the suppressions which are still routinely suffered by women, and insufficiently identify the sorts of other ongoing smotherings and silences which have to be endured by all sorts of other objectified/downtrodden populations (Farganis, 1994). While feminist issues are regularly covered in the field of Tourism Studies by social scientists such as Swain, few feminist commentators have been able to break through the male and managerialist stranglehold that conceivably continues to drive the domain: for instance, in the long-awaited *Encyclopaedia of Tourism*, Kinnaird was only permitted more or less 60 words to define and illustrate the contribution that feminism (in all of its hues) has and can make to our understandings of tourism/culture/heritage/the environment (Jafar, 2000). That is, for instance, about one third of the space allocated to the 'Cruise Lines International Association' entry, and only one sixth of the space allocated to the definition of the 'Council on Hotel Restaurant and Institutional Education' in the field's new reference 'bible'. One may conclude that Tourism Studies clearly does not take itself seriously as a critical field of analysis.

---

**Thinkers on postcolonialism**

Ostensibly, much postcolonialist thought is a thickening of the interest of postmodernist theorists in deconstructing the authoritarian and linearist projections of European/North Atlantic/western culture. Recent thinkers on postcolonialism like the Subaltern Studies group in India object to the elitist articulations of early so-called 'postcolonialists', seeing them as being entrapped entirely or largely within colonialist logocentrisms. Accordingly, the Subaltern Studies group seek to reappraise (and to problematize) the humanist position of seemingly sovereign, *autonomous subjects,* and they generally seek to rewrite the history of colonial/post-colonial places 'from below' in the eyes of those autonomous/ liberated subjects. For instance, Spivak (1996) supports the postmodernist-style re-representation of postcolonial positions, but she is concerned that too many Subaltern theorists ironically remain essentialist themselves, and thereby assume that there is indeed a 'pure' Subaltern voice or a 'true' Subaltern consciousness to be found. Bhabha (1994) may also be interpreted as being a pungently postmodernist thinker on postcolonial matters, notably in terms of his desire to acutely deconstruct the received dichotomies of 'East/West', of 'Centre/Margin', and of 'Self/Other'. By his understanding many postcolonial populations are actually caught in extremely difficult, interstitial positions, restlessly being located 'between cultures'. Drawing on Said, Fanon, and Foucault, Bhabha portrays the ambiguous psychic and awkwardly hybridized locations in which many of the emergent postcolonial peoples of the world now find themselves. Such a mapping of the interstitial locations of culture and heritage has (according to Bhabha) a large relevance for so many sub-cultural groups and 'third space' peoples around the world, if not for all of us. Hence, to Bhabha, such confused postmodern/postcolonial locations of culture and heritage are inevitably restless: while they are characteristically flattened in profile, they are typically capable of double/multiple interpretation, and they can suddenly flicker vibrantly in response to some emergent and often scarcely predictable imperative, impulse or feeling, a fine postmodern representational sympathy, in and of itself. While we await a comprehensive assessment of the import of the work of Spivak and the Subaltern Studies group for tourism/travel, Hollinshead (1998a, 1998b) has attempted to decode the postcolonialist thinking of Bhabha on the hybridity and the ambiguity of peoples/ places/pasts for Tourism Studies. Perhaps, on these refined and precarious matters, he is, however, in these two related papers, often as delicately shadowy and obscure as the cryptic and enigmatic Bhabha, himself!

---

individualistic contributions of the French litero-philosophers Lyotard, Baudrillard, Foucault, Deleuze and Guattari, distinguishing them both from the work of north American intellectuals Bell and Jameson, and from the vast array of feminist and postcolonialist thinkers. In terms of the latter (i.e. the feminist and postcolonialist commentators), the table is put forward on the recognition that the views of feminists and postcolonialist observers generally and variously complement and accentuate postmodernist thought; yet it is also proffered on the understanding that in certain other contexts, particular adherents of feminist and/or postcolonialist theory detach themselves (sometimes delicately, sometimes decidedly and feistily) from commonplace postmodernist outlooks on things, if ever there can be said to be a clear-cut, central postmodern inspection of things (a moot point, in and of itself). Not all the protagonists detailed in Table 9.3 should, therefore, be regarded as being tolerant of each other's assessments either of what postmodernity is, or of what particular 'good', 'benefit' or 'profitable insight' postmodern critiques can shed over and across the world.

Table 9.4 follows closely on from Table 9.3. It distinguishes some of the characteristic reappraisals of and about things that have recently been brought into our consciousnesses, per medium of the new breezes of postmodernist thought. Table 9.4 is predicated on the view that postmodernist cognition comprises a whole family group of new or renewed conceptual winds. It cites a number of whole new or invigorated understandings which postmodernist thought of one sort or another invokes about what is 'really' different or 'truly' distinctive about particular peoples, places and pasts. Those who work in tourism and/or heritage management, and who engage in research into tourism and/or public culture are encouraged to examine Table 9.4 and question of

*Table 9.4* Postmodernity and the politics-of-resistance: instability and incoherence under new invocations of difference

| Certain claimed new or re-caste characteristics in the dominance and suppression of things under the postmodern mood or condition |
| --- |
| 1. **Postmodernity heralds** a new politics of difference<br>*New voices of race*, colour, ethnicity, gender, sexual orientation and other alternative/underground persuasion have emerged from the margins under the postmodern predicament; |
| 2. **The new postmodern** politics of difference compose a perpetual frenzy<br>Under the postmodern mood, *this ceaseless reshuffle* is largely waged over questions of plural, local and immanent legitimacy; |
| 3. **The campaigns and the rhetorics** of different marginal/darkground populations cross-fertilize<br>Under the postmodern condition, *in the effort to destabilize or delegitimate existing elites and assumed authenticities*, the games and plays of different underground interest groups inter-pollinate; |
| 4. **The 'alternative' players and ployers** of the new politics-of-difference are prone to not respect existing jurisdictional and administrative canons<br>*The resultant social and cultural politics*, under the postmodern predicament, is not easy to contain within existing institutional boundaries; |
| 5. **The 'alternative' players and ployers** of the new politics-of-difference are increasingly antagonistic to political systems which impose, or appear to impose, uniformity<br>*Such marginalized individuals and groups* are increasingly alert, under the postmodern mood, to disempowering rhetorics of uniformity, inclusive of their own; |
| 6. **The battle of the marginalized** to replace old elitisms and established dominances is never finally won since it may continue (or lie dormant) in the past as well as being constantly reformulated or merged in the present<br>Often, under the postmodern condition, *new elitisms quickly or quietly replace old elitisms*, or otherwise, dominant populations assume a particular vocal/agitated marginal ill has been dealt with by an early/initial 'solution'; marginal ills have generally been seen to be regularly re-negotiated; |
| 7. **Under the new politics-of-difference** social forces are increasingly aligned in relation to either established rules-of-reason or otherwise to emergent/local knowledge-based discourse<br>*The intimate ties of 'knowledge' to 'situated interest'* are steadily replacing the intimate ties of 'material production' to 'situated interest', under the abandonments of the postmodern moment; |
| 8. **Many individuals and groups** continue to be marginalized by forms of strategic action which are based on distorted communication<br>*The mainstream media continue* to play a huge role in the issuance of privileged or contesting representations of reality and of marginality and thus, under the postmodern predicament, some mediations do not so much change, *ipso facto*, as they accelerate in speed or thicken in influence; |
| 9. **The diversity of voices**, interests and representations within the politics-of-difference is irreducible<br>*What increasingly matters in political action*, under the postmodern mood, is not the battle for equivocality among players and interest groups in fixed situations, but the capacity of players and interest groups to remain strategically unfixed and thereby able to take tactical advantage out of the ambiguities, the incoherences and the instabilities of those sorts of political arrangements which are losing received consensus; |
| 10. **The new politics-of-difference** is not the same as the new politics-of-otherness<br>Under the postmodern condition, *the politics-of-difference continues to be foundational* and continues to privilege *identity per se* over difference. In this respect, a new postpostmodern politics-of-otherness could or should *privilege difference as celebrated dissemblance* or as *championed divergence*, yet, at present, much of the new politics-of-difference still remains essentialist. |

*Source*: Adapted from Hollinshead (1993, pp. 437–8), and originally drawn from insights in Connor (1989), Ross (1988), Foster (1985), among other accounts of the abandonments of postmodernity.

themselves which voices they generally help privilege, uncover or stifle. And they are encouraged to consider who is indeed *made* central and who is *made* peripheral via the mythic structures of history, management and research practice within which they respectively operate.

Let tourism researchers and practitioners not be closed to the important influences and substantive impacts listed. While it will clearly not be possible to test such an extensive set of expectancies within the context of a singular study, the suppositional insight contained within these propositions constitutes an important backdrop to investigations in historical tourism and in heritage tourism. Hopefully, each proposition can be examined rigorously and improved upon by a diversity of tourism researchers over a range of settings.

## POSTMODERNITY AND THE WORTH OF HISTORY

A common view among social theorists is that postmodernity is an unheroic age, an age where the epics, sagas and heroes of past generations are no longer axiomatically revered (Public Service Broadcast, 1992). This acute questioning of the past has been referred to as the loss of a sense of history (Jameson in Stephanson, 1988). It is the view of a number of theorists of postmodernity that the diminution of historical consciousness is part of the way people are differently positioning themselves. Jameson (1988) maintains that for many western individuals, their positioning is increasingly being based upon spatial rather than temporal co-ordinates. Westerners are becoming 'placeless' in terms of their own reflexivity with the historical storylines of their 'own'/ 'inherited' culture (Connor, 1989) and more commonly being 'placed' in terms of the consolidating global, multinational culture.

Contemporaneously, other theorists of postmodernity suggest that the history that has survived to today is being transformed by sheer acts of imaginative will, where this imaginative will is a political will. Baudrillard (1983), for instance, evidences a collapse of the gaps between ideology and history, between appearance and reality and between meaning and representation. Accordingly, for Baudrillard, inherited differences and historical pedigrees are no longer anywhere near so 'effective' in the contemporary western world: such differences are imploding. Grossberg (1988, p. 175) summarizes Baudrillard's views as follows:

> Reality as the site of the origin of effects, desires and powers has drifted away, leaving us in an 'hyperreality' that is always and only a simulacrum. In the simulacrum, nothing exists outside 'the compulsive repetition of the codes'; it is merely that which can be modeled, that which already fits the model, that is positioned as the 'hyperreal'. We live in 'the age of events without consequences'.

Hence, for Baudrillard, image has become more real than reality itself. Historical difference has become unimportant. Historical pedigree is no longer worth much at all. To Baudrillard, heritage has and is certainly being hooliganized. His view is that while the gulf between 'high' and 'low' history is slowly clouding over, it is being made artificially murky at an exceedingly fast pace. Yet, if culture is a force of social control, history and heritage representation are also a form or tool of social control. History and heritage identifications have been used to legitimate what is 'pedigree', what is 'vulgar', what is 'high' and what is 'low'. If history and heritage change and are changed, different forces are likely to benefit in society in terms of the political, economic, symbolic, juridical and other benefits they reap from the telling of history.

In Bell's (1976) neo-conservative judgement, culture and history have been split off from society to function more or less separately. To Bell, the cultural and historical lifeworld have become infected through capitalism by what he called 'modernism', but which others now tend to regard as the unlimited self-realizations and hyper-stimulate sensitivities of postmodernity. For Bell, that is a sorry state of affairs, for his modernist (i.e. postmodernist) culture is no longer consonant with the moral strength of a rational life led purposefully. For others it is the bland recognition that pluralism is replacing the unitary power axes of culture and history: the erstwhile hierarchies of culture and heritage are collapsing (Hebdige, 1986).

So, if not only the position of history and the place of heritage have altered but also their approved forms have changed, different groups and individuals are likely to be gaining. The history and the heritage of peoples and places are proving to be neither so homogeneous nor so monolithic as they were formerly felt to be (Owens, 1985). A wider range of people and populations can share in history's munificence: the promise of postmodernity in terms of heritage is that now actors, new players, new ideas and new imagination can 'fight over, if not infiltrate, every last inch of new historical terrain' (Ross, 1988, p. viii).

## A SUMMARY CROSS-EVALUATION OF HISTORY AND HERITAGE RESEARCH WITH POSTMODERN THEMES AND IDEAS ON POWER AND TRUTH

In this final section, reviewing the recent history and heritage literature on the asymmetries of power and discourse involved in the eugeny of the past, some of the evident mutual impacts of postmodernity upon history and heritage will be inspected. In order to analyse that mutuality for tourism researchers and practitioners, heavy reliance will be made of Fjellman's (1992) account of Walt Disney World as a cultural fantasy landscape which provides a highly valuable synthesis of entrepreneurial and ideological narrative under postmodernity within tourism, leisure and visitor management. The Fjellman text is a lengthy study of who appears to benefit from the invention and reinvention of culture, in which history and heritage play prominent roles. In studying Disney World as a tourism drawcard, Fjellman notes that the Disney Company 'has managed to insinuate its characters, stories and image as a good, clean fun enterprise into the consciousness of millions and around the earth' (p. 398). There is much in Fjellman's specific findings for Florida and Disney that stir thinking about the general creation and recreation of the past, particularly with regard to the way the commodity form directs activity, behaviour and cognition at Disney World under the postmodern influences there, and the way that commodities may also be assumed to dictate participation and response at history/heritage sites. Fjellman indeed deems the commodity form to be 'the taken-for-granted hegemonic truth of our times' (p. 402) in matters of society, culture, ritual and tourism.

Fjellman acknowledges that people invent culture ceaselessly. He explores that fabrication, defabrication and refabrication closely. Drawing from Achenbach, he finds that at sites and places of cultural consumption in the USA 'the line between reality and fiction has become attenuated' (p. 300). And, in assessing the uncertainties between reality and fiction, he judges Disney World, the tourist drawcard *par excellence* to be 'the most ideologically important piece of land in the United States' (p. 10) in terms of the way it essentially reveals and even sets in motion major changes in American patterns and practices of cultural consumption. It is at Disney that the postmoderniza- tion and the commodification of culture occurs at its fastest: consequently, Disney World is the teaching shrine for the corporate world of commodities.

Fjellman maintains that Disney World, as a tourist/visitor magnate, is a behemoth in regard both to the way it reflects cultural consumption and in the way it changes patterns of cultural consumption. Pointing out that its turnstiles clicked over 26 million times in 1988, rendering it 'the most visited tourist site in the world other than Spain' (p. 395) (an odd comparison!), it is, therefore, a site of volume and velocity into which many visitors implicate themselves. Hence, to Fjellman, as commodification has metastasized and 'forced itself into every cell of human life' in the United States, it is at Disney World where the constant metastasis of cultural preference is most in evidence (p. 4). And through the rapidity and the amplitude of that metastasis of commodity and postmodern influence on and in culture, the past is significantly changed at accelerated speed. To Wallace (1985), the Disney companies commit historicide. To Fjellman, history there becomes 'distory', something which is not so much reflexive of Orwell's obvious lies and Orwellian boots 'stomping on an human face', but rather something indicative of Huxley's warnings of the way the world will be made available instead through desire and pleasure. Fjellman's distory – no, Disney's distory – is extreme postmodernization of the past: it is a brave new world of decorative heritage inspired and stimulated through cultivated gratification rather than through totalitarian force.

Thus Fjellman sees distory as:

(a)   a postmodern form of presentation of the past which cultivates in visitors the desire to consume commodified packages of surreal/hyperreal history;

(b)   a postmodern production of spectacle selected and designed for its ease of varied and reproducible sellability;

(c)   a postmodern and self-referential peregrination during which visitors are encouraged to reconstitute themselves through consumption of, and identification with, the preselected symbols of commerce;

(d)   a postmodern set of clarified metastories, subtly condemned and transmitted cinematically, and cleverly, to enforce and reinforce the prescribed Disney worldview;

(e)   a postmodern adaptation of science, literature, geography and history in order to support the 'decent' and 'nationalist' corporate rhetoric and business;

(f)   a postmodern seizure of usable storylines from the past which are decontext- ualized and romanticized and thereby turned into forms of nostalgia that can decorate and be purchased, but which are frequently much diminished in connected meaning;

(g)   a postmodern presentation of that decontextualized history and heritage through the projection of animated, purchasable image through the possession of which the visitor learns to reconstruct himself/herself in accordance with the preferred, defused versions of history presented to him/her;

(h)   a postmodern telling of history and heritage where the differences between the real and the unreal are purposely and effectively blurred, but which is muddled and orderless, and conveyed in volume at precipitate speed and in a repeated fashion;

(i) a postmodern admixture of historical truths and illusions which amuses, but which is muddled and orderless, and conveyed in volume at precipitate speed and in repeated fashion; and

(j) a postmodern exhilarating and paradisal vision of a 'spruced up' past which prepares visitors optimistically for the next challenge of the future (as envisioned for them by Disney and its partner operators), and for which the visitor has scant 'interpretive autonomy'.

## PROSPECT: THE IMPLICATIONS OF 'DISTORY'-STYLE PRESENTATIONS FOR HERITAGE TOURISM

The development of distory (or for present purposes, should it be given as 'distory' *and* 'deritage'?) is of profound relevance to this examination of the construction of truth in the promotion, sale and administration of history and heritage in tourism. What goes on at Disney sites in Florida, California, France and Japan may be extreme cases of the manufacture of heritage in view of the scale of their operations and the weight of expenditure and revenue that pass through the ubiquity of the same distory messages in books, on films, video and merchandising, and the very degree to which Disney ideas are copied elsewhere at other tourism sites around the globe gives distory an epidemic force. Disney is massive in its edifice and in its broadcasting and communicative impact: distory, accordingly, has an extremely sonorous voice in getting certain versions of culture and particular versions of heritage heard. It is not limited by its own geographical or territorial basis; it is presented by Fjellman as the wave of the beaming, the cabling and the publishing future.

The postmodern style of history and heritage, as led by Disney, is 'spectacle': it is a themed and montaged display of simulation and hyperreality. It is the past with a new sort of a truth and a lot of new hues to it. Visitors to Disney, readers and watchers of distory, scanners and zappers of distory, postmonauts all:

> do not quest after an authentic pre-simulational reality but have the necessary dispositions to play in 'the play of the real' and capacity to open up to surface sensations, spectacular imagery, liminoid experiences and intensities without the nostalgia for the real. (Featherstone, 1991, p. 60)

The success of distory and of what we may call 'deritage' (though Fjellman, himself, does not use the term), as measured in sales and at the turnstiles, raises the practical question as to how real need be presented history and illuminated heritage to work in the postmodern marketplace in tourism. Yet they also raise the philosophical question as to how real any history narrative or heritage storyline is anywhere, anyway, anytime. In putting distory under intensive scrutiny, Fjellman (1992) finds that its truth and its 'lies' are becoming indistinguishable; yet perhaps Disney World is all only an extended and particularly colourful case of what has been happening in the construction of history and heritage all along, down the centuries (or up the centuries, as modernists would possibly have it).

One could argue, then, that the distory and the deritage presentations of today in tourism offer nothing new. There is no change in form, only an alteration of degree. When Fjellman echoes Baudrillard, and emphasizes that at Disney under Hyperreality, illusion is no longer possible because reality, itself, is no longer possible, we need to recall that there never has been one all-purpose unchallengeable reality underpinning accounts of the history and the heritage of peoples and places. It is a perspectival impossibility: people in any age are never, ever likely to agree on what happened in the past. What has changed is the extent to which the amplitude of signage (of all sorts and communicative methods) at Disney, specifically, and under postmodernity, in general, produces spectacle at a faster and thicker rate. And that spectacle can be illusion or it can be truth. One could conclude, then, that under distory and deritage, and, indeed, under the mood or condition of postmodernity, there is not so much a falsification of the past as a technological reinvention of it: distory and deritage are not as much truthless representations as they are a-truthful ones. Under distory and under deritage, and under the era or climate of postmodernity, one could observe that history and heritage are dependent upon authority: 'histories remain in force when they are supported by enough authority, whether the information on which their claims rest is real, false or incomplete' (Fjellman, 1992, p. 62). At Disney World, that authority is contained, it is claimed and held by those who design and adumbrate the commodity form. In this fashion at Disney, history-via-distory and heritage-via-deritage act 'as a shell for decontextualized, digitalizing 'hard-path' technologies' (*ibid.*, pp. 24–5). Authority over the past, there, lies within *techne*: that, to many, is a highly dangerous eventuality.

But the postmodernization of history at Disney is no mild acceleration of technological artistry. To Fjellman, distory and the project of commodity aesthetics are military. Disney World is not an accidental shrine for yesteryear, or a nature, or for global possibility, it is an intended shrine for preferred and esteemed versions of those very things. It is a shrine to the religion of desire. For Fjellman, to reiterate, Disney is Huxley's vision of the Brave New World, 'one based on the reinforcement of desired behaviour by reward'. It speaks up for a world where the corporate commodifiers and cross-marketing referential partners have been able to purloin the cultural icons from past history and from accumulated heritage, or otherwise have been able to invent new cultural icons within forms of pasteurized history and of, perhaps, 'hygienic heritage'. And all that postmodern ballyhoo in the commodified tourism of central Florida, and elsewhere, has been conducted with warlike zest. The zeal behind the telling of distory does not stem from any disinterest in or neutrality about the past.

Over the centuries, historians and heritage interpreters of various sorts have widely and repeatedly failed to recognize the role of the human mind in the production of knowledge and the creation of storylines on yesteryear (Preiswerk and Perrot, 1978, p. 269). Fjellman's insights on distory have an important value in bringing these issues, and these subtle and not so subtle acts of eugeny, to a head. The neutrality of communicated historical facts is just that more transparent under distory and pastiche of deritage; the false neutrality of historical truths is just a bit easier to see through, there at Disney World. After Fjellman, historical truth and heritage veracity may now not be seen to be so different from historical lies and from heritage falsehood. With history and heritage now proving to be so episodic and so changeable on central stage under their commodified guise as distory and deritage (and under other presentations of pastiche tourism elsewhere), both reality and illusion are now that little bit easier to spot as being the product of soldiery and sanguinary intent.

Yet, distory, deritage, and other postmodernity narratives in the simulacra of tourism, are not just matters of the kinetic mosaic of the post-industrial/service-sector age (Fjellman, 1992, p. 360). The lesson to be learnt for tourism research and practice from the Disney and other postmodern kaleidoscopic treatments of the past is not simply one about contemporary theatre posing as truth. If this postmodern age can muster up its own conception of what is really important in and of the past, then any age can, and any political grouping can rearrange and reassemble the inheritance of peoples and places. And, in this sense, the architects and the designers of emergent storylines in tourism are no longer just receiving second-storey players, thereby they are also first-storey communicators in the manipulation of the past.

It is conceivable that, hereafter, plural interpretation will become even more significant and commonplace in the telling of the past in travel and tourism around the globe. If hierarchical order over society continues to crumble as it has conceivably done during the twentieth century, the scope for multiple truths (in tourism exhibitory and in travel presentations) will continue to widen. History and heritage accounts will be omniform and protean more often, in more tourism places, and on more tourism occasions. History and heritage will not be seen as singular entities, preciously protected from the world; they are part of the human, known world, and they are constructed differentially over time and place through the changing vicissitudes of authority and cohesion in society. Wider worldviews always, inevitably, affect how the past is construed, and they will do so in the tourism narratives of future generations. The current, loudest ballyhoo on and about the past in tourism under postmodernity is heavily corporate, and is heavily commodified in its aesthetics. The succeeding ballyhoo may be even more corporate and even more embedded within the commodity form. Or, then, the past might be something else again: the kinetics may be something else, and then legitimated from some other source of authority entirely.

Disney's 'duture' (future) will not really help us (today) to know. Therefore, its visions can only help and hinder our present capacity to imagine, as they cleverly, technologically and gratifyingly insinuate themselves into our personal conceptions of what will be important, just as the bricolage of distory and the pastiche of deritage seek to tell us cleverly, technologically and gratifyingly, what was (and is) important. And the new pasts roll and cavort on.

## CERTAIN CAVEATS ON POSTMODERN UNDERSTANDING

During the last two decades of the twentieth century, the number of social scientists who made considerable use of postmodern styles of analysis expanded exponentially. A broad and mixed church of 'soft-science' theoreticians like Stephen Fjellman have harnessed the new and frequently insurrectionary logics of and about truth, right and power that course through the recent continental writings of Lyotard, Baudrillard, Foucault, Deleuze, Guattari and others. In the light of that new and renewed logic, they have generated whole new understandings regarding our identities, our affiliations, our collectivities, our new transnational bonds of association and our fresh aspirations. Clearly, these new intelligences about hyperreal culture (after Baudrillard), about pastiche styles of living (after Jameson) and about unsuspected agents of normalcy (after Foucault), et cetera, have catalysed our cognitions about the subtle ways the past, present and future are discriminatingly but penetratingly appreciated; and they have catalysed our insights into the way particular sites or storylines can be discriminatingly but penetratingly re- or de-celebrated.

Yet, all too frequently, the endeavour to announce new postmodern perceptions in and over things has become an underregulated 'game' of claimed liberated critique. Too frequently, these newly invigorated and largely relativistic reassessments run away with themselves. Thus, Table 9.5 is now provided to help readers recognize some of the cardinal dangers involved in the unfettered indulgence in postmodern outlooks.

*Table 9.5* Some postmodern problematics: certain major difficulties with postmodernist lines of thought

| |
|---|
| ***Under postmodernism, meaning destructs***<br>Some opponents of postmodernist thought censure it because it offers no values which transcend time, place and specific interests, and so cannot readily be used to justify political action. Thus collective postmodern critique is regarded as 'running rampant' without political direction, being destructive of consummate meaning. Consonantly, such opponents maintain that 'extreme' postmodernists like Baudrillard can only write about fleeting feelings or about isolated/fragmented experiences: treatise-writers like Baudrillard and Barthes are seen to have little measured understanding to ever contribute substantively to our understanding of patterned social phenomena. |
| ***Under postmodernism, anything goes***<br>Just as postmodern commentators like Baudrillard write of an 'anything goes' culture characterized by immediacy, disorientation and indifference, so critics of these writers say they themselves (i.e. Baudrillard and company) indeed write with their own 'anything goes' absence of gravity. While the postmodernist writers talk of a contemporary culture which annihilates all referents and dissolves the boundaries between fantasy and fact, so they are themselves accused of writing with the same over-free hand. The rejection (by Baudrillard and company) of what others regard as the basic assumption of social theory despoils the opportunity for the engagement of postmodernist thought with other late/contemporary social theories (Antonio, 1991). |
| ***Under postmodernism, obscure metaphysics triumphs***<br>Taken *in toto*, the body of postmodernist theory is incoherent and all-too-frequently contradictory, a result of many postmodernists either writing too loosely, or of dabbling in abstruse and speculative incorporealities. To Giddens (1987), the postmodernists' arch-tool of *deconstruction* (after Derrida) is 'a dead tradition of thought', and *the hyperreal* is likewise dismissed by Harvey as being so banal in its conceptuality that it (ironically) needs its own poetic hyper-rhetoric to describe it! To the adversaries of postmodernist thought, there is no simply clear consensus anywhere as to what is postmodernity. |
| ***Under postmodernism, there is only discourse***<br>Dissentient voices against postmodernist thought tend to conclude that postmodernist assessments of culture and society are commonly as flat and non-dimensional as the simulated worlds of image which postmodernist observers prefer to write about. By this, it is generally meant that to theorize about postmodernity, one must accept an extremely broad and complex mix of phenomena, geographical situations, and periodic contexts. Thus postmodernist accounts are frequently dismissed because of the very 'convenient' width of this purview. Such postmodernist outlooks do not sufficiently go into local matters of production, and are condemned for largely remaining as scarcely situated or as unsituated text. And, following such critique further, the majority of postmodernist accounts tend to be ungrounded in terms of economic and class relations, remaining only as ever-shifting forms of essayist discourse (Kaplan, 1988). |
| ***Under postmodernism, international understanding is denied***<br>Gitlin (1989) is dissatisfied with most postmodernist commentary because it abandons the quest for unity of vision in social science, and for continuity in/of human understanding. Fraser and Nicholson (1988) concur with this view, and bemoan the fact that the commonplace postmodernist rage against totality inevitably frustrates the winning of global outlooks from postmodern conceptualities, sufficient to ever significantly advance critical social theory. Thus, such disputants against postmodernist thought are inclined to rail against the absence of a or any 'language' in postmodernist thought that can embrace the threads of shared and international life across the world, or of shared human living across the ages. |

*Under postmodernism, negativism thrives*
Although postmodernist thought is regularly praised for its pluralisms, it is regularly upbraided for failing to elaborate new avenues by which the suppressed/disadvantaged can go about societal reformation: in fact, to outsiders, postmodernist thinkers rarely seem interested in helping the subordinated *pragmatically* out of the dilemmas they have to endure. The war of Lyotard and Baudrillard *et al.* is not then seen to be decently *emancipatory*, while the work of Foucault is not only seen to be non-normative, it also is censured for being typically *non-positive* (Best, 1994). In these ways Baudrillard, Lyotard and Foucault are damned for their routine pessimisms (Antonio and Kellner, 1994), and for seemingly condemning everything yet proposing nothing buoyant or expectant in its stead. Hence, adversaries of postmodernist thought suggest that postmodernist logic needs to have its natural erosive 'hermeneutics of suspicion' conjoined by a more helpful and counter-balancing 'hermeneutics of affirmation'. Then, the antagonists of postmodernist truths argue, postmodernist thought would indeed do us all a pro-bono service: it could/would in fact tell us which demon to follow (Farganis, 1994)!

*Under postmodernism, people do not matter*
In a famous denunciation of postmodernist thought (and of theorizations about post-Marxism, post-structuralism, post-Fordism and post-industrialism), the Marxist theoretician Callinicos suggested that such post-isms are no more than the ideological mainstay of a rising intellectual elite. Callinicos (1990) suggests that the experiences of such a removed elite are entirely esoteric, and consequently remote from the proper work 'of the [real] revolutionary project'. Numerous other observers (not all of them Marxists, themselves) have suggested that the work of Baudrillard and of other leading French litero-philosophers of and about postmodernity is like the make-believe work of Adorno – it is largely 'depopulated' fiction (Billig, 1994). Perhaps Cloud (1994) is even more pointedly dismissive of 'the great subversive' Foucault for the radical and ubiquitous *anti-humanism* of his (Foucault's) postmodernist thinking. Clegg (1991) joins Cloud in weighing in against Foucault, and finds that Foucault's maverick lack of concern for human action repeatedly forestalls the chance of there being any possibility of transformative conscious political endeavour arising from his (Foucault's) libertine insights.

*Under postmodernism, some epics are better than others!*
The final stricture against postmodernist thought largely targets the thinking of Lyotard, whose early and pioneering postmodernist logic – as was observed above in Table 9.3 – saw no place for meta-narrative during the so-called postmodern moment. In this fashion, such doubters argue that Lyotard's postmodernist logic tends to end up preaching against itself, *in toto*: they ironically adjudge the logic of Lyotard to constitute *a vibrant continental theory* which denounces the need for *vibrant continental theories*. Thus, while Lyotard is seen to dissent against the 'epic' or universal claims of modernity, his own postmodernist thinking is found to comprise an 'epic' in and of itself (Ross, 1988)! Lyotard might claim to attack the generalization principles which drive the universalisms of modernity, yet his own postmodernist treatise is seen to encompass something of a generalized and universalist narrative 'of grand *meta* proportions' itself.

Table 9.5 lists eight of the key difficulties which are often raised against the seeming crapulence of over-intoxicated postmodernist analysis. While those who wish to research the iconographies and the iconologies of the past (as they are signified in the heritage tourism of the present) are certainly to be encouraged to acquaint themselves with the new wakeful insights which drift into Tourism Studies on various sorts of Barthesian or Bhabhian postmodern breezes, they should maintain a healthy circumspection about gulping down postmodernity as a *force majeure*. As the eight cardinal objections of Table 9.5 suggest, rampant postmodern thinking can leave us with a host of negativities and destructivities, as these new airy postmodern breezes penetrate our local fogs and our domain mists, or as they creep up to swirl over and past us.

For some, the new, admixed and generally insouciant styles of postmodern thought have helped us to re-decipher the whole history and condition of humanity. For others, as Table 9.5 evinces, the whole postmodern game has just been a free-and-easy play of vacant discourse. The jury is still out, then, on whether postmodern thoughtlines have, overall, been a helpful theoretical 'windfall' for the humanities, to thereby, in Tourism

Studies for instance, widen our understandings of whom we all are, and deepen our insights into what we seek to project, to celebrate or to visit.

Now that the winds of postmodern thought have come (and still linger among us?), many of us in Tourism Studies are steadily learning to much more frequently and wittingly self-superintend the truths we work to in our tourism management practice and tourism research practice: yes, even in the Punch-and-Judy and Mickey Mouse Fjellmanic realms of Tourism Studies. Perhaps, by definition, that increasing self-surveillance means that the breezy occurrence of the recent postmodern draughts and the pluralistic zephyrs of postmodern thought have been an aggregate 'plus' for us, despite the discrepancies of logic and impact alluded to in Table 9.5. Perhaps our understanding of history and heritage (as of all human and societal things) has indeed been animated and vivified. But, as Table 9.5 warns, one can easily get breathless thinking about all of these new reflexive possibilities and these new relative potentialities for things. One can run too far and too fast with one's Lyotardian distrust of metanarrative, or with one's Baudrillardian distaste for the assumed power of the sign over ourselves. As Table 9.5 suggests, one can run too swiftly with the postmodern breezes at one's back, to thereby suddenly lose one's way back, never able to return to old domains of understanding, or, indeed, to *any* collective domain of understanding.

As this endnote is penned in the middle of 2001, one windy night in the midst of an English summer (see, we even have postmodern weather, now!), one wonders what we will all think of all these postmodern postulations in posterity. One wonders just what our grandchildren and great-grandchildren (i.e. our post-children?) will think of the interpretive turns, the textual turns, and the rhetorical turns which good and wise postmodernist logicians have empowered themselves to indulge in at the turn of the millennium. Roll on 2101, and 2201, theorists of Our Future; do give us your judgement on the deep postmonautics of Our Present. Pray tell us, in general, where truth headed, and where hyperreality and pastiche ended up? And inform us, in particular, about the future heritage of our Cultural Tourism truth-making. Did Lyotard lie around for long? Did we soon forget Foucault? Was Deleuze deluded?

## Chapter 10

# 'The time of our lives' or time for our lives: An examination of time in holidaying

*Chris Ryan*

## INTRODUCTION

It is often said that holidays represent a period when we can 'have the time of our lives'. It is a commonly used expression, but what does it mean? This final chapter takes a look at this expression by examining the question of time *in* holidays as distinct from time *on* holiday. This is a pertinent question because if holidays are periods of special experiences outside of daily life, then possibly one explanation of this uniqueness is that holiday-makers, freed from their normal constraints, might have a different perception of time. Again, the very expression 'the time of our lives' implies a specific concept of time – it is '*the* time' in the meaning of *the event* or *happening*. It implies that time is not just a chronological sequence, but also a social construct.

The chapter thus considers what is meant by 'time', and reviews some of the literature about the subject. In the first edition of this book, comment was made upon the relative scarcity of references to time within the tourism literature. It was as if no-one had thought to consider the implications of the common statement quoted above. Indeed, it was asked whether examination of the phrase was worth pursuing. It was argued that it was not possible to conclude that the question has no meaning until an answer is considered, that there is a curious symbiosis between questions and answers. The nature of the question can prejudge the answer. Some six years later much truth still remains within the original contention, although in one area, that of a postmodern analysis of time-space compression that characterizes tourism, there exists a literature, albeit much of it not replicated (at the time of writing, 2001) in the main tourism journals. Equally, it can be noted, some of the key texts in this area (such as that of Lash *et al.* (1998), entitled *Time and Value*) are able to devote a whole book to the subject of time without reference to the time-space compression that is symptomatic of tourism. Therefore, after reviewing some concepts of time, the chapter will conclude the book by reviewing briefly some of the points made in earlier chapters.

## SOME CONCEPTS OF HOLIDAY TIME

Some holidays are sold as 'a once-in-a-lifetime experience'. So what is the nature of this time? It has been argued that holidays represent special periods in people's lives when the constraints of everyday life are, if not forgotten, at least relaxed. For many people holidays are a period when it is possible to reclaim time. In an unpublished survey of 1127 holiday-makers of the east Midlands, the author found that some respondents spoke of their holidays as relaxing in the sense that they had a feeling of not being time-constrained in their activities – they did not have to do things – there was no imposition made upon them. As already noted, Crompton (1979) spoke of holidays as periods of family bonding, and some respondents specifically referred to this motivation in such terms as: 'It was nice to have time to play with the children'; 'It was a pleasure to have time with my wife.'

It has been argued that holidays represent a valid area of research not only for what such studies reveal about holiday behaviours, but also for what that behaviour reveals about wider contemporary social life. Earlier writers, such as Shaw (1990) and Kay and Jackson (1990), have referred to and researched the phenomenon of the 'harried leisure class'. In Chapter 2, research relating to constraints upon female leisure was mentioned, wherein it was noted that some women develop coping behaviours to balance competing demands upon their time.

Holidays are a temporal experience in many ways. Some include:

(a)   freedom from constraints imposed by perceived or actual lack of time;
(b)   holidays as the passing of time – holidays have a chronological sequence;
(c)   holidays as an experience of time – the elasticity of time; and
(d)   holidays as possessing temporal boundaries beyond the duration of the stay at the destination – holidays are anticipated and remembered.

With reference to this last point, it has become a cliché that a holiday begins with the last holiday – the recent vacation experience and the re-immersion into the 'daily world' often creates a longing for the next holiday. As shown in Chapter 3, the holiday is a learning experience with which the holiday-maker can establish criteria for assessing the promise of locations and destinations of the future. There is an overlap of reliving the recent past through the use of souvenirs and the claiming of recently developed photographs, and the anticipation of the next period of holidaying. Hence, as argued in Chapter 4, the visit to the travel agent is also part of the holiday experience.

Holidays also possess a curious 'elasticity' in our experience of time. The sense of a 'good time' is that it possesses an experience of the infinite. The contemplation of waves breaking on rocks, the view of majestic scenery – all such experiences can create a sense of 'timelessness'. Equally, good companionship, a sense of social closeness, can produce a feeling of participating in, and wanting to extend, a perpetual process of the 'holiday society' in which the tourist finds himself – a special type of society where basic needs are met by 'service providers' which permits a fulfilling social relationship to flourish. Yet the date of return can arrive quickly, and it seems like only yesterday that the holiday-maker was starting on his holiday.

Such senses of time are very different to the eternity of time produced by boredom, when time seems to 'hang heavy'; a never-ending period with little promise of it stopping. So holidays possess qualitative aspects to time, or a 'flow' that permits special experiences to be had.


## TIME AS A SOCIAL CONSTRUCT

So, if holidays are indeed about having 'the time of our lives', they possess curious attributes of time, which perhaps necessitates a closer examination of what is meant by 'time'. But to so examine a phenomenon that is so common to us all that we fail to comment upon it, implies that the question of 'What is time?' has value. In one sense Hollinshead, in Chapter 9, has already approached this question – the time of the past is a manipulated, social time, in that the chronological sequencing of history as measured by the happening of events is interpreted by the present. Implicit in both Hollinshead's analysis and in the above introduction is the notion that time possesses not only a flow in and of itself, but also within human experiences, a specific social construction. Adam (1994) has drawn a distinction between 'organic' and 'artefactual' time. She writes that:

> Time in the natural environment is characterised by rhythmic variation, synchronization and an all-embracing, complex web of interconnections. Linear sequences take place but these are part of a wider network of cycles as well as finely tuned and synchronized temporal relations where ultimately everything connects to everything else: the structure of an ecological system is temporal and its parts resonate with the whole and vice-versa. Rhythmicity, therefore, forms nature's silent pulse. (pp. 94–5)

On the other hand, artefactual time is the time measured by watches and clocks – a resource to be used. Therefore this concept of time, argues Adam, becomes a product, not a process, and has the result that the user of time becomes separated from the processes of organic time. Associated with the rationalization of scientific processes that have characterized western thought, the creation of linear perspectives have had value in gaining knowledge by demarcating differences between past, present and future, and by laying an emphasis upon longevity (e.g. of transmission of knowledge into the future). Yet, at the same time, argues Adam (1994) the result has been a process of disembedding, detemporalization and externalization.

Certainly it would appear that there are differences in the time being taken for holidays. Chapter 1 referred to the holidaying periods of the past, for example 'Saint Monday'. The current time patterns of holidays seem to have been established in the modern period of industrialization, and the 'package holiday' of the jet travel era has been established only since the 1950s. There is anthropological evidence that different peoples have different perspectives of time. Whorf (1956) pointed out that the Hopi Indians of the USA do not have a word for time. Evans-Pritchard's (1969) study, undertaken in the late 1930s of the *Nuer*, argued that the *Nuer* conceptualized time as being ecological and socio-structural – that it was based upon the seasons and the appropriateness of rite. In current work on Maori tourism Ryan notes the different time perspective of Maori. For example, the late Emily Schuster, a revered expert in *kahu-taniko* (cloaks) and *raranga* (baskets), who taught these skills of traditional finger weaving at the New Zealand Maori Arts and Crafts Institute, Rotorua, was at pains to point out to the author that a piece of *taniko* work could easily take two years to complete. There would be a proper time for the collection of the flax, a proper time for the collection of the dyes, a proper time for the soaking of the flax, and for the commencement of the work. These 'proper' times were determined, like the case of the *Nuer*, by ecological processes associated with the seasons, and by social processes involving approval by those with *mana* (a spiritual authority). For Maori, there is a sense of time being shared with the ancestors, of a continuing process which yet also encompasses the observed patterns of the seasons.

Arguably, similar concepts of time were found in early western civilizations that were agriculturally based; that there is indeed a 'season for all things'. But what is probably not beyond dispute is that the contemporary notion of time is more diverse; encompassing possibly some remnant of such past notions of time, but also certainly including more mechanistic components of time as a unit of measurement.

However, to perceive holidays as representing opportunities for an escape from the mechanistic interpretation of time to one more akin to that of indigenous peoples is too simplistic. Berger (1984) recognizes part of the problem, stating:

> The explanation [of time] offered by contemporary European culture – which, during the last two centuries, has increasingly marginalised other explanations – is that which constructs a uniform, unilinear law of time applying to all events, and according to which all 'times' can be compared and regulated. This law maintains that the Great Plough and the famine belong to the same calculus, a calculus that is indifferent to both. It also maintains that human consciousness is an event, set in time, like any other. Thus an explanation whose task is to 'explain' the time of consciousness, treats that consciousness as if it were as 'passive' as a geological stratum. (pp. 9–10)

As previously noted, such a view stems from a positivist tradition developed in the modern era. Hollinshead has argued that heritage is a specific interpretation of past events, selected from the past with the eyes of the present. So, too, it might be said of the holiday experience itself. If, as argued in Chapter 2, there is a strong motivation to achieve a satisfactory holiday, the perception of past holidays will be selective, identifying more strongly the positive experiences and diminishing the unacceptable. But does this process of selectivity of events affect the perceptions of experienced time? Additionally, does not such an argument imply that time is solely a subjective experience, lacking an independent existence not associated with humans? In short, if Berger argues that time has been seen as 'uniform' and 'indifferent', does an alternative thesis have to restate time as having a basis solely in subjective experience?

So far the discussion of time has indicated various perceptions – it is independent and indifferent to humans, or it is based solely in the human experience. Moreover, anthropological evidence suggests that differences exist between contemporary urban-based societies, and those with perceptions of time based upon clear, observable seasonal and annual change. A review of the literature indicates a number of variations upon these themes. For example, Lauer (1981) has argued that time is a social construct with multiple dimensions. As an example, it is argued (p. 99) that 'waiting time' can be used to emphasize the power of the person who creates a need for another to wait. Thus time is a social resource used to serve purposes of enforcing power relationships. One of the best examples of 'waiting time' in tourism, and one which reinforces the subordinate role of the tourist, is the 'check in' time required by charter airlines. It is often longer than that required by commercial flights, and subject to more frequent delays. Indeed, long delays can create a sense of 'powerlessness' on the part of the unfortunate holiday-maker.

Schöps is another writer who emphasizes the social dimensions of time, but from the perspective of organizational structures. For Schöps (1980) time is an asset which is planned – it is a basis upon which humans measure duration, sequence, synchronization, and periodicity – it is the social need to co-ordinate activities over time which gives rise to its measurement. This approach too has implications for holidays and their experience. It has been argued that holidays represent opportunities to escape from this facet of time; but, equally, some types of holidays generate intense needs to adhere to schedules. For example, a coach tour maintains a schedule of stops and visits over perhaps several weeks. The schedule can only be maintained by the co-operation of the holiday-makers. It is part of Schöps's analysis of time that failure to adhere to agreed 'times' can merit the imposition of penalties – and so it is with the coach party. These penalties vary. A decision by a party to linger at one spot means that less time is spent at another location. Social pressures might be placed on the individuals within the tour party who cause a coach to be late when leaving a destination, even perhaps to the point of becoming 'social outcasts'. Finally, the coach party itself may be the victim of the coach driver, who may have different time dimensions as a 'worker' to those of the 'holiday-makers'.

Elias (1984) is one writer who recognizes a duality within time. On the one hand there is the natural time of the planetary system – the revolutions around the sun – and the biological clock with the processes of ageing and the irreversible processes towards death. On the other hand there is social time – the time of change exhibited by past events. Elias argues that our experience of time is a synthesis between these two dimensions, that time is a highly sophisticated construct for the co-ordination of the body, person, society and nature. Time is hence a measure, a control, a regulator and a synchronization – it permits us to develop points of reference out of a continuous flow. Time consists of both earlier and later stages, but it also involves the observer. For Elias there is no distinction between the natural processes of time, on the one hand, and humans on the other – the synthesis that is constructed is one where humans are not only part of nature, but *are* nature at a higher level of integration. Thus Elias writes that 'Everything that happens in the human sphere is now experienced and represented by human symbols' (1982, p. 855) and a developing synthesis results, from which the 'natural origins' of time are combined with human awareness of the state of awareness.

Schutz implies that 'the awareness of awareness' is an aspect of self, so that

> We cannot approach the realm of the Self without an act of reflective turning. But what we grasp by the *reflective* act is never the present of our stream of thought ...; it is always its past ... The whole present, therefore, and also the vivid present of our Self, is inaccessible for the reflective attitude. We can only turn to the stream of our thoughts as if it had stopped with the last grasped experience. In other words, self consciousness can only be experienced *modo praeterito*, in the past tense. (Schutz, 1971, pp. 172–3)

It is not new to comment that we are the sum of our experiences. Indeed, that is why holidays are so important, for, as argued in Chapter 1, holidays possess the potential for catharsis. What Schutz adds to this comment is that we are the sum of our pasts; that the very act of contemplation is, as an act of the present, a contemplation of the past and which act, in turn, becomes a part of our past. If there is a selection from the past, to meet the needs of the present, so, too, the holiday-maker creates a self from a selective awareness of the holiday experience. This 'holiday self', however, can also create expectations of the future, but following Schutz, it appears that our expectations of the future are based upon constructs of the past. Adams (1990) argues that:

We *are* time and this fact unites us with all other rhythmically organised beings. Together with plants and animals we *are aware* of time and experience it. As human beings we *have a relationship* to time and we reckon time. As members of Western industrial societies *we create time* as a resource, as a tool, and as an abstract exchange value. (p. 161)

## HOLIDAYS: PERIODS OF FREE TIME

So, given this understanding of time, what does it mean to say that 'we have the time of our lives while on holiday'? One of the interesting aspects of holidays is that it permits holiday-makers to create new senses of time. Like a recent lottery winner of over £20 million in the UK (a worker who had had to rise early in the morning for over twenty years) who commented that he 'was now free of the clock' (BBC TV News, 11 July 1995), the holiday-maker is able to be free of the clock to develop a new time – holiday time.

Holiday time is thus both a chronological sequence and a social construct. But as a social construct it can change the perceptions of the chronological sequencing even while it is unable to change a sense of passing events. Holiday-makers have 'the time of their lives' because they attribute a special significance to holidays. Thus, it is not possible to separately analyse a concept of 'time' on holidays without reference to the issues discussed elsewhere in this book – holidays do not make sense as a means of passing time without reference to the motivations of the holiday-makers. Soares (1998) provides a specific example of this when recounting his experiences of hosting Swedish visitors at his home in Brazil. He notes that 'Actually it was a Brazilian party from the point of view of the Swedish imagination, through which they were trying to experience their own identity from a distance, from an inversion, turning it upside down' (Soares, 1998, p. 131).

The holiday is a process of displacement, and the displacement into another place and a special time creates an imaginary otherness wherein the tourist acts out roles to which he or she provides meaning, a meaning structured within a framework informed by various notions, many of which are derived from entertainment media. Ryan (2001) writes of visitors to sites of indigenous peoples' cultures that

> it is as if they are collecting yet more mementoes for a scrap book of travel memories, that can be potentially very important, but for many are simply matters of the moment, an entertainment, and a curio. It is a commonplace in the academic literature relating to cultural tourism that the places and cultures tourists visit are being packaged for consumption, are visually and aurally consumed and are thirdly being consumed in the sense of being exhausted as rubric and ritual are made devoid of their original meanings. But, as Urry (1995, p. 2) has argued, it is possible for localities to consume one's identity so that such places become almost *all-consuming* places. (Ryan, 2001)

If holidays are times of performance informed by the wider neural structures of perceptions of what performance is, as modelled by Hollywood, then it is of little surprise that tourism products exist to turn tourist into actor, and actor into star. Tinseltown Studios in Anaheim worked on the premise that the tourist was the star attending the Oscars, and in ludic postmodern irony, 'fans' that mobbed the 'stars' were out-of-work 'wannabe' actors of whom several may have entertained the wish to be stars. So tourists were interviewed on the red carpet, waved to fans, and showed the anxieties of potential Oscar winners when the names of nominees were read out. But to add to the confusion of facts and perceived realities, this product ceased operating in 1999 due to 'disappointing demand' and the faux movie studio has now reopened as an 'intimate' theatre seating 1400 for concerts; but advertises, as part of its uniqueness, its history as the place 'where every guest is a star'.

Tourism, perhaps more than most activities, engages in exercises of subjectivity. As the tourist seeks a role in a place of difference in a temporal finity, then by the act of not being that which they normally are, the tourist engages in an act of becoming something new. Upon departure from the temporary, the tourist returns to the non-holiday time and place with a new experience. The role play of holiday is a process of change. As Von Weizsäcker wrote (1946/1990, p. 181), 'An antilogical state of things is ... such that both an assertion and its negation are true ... If for instance I say "I am becoming", and at the same time I say "little by little I am dying", both things are true ... the living is always something permanent that changes.' Tourism experiences possess this attribute of the antilogical.

Hence holidays do not make sense without reference to non-holiday time. The tourist provides their meaning by comparison with not being a tourist – the *choraster* of Wearing and Wearing (1996) imputes meaning to new space in ways informed by old space, and the meanings so derived become hybridizations of meaning that, in turn, inform perceptions of the yet to be experienced. What, however, tourism imposes upon the tourist is a continuous sense of the present – the time of our lives is an experience of displaced time by reason of an emphasis upon the present – this is a *special* time within which are fulfilled the motives of learning, relaxation or hedonism. It is structured selfishness or subjectivity, commonly (but not always) aided and abetted by structures of spectacle (for example, see the interpretation of viewing platforms at Fogg Dam by Ryan *et al.* 2000). The 'presentism' (Maffesoli, 1998) of tourism, therefore, requires little rituals of re-absorption into the other realities of non-holiday time. Equally, it is the enactment of such rituals that signifies the passing of time – time is measured by absence and/or presence of things and thoughts external and internal to the actor that is the tourist.

Many writers, including the present author, have commented upon the ethnomethodological significance of holidays. Indeed, to take a somewhat extreme example, Ryan and Kinder (1995) argued that an understanding of why tourists visited prostitutes in Auckland could not be achieved without reference to prevailing concepts of male and female sexual and social relations as well as noting that the holiday was a period of escape. So, when asked what did it mean to 'have the time of one's life', a number of people answered that it meant to have something memorable; that, in essence, the concept of time being used was one of storing a specific event in the mind to use in the future as a positive memory. So, it appears that, at least in holidaying, Schutz's concept of the reflexive nature of time needs to be amended to take into account the use of the past to create assets for the future. If, as Adam argues, we are time, then time possesses not just the past and the present, but also the future. Part of the social constructing of time that holiday-makers are able to perform is to develop memories for future use. It also implies something further about the nature of holidays. If holidays are concerned with the search for the memorable, then it implies that the memorable is lacking for much of daily life.

Again, this lack of the memorable implies potentially different dimensions to the use of time when on holiday. Time can be viewed as being more than simply a sequence of events. Our experience of time is also shaped by the vividness of the event. It is commonly reported by racing drivers or others facing accidents that the event appears to unfold in 'slow motion' – to the outside observer the event appears to take but a fraction of time – but to the participant the event is stretched in time as if to prepare the driver for possible death. At a less intense level successful holidays can possess this curious elasticity of time – a combination of the intensity of the event and the perceived time taken for the happening to take place. To have 'the time of one's life' thus creates a number of different implications for our understanding of the experience of time in holidays, and hence of the experience of holidays. Giddens (1984, 1985, 1990, 1991) has characterized time as possessing five features:

1. the zoning of time-space in relationship to routinized social practice;
2. the concept of presence-availability;
3. time-space distanciation – the processes by which time is stretched over longer or shorter spans of time and space (and thus the significance of the web in globalization);
4. time-space edges – the points of contact and dialogue between different cultures; and
5. the power-containers – the storage capacity for time and space.

Much of this has been previously discussed, but it can also be noted that tourist assets possess a specific and peculiar 'storage capacity' by reason of a deliberate packaging of heritage, history and culture as product for touristic (and capitalistic) purposes. Lash and Urry (1994) comment that Giddens provides no explanation of why people travel, seek to 'save time', or why covering 'space' might be of 'interest'. They write that 'Giddens does not examine how time-space changes will often have the consequence, not merely of heightening distanciation, but also of helping to encourage resistance, opposition, pleasure, autonomy or a sense of deprivation' (Lash and Urry, 1994, p. 235). The contemporary tourist may travel through a space that is already familiar within certain perceptual maps and images that the tourist already perceives due to the representations of place through the modern media of television, film, internet, newspapers and magazines, and is perhaps cocooned in a tourist bubble. The existential derived past is brought into a present of immediate interaction with place that is conducted through a dialogue between one party for whom this is a normal, everyday occurrence (the 'host' – or the tourist industry intermediary), and the other for whom this is an image made into a reality (the tourist). The present interaction is partially shaped by a network comprising past images delivered through mediated structures to become a further past that informs evolving present and future interpretations of that place. The uniqueness of the tourist interaction is the dis-located space occupied by the tourist – a geographical space not previously bodily occupied by the tourist, a space of the imagination now made physical, a perception of space that may or may not be congruent with that previously envisaged. The evaluation of those boundaries contains the potentials for pleasure, opposition and resistance (or acquiescence) identified by Lash and Urry, or for catharsis previously identified in this book. To add to the conceptualization of these junctions of space and time, reference can be made to the notion of frames identified by Goffman (1967). The tourist–other person interaction occurs with a structure of frames – layers of intentional or unintentional structured meanings by which the individual makes sense of their world. Yet the meaning emerges through a transformation of frames. So, for the tourist guide the tourist is first a mental framework of 'the' tourist, but over the time of the interaction becomes, perhaps, the individual personality, yet is a memory that quickly fades when faced with continuing streams of tourists. For the tourist, though, the importance attributed to the place may mean that the 'guide' retains a personality over time. For Goffman (1974) the issue was how to mediate a way between hyper-relativism on the one hand and the objective determinism of conventional sociology on the other. Consequently, he discussed not only a classification of frames (such as 'fabrications') but also points of frame-breaks and tolerances for frames. Tourism presents a series of such breaks of framing wherein the tourist is taken from the time of 'here and daily now' into a time of 'here and specially structured place and time' (Disney World, a Wild West show, Tinseltown) – a disjuncture of time and place – or a frame-break, made possible by the tolerance that is knowingly exercised for the most part by Urry's ludic, postmodern tourist. Given these tolerances, then meanings and cultures associated with product change. Eyerman (1999) provides examples of moving culture with reference to gospel songs, but so, too, do spaces possess changing meanings for those who use them. For example, London Docklands become new zones of art- and business-oriented precincts that differ from former areas of low-income residences (Hall and Page, 1999).

As Wang (2000, p. 112) comments, 'Holiday making is a re-organisation of experiences'. It is a cultural construction of alternative temporalities.' It might therefore be said that 'successful' holidays involve the following concepts of time:

1. possible freedom from the usual regulatory constraints of time;
2. the sense of time is shaped by the vividness of the experience of events;
3. time is a social construct, and thus within holidays is sensed as a consequence of the social interactions that take place;
4. holidays possess the potential to experience time in a way more akin to the concepts of time associated with indigenous peoples – that is, time as a natural phenomenon associated with rhythms of, if not the seasons, at least rhythms not imposed by daily work patterns;
5. holidays represent opportunities when, within short periods of calendar time, it is possible to experience time as other than fixed units of measurement – that is, time seems to speed up or slow down;
6. holidays possess the opportunity to create memorable time;
7. thus, holiday time can be used to create positive memories which are assets for the future, that is the past is linked to the future through resource building for future presents. By 'future presents' is meant that, as humans cannot experience the future, we can only utilize the past at a given present time; and some of those 'given presents' have yet to happen;
8. that time, which is a social construct, contributes to concepts of self; thereby reinforcing the importance of holidays as periods of potential self-awareness;
9. holiday time is subject to transformations of frames.

(Goffman, 1967, 1974)

However, while all of this may mean that the holiday-maker enjoys time in a way not normally done, there is a paradox present that has been implied by other contributors to this book. It has been shown that the travel agent is important in the early stages of the holiday. Equally, Baum argues that the role of the representatives of the tourist industry and the training such staff have are important factors in shaping the tourist experience. Getz and Cheyne argue that the construction of events can artificially create events to be experienced, while Page notes the significance of the place itself within an urban setting. So, what is the paradox? It is that while the holiday-maker may seek to free him or herself from the normal constraints of time, it is done so within a constrained period. The freedom from regulatory time that is presented by holidays is, itself, for most people, constrained by a need to return to their normal daily lives at some point. Hence, in order to obtain the maximum return from this period of unconstraint, many holiday-makers will plan their time. Both time and space are individually, as well as jointly, compressed.

The implications of time that have been identified above are not all pertinent to every type of holiday. It has already been mentioned that the coach tour implies adherence to schedules based upon a measurement of time. The concept of a freedom of time is contrary to the processes noted earlier in discussions about leisure, where some writers have noted an industrialization of leisure time and, by implication, of holiday times. And even where the freedom from regulatory time exists, as Page, Baum, Getz and Cheyne have noted, this freedom, this perception of different types of time, this access to a memorable time, may have been the result of planning, of conscious decisions and the machinations of organized business and governmental organizations. So, to the above list must be added:

10. planned time. This has a number of different dimensions. There is the planning undertaken by the tourist prior to, and while on, holiday. It is a form of regulatory time, but differs from that of daily life in that it is negotiated to a greater degree than normal by the holiday-maker. Secondly, there is the planning of time undertaken by the organizers and providers of tourist experiences. Thus, for example, planners might promote a festival at a given time in order to extend the season or fill hotel accommodation during the 'off season';

11. manipulated or systematic time. This can be regarded as a subset of planned time, but it differs in that it envisages the tourist as the subject of planned time rather than a participant in the planning. Hence the initiative for manipulated time rests with the industry providers. One example of manipulated time is the case of the tourist whose flight departs late in the afternoon or the night, yet whose hotel checkout time is 10.00 a.m. in the morning. The times are determined not for the convenience of the tourist, but for the staffing and other schedules of the accommodation and flight providers. It is what might be called 'systematic time' imposed upon 'free time' of the tourist.

## CONCLUSIONS

To complete a book on the experience of holidays by reference to concepts of time seems pertinent in many different ways, as it implies a reversion to earlier concerns. It has been noted above that holidays are periods with potential for different experiences of time – literally to have not simply the time *of* our lives, but time *for* our lives. In the first chapter it was argued that holidays have changed over time not only in the way in which we take holidays – a process which reflects changes in societies and opportunities created by changing technologies – but in the demands that holidays are asked to satisfy. A postmodernistic society is one of flux, with few fixed signposts by which one can measure the impact of change. Holidays thus represent important periods when tourists can continue to play the role of the post-tourist described by Urry (1990) – a ludic involvement of role change, or to opt out of this role in seeking to reconfirm family ties or a sense of self as earlier described by researchers such as Crompton (1979). It is one of the paradoxes of a postmodernist analysis that the recognition of varying structures and roles implies a persistence of past attitudes as well as the construction of new modes of thinking. Over time, it is true, a new 'Gaze' can develop unlike that of earlier periods, but in contemporary society heterogeneity includes temporary stasis as well as change – indeed it is the objects of stasis that are the measures of change. So, in holidaying, we can duplicate the experiences of the recent past by continuing the traditions of building sandcastles on the beach, and create new experiences by travelling to foreign places not immediately accessible to past generations, and using new technologies not available until but recently.

Yet, at the heart of much of this activity, as Baum pointed out, the quality of social interaction in holidaying is still very important. Thus the holiday experience is one of meeting and being helped by people. Of these, the representatives of the tourist industry are significantly important, as they act as the 'gatekeepers' and 'sign posters' to desired holiday experiences. They are the 'sign posters' in that they identify those things that are worth doing, and those that are not. They are the 'gatekeepers' in that their local knowledge aids the tourist in gaining access to the appropriate places and people. As Baum then points out, the quality of this interaction is important, and, in turn, a significant variable is the training that such people possess. The 'tourist experience' is thus dependent upon a 'staff experience' of training that permits an empathy with the needs of the tourist.

Such empathy also needs to be shown by significant 'gatekeepers' and 'sign posters' at the start of the holiday experience, and indeed it can be argued that the holiday begins with the tourists' interaction with such people, namely the travel agent. Cliff and Ryan thus examined the role of the travel agent, and presented research findings that showed that significant differences in experiences existed right from the outset of the holiday in the way in which different agency services were being perceived by their clients. However, the use of a ServQual model implies the creation of expectations, and expectations can only be related to motivations – thus it was necessary to examine the relationship between motivations and subsequent holiday behaviours.

Throughout much of the book there has been a theme that motivations shape perceptions and behaviours, and this was ably demonstrated by Hollinshead in his analysis of heritage tourism. His themes also fitted much else of the book in terms of its use of postmodernistic concepts to analyse 'distory', a selective representation of the past that offers examples of not simply a manipulation of holiday time as described above, but also a manipulation of the myths of a culture. And so, too, perhaps other strands within the book have come to the fore at various times. It has been argued in several places that to understand the tourist experience requires an understanding of the non-holiday aspects of our lives; and in that sense a concentration upon the nature of holidays can only create a partial understanding of what constitutes the 'tourist experience'. Krippendorf, in his book *The Holidaymakers*, utilized Durkheim's concepts to argue that the type of tourism that exists today arises from the nature of contemporary society; that to understand tourism it is important to examine what people seek to escape from and what they are drawn to. There is much truth in this, but the opposite process can also be applied; such is the symbiosis between holiday and non-holiday time. By examining the tourist experience it is possible to examine more closely the nature of contemporary society and the roles adopted by humans within it.

It is to be noted that it has not proven possible to fully examine all of these relationships, but in one sense that was not the purpose of the text. In the Preface it was written that the direction given to the participating authors was to review the literature, and *to speculate* in order to raise questions for discussion by students and researchers in tourism. The authors are aware that the speculation engaged in was but partial, for there are many other aspects of the tourist experience that have not been examined. It has been assumed that much of the holiday experience has been positive, but that is not always the case. Accidents and ill health do occur on holidays, and when in strange countries, such things become even more serious. Many writers have described tourism as a tension between the seeking of the new and the retention of the familiar, but for many females that tension becomes sharper because of a real sense of fear that can inhibit their travel patterns if they are travelling alone. It has also been assumed that the tourists are engaged in legitimate recreational pursuits, but the sense of release that has been mentioned can also lead to, as Ryan and Kinder (1995) have described, behaviours that involve the 'fuzzy legal', if not the illegal.

Additionally, to speculate in order to raise questions is an easy task, for it does not require the formulation of answers or even, possibly, an assessment of the importance of the question; but it is contended that such speculation is not without a role in contributing to discussion about the complexities of holiday-making. Thus, in many senses, although this is the end of the text, it is not the end of the task, for the ideas and concepts included in the text need to be revisited and structured in such a way as to permit further research to be undertaken. If the book does prompt such research it will be thought to have achieved a task of some value.

# References

Abrahams, R. (1987) 'An American vocabulary of celebrations', in A. Falassi (ed.), *Time Out of Time: Essays on the Festival*. Albuquerque: University of New Mexico Press, pp. 173–83.

Adam, B. (1990) *Time and Social Theory*. Cambridge: Polity Press.

Adam, B. (1994) 'Running out of time: global crisis and human engagement', in M. Redclift and T. Benton (eds), *Social Theory and the Global Environment*. London: Routledge, pp. 92–112.

Adams, R. L. A. (1973) 'Uncertainty in nature, cognitive dissonance, and the perceptual distortion of environmental information: weather forecasts and New England beach trip decisions'. *Economic Geography*, **49**, 287–97.

Ajzen, I. and B. L. Driver (1992) 'Application of the theory of planned behaviour to leisure choice'. *Journal of Leisure Research*, **24**(3), 207–24.

Albrecht, C. and R. Zemke (1985) *Service America*. Homewood, IL: Dow Jones-Irwin.

Aldskogius, H. (1977) 'A conceptual framework and a Swedish case study of recreational behaviour and environmental cognition'. *Economic Geography*, **53**, 163–83.

Alford, P. (2000) 'E-business in the travel industry'. *Travel and Tourism Analyst*, August.

Allport, G. W. (1937) *Personality: A Psychological Interpretation*. New York: Holt.

Allport, G. W. (1955) *Becoming: Basic Considerations for a Psychology of Personality*. New Haven, CT: Yale University Press.

Allport, G. W. (1961) *Pattern and Growth in Personality*. New York: Holt, Rinehart and Winston.

Anon. (1993) 'Novotel overhauls management culture'. *Caterer and Hotelkeeper*, 19 August, 22.

Antonio, R. J. (1991) 'Postmodern storytelling vs pragmatic truth-seeking: the discursive basis of social theory'. *Sociological Theory*, **9**, 154–68.

Antonio, R. J. and D. Kellner (1994) 'The future of social theory and the limits of postmodern critique', in D. R. Dickens and A. Fontana (eds), *Postmodernism and Social Inquiry*. New York: Guilford Press, pp. 127–154.

Aotearoa Maori Tourism Federation (1994) *Position Paper: The Protection of Cultural and Intellectual Property Rights of Maori Within the Tourism Industry*. Rotorua: Aotearoa Maori Tourism Federation.

Aotearoa Maori Tourism Federation (1995) *Report on the Current Market Position of Maori Tourism Product*. Rotorua: Aotearoa Maori Tourism Federation.

Argyle, M., A. Furnham and J. A. Graham (1981) *Social Situation*. Cambridge: Cambridge University Press.

Ashley, D. (1994) 'Postmodernism and antifoundationalism', in D. R. Dickens and A. Fontana (eds), *Postmodernism and Social Inquiry*. New York: Guilford Press, pp. 53–75.

Ashworth, G. J. (1989) 'Urban tourism: an imbalance in attention', in C. P. Cooper (ed.), *Progress in Tourism, Recreation and Hospitality Management*, Vol. 1. London: Belhaven, pp. 33–54.

Ashworth, G. J. (1992) 'Is there an urban tourism?' *Tourism Recreation Research*, **17**(2), 3–8.

Ashworth, G. J. and T. Z. de Haan (1986) *Uses and Users of the Tourist-Historic City*. Field Studies 10. Groningen: Faculty of Spatial Sciences.

Ashworth, G. J. and J. Tunbridge (1990) *The Tourist-Historic City*. London: Belhaven.

Ashworth, G. and J. Tunbridge (2000) *The Tourist-Historic City: Retrospect and Prospect of Managing the Heritage City*. Oxford: Pergamon.

Ashworth, G. J. and H. Voogd (1994) 'Marketing of tourism places: What are we doing?', in M. Uysal (ed.), *Global Tourist Behavior*. New York: International Press Ltd, pp. 5–20.

Aziz, H. (1995) 'Understanding attacks on tourists in Egypt'. *Tourism Management*, **16**(2), 91–6.

Backman, S. J., R. B. Ditton, R. Kaiser and J. Fletcher (1986) 'An investigation of benefits sought at Texas Beaches', in W. Benoy Joseph, L. Moutinho and I. R. Vernon (eds),

*Proceedings of Tourism Services Marketing: Advances in Theory and Practice*. Academy of Marketing Science and Marketing Department of Cleveland State University, pp. 53–62.

Backman, K., S. Backman, M. Uysal and K. Sunshine (1995) 'Event tourism: an examination of motivations and activities'. *Festival Management and Event Tourism*, 3(1), 15–24.

Bagguley, P., J. Mark-Lawson, D. Shapiro, J. Urry, A. Walby and A. Wardle (1990) *Restructuring: Place, Class and Gender*. London: Sage.

Bakhtin, M. M. (1984) *Rabelais and his World* (trans. H. Iswolsky) Bloomington: Indiana University Press.

Bale, J. (1989) *Sports Geography*. New York: E. and F. N. Spon.

Barker, M., S. J. Page and D. Meyer (forthcoming). 'Evaluating the impact of the 2000 America's Cup on Auckland'. *Event Management*.

Barraclough, G. (1978) *Main Trends in History*. New York: Holmes and Meier.

Barthes, R. (1973) *Mythologies* (trans. Annette Lavers). London: Paladin.

Bateson, C. (1959) *The Convict Ships 1787–1868*. Sydney: The Library of Australian History.

Baudrillard, J. (1975) *The Mirror of Production* (trans. Mark Poster). St Louis: Telos Press.

Baudrillard, J. (1981) *For a Critique of the Political Economy of the Sign*. St Louis, MO: Telos Press.

Baudrillard, J. (1983) *Simulations*. New York: Semiotext Inc.

Baudrillard, J. (1988) *America*. London: Verso.

Baum, T. (1995) *Managing Human Resources for the European Tourism and Hospitality Industry: A Strategic Approach*. London: Chapman and Hall.

Baum, T. (1996) 'Unskilled work and the hospitality industry: myth or reality?' *International Journal of Hospitality Management*, 15(3), 207–10.

Bauman, Z. (1992) *Intimations of Postmodernity*. London: Routledge.

Bauman, Z. (1993) *Postmodern Ethics*. Oxford: Blackwell.

Beard, J. G. and M. G. Ragheb (1982) 'Measuring leisure attitude'. *Journal of Leisure Research*, 14(2), 155–167.

Beard, J. G. and M. G. Ragheb (1983) 'Measuring leisure motivation'. *Journal of Leisure Research*, 15(3), 219–28.

Bell, D. (1976) *The Cultural Contradictions of Capitalism*. New York: Basic Books.

Bell, D. (1978) *The Cultural Contradictions of Capitalism*. New York: Basic Books.

Bennett, T. (1988) 'Museums and the "people"', in R. Lumley (ed.), *The Time-Machine: Putting Cultures on Display*. London: Comedia/Routledge, pp. 63–86.

Benson, S. P., S. Brier, R. Entenmann, W. Goldstein and R. Rozenweig (eds) (1981) Editors' introduction. *Radical History Review*, 25, October, pp. 3–4.

Berger, J. (1984) *And our Faces, My Heart, Brief as Photos*. London: Writers and Readers.

Best, S. (1994) 'Foucault, postmodernism and social theory', in D. R. Dickens and A. Fontana (eds), *Postmodernism and Social Inquiry*. New York: Guilford Press, pp. 25–52.

Best, S. and D. Kellner (1991) *Postmodern Theory: Critical Interrogations*. New York: Guilford Press.

Bhabha, H. (1994) *The Location of Culture*. London: Routledge.

Billig, M. (1994) 'Sod Baudrillard! or ideology critique in Disney World', in H. W. Simons and M. Billig (eds), *After Postmodernism: Reconstructing Ideological Critique*. London: Sage, pp. 150–71.

Billig, M. and H. W. Simons (1994) 'Introduction', in H. W. Simons and M. Billig (eds), *After Postmodernism: Reconstructing Ideological Critique*. London: Sage, pp. 1–11.

Bitner, M. J. and B. H. Booms (1982) 'Trends in travel and tourism marketing: the changing structure of distribution channels'. *Journal of Travel Research*, spring, 39–44.

Bitner, M. J., Booms, B. H. and M. Tetreault (1990) 'The service encounter: diagnosing favorable and unfavorable incidents'. *Journal of Marketing*, January, 71–84.

Bitran, G. and M. Lojo (1993) 'A framework for analysing the quality of customer interface'. *European Management Journal*, 11(4), 385–96.

Blank, U. and M. Petkovich (1980) 'The metropolitan area: a multifaceted travel destination complex', in D. Hawkins, E. Shafer and J. Ravelstad (eds), *Tourism Planning and Development Issues*. Washington DC: George Washington University, pp. 393–405.

Blank, U. and M. Petkovich (1987) 'Research on urban tourism destinations', in J. B. Ritchie and C. Goeldner (eds), *Travel, Tourism and Hospitality Research: A Handbook for Managers and Researchers*. New York: Wiley, pp. 165–77.

Bloch, M. (1949) *Apologie pour l'histoire, ou métier d'historien* (posthumous publication). Paris: Armend Colin. English translation by P. Putnam (1994) Historian's Craft. New York: Knopf.

Boggiano, A. K. and T. S. Pittman (1992) 'Divergent approaches to the study of motivation and achievement: the central role of extrinsic/intrinsic orientations', in K. Boggiano and T. S. Pittman (eds), *Achievement and Motivation: A Social-Developmental Perspective*. Cambridge, MA: Cambridge University Press, pp. 268–73.

Bolton, R. N. and J. H. Drew (1991) 'A multistage model of customers' assessments of service quality and value'. *Journal of Consumer Research*, **17**(4), 375–84.

Bordessa, R. (1993) 'Geography, postmodernism and environmental concern'. *The Canadian Geographer*, **37**(2), 147–55.

Borsay, P. (1989) *The English Urban Renaissance*. Oxford: Clarendon.

Bossen, C. (2000) 'Festival mania, tourism and nation building in Fiji: the case of the Hibiscus Festival, 1956–1970'. *Contemporary Pacific*, **12**(1), spring, 123–54.

Boulding, W., A. Kalra, R. Staelin and V. A. Zeithaml (1993) 'A dynamic process model of service quality: from expectations to behavioural intentions'. *Journal of Marketing Research*, **30**, February, 7–27.

Bramwell, B. (1998) 'User satisfaction and product development in urban tourism'. *Tourism Management*, **19**(1), 35–48.

Breitbart, E. (1981) 'From the panorama to the diorama: notes on the visualization of history'. *Radical History Review*, October, 115–25.

Brocx, M. (1994) *Visitor Perceptions and Satisfaction Study*. winter 1993. Auckland: Tourism Auckland.

Brodribb, S. (1993) *Nothing Matters: A Feminist Critique of Postmodernism*. North Melbourne, Australia: Spinifex Press.

Brown, R. H. (1994) 'Reconstructing social theory after the postmodern critique', in H. W. Simons and M. Billig (eds), *After Postmodernism: Reconstructing Ideological Critique*. London: Sage, pp. 12–37.

Brown, T. J., G. A. Churchill, Jr and J. P. Peter (1993) 'Improving the measurement of service quality'. *Journal of Retailing*, **69**, spring, 127–39.

Buck, E. (1993) *Paradise Remade: The Politics of Culture and History in Hawai'i*. Philadelphia: Temple University Press.

Buckley, P. and S. Witt (1989) 'Tourism in difficult areas II: case studies of Calderdale, Leeds, Manchester and Scunthorpe'. *Tourism Management*, **10**(2), 138–52.

Burns, P. M. (1997) 'Hard-skills, soft-skills: undervaluing hospitality's "Service with a Smile"'. *Progress in Tourism and Hospitality Research*, **3**, 239–48.

Burtenshaw, D., M. Bateman and G. J. Ashworth (1991) *The City in West Europe* (2nd edn). Chichester: Wiley.

Butler, J. (1997) *Excitable Speech: The Politics of the Performative*. London: Routledge.

Butler, R. and B. Mao (1997) 'Seasonality in tourism: problems and measurement', in P. Murphy (ed.), *Quality Management in Urban Tourism*. Chichester: Wiley, pp. 9–24.

Butler, R. and D. Pearce (1993) *Tourism Research: Critiques and Challenges*. London and New York: Routledge.

Buzzard, J. (1993) *The Beaten Track: European Tourism, Literature and the Ways to 'Culture', 1800–1918*. London: Lutterworth Press.

Caffyn, A. and J. Lutz (1999) 'Developing the heritage tourism product in multi-ethnic cities'. *Tourism Management*, **20**(2), 213–21.

Callinicos, A. (1990) *Against Postmodernism: A Marxist Critique*. New York: St. Martin's Press.

Cantwell, M. L. and M. M. Sanik (1993) 'Leisure before and after parenthood'. *Social Indicators Research*, **30**, 139–47.

Carlson, A. (1998) 'America's growing observance of Cinco de Mayo'. *Journal of American Culture*, **21**(2), 7–16.

Carlzon, J. (1987) *Moments of Truth*. Cambridge, MA: Ballinger.

Carman, J. M. (1990) 'Consumer perceptions of service quality: an assessment of the SERVQUAL dimensions'. *Journal of Retailing*, **66**, 33–55.

Carr, E. H. (1961) *What is History*. Harmondsworth: Macmillan.

Cartwright, R. (1996) 'Travellers' diarrhoea', in S. Clift, S. J. Page and N. Clark (eds), *Health and the International Tourist*. London and New York: Routledge, pp. 44–66.

Centre for Leisure Research, Dunfermline College of Physical Education (1984) *Crowd Behaviour at Football Matches: A Study in Scotland*. For the Football Trust.

Chamot, E., L. Toscani, and A. Rougemont (1998) *Public Health: Importance and Risk Factors for Cercarial Dermatitis Associated with Swimming in Lake Leman at Geneva, Switzerland*. Geneva: Institute of Social and Preventive Medicine.

Charlton, B. G. (1998) 'Peak experiences, creativity and the *Colonel Flastratus* phenomenon'. *Abraxis*, **14**, 10–19.

Churchill, D. (1994) 'Time to upgrade'. *The Sunday Times Style and Travel*, 22 May, p. 38.

Clark, N., S. Clift and S. J. Page (1993) *A Safe Place in the Sun? Health Precautions, Behaviours and Health Problems of British Tourists in Malta*. Centre for Health Education and Research/ Centre for Tourism Studies, Canterbury Christ Church College, Kent, UK, CT1 1QU.

Cleere, H. F. (1989a) 'Preface', in H. F. Cleere (ed.), *Archaeological Heritage Management in the Modern World*. London: Unwin Hyman, pp. xxiii–xxiv.

Cleere, H. F. (1989b) 'Introduction: the rationale of archaeological heritage management', in H. F. Cleere (ed.), *Archaeological Heritage Management in the Modern World*. London: Unwin Hyman, pp. 1–22.

Clegg, S. (1991) 'The remains of Louis Atthusser'. *International Socialism*, **53**, winter, 57–78.

Clewer, A., A. Pack and M. T. Sinclair (1992) 'Price competitiveness and inclusive tour holidays', in P. Johnson and B. Thomas (eds), *Choice and Demand in Tourism*. London: Mansell, pp. 123–44.

Cliff, A. D. and C. Ryan (1994) 'Do travel agencies measure up to customer expectation? An empirical investigation of travel agencies' service quality as measured by SERVQUAL', in J. Buchanan-Cheyne and C. Ryan (eds), *Proceedings of Tourism Down Under*, Massey University, 6–9 December, pp. 553–78.

Cloud, D. L. (1994) 'Socialism of the mind: the new age of post-Marxism', in H. W. Simons and M. Billig (eds), *After Postmodernism: Reconstructing Ideological Critique*. London: Sage, pp. 222–52.

Cockerell, N. (1997) 'Urban tourism in Europe'. *Travel and Tourism Analyst*, **6**, 44–67.

Cohen, E. (1982) 'Marginal paradises: bungalow tourism on the islands of Southern Thailand. *Annals of Tourism Research*, **9**(2), 189–228.

Connor, S. (1989) *Postmodernist Culture: An Introduction to Theories of the Contemporary*. Oxford: Basil Blackwell.

Cook Johnson, G. (1991) *How Service Leaders Empower their Employees*. Toronto: Reacon.

Cooper, C. P. (1981) 'Spatial and temporal patterns of tourist behaviour'. *Regional Studies*, **15**(5), 359–71.

Crompton, J., (1979) 'Motivations for pleasure vacations'. *Annals of Tourism Research*, **6**, 408–24.

Crompton, J. L. (1992) 'Structure of vacation destination choice sets'. *Annals of Tourism Research*, **19**(3), 420–34.

Crompton, J. L. (1993) 'Choice set propositions in destination decisions'. *Annals of Tourism Research*, **20**(3), 461–76.

Crompton, J. L. and P. K. Ankomah (1993) 'Choice set propositions in destination decisions'. *Annals of Tourism Research*, **20**(3), 461–77.

Crompton, J., and S. McKay (1997) 'Motives of visitors attending festival events'. *Annals of Tourism Research*, **24**(2), 425–39.

Crook, S., J. Pakulski and M. Waters (1992) *Postmodernisation: Change in Advanced Society*. London: Sage.

Crouch, C. and A. Marquand (eds) (1995) *Reinventing Collective Action*. Oxford: Basil Blackwell.

Csikszentimihalyi, M. (1975) *Beyond Boredom and Anxiety*. San Francisco, CA: Jossey-Bass.

Csikszentimihalyi, M. and I. S. Csikszentimihalyi (eds) (1988) *Optimal Experience: Psychological Studies of Flow in Consciousness*. Cambridge, MA: University of Cambridge Press.

Cunneen, C. and R. Lynch (1988) 'The social meanings of conflict in riots at the Australian Grand Prix motorcycle races'. *Leisure Studies*, **7**(1), 1–19.

Cunningham, H. (1980) *Leisure in the Industrial Revolution, 1780–1880*. London: Croom Helm.

Cunningham, H. (1990) 'Leisure and culture', in F. M. L. Thompson (ed.), The Cambridge Social History of Britain, 1750–1950, vol. 2, *People and their Environment*. Cambridge: Cambridge University Press.

Curry, M. R. (1991) 'Postmodernism, language, and the strains of modernism'. *Annals of the Association of American Geographers*, **8**(2), 212.

Damousi, J. (1995) 'Chaos and order: gender, space and sexuality on female convict ships'. *Australian Historical Studies*, **26**(104), April, 351–72.

Dann, G. (2000) 'Overseas holiday hotels for the elderly: total bliss or total institution?', in M. Robinson, P. Long, N. Evans, R. Sharpley and J. Swarbrooke (eds), *Motivations, Behaviours and Tourist Types: Reflections on International Tourism*. Sunderland: Business Education Books and Centre for Tourism, University of Northumbria, pp. 83–94.

Dann, M. S. (1977) 'Anomie, ego-enhancement and tourism'. *Annals of Tourism Research*, **4**, 184–94.

Davidson, P. (1996) 'The holiday and work experiences of women with young children'. *Leisure Studies*, **15**(2), 89–103.

Dawood, R. (1993) 'Preparation for travel', in R. Behrens and K. McAdam (eds), *Travel Medicine*. London: Churchill Livingstone.

Dear, M. and S. Flusty (1998) 'Postmodern urbanism'. *Annals of the Association of American Geographers*, **88**(1), 50–72.

Deem, R. (1996) 'Women, the city and holidays'. *Leisure Studies*, **15**(2), 105–19.

Deleuze, G. and F. Guattari (1972) *Anti-Oedipus*. Paris: Editions de Minuit. [English translation, London, Athlone Press, 1984]

Deleuze, G. and F. Guattari (1980) *A Thousand Plateaus: Capitalism and Schizophrenia*. Paris: Editions de Minuit. [English translation, London, Athlone Press, 1988]

Derrida, J. (1976) *Of Grammatology* (trans. Gayatri Chakravorty Spivak). Baltimore: Johns Hopkins University Press.

Dickens, D. R. (1994) 'North American theories of postmodern culture', in D. R. Dickens and A. Fontana (eds), *Postmodernism and Social Inquiry*. New York: Guilford Press, pp. 76–100.

Diener, E. (1992) *Assessing Subjective Well Being: Progress and Opportunities*. Unpublished paper, University of Illinois.

Diener, E., C. R. Colvin, W. Pavot and A. Allman (1991) 'The psychic costs of intense positive emotions'. *Journal of Personality and Social Psychology*, **61**, 492–503.

Diener, E. and C. Diener (1996) 'Most people are happy'. *Psychological Science*, **7**, 181–5.

Diener, E. and M. Diener (1995) 'Cross-cultural correlates of life satisfaction and self-esteem'. *Journal of Personality and Social Psychology*, **68**, 653–63.

Diener, E. and R. J. Larsen (1984) 'Temporal stability and cross-situational consistency of affect, behavioral and cognitive responses'. *Journal of Personality and Social Psychology*, **47**, 871–83.

Diener, E. and R. E. Lucas (2000) 'Subjective emotional well-being', in M. Lewis and J. M. Haviland (eds), *Handbook of Emotions* (2nd edn). New York: Guilford, pp. 325–37.

Douvis, J., A. Yusof and S. Douvis (1999) 'An examination of demographic and psychographic profiles of the sport tourist'. *The Cyber-Journal of Sport Marketing*.

Downs, R. (1970) 'Geographic space perception: past approaches and future prospects'. *Progress in Geography*, **2**, 65–108.

Driver, B. L. (1977) 'Item Pool for Scales Designed to Quantify the Psychological Outcomes Desired and Expected from Recreation Participation'. Unpublished paper, USDA Forest Service, Rocky Mountain Forest and Range Experiment Station, Fort Collins, Colorado.

Elias, N. (1984) *Über die Zeit* (trans. H. Fliessbach and M. Schröter). Frankfurt am Main: Suhrkamp.

English Tourist Board/Employment Department (1991) *Maintaining the Balance*. London: English Tourist Board/Employment Department.

Evans-Pritchard, E. E. (1969) First published 1940. *The Nuer: A Description of the Modes of Livelihood and Political Institutions of a Nilotic People*. New York: Oxford University Press.

Ewen, S. (1988) *All Consuming Images: The Politics of Style in Contemporary Culture*. New York: Basic Books.

Eyerman, R. (1999) 'Moving culture', in M. Featherstone and S. Lash (eds), *Spaces of Culture*. London: Sage Publications, pp. 116–37.

Falassi, A. (ed.) (1987) *Time Out of Time: Essays on the Festival*. Albuquerque: University of New Mexico Press.

Farganis, S. (1994) 'Postmodernism and feminism', in D. R. Dickens and A. Fontana (eds), *Postmodernism and Social Inquiry*. New York: Guilford Press, pp. 101–26.

Faulkner, B. and Ryan, C. (eds) (1999) 'Special issue: research methods and conceptualisations'. *Tourism Management*, **20**(1), 3–6.

Featherstone, M. (1991) *Consumer Culture and Postmodernism*. London: Sage.

FECTO (2000) http://www.europeancitiestourism.com

Feifer, M. (1985) *Going Places*. London: Macmillan.

Festinger, L. (1957) *A Theory of Cognitive Dissonance*. Stanford: Stanford University Press.

Fischer, C. S. (1994) 'Changes in leisure activities, 1890–1940'. *Journal of Social History*, **27**(3), 453–76.

Fishbein, M. (1967) *Readings in Attitude Theory and Measurement*. New York: John Wiley and Sons.

Fjellman, S. (1992) *Vinyl Leaves: Walt Disney World and America*. Boulder, CO: Westview Press.

Flax, J. (1990) *Thinking Fragments: Psychoanalysis, Feminism, and Postmodernism in the Contemporary West*. Los Angeles and Oxford: University of California Press.

Foresta, R. A. (1984) *America's National Parks and their Keepers*. Washington, DC: Resources for the Future.

Formica, S. and S. Murrmann (1998) 'The effects of group membership and motivation on attendance: an international festival case'. *Tourism Analysis*, **3**, 197–207.

Formica, S. and M. Uysal (1998) 'Market segmentation of an international cultural-historic event in Italy'. *Journal of Travel Research*, **36**(4), 16–24.

Foster, H. (1985) *Postmodern Culture*. London: Pluto.

Foster, K. (1991) 'Not just a job'. *Managing Service Quality*, May, 223–7.

Foucault, M. (1972) *The Archaeology of Knowledge*. London: Tavistock.

Foucault, M. (1976/1978) *The History of Sexuality: An Introduction*. Volume 1. English translation, 1978. New York: Random House.

Foucault, M. (1978) *Naissance de la clinique: une archéologie de regard médica*. Paris: Presses Universitaires de France.

Foucault, M. (1975/1979) *Discipline and Punish*. (trans. Alan Sheridan). Harmondsworth: Penguin.

Foucault, M. (1980) *Power/Knowledge: Selected Interviews and Other Writings* (trans. Colin Gordon *et al.*). New York: Porthean.

Fox, N. J. (1993) *Postmodernism, Sociology and Health*. Buckingham: Open University Press.

Fox, J. and J. Crotts (1990) 'A longitudinal investigation into script developments and the evaluation of a service'. *Proceedings of the 21st Annual Decision Science Institute*. San Diego, CA, June 15.

Frankl, V. E. (1962) *Man's Search for Meaning: An Introduction to Logotherapy*. Boston, MA: Beacon Press Inc.

Frankl, V. E. (1997) *Man's Search for Ultimate Meaning*. New York: Perseus Book Publishing.

Fraser, N. (1989) 'Talking about needs: interpretive contests as political conflicts in welfare-state societies'. *Ethics*, **99**, 291–313.

Fraser, N. and L. Nicholson (1988) 'Social criticism without philosophy: an encounter between feminism and postmodernism'. *Theory, Culture and Society*, **5**, 573–94.

Frisch, M. H. (1981) 'The memory of history'. *Radical History Review*, **25**, October: 9–23.

Fussell, P. (1982) *Abroad: British Literary Travelling Between the Wars*. New York: Oxford University Press.

Getz, D. (1991) *Festivals, Special Events, and Tourism*. New York: Van Nostrand Reinhold.

Getz, D. (1993) 'Planning for tourism business districts'. *Annals of Tourism Research*, **20**, 583–600.

Getz, D. (1997) *Event Management and Event Tourism*. New York: Cognizant.

Gibbins, J. R. and B. Reimer (1995) 'Postmodernism', in J. van Deth and E. Scarborough (eds), *The Impact of Values*. Oxford: Oxford University Press.

Gibbins, J. R. and B. Reimer (1999) *The Politics of Postmodernity: An Introduction to Contemporary Politics and Culture*. London: Sage.

Gibson, H. (1998) 'Active sport tourism: who participates?' *Leisure Studies*, **17**, 155–70.

Giddens, A. (1984) *The Constitution of Society*. Cambridge: Polity Press.

Giddens, A. (1985) *The Nation State and Violence*. Cambridge: Polity Press.

Giddens, A. (1987) 'Structuralism, post-structuralism and the production of culture', in A. Giddens and J. Turner (eds), *Social Theory Today*. Stanford, CA: Stanford University Press, pp. 195–223.

Giddens, A. (1990) *The Consequences of Modernity*. Cambridge: Polity Press.

Giddens, A. (1991) *Modernity and Self-Identity*. Cambridge: Polity Press.

Gilbert, D. and I. Joshi (1992) 'Quality management and the tourism and hospitality industry', in C. Cooper and A. Lockwood (eds), *Progress in Tourism, Recreation and Hospitality Management*, Vol. 4. London: Belhaven, pp. 149–68.

Gillis, K. and R. Ditton (1998) 'Comparing tournament and nontournament recreational billfish anglers to examine the efficacy of hosting competitive billfish angling events in southern Baja, Mexico'. *Festival Management and Event Tourism*, **5**(3), 147–58.

Gitelson, R., D. Kerstetter and N. E. Kiernan (1995) 'Evaluating the educational objectives of a short-term event'. *Festival Management and Event Tourism*, **3**(1), 9–14.

Gitlin, T. (1989) 'Postmodernism: roots and politics'. *Dissent*, **36**, 100–8.

Godbey, G. (1994) *Leisure in Your Life: An Exploration*. Venture: State College, PA.

Goffman, E. (1967) *Interaction Ritual*. Harmondsworth: Penguin.

Goffman, E. (1974) *Frame Analysis: An Essay on the Organization of Experience*. New York: Harper & Row.

Gold, J. and M. Gold (1995) *Imagining Scotland: Tradition, Representation and Promotion in Scottish Tourism Since 1750*. Aldershot: Scholar.

Gold, J. and S. Ward (eds) (1994) *Place Promotion: The Use of Publicity and Marketing to Sell Towns and Regions*. Chichester: Wiley.

Goldman, R. and S. Papson (1994) 'The postmodernism that failed', in D. R. Dickens and A. Fontana (eds), *Postmodernism and Social Inquiry*. New York: Guilford Press, pp. 224–54.

Graefe, A. R. and J. J. Vaske (1987) 'A framework for managing quality in the tourist experience'. *Annals of Tourism Research*, **14**, 389–404.

Gray, H. P. (1970) *International Travel: International Trade*. Lexington: Lexington Books.

Green, B. and L. Chalip (1998) 'Sport tourism as the celebration of subculture'. *Annals of Tourism Research*, **25**(2), 275–91.

Greer, G. (1999) *The Whole Woman*. London: Transworld Publishers/Doubleday.

Gronroos, C. (1990) *Service Management and Marketing*. Cambridge, MA: Lexington Books.

Grossberg, L. (1988) 'Putting the pop back into postmodernism', in A. Ross (ed.), *Universal Abandon? The Politics of Postmodernism*. Minneapolis: University of Minnesota Press.

Guy, B. S. and W. W. Curtis (1986) 'Consumer learning or retail environment: a tourism and travel approach'. Conference paper presented at the American Academy of Marketing Conference, Cleveland University. *Tourism Services Marketing, Advances in Theory and Practice* (ed. W. Benoy Joseph). American Academy of Marketing Conference/Cleveland University.

Hall, C. M. (2000) *Tourism Planning: Policies, Processes and Relationships*. Harlow: Prentice-Hall.

Hall, C. M. and C. Hamon (1996) 'Casinos and urban redevelopment in Australia'. *Journal of Travel Research*, **34**(3), 30–6.

Hall, C. M. and S. J. Page (1999) *The Geography of Tourism and Recreation: Environment, Place and Space*. London and New York: Routledge.

Hall, C. M. and S. J. Page (2002) *Managing Urban Tourism*. Harlow: Pearson Education.

Hall, M. (1914/2000) 'A woman in the antipodes', extract in L. Wevers (ed.), *Travelling to New Zealand: An Oxford Anthology*. Auckland: Oxford University Press.

Hampden, T. C. (1971) *Radical Man*. London: Duckworth.

Hannigan, J. (1998) *Fantasy City*. London: Routledge.

Haraway, S. (1990) 'A manifesto for Cyborgs', in *Feminism/Postmodernism*. New York: Routledge.

Hartsock, N. (1987) 'Rethinking modernism: minority vs majority theories'. *Cultural Critique*, 7, fall, 187–206.

Harvey, D. (1989) *The Condition of Postmodernity*. Oxford: Blackwell.

Haukeland, J. V. (1990) 'Sociocultural impacts of tourism in Scandinavia'. *Tourism Management*, 5, 207–14.

Havitz, M. and Dimanche, F. (1990) 'Propositions for testing the involvement construct in recreation tourism contexts'. *Leisure Sciences*, 12, 179–95.

Haynes, R. (1980) *Geographical Images and Mental Maps*. London: Macmillan.

Haywood, K. M. and T. E. Muller (1988) 'The urban tourist experience: evaluating satisfaction'. *Hospitality Education and Research Journal*, 12(2), 453–9.

Heady, B. and A. Wearing (1989) 'Personality, life events and subjective well being: toward a dynamic equilibrium model'. *Journal of Personality and Social Psychology*, 57, 731–9.

Hebdige, R. (1986) 'Postmodernism and "the other side"'. *Journal of Communication Inquiry*, 10, summer, 78.

Henderson, K. A. (1991) 'The contributions of feminism to an understanding of leisure constraints'. *Journal of Leisure Research*, 24(3), 119–37

Henderson, K. A. (1994) 'Perspectives on analysing gender, women and leisure'. *Journal of Leisure Research*, 26(2), 119–37.

Henderson K. A., D. Stalnaker and G. Taylor (1988) 'The relationship between barriers to recreation and gender-role personality traits for women'. *Journal of Leisure Research*, 20, 69–80.

Heung, V. and H. Qu (1998) 'Tourism shopping and its contribution to Hong Kong'. *Tourism Management*, 19(4), 383–6.

Hewison, R. (1987) *The Heritage Industry: Britain in a Climate of Decline*. London: Methuen.

Hibbert, C. (1987) *The Grand Tour*. London: Channel 4 TV/Methuen.

Higgs, E. (1986) 'Domestic service and household production', in A. V. John (ed.), *Unequal Opportunities: Women's Employment in England 1800–1918*. Oxford: Basil Blackwell.

Hirschman, E. C. (1984) 'Leisure motives and sex roles'. *Journal of Leisure Research*, 16(3), 209–23.

Hollinshead, K. (1993) *The Truth About Texas: A Naturalistic Study of the Construction of Heritage*. Unpublished doctoral dissertation. College Station, Texas: Department of Recreation, Park and Tourism Sciences, Texas A&M University.

Hollinshead, K. (1994a) *Fjellman and Distory: The 'Postmodern'/'Culture redux' Concept of History in 'Vinyl Leaves'*. The XIII World Congress of Sociology: The 1994 Bielefeld Conference.

Hollinshead, K. (1994b) *The Truth about Texas: A Naturalistic Study of the Construction of Heritage*. Paper given at Tourism: The State of the Art, Conference, 10–14 July, Strathclyde University, Scotland.

Hollinshead, K. (1998a) 'Tourism, hybridity, and ambiguity: the relevance of Bhabha's "third space" cultures'. *Journal of Leisure Research*, 30(1), 121–56.

Hollinshead, K. (1998b) 'Tourism and the restless peoples: a dialectical inspection of Bhabha's halfway populations'. *Tourism, Culture and Communication*, 1(1), 49–77.

Hollinshead, K. (1999) 'Surveillance of the worlds of tourism: Foucault and the eye-of-power'. *Tourism Management*, 20(1), 7–24.

Hollis, G. and J. Burgess (1977) 'Personal London: students perceive the urban scene'. *Geographical Magazine*, 50(3), 155–61.

Holmes, P. R. and D. Kay (1997) *Bacteria in Recreational Waters: A Regulator's Concerns. Coliforms and E-coli: Problem or Solution*. Hong Kong: Environmental Protection Department, Government of Hong Kong.

Horna, J. L. A. (1994) *The Study of Leisure: An Introduction*. Toronto: Oxford University Press.

Horne, D. (1986) *The Public Culture: The Triumph of Industrialisation*. London: Pluto.

Houston Television Channel 8 Public Service Broadcast (1992) *Art of the Western World*.

Howard, J. A. and J. N. Sheth (1969) *Theory of Buyer Behaviour*. New York: John Wiley and Sons.

Hughes, E. C. (1971) *The Sociological Eye*. Chicago: Aldine.

Hughes, H. (1998) 'Theatre in London and the inter-relationship with tourism'. *Tourism Management*, **19**(6), 445–52.

Hughes, H. (2000) *Arts, Tourism and Entertainment*. Oxford: Butterworth-Heinemann.

Hughes, H. S. (1963) 'The historian and the social scientist', in A. V. Riasanovsky and B. Riznik (eds), *Generalizations in Historical Writing*. Philadelphia, PA: University of Philadelphia Press.

Huizinga, J. (1950) *Homo Ludens: A Study of the Play Element in Culture*. Boston: Beacon Press.

Iacobucci, D., K. A. Grayson and A. Ostrom (1994) 'The calculus of service quality and customer satisfaction: theoretical and empirical differentiation and integration', in T. A. Swartz, D. E. Bowen and S. W. Brown (eds), *Advances in Services Marketing and Management*, Vol 3. Greenwich, CT: JAI Press, pp. 1–67.

Institut National de Recherche sur les Transports et leur Sécurité (INRETS) (1996) *Le Tourisme Urbain – Les Pratiques des Francais*. Rapport No. 208. Paris: Institut National de Recherche sur les Transports et leur Sécurité.

Iso-Ahola, S. (1982) 'Towards a social psychology of tourism motivation: a rejoinder'. *Annals of Tourism Research*, **9**, 256–61.

Jackson, E. (1983) 'Activity specific barriers to recreation participation'. *Leisure Sciences*, **6**, 47–60.

Jackson, E. (1988) 'Leisure constraints: a survey of past research'. *Leisure Sciences*, **10**, 203–15.

Jafari, J. (ed.) (2000) *Encyclopaedia of Tourism*. London: Routledge.

Jameson, F. (1982/1991) *Postmodernism, or the Cultural Logic of Late Capitalism*. Durham: Duke University Press.

Jameson, F. (1983) 'Postmodernism and consumer society', in H. Foster (ed.), *The Anti-Aesthetic*. Port Townsend: Washington Bay Press, pp. 111–25.

Jameson, F. (1984) 'Postmodernism, or the cultural logic of late capitalism'. *New Left Review*, **146**, 53–92.

Jansen-Verbeke, M. (1986) 'Inner-city tourism; resources, tourists and promoters'. *Annals of Tourism Research*, **13**(1), 79–100.

Jarvis, J. F. (1993) *The Rise of the Devon Seaside Resorts, 1750–1900*. Exeter: University of Exeter Press.

Jenkins, J. and D. Walmesley (1993) 'Mental maps of tourists: a study of Coffs Harbour'. New South Wales, *GeoJournal*, **29**(3), 233–41.

Johnson, R. (1991) 'A strategy for service – Disney style'. *The Journal of Business Strategy*, **12**(5), 38–44.

Johnston, R. (1981) 'Urbanisation', in R. Johnston, D. Gregory, P. Haggett, D. Smith and D. Stoddard (eds), *The Dictionary of Human Geography*. Oxford: Blackwell, pp. 363–4.

Johnston, R. J., D. Gregory and D. M. Smith (1994) *The Dictionary of Human Geography*. Oxford: Basil Blackwell.

Jones, D. (1985) 'Maplin's was never like this'. *News of the World*. Reproduced in Butlin's Holidays Students' Guide, spring.

Kahneman, D., P. Slovic and A. Tversky (1982) *Judgement Under Uncertainty: Heuristic and Biases*. New York: Cambridge University Press.

Kanter, R. M. (1983) *The Changing Masters: Innovation and Entrepreneurship in the American Corporation*. New York: Simon and Schuster.

Kaplan, E. A. (1988) 'Introduction', in E. A. Kaplan (ed.), *Postmodernity and its Discontents*. London: Verso, pp. 1–9.

Kay, T. and G. Jackson (1990) 'The operation of leisure constraints', paper presented at the 6th Canadian Congress on Leisure Research, University of Waterloo, Ontario.

Kelly, G. A. (1955) *The Psychology of Personal Constructs*. New York: Norton.

Kelly, J. and J. Kelly (1994) 'Multiple dimensions of meaning in the domains of work, family and leisure'. *Journal of Leisure Research*, **26**, 250–74.

Kent, P. (1990) 'People, places and priorities: opportunity sets and consumers' holiday choice', in G. J. Ashworth and B. Goodall (eds), *Marketing Tourism Places*. London: Routledge, pp. 42–62.

Kerstetter, D. and P. Mowrer (1998) 'Individuals' reasons for attending First Night, a unique cultural event'. *Festival Management and Event Tourism*, **5**(3), 139–46.

Kim, E. (1994) 'Korean outbound tourism'. Conference proceedings, *Tourism Down Under: A Tourism Research Conference*, 6–9 December. Department of Management Systems, Massey University, Palmerston North, New Zealand, pp. 71–92.

Kim, E., P. L. Pearce, A. M. Morrison and J. T. O'Leary (1996) 'Mature vs. youth travelers: The Korean Market'. *Asia Pacific Journal of Tourism Research*, 1(1), 102–12.

Kotler, P., D. Haider and I. Rein (1993) *Marketing Places: Attracting Investment, Industry and Tourism to Cities, States and Nations*. New York: Free Press.

Krausse, G. (1998) 'Waterfront festivals: a spectator analysis of event tourism in three New England cities'. *Festival Management and Event Tourism*, 5(4), 171–84.

Krippendorf, J. (1989) *The Holidaymakers: Understanding the Impact of Leisure and Travel*. London: Heinemann.

Laing, A. (1987) 'The package holiday participant: choice and behaviour'. Unpublished PhD thesis, Hull University.

Langer, E. J. and H. Newman (1979) 'The role of mindlessness in a typical social psychological experiment'. *Personality and Social Psychology Bulletin*, 5, 295–9.

Langer, E. J. and A. T. Piper (1987) 'The prevention of mindlessness'. *Journal of Personality and Social Psychology*, 52, 269–78.

Lasch, C. (1979) *The Culture of Narcissism: American Life in an Age of Diminishing Expectations*. New York: Warner Books.

Lash, S., A. Quick and R. Roberts (eds) (1998) *Time and Value*. Oxford and Malden, MA: Blackwell.

Lash, S. and J. Urry (1987) *The End of Organised Capitalism*. Cambridge: Polity.

Lash, S. and J. Urry (1994) *Economies of Signs and Space*. London: Sage.

Lashley, C. (1997) *Empowering Service Excellence. Beyond the Quick Fix*. London: Cassell.

Laslett, P. (1965) *The World We Live In*. London: Methuen.

Lauer, R. H. (1981) *Temporal Man: The Meaning and Use of Social Time*. New York: Praeger.

Law, C. M. (1992) 'Urban tourism and its contribution to economic regeneration'. *Urban Studies*, 29(3/4), 599–618.

Law, C. M. (1993) *Urban Tourism: Attracting Visitors to Large Cities*. London: Mansell.

Law, C. (ed.) (1996) *Tourism in Major Cities*. London: International Thomson Business Press.

Lawton, G. and S. J. Page (1997) 'Analysing the promotion, product and visitor expectations of urban tourism: Auckland New Zealand as a case study'. *Journal of Travel and Tourism Marketing*, 6(314), 123–42.

Le Blanc, G. (1992) 'Factors affecting customer evaluation of the service quality in travel agencies: an investigation of customer perceptions'. *Journal of Travel Research*, spring, 10–16.

Leiper, N. (1990) *Tourism Systems*, Department of Management Systems, Occasional Paper 2, Massey University, Auckland.

Leiper, N. (2000) 'Tourist', in J. Jafari (ed.), *Encyclopedia of Tourism*. London: Routledge, pp. 589–90.

Leiss, W. (1983) *The Icons of the Marketplace: Theory, Culture and Society*. London: Routledge.

Lencek, L. and G. Bosker (1998) *The Beach: A History of Paradise on Earth*. London: Secker and Warburg.

Lewis, R. and R. Chambers (1989) *Marketing Leadership in Hospitality*. New York: Simon and Schuster.

Light, D. (1996) 'Characteristics of the audience for "events" at a heritage site'. *Tourism Management*, 17(3), 183–90.

Lodge, D. (1991) *Paradise News*. London: Penguin Books.

Lodge, D. (1996) *Therapy: A Novel*. London: Penguin Books.

Lorentz, S. (1974) (?) *Reconstruction of the Old Town Centres of Poland*. Historic Preservation Today.

Loundsbury, J. W. and C. P. Franz (1990) 'Vacation discrepancy: a leisure motivation approach'. *Psychological Reports*, 66(2), 699–702.

Loundsbury, J. W. and L. Hoopes (1988) 'Five year stability of leisure activity and motivation factors'. *Journal of Leisure Research*, 20(2), 118–34.

Loundsbury, J. W. and J. R. Polik (1992) 'Leisure needs and vacation satisfaction'. *Leisure Studies*, 14, 105–19.

Lowenthal, D. (1985) *The Past is a Foreign Country*. Cambridge: Cambridge University Press.

Lowenthal, D. (1989) 'Heritage revisited: concluding address', in D. L. Uzzell (ed.), *Heritage Interpretation, Vol. 2, The Visitor Experience*. Papers from the Second Congress on Heritage Presentation and Interpretation, Coventry, England. London: Belhaven Press, pp. 212–16.

Lumley, R. (1988) *The Museum Time Machine: Putting Cultures on Display*. London: Comedia/ Routledge.

Lutz, R. J. and C. Ryan (1996) 'The impact inner city tourism projects: the case of the International Convention Centre, Birmingham, UK', in P. Murphy (ed.), *Quality Management in Urban Tourism*. Chichester: John Wiley, pp. 41–54.

Lynch, K. (1960) *The Image of the City*. Cambridge, MA: MIT Press.

Lynch, K. (1972) *What Time is This Place*. Cambridge, MA: MIT Press.

Lyotard, J. F. (1984) [1979] *The Postmodern Condition: A Report on Knowledge* (trans. G. Bennington and B. Massumi). Manchester: Manchester University Press.

MacAloon, J. (1984) 'Olympic Games and the theory of spectacle in modern societies', in J. MacAloon (ed.), *Rite, Drama, Festival, Spectacle: Rehearsals Towards a Theory of Cultural Performance*. Philadelphia: Institute for the Study of Human Issues, pp. 241–80.

McBride, G. B., C. E. Salmond, D. R. Bandaranyake, S. J. Turner, G. D. Lewis and D. G. Till (1998) 'Health effects of marine bathing in New Zealand'. *International Journal of Environmental Health Research*, **8**(3), 173–89.

MacCannell, D. (1976) *The Tourist: A New Theory of the Leisure Class*. London: Macmillan.

McInnes, A. (1988) 'The emergence of a leisure town, Shrewsbury, 1600–1760'. *Past and Present*, **120**, 53–87.

McNeil, J. K., M. J. Stones and A. A. Kozma (1986) 'Subjective well being in later life, Issues concerning measurement and prediction'. *Social Indicators Research*, **18**, 35–70.

Madrigal, R., M. E. Havitz and D. R. Howard (1992) 'Married couples' involvement with family vacations'. *Leisure Sciences*, **14**, 287–301.

Maffesoli, M. (1998) 'Presentism – or the value of the cycle', in S. Lash, A. Quick and R. Roberts (eds), *Time and Value*. Oxford: Blackwell Publishers, pp. 103–11.

Mahesh, V. S. (1988) 'Effective human resource management: key to excellence in service organizations'. *Vikalpa*, **13**(4), 9–15.

Mahesh, V. S. (1994) *Thresholds of Motivation*. New York: McGraw-Hill.

Mannell, R. and S. Iso-Ahola (1987) 'Psychological nature of leisure and tourist experiences'. *Annals of Tourism Research*, **14**, 314–31.

Mannell, R., J. Zuzanek and R. Larson (1988) 'Leisure states and "flow" experiences: testing perceived freedom and intrinsic motivation hypotheses'. *Journal of Leisure Studies*, **20**(4), 289–304.

Manning, F. (ed.) (1983) *The Celebration of Society: Perspectives on Contemporary Cultural Performance*. Bowling Green, Ohio: Bowling Green University Popular Press.

Mansfeld, J. (1999) 'Consuming spaces', in R. Le Heron, L. Murphy, P. Forer and M. Goldstone (eds), *Explorations in Human Geography: Encountering Place*. Auckland: Oxford University Press, pp. 318–43.

Mansfield, S. (1990) 'Customer care in tourism and leisure'. *Insights*. London: The English Tourist Board.

Mansfield, Y. (1992) 'From motivation to actual travel'. *Annals of Tourism Research*, **19**, 399–419.

Marshal Macklin Monaghan (1993) *Spectator Sporting Activities in Canada from a Tourism Perspective*. Ottawa: Tourism Canada.

Maslow, A. (1970) *Motivation and Personality* (2nd edn). New York: Harper.

Maslow, A. H. (1979) *The Journals of A. H. Maslow* (ed. R. J. Lowry for The International Study Project Inc. in co-operation with Bertha G. Maslow). Monterey, CA: Brooks/Cole Pub. Co.

Massey, D. (1994) *Space Place and Gender*. Oxford: Polity Press.

Mazanec, J. (ed.) (1997) *International City Tourism: Analysis and Strategy*. London: Pinter.

Meethan, K. (1996) 'Consumed in civilised city'. *Annals of Tourism Research*, **32**(2), 22–40.

Mercer, C. (1983) 'A poverty of desire: pleasure and popular politics', in T. Bennett (ed.), *Formations of Pleasure*. London: Routledge and Kegan Paul, pp. 84–101.

Mercer, D. (1991) 'Discretionary travel behaviour and the urban mental map'. *Australian Geographical Studies*, **9**, 133–43.

Merquior, J. G. (1985) *Foucault*. London: Fontana.

Middleton, V. T. C. (1988) *Marketing in Travel and Tourism*. Oxford: Heinemann Professional Publishing Ltd.

Mill, R. C. and A. M. Morrison (1985) *The Tourism System: An Introductory Text*. Englewood Cliffs, NJ: Prentice-Hall International.

Mills, A. S. (1985) 'Participant motivations for outdoor recreation: a test of Maslow's theory'. *Journal of Leisure Research*, **17**, 184–99.

Mohr, K., K. Backman, L. Gahan and S. Backman (1993) 'An investigation of festival motivations and event satisfaction by visitor type'. *Festival Management and Event Tourism: An International Journal*, **1**(3), 89–97.

Monk, J. (1992) 'Gender in the landscape: expressions of power and meaning', in K. Anderson and F. Gale (eds), *Inventing Places: Studies in Cultural Geography*. Melbourne: Longman Cheshire, pp. 123–38

Morgan, R. (1999) 'A novel, user-based rating system for tourist beaches'. *Tourism Management*, **20**(4), 393–410.

Morrison, A. M. (1989) *Hospitality and Travel Marketing*. Albany, NY: Delmar.

Moynahan, B. (1983) *Fool's Paradise*. London: Pan Books.

Mullins, P. (1991) 'Tourism urbanization'. *International Journal of Urban and Regional Research*, **15**(3), 326–42.

Murphy Jr, C. F. (1990) *Descent into Subjectivity: Studies of Rawls, Dworkin and Unger in the Context of Modern Thought*. Wakefield, New Hampshire: Longwood Academic.

Murphy, L. (1999) 'Visioning of cities', in R. Le Heron, L. Murphy, P. Forer and M. Goldstone (eds), *Explorations in Human Geography: Encountering Place*. Auckland: Oxford University Press, pp. 289–317.

Murphy, P. (ed.) (1997) *Quality Management in Urban Tourism*. Chichester: John Wiley and Sons.

Murray, H. A. (1938) *Explorations in Personality*. New York: Oxford University Press.

Myers, D. G. (1990) *Social Psychology* (3rd edn). New York: McGraw-Hill.

Nietzsche, F. (1967) (trans. W. Kaufmann) *Ecce Homo*. Harmondsworth: Penguin.

Nogawa, H., Y. Yamaguchi and Y. Hagi (1996) 'An empirical research study on Japanese sport tourism in sport-for-all events: case studies of a single-night event and a multiple-night event'. *Journal of Travel Research*, **35**, 46–54.

Normann, R. (1984) *Service Management*. New York: John Wiley.

Oliver, R. L. (1993) 'A conceptual model of service quality and service satisfaction: compatible goals, different concepts'. *Advances in Services Marketing and Management*, **2**, 65–85.

Oppermann, M., K. Din and S. Amri (1996) 'Urban hotel location and evolution in a developing country'. *Tourism Recreation Research*, **21**(1), 55–63.

Osgood, D. W. and H. Lee (1993) 'Leisure activities, age and adult roles across the lifespan'. *Loisir et Société*, **16**(1), 181–208.

Owens, C. (1985) 'The discourse of others: feminism and postmodernism', in H. Foster (ed.), *The Postmodern Culture*. London: Pluto.

Page, S. J. (1994a) *Place-marketing and Town Centre Management: A New Tool for Urban Revitalisation*. Marketing Educators Conference Proceedings, University of Waikato, Hamilton, New Zealand.

Page, S. J. (1994b) 'Waterfront revitalisation in London: market-led planning and tourism in London Docklands', in S. Craig-Smith and M. Fagence, (eds), *Recreation and Tourism as a Catalyst for Urban Waterfront Development*. Connecticut: Greenwood Publishing, pp. 54–73.

Page, S. J. (1995) *Urban Tourism*. London: Routledge.

Page, S. J. (2000) 'Urban tourism', in C. Ryan and S. J. Page (eds), *Tourism Management: Towards the New Millennium*. Oxford: Pergamon, pp. 197–202.

Page, S. J. (2002) 'Urban tourism: evaluating the tourists' experience of urban places', in C. Ryan (ed.), *The Tourist Experience – A New Approach*. London: Continuum, pp. 112–36.

Page, S. J., P. Brunt, G. Busby and J. Connell (2001) *Tourism: A Modern Synthesis*. London: Thomson Learning.

Page, S. J. and C. M. Hall (2002) *Managing Urban Tourism*. Harlow: Pearson Education.

Page, S. J. and R. Hardyman (1996) 'Place marketing and town centre management: a new tool for urban revitalisation'. *Cities: The International Journal of Urban Policy and Planning*, **13**(3), 153–64.

Page, S. J. and D. Meyer (1995) 'Tourist accidents: an exploratory analysis'. Unpublished paper, Department of Management Systems, Albany Campus, Massey University, New Zealand.

Page, S. J. and M. T. Sinclair (1989) 'Tourism accommodation in London: alternative policies and the Docklands experience'. *Built Environment*, **2**, 125–37.

Palmer, L. (1998) *Land Rights, Land Ethics and the 'Tourist Interest'*, in Kakadu National Park, paper presented in the CINCRM Seminar series, October 13. Darwin: Northern Territory University.

Parasuranam, A., V. A. Zeithaml and L. L. Berry (1985) 'A conceptual model of service quality and its implications for future research'. *Journal of Marketing*, **49**, fall, 41–50.

Parasuraman, A., V. A. Zeithaml and L. L. Berry (1988) 'SERVQUAL: a multiple-item scale for measuring consumer perceptions of service quality'. *Journal of Retailing*, **64**, 12–37.

Parasuraman, A., V. A. Zeithaml and L. L. Berry (1991) 'Refinement and reassessment of the SERVQUAL scale'. *Journal of Retailing*, **67**, 420–50.

Parasuraman, A., V. A. Zeithaml and L. L. Berry (1994a) 'Alternative scales for measuring service quality: a comparative assessment based on psychometric and diagnostic criteria'. *Journal of Retailing*, **70**(3), 201–30.

Parasuraman, A., V. A. Zeithaml and L. L. Berry (1994b) *Moving Forward in Service Quality Research: Measuring Different Customer-Expectation Levels, Comparing Alternative Scales, and Examining the Performance-Behavioral Intentions Link*. Marketing Science Institute Working Paper, report no. September, 94–114.

Parasuraman, A., V. A. Zeithaml and L. L. Berry (1994c) 'Reassessment of expectations as a comparison standard in measuring service quality: implications for further research'. *Journal of Marketing*, **58** (January), 111–24.

Pearce, D. G. (1987) *Tourism Today: A Geographical Analysis*. London: Longman.

Pearce, D. G. (1993) 'Introduction', in R. Butler and D. Pearce (eds), *Tourism Research: Critiques and Challenges*. London and New York: Routledge, pp. 1–8.

Pearce, D. G. (1998) 'Tourist districts in Paris: structure and functions'. *Tourism Management*, **19**(1), 49–66.

Pearce, D. G. and R. W. Butler (eds) (1993) *Tourism Research: Critiques and Challenges*. London: Routledge.

Pearce, P. L. (1977) 'Mental souvenirs: a study of tourists and their city maps'. *Australian Journal of Psychology*, **29**, 203–10.

Pearce, P. L. (1981) 'Route maps: a study of travellers' perceptions of a section of countryside'. *Journal of Environment Psychology*, **1**, 141–55.

Pearce, P. L. (1982) 'The social psychology of tourist behaviour'. *International Series in Experimental Psychology*, Vol. 3. Oxford: Pergamon Press.

Pearce, P. L. (1988) *The Ulysses Factor: Evaluating Visitors in Tourist Settings*. New York: Springer Verlag.

Pearce, P. L. (1993) 'Fundamentals of tourist motivation', in D. G. Pearce and R. W. Butler (eds), *Tourism Research: Critiques and Challenges*. London: Routledge, pp. 113–34.

Pearce, P. L. and M. L. Caltabiano (1983) 'Inferring travel motivation from travelers' experiences'. *Journal of Travel Research*, **22**(2), fall, 16–21.

Pearce, P. L. and G. Moscardo (1999) 'Understanding ethnic tourists'. *Annals of Tourism Research*, **26**(2), 416–34.

Pitts, B. (1999) 'Sports tourism and niche markets: identification and analysis of the growing lesbian and gay sports tourism industry'. *Journal of Vacation Marketing*, **5**(1), 31–50.

Pitzinger, B., R. Steffen and A. Tschopp (1991) 'Incidence and clinical features of travellers' diarrhoea in infants and children'. *Pediatric Infectious Disease Journal*, **10**(1), 719–23.

Plog, S. C. (1977) 'Why destinations rise and fall in popularity', in E. M. Kelly (ed.), *Domestic and International Tourism*. Institute of Certified Travel Agents, Wellesley, MA, pp. 26–8.

Plog, S. C. (1990) 'A carpenter's tools: an answer to Stephen L. J. Smiths's review of psychocentricism/allocentrism'. *Journal of Travel Research*, **28**(4), spring, 43–4.

Plumb, J. H. (1970) *The Death of the Past*. Boston, MA: Macmillan.

Pooley, J. (1979) *The Sport Fan: A Social-Psychology of Misbehaviour*. The Canadian Association for Health, Physical Education and Recreation. Published by the University of Calgary.

Poon, A. (1993) *Tourism, Technology and Competitive Strategies*. Wallingford: CABI.

Powell, J. M. (1978) *Mirrors of the New World: Images and Image Makers in the Settlement Process*. Canberra: Australian National University Press.

Preiswerk, R. and D. Perrot (1978) *Ethnocentrism and History: Africa, Asia and Indian America in Western Textbooks*. New York: Nok.

Preston-Whyte, R. (2001) 'Constructed leisure space: the seaside at Durban'. *Annals of Tourism Research*, **28**(3), 581–96.

Priest, S. and C. Bunting (1993) 'Changes in perceived risk and competence during whitewater canoeing'. *Journal of Applied Recreation Research*, **18**(4), 265–80.

Pritchard, A. and N. J. Morgan (2000) 'Privileging the male gaze: gendered tourism landscapes'. *Annals of Tourism Research*, **27**(4), 884–905.

Province of British Columbia (1992) *Report of the Task Force on Public Order*. Victoria, BC: Ministry of Attorney General.

Ragheb, M. G. and J. G. Beard (1983) 'Measuring leisure attitudes'. *Journal of Leisure Research*, **14**, 155–62.

Raybould, M. (1998) 'Participant motivation in a remote fishing event'. *Festival Management and Event Tourism*, **5**(4), 231–41.

Riley, R. W. (1994) 'Movie-induced tourism', in A. V. Seaton *et al.* (eds), *Tourism: The State of the Art*. Chichester: John Wiley, pp. 453–8.

Ritzer, G. (1993) *The McDonaldization of Society: An Investigation into the Changing Characteristics of Contemporary Social Life*. Thousand Oaks, CA: Pine Forge Press.

Roche, M. (1992) 'Mega-events and micro-modernisation: on the sociology of the new urban tourism'. *British Journal of Sociology*, **43**(4), 563–600.

Rodman, H. (1963) 'The lower class value stretch'. *Social Forces*, **45**, 205–15.

Rogers, C. R. (1959) 'A theory of therapy, personality, and interpersonal relationships, as developed in the client-centered framework', in S. Koch (ed.), *Psychology: A Study of Science*, vol. 3. New York: McGraw-Hill, pp. 185–256.

Rojek, C. (1985) *Capitalism and Leisure Theory*. London: Tavistock Press.

Rojek, C. (1993) *Ways of Escape: Modern Transformations in Leisure and Travel*. Basingstoke: Macmillan.

Rorty, R. (1989) *Contingency, Irony and Solidarity*. Cambridge: Cambridge University Press.

Rose, G. (1993) *Feminism and Geography: The Limits of Geographical Knowledge*. Cambridge: Polity Press.

Ross, A. (1988) *Universal Abandon? The Politics of Postmodernism*. Minneapolis: University of Minnesota Press.

Ross, G. (1991) 'School leavers and their perceptions of employment in the tourism/hospitality industry'. *Journal of Tourism Research*, **2**(1), 28–35.

Ross, G. (1994) *The Psychology of Tourism*. Melbourne: Hospitality Press.

Ryan, C. (1991) *Recreational Tourism: A Social Science Approach*. London: Routledge.

Ryan, C. (1992) *Tourism, Terrorism and Violence: The Risks of Wider World Travel*. Conflict Study 244. London: Research Institute for the Study of Conflict and Terrorism.

Ryan, C. (1993) *Tourism and Terrorism in Egypt and Kenya: Conflict Update*. London: Research Institute for the Study of Conflict and Terrorism.

Ryan, C. (1994) 'Leisure and tourism: the application of leisure concepts to tourist behaviour: a proposed model'. Paper at Tourism: The State of the Art, Strathclyde University, July (a version of which was published in A. Seaton, *et al.* (eds) (1994) *Tourism: The State of the Art*. Chichester: Wiley, pp. 294–307).

Ryan, C. (1995a) 'Learning about tourists from conversations: the over 55s in Majorca'. *Tourism Management*, **16**(3), 207–16.

Ryan, C. (1995b) 'Beaches, life-stage marketing', in M. Conlin and T. G. Baum (eds), *Island Tourism*. Chichester: John Wiley and Sons, pp. 79–93.

Ryan, C. (1995c) 'What is the island tourist product?' Proceedings, International Island Tourism Forum, Centre for Tourism and Innovation Research, Bermuda College, November.

Ryan, C. (1995d) *Researching Tourism Satisfaction: Issues, Concepts, Problems.* London: Routledge.

Ryan, C. (1996) 'Market research in tourism: shifting paradigms for new concerns', in L. Moutinho (ed.), *Marketing Research in Tourism*, Hemel Hempstead: Prentice-Hall.

Ryan, C. (1997a) 'Rural tourism in New Zealand: rafting in the Rangitikei at River Valley Ventures', in S. J. Page and D. Getz (eds), *The Business of Rural Tourism: International Perspectives.* London: International Thomson Business Press, pp. 162–87.

Ryan, C. (1997b) 'Maori and tourism: a relationship of history, constitutions and rites'. *Journal of Sustainable Tourism*, 5(4), 257–79.

Ryan, C. (1998) 'The travel career ladder: an appraisal'. *Annals of Tourism Research*, 25(4), 936–57.

Ryan, C. (1999) 'From the psychometrics of SERVQUAL to sex: measurements of tourist satisfaction', in A. Pizam and Y. Mansfield (eds), *Consumer Behavior in Travel & Tourism.* Binghamton, New York: Haworth Press, pp. 267–86.

Ryan, C. (2001) 'Entertainment, globalisation and mutant messages: the search for edutainment and tourism based on indigenous peoples' culture'. Paper presented at the conference of the International Academy for the Study of Tourism, Institute of Tourism, Macau, July.

Ryan, C. and S. Birks (2000) *Passengers at Hamilton International Airport.* Unpublished report for Hamilton International Airport, Hamilton, New Zealand. Hamilton: University of Waikato.

Ryan, C. and A. Cliff (1996) 'Differences between users and non-users on the expectation items of the ServQual Scale: an application to travel agencies'. *Annals of Tourism Research*, 23(4), 931–4.

Ryan, C. and A. Cliff (1997) 'Do travel agencies measure up to customer expectation? An empirical investigation of travel agencies' service quality as measured by SERVQUAL'. *Journal of Travel and Tourism Marketing*, 6(2), 1–32.

Ryan, C. and I. Glendon (1998) 'Application of Leisure Motivation Scale to tourism'. *Annals of Tourism Research*, 25(1), 169–84.

Ryan, C. and C. M. Hall (2001) *Sex Tourism: Liminalities and Marginal Peoples.* London: Routledge.

Ryan, C., K. Hughes and S. Chirgwin (2000) 'The gaze, spectacle and eco-tourism'. *Annals of Tourism Research*, 27(1), 148–63.

Ryan, C. and R. Kinder (1995) 'The Deviant Tourist and The Crimogenic Place', in A. Pizam and Y. Mansfield (eds), *Tourism, Crime and International Security Issues.* Chichester: Wiley.

Ryan, C. and R. Kinder (1996) 'Sex, tourism and sex tourism: fulfilling similar needs?' *Tourism Management*, 17(7), 507–18.

Ryan, C. and E. Robertson (1996) 'New Zealand students as tourists: food poisoning, sunburn, drugs, drink and sex'. Paper for Australian Tourism Research Conference, Southern Cross University, NSW.

Ryan, C. and E. Robertson (1997) 'The New Zealand student-tourist and risk behaviours', in S. Clift and P. Grawboski (eds), *Tourism and Health: Risks, Research and Responses.* London: Mansell, pp. 119–39.

Rybczynski, W. (1991) 'Waiting for the weekend'. *The Atlantic Monthly*, August, pp. 35–52.

Saleh, F. and C. Ryan (1992) 'Conviviality: a source of satisfaction for hotel guests? An application of the Servqual model', in P. Johnson and B. Thomas (eds), *Choice and Demand in Tourism.* London and New York: Mansell, pp. 107–22.

Saleh, F. and C. Ryan (1993) 'Jazz and knitwear: factors that attract tourists to festivals'. *Tourism Management*, 14(4), 289–97.

Sartre, J. P. (1957/1984) *Existentialism and Human Emotions.* New York: Carol Publishing Group.

Schlosser, E. (2001) *Fast Food Nation.* London: Allen Lane.

Schöps, M. (1980) *Zeit und Gesellschaft.* Stuttgart: Ferdinand Enke Verlag.

Scott, D. (1996) 'A comparison of visitors' motivations to attend three urban festivals'. *Festival Management and Event Tourism*, 3(3), 121–8.

Scott Haine, W. (1994) 'The development of leisure and the transformation of working-class adolescence, Paris, 1830–1940'. *Journal of Family History*, 17(4), 451–76.

Sefton, J. M. (1989) *Examining the Factor Invariance of Ragheb and Beard's Leisure Satisfaction and Leisure Attitude Scales.* Unpublished paper, Office of Research Services, University of Saskatchewan, June.

Sefton, J. M. and T. L. Burton (1987) 'The measurement of leisure motivations and satisfaction: a replication and an extension'. *Leisure Studies Division: The Fifth Canadian Congress on Leisure Research.* Hailfax: Dalhousie University.

Seymour, D. (2000) 'Emotional labour: a comparison between fast food and traditional service work'. *International Journal of Hospitality Management*, **19**(2), 159–71.

Shaw, G. and A. Williams (1994) *Critical Issues in Tourism: A Geographical Perspective.* Oxford: Blackwell.

Shaw, S. M. (1990) 'Where has all the leisure gone? The distribution and redistribution of leisure', Keynote paper presented at the 6th Canadian Congress on Leisure Research, University of Waterloo, Ontario, pp. 1–4.

Shaw, S. M. (1992) 'Dereifying family leisure: an examination of women's and men's everyday experiences and perceptions of family time'. *Leisure Sciences*, **14**(4), 271–86.

Shields, R. (1991) *Places on the Margin.* London and New York: Routledge.

Shostack, G. L. (1985) 'Planning the service encounter', in J. A. Czepiel, M. R. Solomon and C. F. Suprenant (eds), *The Service Encounter.* New York: Lexington Books, pp. 243–54.

Shrew, R. S. and N. Chaimongkol (1993) 'The socio-demographic characteristics of Thai sex workers in Auckland'. Paper presented to the New Zealand Venerological Association Conference.

Simmel, G. (1903) 'Die Grossstädte und das Geistesleben', in von Bücher, K., F. Ratzel, G. V. Mayr, H. Waentig and G. Simmel (eds), *Die Grosstadt.* Dresden: Gehe-Stiftung zu Dresden, winter, pp. 185–206.

Simmel, G. (1909/1950) 'The metropolis and mental life', in Kurt Wolff (trans.) *The Sociology of Georg Simmel.* New York: Free Press.

Sincich, T. (1992) *Business Statistics by Example.* New York: Maxwell Macmillan International.

Slavson, S. R. (1948) *Recreation and the Total Personality.* New York: Association Press.

Smith, S. L. J. (1990) *Dictionary of Concepts in Recreation and Leisure Studies.* New York: Greenwood Press.

Smith, V. K., Z. XiaoLong and R. B. Palmquist (1997) 'Marine debris, beach quality and non-market values'. *Environmental and Resource Economics*, **10**(3), 223–47.

Soares, L. E. (1998) 'Staging the self by performing the other: global fantasies and the migration of the projective imagination', in S. Lash, A. Quick and R. Roberts (eds), *Time and Value.* Oxford: Blackwell Publishers, pp. 130–46.

Soja, E. (1989) *Postmodern Geographies: The Reassertion of Space in Critical Social Theory.* London: Verso.

Soja, E. (1996) 'Los Angeles 1965–1992: the six geographies of urban restructuring', in A. Scott and E. Soja (eds), *The City: Los Angeles and Urban Theory at the End of the Twentieth Century.* Los Angeles: University of California Press, pp. 426–62.

Sontag, S. (1978) *Illness as Metaphor.* New York: Farrar, Strauss and Giroux.

Sparrowe, R. (1994) 'Empowerment in the hospitality industry: an exploration of antecedents and outcomes'. *Hospitality Research Journal*, **17**(3), 51–74.

Spivak, G. (1996) 'Subaltern studies: deconstructing historiography', in D. Landry and G. McLean (eds), *The Spivak Reader.* London: Routledge, pp. 203–35.

Sprawson, C. (1992) 'Everything going swimmingly'. *The Independent Weekend*, 23 May.

Squires, J. (ed.) (1993) *Principled Positions: Postmodernism and the Recovery of Values.* London: Lawrence and Wishart.

Stabler, M. (1990) 'The concept of opportunity sets as a methodological framework for the analysis of selling tourism places: the industry view', in G. J Ashworth and B. Goodall (eds), *Marketing Tourism Places.* London: Routledge, pp. 23–41.

Stansfield, C. A. (1964) 'A note on the urban-nonurban imbalance in American recreational research'. *Tourist Review*, **19**(4), 196–200.

Stea, R. and R. Downs (1970) 'From the outside looking in at the inside looking out'. *Environment and Behaviour*, **2**, 3–12.

Steinecke, A. (1993) 'The historical development of tourism in Europe', in W. Pompl and P. Lavery (eds), *Tourism in Europe: Structures and Developments*. Wallingford: CABI.

Stephanson, A. (1988) 'Regarding postmodernism: a conversation with Frederic Jameson', in A. Ross (ed.), pp. 3–30.

Suh, S. H., Y.-H. Lee, Y. Park and G. C. Shin (1997) 'The impact of consumer involvement on the consumers' perception of service quality: focusing on the Korean hotel industry'. *Journal of Travel and Tourism Marketing*, **6**(2), 33–52.

Survey Research Associates (1991) *London Docklands Visitor Survey: Summary of Findings*. London: London Docklands Development Corporation.

Swarbrooke, J. (1992) 'The impact of British visitors on rural France: Proceedings of *Tourism in Europe: The 1992 Conference*'. University of Northumbria at Newcastle: Centre for Tourism Studies.

Swiecimski, J. (1989) 'Truths and untruths in museum exhibitions', in D. L. Uzzell (ed.), *Heritage Interpretation, Vol. 2, The Visitor Experience*. Papers from the Second Congress on Heritage Presentation and Interpretation (Coventry, England). London: Belhaven Press, pp. 203–11.

Taylor, S. A. (1997) 'Assessing regression-based importance weights for quality perceptions and satisfaction judgements in the presence of higher order and/or interaction effects'. *Journal of Retailing*, **73**(1), 135–59.

Taylor, S. A. and T. L. Baker (1994) 'An assessment of the relationship between service quality and customer satisfaction in the formation of consumers' purchase intentions'. *Journal of Retailing*, **70**(2), 163–78.

Theweleit, K. (1987) *Male Fantasies*, Vol. 1, *Women, Floods, Bodies and History*. Cambridge: Polity Press.

Timothy, D. and G. Wall (1995) 'Tourist accommodation in an Asian historic city'. *Journal of Tourism Studies*, **6**(2), 63–73.

Towner, J. (1985) 'The history of the grand tour'. *Annals of Tourism Research*, **12**(3), 310–16.

Towner, J. (1994) 'Tourism history: past, present and future', in A. V. Seaton *et al.* (eds), *Tourism: The State of the Art*. Chichester: John Wiley, pp. 721–8.

Travel Industry Association of America (1999) *Profile of Travellers Who Attend Sports Events*. Washington, DC.

Turner, V. (1982) *From Ritual to Theater: The Human Seriousness of Play*. New York: PAJ Publications.

Turner, V. (1983) 'Carnival in Rio: Dionysian drama in an industrializing society', in F. Manning (ed.), *The Celebration of Society: Perspectives on Contemporary Cultural Performance*. Bowling Green, Ohio: Bowling Green University Popular Press, pp. 31–9.

Tyler, D., Y. Guerrier and M. Robertson (eds) (1998) *Managing Tourism in Cities: Policy, Process and Practice*. Chichester: John Wiley and Sons.

Urry, J. (1990) *The Tourist Gaze*. London: Sage Publications.

Urry, J. (1995) *Consuming Places*. London: Routledge.

Urry, J. (1997) 'Review of *The Tourist Experience*'. *Regional Studies*, **31**(8), Nov, 825.

Urry, J. (2000) 'The global media and cosmopolitanism'. Paper presented at Transnational America Conference, Bavarian American Academy, Munich, June 2000, http://www.comp. lancaster.ac.uk/sociology/soc056ju.html.

Uysal, M., K. Backman, S. Backman and T. Potts (1991) 'An examination of event tourism motivations and activities'. *New Horizons Conference Proceedings*, University of Calgary, 203–18.

Uysal, M., L. Gahan and B. Martin (1993) 'An examination of event motivations: a case study'. *Festival Management and Event Tourism: An International Journal*, **1**(1), 5–10.

Van der Borg, J., P. Costa and G. Gotti (1996) 'Tourism in European heritage cities'. *Annals of Tourism Research*, **23**(2), 306–21.

Veenhofen, R. (1993) *Happiness in Nations*. Rotterdam: Risbo.

Verhoef, M. J., E. J. Love and M. S. Rose (1992) 'Women's social roles and their exercise participation'. *Women and Health*, **19**(4), 15–29.

Vetter, F. (ed.) (1985) *Big City Tourism*. Berlin: Dietrich Verlag.

Von Weizsäcker, V. (1946/1990) 'Anonyma scriptura', in T. Henkelmann (ed.), *Filosofia della Medicina*. Milan: Guerini e Associati, pp. 175–84.

Vukonić, B. (1996) *Tourism and Religion*. Oxford: Pergamon.

Wahlers, R. G. and M. J. Etzel (1985) 'Vacation preference as a manifestation of optimal stimulation and lifestyle experience'. *Journal of Leisure Research*, **17**, 283–95.

Wallace, M. (1981) 'Visiting the past: history museums in the USA'. *Radical History Review*, October, 63–100.

Wallace, M. (1985) 'Mickey Mouse history: portraying the past at Disney World'. *Radical History Review*, **32**, 33–57.

Wallerstein, I. (1980) 'Maps, maps, maps: review of G. Barrouclough's edited text, *The Times Atlas of World History*'. *Radical History Review*, **24**, fall, 155–9.

Walmesley, D. J. and J. Jenkins (1992) 'Tourism cognitive mapping of unfamiliar environments'. *Annals of Tourism Research*, **19**(3), 268–86.

Walmesley, D. J. and G. J. Lewis (1993) *People and Environment: Behavioural Approaches in Human Geography* (2nd edn). London: Longman.

Wang, N. (2000) *Tourism and Modernity: A Sociological Analysis*. Oxford: Pergamon Press.

Ward, C. and D. Hardy (1986) *Goodnight Campers: The History of the British Holiday Camp*. London: Mansell.

Ward, S. (1998) *Selling Places: The Marketing and Promotion of Towns and Cities 1850–2000*. London: E. & F. N. Spon.

Warhurst, C., D. Nickson, A. Witz and A. M. Cullen (2000) 'Aesthetic labour in interactive service work: some case study evidence from the 'New Glasgow'. *Service Industries Journal*, **20**(3), 1–18.

Wearing, B. and S. Wearing (1996) 'Refocusing the tourist experience: the flâneur and the choraster'. *Leisure Studies*, **15**, 229–43.

Webster, F. (1995) 'Tourism academic works'. *Times Higher Educational Supplement*, 10 March 1995, p. 24.

Wessman, A. E. and D. F. Ricks (1966) *Mood and Personality*. New York: Holt.

West, R. (1988) 'The making of the English working past: a critical view of the Ironbridge Gorge Museum', in R. Lumley (ed.), *The Time-Machine: Putting Cultures on Display*. London: Comedia/Routledge, pp. 36–62.

Wheeller, B. (1990) 'Is responsible tourism appropriate'. Proceedings of Tourism Research into the 1990s. University College, University of Durham.

Wheeller, B. (1993) 'Sustaining the ego'. *Journal of Sustainable Tourism*, **1**(2), 121–30.

White, B., C. Cox and C. Cooper (1992) *Women's Career Development: A Study of High Flyers*. Oxford: Blackwell Publishers.

Whorf, B. L. (1956) *Language, Thought and Reality: Selected Writings*. Cambridge, MA: Technology Press of the Massachusetts Institute of Technology.

Wickens, E. (1994) 'Consumption of the authentic: the hedonistic tourist in Greece', in A. V. Seaton *et al.* (eds), *Tourism: The State of the Art*. Chichester: John Wiley, pp. 818–25.

Wickens, E. (1999) *Tourists' Voices: A Sociological Analysis of Tourists' Experiences in Chalkidiki, Northern Greece*. Oxford Brookes University. Unpublished PhD thesis.

Wickens, E. (2000) 'Rethinking tourists' experiences', in M. Robinson, P. Long, N. Evans, R. Sharpley and J. Swarbrooke (eds), *Motivations, Behaviour and Tourist Types*. Morpeth: Centre for Travel and Tourism, University of Northumbria and Sunderland: Business Education Publishers Ltd, pp. 455–72.

Williams, R. (1990) *Notes on the Underground: An Essay on Technology, Society and the Imagination*. London: MIT Press.

Wöber, K. (2000) 'Standardising city tourism statistics'. *Annals of Tourism Research* **27**(1), 51–68.

Wolff, J. (1985) 'The invisible flâneuse: women and the literature of modernity'. *Theory, Culture and Society*, **2**, 37–45.

Wolper, D. (1980) *On Location* (interview of David Wolper), January/February, pp. 83–8.

Wood, R. C. (1997) *Working in Hotels and Catering* (2nd edn). London: Routledge.

Woods, T. (1999) *Beginning Postmodernism*. Manchester: Manchester University Press.

Woodside, A. G. and S. Lysonski (1989) 'A general model of traveler destination choice'. *Journal of Travel Research*, **27**(4), 8–14.

Woodside, A. and R. MacDonald (1993) 'General systems framework of customer choice and behavior processes for tourism services'. Conference paper for *Decision Making Processes and*

*Preference Changes of Tourists: Intertemporal and Intercountry Perspectives Conference*, at Institute of Tourism and Service Economics, University of Innsbruck, Nov. 25–7.

Wright, P. (1985) *On Living in an Old Country: The National Past in Contemporary Britain.* London: Verso.

Würstermeyer, M. (1967) *Die 'Annales': Grundsätze un Methoden ihres 'neun Gesschichtswissenschaft'*, Vierteljahrschift für sozial-und Wirtschaftgeschicte, Liv., pp. 1–45.

Yerkes, R. N. and J. D. Dodson (1908) 'The relation of strength of stimulus to rapidity of habit formation'. *Journal of Comparative Neurological Psychology*, **18**, 459–82.

Yiannakis, A. and H. Gibson (1992) 'Roles tourists play'. *Annals of Tourism Research*, **19**(2), 287–303.

Yin, R. (1994) *Case Study Research: Design and Methods* (2nd edn). London: Sage.

Ziehe, T. (1986) *Ny Ungdom: Om ovanliga laro processer*. Stockholm: Norstedts.

# Index